BISON
BOOKS

JOHN McGRAW

Charles C. Alexander

University of Nebraska Press
Lincoln and London

The paper in this book meets the minimum requirements of American
National Standard for Information Sciences—Permanence of Paper for
Printed Library Materials, ANSI Z39.48-1984.

First Bison Book printing: 1995
Most recent printing indicated by the last digit below:
10   9   8   7   6   5   4   3   2   1

Library of Congress Cataloging-in-Publication Data
Alexander, Charles C.
John McGraw / Charles C. Alexander.
p.   cm.
Originally published: New York, N.Y., U.S.A.: Viking, 1988.
Includes bibliographical references (p.   ) and index.
ISBN 0-8032-5925-5 (alk. paper)
1. McGraw, John Joseph, 1873–1934.   2. Baseball managers—United
States—Biography.   3. New York Giants (Baseball team)—History.   I.
Title.
GV865.M3A75   1995
796.357′092—dc20
[B]
94-23951
CIP

Reprinted by arrangement with Charles C. Alexander.

*For Dwain, Georgia, Victor
Travis, and Herbert Erwin,*

*and to the memory
of D. A. Erwin (1907–1987)*

ACKNOWLEDGMENTS

AGAIN EUGENE C. MURDOCK, recently retired from the history faculty of Marietta College, and Warren F. Kimball, Rutgers University-Newark, were willing to take the time to read, comment upon, and (blessedly) correct my work. I'm deeply obligated to both of them not only this time around but for many past favors. The staff of the National Baseball Library, Cooperstown, New York, again gave me prompt, friendly, and indispensable assistance. It was a particular pleasure to visit St. Bonaventure University and use the materials in the archives there concerning John McGraw and Hugh Jennings, two of that institution's most illustrious alumni. My thanks also go to the staffs of the Enoch Pratt Free Library, Baltimore, and the Alden Library, Ohio University. People in various places across the country were kind enough to share with me their personal recollections of John and Blanche McGraw and their times. I thank them collectively here and acknowledge them individually in the bibliography. The students in my course in American Baseball History, which I teach every spring at Ohio University, have helped me to bring into focus my thinking not only about McGraw but about more general issues having to do with baseball's evolution and its relation to American life.

And one more time, I express my loving thanks to JoAnn Erwin Alexander. She knows what she's meant for all these many years—so do a lot of other people. But it's my joy to remind her from time to time, as I do on this occasion.

C.C.A.
Athens, Ohio
July 1987

CONTENTS

Errata

P. 37, lines 23–25: Brouthers . . . had led the National League in batting four times. *Add:* and the American Association once

P. 104, line 23: his [Honus Wagner's] six National League batting titles *should read* his eight National League batting titles

P. 116, lines 22–23: Born Cornelius Alexander McGillicuddy in 1862 in East Brookline, Massachusetts *should read* Born . . . in East Brookfield, Massachusetts

P. 244, line 19: WYG in Schenectady *should read* WGY in Schenectady

JOHN McGRAW

Prelude

A SOGGY JUBILEE

IT WAS PLANNED as a gala event. A Silver Jubilee Celebration Committee, chaired by the ubiquitous baseball ghostwriter Christy Walsh, had worked for weeks arranging festivities to commemorate the twenty-fifth anniversary of John McGraw's first game as manager of the New York Giants. Unfortunately for McGraw and for the many people who claimed him as their friend, Tuesday, July 19, 1927, was overcast and humid from the start. Rain fell on the parade of civic and baseball dignitaries who rode in open automobiles from Times Square north to the Polo Grounds, a distance of about four and one-half miles. A crowd of some 25,000, swelled by the free admission of several thousand disabled veterans of the World War and children from the city's orphanages, occupied somewhat less than half the seats in the big horseshoe-shaped ballpark.

The Giants were scheduled to play the Chicago Cubs at three o'clock that afternoon. Under threatening skies, the start of the game had to wait on protracted commemorative activities. First, two teams of Broadway entertainers played burlesque baseball until master of ceremonies Joe Humphreys, worried about the delays and weather, cut short the antics of such headliners as George M. Cohan, Eddie Cantor, Victor Moore, and Julius Marx (who'd recently adopted the nickname "Groucho"). Humphreys announced that the celebrity pie-eating contest and a hundred-yard dash by a platoon of briefly clad chorus girls would have to be canceled, and then turned the ceremonies over to James J. Walker. New York's effervescent mayor, always at his best at such times, introduced Kenesaw Mountain Landis, baseball's commissioner; John K. Heydler, president of the National League; and presidents Charles Stoneham of the Giants, Emil Fuchs of the Boston Braves, William F. Baker of the

1

Philadelphia Phillies, Thomas Shibe of the Philadelphia Athletics, William Veeck of the visiting Cubs, and Jacob Ruppert of the New York Yankees, the Giants' American League rivals just across the Harlem River in the Bronx.

Jimmy Walker had decided to include Commander Richard Byrd and Clarence Chamberlin in the home-plate ceremonies. In 1926 Byrd had become the first man to pilot an aircraft to the North Pole. In the last few weeks, first Chamberlin and then Byrd had flown from New York across the Atlantic to the European mainland. Of course, Charles Lindbergh, in May, had been the first to accomplish that feat, and he had done it alone, whereas Chamberlin and Byrd had flown with other crew members in larger aircraft. But in the aviation mania of the times, the second and third trans-Atlantic flyers had received welcomes from the city of New York almost on the scale accorded Lindbergh. After two days of parades and banquets, Byrd and Chamberlin scarcely needed more cheers. Their presence took a little away from an occasion that was supposed to belong only to John McGraw.

It was drizzling by the time McGraw himself, fifty-four years old but looking older, almost totally white-haired, paunchy but still dapper in tan suit and two-toned shoes, joined the semi-circle of notables at home plate. In the name of the baseball fans of the city of New York, Walker presented to McGraw a four-foot-high silver loving cup, with an inscription to the "master of baseball men, 1902–1927, in recognition of his human qualities."[1] Roger Bresnahan, the star catcher of McGraw's early New York teams and now his chief assistant, presented a silver service on behalf of the current Giants players. The Lambs' Club, a convivial fraternity of mostly theatrical people, gave fellow-member McGraw a silver platter, while the Polo Grounds ushers added a silver cane.

It would be another three years before the Polo Grounds had an electrically amplified loudspeaker system, so that McGraw's thank-yous and acknowledgments of his former ballplayers sitting in box seats near the Giants first-base dugout were inaudible to the great majority of the spectators. After several minutes, people in various sections began to call for Hughey Jennings. As the cries of "Hughey, Hughey!" resounded over the ballpark, a frail little man whose flaming red hair was now mostly gray made his way slowly down to the field. Once McGraw's teammate and buddy on the legendary Baltimore Orioles of the 1890s, later a fiery manager of the Detroit Tigers in the American League, and until a couple of seasons ago McGraw's right-hand man on the Giants,

Jennings was now battling tuberculosis and had to lean on a cane as he joined the others at the plate. But he was able to smile and wave to the crowd as the photographers snapped a group of men in which McGraw, the shortest among them, was less than conspicuous.

The drizzle continued throughout the ballgame, which started some forty-five minutes late. McGraw's players were unable to give him the twenty-fifth anniversary present he wanted most—a victory. As the playing field grew soggier and soggier, McGraw sat in a corner of the dugout and watched the Cubs pound three Giants pitchers and win 8–5, the big hit being Charles "Gabby" Hartnett's three-run homer. The Giants' record dropped to 47–43, good for no better than fourth place.

In the last two months of the season of 1927, the Giants would play much better baseball and end up missing a National League championship by only a game and a half. In 1928 they would fall short by only two games. McGraw had already managed his last pennant winner— back in 1924. After that his ball clubs were like the elaborately planned McGraw Silver Jubilee: impressive on paper but with enough flaws to keep them from being what they might have been.

Yet even though McGraw would never again lead a team into the World Series, his reputation as baseball's premier manager would endure among veteran sportswriters, old ballplayers, and ordinary fans. Some people, especially Philadelphia partisans, might hold out for Connie Mack, who would manage his Athletics to nine American League pennants against McGraw's ten National League titles. Mack's teams won five World Series to McGraw's three, but they also finished last or next to last thirteen times in Mack's fifty-year reign in Philadelphia. In twenty-nine full seasons in New York, McGraw had one last-place team; and only one other time did his ball club finish lower than fourth place.[2] As Mack himself put it at a banquet for McGraw a few days before the Silver Jubilee celebration, "There has been only one McGraw, and there has been only one manager—and his name [is] McGraw."[3]

But McGraw's fame rested on far more than his year-by-year record. In a period in American history when baseball was far and away the nation's leading sport, in numbers of both spectators and participants, McGraw epitomized what a baseball manager was supposed to be: smart, shrewd, pugnacious, tough and demanding with his players. McGraw's baseball intelligence—his judgment of players, his ability to make the right move at just the right time, his insistence that his men follow his dictates on (and off) the field—became legendary. "When you train under most managers," remarked Rogers Hornsby in the spring of the one year he played for McGraw, "you merely get yourself in good physical condition. When you train under McGraw, you learn baseball." "I always thought McGraw was sort of on the genius side," Frank Frisch said as he looked back on his time with the Giants. "Give him the [military] uniform," wrote one admirer in 1911, "and you would see Napoleon— the attitude, the quiet decision, the folded arms, and even the funny little protruding stomach—all are there." It was nearly inevitable that the New York baseball writers should dub him (somewhat redundantly) "the little Napoleon."[4]

It was McGraw's fiercely combative temperament that contemporaries remembered best. "The only road to popularity is to win," he declared. "The man who loses gracefully loses easily. Sportsmanship and easygoing methods are all right, but it is the prospect of a hot fight that brings out the crowds. Personally I never could see this idea of taking a defeat philosophically. . . . once a team of mine is on the diamond I want it to fight. Namby-pamby methods don't get much in results."[5] Long after his death, the image lingered of a fat little man charging across the field, waving his short arms and yelling in an umpire's face, stamping his feet and generally disturbing what might otherwise have been a peaceful afternoon. McGraw never struck an umpire—at least not on the playing field. But his ability to heap verbal abuse on the beleaguered arbiters was unmatched. "McGraw," complained Arlie Latham during one of his brief stints as a National League umpire, "eats gunpowder every morning and washes it down with warm blood." For the veteran reporter John B. Sheridan, who watched him as a player and manager for thirty years, McGraw "always acted like an angry hornet on the baseball field. He spared no man, least of all himself." McGraw's acid tongue, Sheridan added, "would burn holes in nickel twelve inches thick."[6]

Indeed McGraw spared nobody—neither umpires, players on opposing teams, fans in enemy ballparks, nor his own players. Over the years some of the men who played for him rebelled against his overbearing ways. By far the greater number accepted his authority; whatever else they might think about him, they knew that his teams were consistent winners and, at least before the emergence of the Yankees powerhouse in the early Twenties, baseball's biggest moneymakers. His players endured his tongue-lashings, his efforts to control their every movement on the ballfield, his snooping into their lives away from the ballpark. Characteristically awed by McGraw when they first came to him as young players, many developed a warm admiration, even a love for the man. He sought to cultivate not only baseball knowledge and skills but a professional attitude, maturity, and self-respect. "McGraw," said out-fielder Benny Kauff in 1916, after his first season with the Giants, "has taught me that baseball is a serious profession, requiring the best years of a man's life, and that the man is a fool if he doesn't take the game seriously." "An important part of McGraw's capacity for leadership," observed the well-known political columnist and onetime sportswriter Heywood Broun when McGraw died, "[was] that he could take kids out of coal mines and wheat fields and make them walk and talk and chatter and play ball with the look of eagles."[7]

By the standards of the times, McGraw's players were paid well, and he also insisted on first-class accommodations for them on road trips. In exchange, he demanded absolute commitment to winning, within the rules and by ethical means if possible, but by whatever means were necessary. That was the way he had played and the way he managed.

In 1890, when seventeen-year-old McGraw left Truxton, New York, to become a professional ballplayer, the sport of baseball was still raw and disorderly. With only one umpire responsible for watching everything that happened on the field, it was accepted behavior for runners to cut inside bases without touching them, for basemen to block, trip, and hold runners, and above all for players to assault and revile the umpire with impunity. Small and (in his playing days) on the thin side, never con-stitutionally robust, high-strung, quick-tempered, McGraw was usually, as Sheridan said, "worn to a shred" by the middle of the season.[8] Not gifted with great athletic ability, McGraw made himself into one of the top players of the 1890s—and one of the most aggressive. The Baltimore Orioles for which he starred at third base were arguably the rowdiest, most contentious ball club ever assembled. McGraw gained a reputation as the rowdiest of them all, the worst umpire-baiter in the game's history.

In simplest terms, umpires were his natural enemies, men to be tricked, bluffed, brow-beaten, intimidated any way possible. "Kicking" was not only an acceptable but an essential part of the game, a basic tactic to be used with deliberate intent. What McGraw called "judicious kicking" had to be done as carefully as base-running or bunting. Winning teams, he believed, always had "good kickers." But he also believed that "kickers are born and not made. . . ." By keeping the umpires alert, he contended in 1896, an artful kicker could gain his ball club as many as fifty additional runs in a season.[9]

As a manager McGraw encouraged aggressiveness not only at bat and afield but in dealing with umpires as well. He always maintained that club owners ought to be willing to pay whatever fines players might incur from the league office for their run-ins with umpires. That way, "The players are not afraid to stand up for their rights, and the result is they play with more ginger."[10]

Highly competitive people, people for whom getting ahead and staying there is the most important thing in life, often find it hard to turn off the juices when the work day ends. McGraw, though, seems to have been able, most of the time, to change demeanors once he left the ballpark. Blanche Sindall McGraw remained his loving and adoring companion until his death after thirty-two years of marriage. McGraw seems to have been an equally devoted husband, at least as devoted as it was possible for a man to be who was away from home nearly half the time. Numerous people who knew him well testified to his being, in Frank Frisch's words, "night and day off the field from what he was on the field." Branch Rickey (who built the St. Louis Cardinals farm system mainly to counter the Giants' ability to buy talent) found McGraw to be "quiet-spoken, almost disarmingly so" when he was not in a ballgame. In 1908 a Chicago writer described McGraw as having a Jekyll-and-Hyde personality: In uniform he was "the incarnation of rowdyism, the personification of meanness and howling blatancy"; off the field he was "the kindliest, most generous and most sympathetic of men."[11]

McGraw out of uniform was not always such a gentle soul. He could be thoughtless, surly, and belligerent, particularly on those not-uncommon occasions when he had too much to drink. But there was also much truth in what his friends often said about him: "He's the toughest loser in the world and the easiest to touch."[12] With indigent old ballplayers or their widows or almost anybody else who came to him asking for help, McGraw was unfailingly solicitous and usually ready with a sizable handout. He showed little interest in organized philanthropy, but the inordinate sums he gave away over the years to individual petitioners and the sorely needed jobs he found for men who'd once played with, against, or under him were well known within his circle of friends.

That circle was a very big one. McGraw knew people all over the United States, as well as in Cuba (virtually his off-season home in the

1920s) and—because of two highly publicized overseas baseball tours—
Europe and Asia. As the leader of the favorite sports team in the city
that had long since become the nation's media capital, McGraw was in
a position where nearly everything he did drew press attention. He was
an international celebrity, one of the best-known personalities of his
time.

If his friends were legion, they were also motley. McGraw loved to
gamble, especially on horses. For almost all of his adult life, he gambled
openly and inveterately. His gambling habits, together with his weakness
for others' hard-luck stories, mostly explain why, for all the money he
made in baseball, he left his wife only moderately well off. Some of his
favorite people were bookies and racetrack touts. He had close asso-
ciations with various big-time gamblers, track and casino owners, and
real estate hustlers. For the last fourteen years that he managed the
Giants, he worked with a club president who had made his fortune mainly
in questionable securities trading and a club treasurer who finally had
to resign from his city magistracy after being implicated in a variety of
corrupt practices.

McGraw never cared much about a man's reputation if he liked him.
However admirable that attitude might be in some circumstances, McGraw's
carelessness in choosing his friends left him open to hints and whispers
of scandal several times during his career. He seemed to have an actual
affinity for ballplayers of doubtful honesty, convinced that, as he sought
to do with a succession of hard drinkers, he could get them to play up
to full potential after other managers had failed. In short, McGraw never
was willing to put as much distance as he should have between himself
and elements inside and outside baseball that could and sometimes did
damage the integrity of the sport.

John McGraw was an amalgam of virtues and vices. But as is usually
the case with people whose lives take place mainly in public, both
McGraw's best and his worst qualities were continually being magnified.
He was perhaps the single most significant figure in baseball's history
before Babe Ruth transformed the game with his mammoth home runs
and unparalleled showmanship. In the 1920s Ruth made the New York
Yankees franchise a glowing success, but earlier in the century McGraw
had taken the moribund Giants and quickly built them into America's
richest and most famous sports team. It was a team that closely reflected
his temperament and style. As Christy Mathewson, the finest pitcher of
his day and McGraw's favorite player, once remarked, "The club *is*

McGraw." In various ways all of baseball came to show McGraw's influence. In the view of John B. Sheridan, "no man has ever laid the impress of his ego, his psyche, his soul, his animating spirit upon baseball as [has] John Joseph McGraw. . . ."[13]

McGraw's career as player and manager spanned two distinct eras: the raucous and rough-hewn baseball that still prevailed in the late nineteenth and early twentieth centuries, and the mature, firmly anchored big-business and big-time sport of the post—World War I decade. McGraw saw baseball move out of the wooden ballparks of the Nineties, fire traps that held at most 15,000 spectators, into the big steel-and-concrete baseball palaces epitomized in the 1920s by the rebuilt Polo Grounds and the new Yankee Stadium. He was an intimate part of the game's evolution from the lusty hitting of the Nineties, through the dead-ball years, dominated by pitching and base-running and "inside baseball," on into a style of play based on the advent of the lively ball and featuring home runs and reliance on the "big inning." McGraw proved himself a winner, whether playing or managing, and regardless of what style of baseball was in favor. His life opens a window on a rich and colorful half-century in baseball and American society.

One

---·---

"AS GOOD AS THEY COME"

THROUGHOUT THE NINETEENTH CENTURY the United States was chronically short of labor to fuel its robustly growing economy, and welcomed nearly all the Europeans who wanted to come. Those people already here, no matter how shallow their own roots, habitually looked with suspicion and often contempt on the successive waves of immigrants who came after them. In the late 1840s, Roman Catholics, mainly from southern Ireland and the southern German states, began to arrive in large numbers. Hundreds of thousands came to a country in which Protestantism had always been the overwhelmingly dominant religious influence.

Of the various immigrant groups coming in the century's middle decades, the Irish Catholics generally had the worst time of it. Mostly destitute when they got off the boat and professing a faith that vast numbers of Americans held to be alien and dangerous, the Irish took the lowest-paying jobs and crowded into the rundown sections of the seaports and industrializing cities, where jobs were most readily available. Some prospered and managed to rise in a society where increasingly money and money alone influenced social standing. But most Irish families persisted in poverty into the second generation and often long beyond.

Not all of the Irish became permanent city dwellers. Quite a few ended up in small towns throughout the northeastern and midwestern states, people seeking a better chance. One immigrant seeking another new start was John McGraw, a widower in his mid-thirties, who in 1871 came to the town of Truxton in Cortland County, New York. Not much is known about the prior circumstances of his life. Fifteen or so years

9

earlier he and an older brother, Michael, had come over from Ireland. They arrived in time for the Civil War, into which John McGraw, at least, was drawn as a recruit for the Army of the Union. Somewhere along the line, probably not long after the war, he married. After losing his wife in childbirth, he found his way with a baby daughter to the valley of the little Tioughnioga River, apparently in the hope that he might find a teaching job and thereby make use of the ten or twelve years of Catholic schooling he had received in Ireland. But no teaching job was to be had.

So John McGraw went to work helping build the railroad originally called the Midland and, under a subsequent corporate reorganization, renamed the Elmira, Cortland & Northern, connecting Elmira to the southwest with Canastota on the main New York Central line. When the stretch of track through the Tioughnioga Valley was finished, he stayed on with the E, C & N as a maintenance worker, tending the roadbed and track. Paid nine dollars for a sixty-hour work week, he was able to provide for himself and his daughter. Well enough, in fact, so that he could start thinking about remarriage. It took him only a short time to find another wife, a young woman just out of her teens named Ellen Comerfort, from a local Catholic family. The new husband, wife, and stepdaughter moved into a little rented house on West Hill, about two miles from the center of town. In that house on April 7, 1873, Ellen Comerfort McGraw bore her first child, a boy with an abundance of black hair and eyes that were so dark brown everybody would always say they were black. They named him John, after his father, and Joseph, for the baby's grandfather in Ireland.

John McGraw, the father, was better educated than most people of his day, sober, hard-working, devoutly Catholic. He deserved to do better in his adopted country. He might have, too, if his family hadn't quickly outgrown his ability to care for more than its most minimal needs. In less than twelve years, seven more McGraws—three boys and four girls—were born on West Hill. The McGraws may have had their moments of light-heartedness and warm, loving companionship; but the main ingredients of their lives were toil and denial: managing week by week to have food on the table and enough clothing to protect against the region's harsh winters.

In the 1870s and 1880s, Truxton, New York, was no isolated village. It was only eleven miles by railroad into the county seat at Cortland, and within an hour and a half (with a train change at Rippleton), one could reach Syracuse, a real city. Truxton's population was close to four hundred, enough to support a bank, a two-story tavern and hotel owned by Mary Goddard in the center of town, a smaller inn-boardinghouse, several grocery stores, a livery stable, and three churches—Methodist, Northern Baptist, and Roman Catholic. About a fifth of Truxton's population was foreign-born. (There were no black residents at all.) Of the foreign-born, most were Irish and nearly all Catholic.

St. Patrick's Church, a mock-Tudor edifice whose outsized spire and belfry gave it a top-heavy appearance, was where John and Ellen McGraw brought their children unless the road from West Hill was impassable. As an altar boy, Johnny McGraw was supposed to be there regardless of what the road was like. In winter he had to rise well before dawn, dress himself in the dark, and trudge through the snow to assist the priests who came from Cortland to say Mass and hear confessions.

By all accounts the boy was well liked. He was courteous and conscientious as he went about the village in his shabby clothes, doing odd jobs for dimes and quarters and helping out as best he could in a family that almost every year added another. The circumstances of the hardworking McGraws elicited sympathy from many of the townfolk but little else. Like the rest of the area's poor, the McGraws were supposed to take care of themselves and expect nothing from outside sources.

If it was a period when poor people basically had to fend for themselves, it was also one in which children usually looked after their own recreations and entertainments, uninhibited by organizing and supervising adults. And it was a period when, across the United States, in little places like Truxton and big cities as well, boys loved to get together and throw and catch and knock around a baseball. Johnny McGraw managed to save a dollar and send off to the recently founded Spalding brothers' company in Chicago for one of their cheaper-model balls. Everywhere he went he carried that ball tucked into a hip pocket, and whenever he could he played with village boys on the school lot. Townspeople soon became used to the sight and sound of the pint-sized McGraw boy hurling his ball against the shed behind the Methodist church in the deepening twilight, after all the others had been called home.

In the winter of 1884–85, a diphtheria epidemic moved through the Tioughnioga Valley, closing local schools and churches and causing people to lock their doors and avoid contact with others as much as possible. The McGraw family was one of the hardest hit. Within a few days after giving birth to a baby girl, her eighth child, Ellen McGraw

came down with a high fever and severe sore throat. In another two days
she was dead. A week later thirteen-year-old Anna also died, choking
and gasping as her father and stepbrothers and stepsisters watched
helplessly. By the end of January three more McGraw offspring had
succumbed. Then the sickness finally passed, and people came up the
hill to do what they could for the children and their dazed and bitter
father. They convinced him that he would be better off moving into town,
particularly so he could get somebody to look after the baby girl who
had miraculously survived. Johnny McGraw, at age eleven, became a
full-fledged town boy, moving with his father and his two younger brothers
and two sisters into a frame house across Truxton's main street from
Mary Goddard's hotel.

What had been a hard life now became a lot harder. Johnny was
expected to do more than ever to help support his family. His father
had little time for him, little patience with his still-childish moments,
no use at all for the boy's passion for baseball. He gave his son floggings
for collecting piles of stones from the nearby railroad bed, stones the
boy liked to slap around with a stick as he sought to improve his batting
skill. Father and son quarreled incessantly about the amount of time the
boy spent playing foolish games when he was needed for chores around
the house. On several occasions Johnny McGraw's long hits broke neigh-
bors' window panes; each time his father had to come up with fifteen
cents to cover the damage.

One night in the early fall of 1885, when Johnny McGraw was still
only twelve, his father paid a caller for one more broken pane and then
turned on his son in what seemed like a murderous rage. He grabbed
the boy and threw him into a corner of the little front room, then jerked
him up and began slapping and punching him. The boy managed to
break free and get upstairs, where he crammed some possessions into
a sack. Bolting back down the stairs, he got past the man and out the
front door. After a dash through rain and mud across the road, he reached
the side alley of the Truxton House and found refuge in the kitchen of
Mary Goddard.

Mary Goddard was a kind-hearted woman in her late thirties. Widowed
a few years earlier, she was now trying to raise two sons of her own
while she operated the two-story hotel in white clapboard with green
shutters that was the best accommodation to be found between Cortland
and Cazenovia. When John McGraw came looking for his son, she
persuaded him that the sensible thing was to let the boy remain with

her. When he left the Truxton House that day, John McGraw may have realized that his son's flight was the beginning of the breakup of what remained of his family.

Over the next few years Johnny McGraw watched his brothers and sisters move out of the house across the road and into other people's homes. Finally his father also moved, and from then on the boy rarely saw him. Meanwhile, Johnny thrived under Mary Goddard's care. Besides attending the local school, he took on a variety of responsibilities at the hotel and eventually got the Cortland distributors of the Elmira *Telegraph*, the area's only daily newspaper, to make him their Truxton delivery agent. That meant that sometimes he had to brave snowstorms to get the paper to the farmers outside town, but the money made it worthwhile. He also got a job as a "butcher boy" on the E, C & N, selling magazines, candies, frúits, and other items out of a big basket. Catching the train at Truxton after his morning chores, he peddled his goods among the passengers on the Cortland–Elmira run, killed a three-hour layover (often by finding some local boys to play ball with), and then worked the passengers back to Cortland. He usually was home in time for evening chores at Mrs. Goddard's.

He had enough money to buy new baseballs and the annual guides published by the Spalding company. Poring over those guides late at night, he memorized the year-by-year rules changes instituted in the National League and its rival major league, the American Association, as professional baseball's leaders continued to alter the sport that had already become the nation's favorite. Young McGraw prided himself on knowing those rules, knowing them so well that he could overawe his playmates in any dispute and stump the town's adult baseball enthusiasts as well. As he grew stronger and tougher (though not much bigger), he became the best player on the school team. The summer after he turned sixteen, he began playing for the Truxton town team, known as the Grays and managed by Albert "Bert" Kenney, owner of a local boardinghouse. The boy could play anywhere in the infield or outfield, but his ability to throw a big-breaking curve ball made him, at 105 pounds, the team's star pitcher.

He worked hard and stayed almost impossibly busy. The Goddard quarters at the back of the hotel provided warmth, a safe place, and plenty to eat; sometimes the O'Connor family, who lived a short distance down the road, also fed him. But young McGraw lacked parental affection, concern, and guidance, lacked much of anything to care for or about outside of himself. Nobody was going to look out for his interests if he didn't. So he had no compunction at all about terrorizing a Freeville boy who horned in on his trade by selling sandwiches and candies through the train windows. If he could hustle an extra dollar by showing a gullible traveler that a curve ball really did curve, as he did during a stop on the E, C & N one day, then he eagerly seized the chance. When the manager of the town team at East Homer, five miles to the south, wanted him to pitch a Saturday game, McGraw refused to go unless he received five dollars and transportation from and back to Truxton, an exorbitant arrangement in the penurious world of town baseball. It was his first big moment: arriving by buggy to the applause of the East Homer crowd, pitching and winning his game, collecting his pay, and riding triumphantly from the grounds.

In late-nineteenth-century America, young Irish Catholic males had four main paths of advancement open to them: politics, police work, the priesthood, and professional sports. Opportunities in politics and the police were most readily available in the cities, where masses of Irish voters gave their allegiance to Irish-dominated political organizations, of which Tammany Hall in New York City was the most famous—and infamous. Getting on as a policeman usually depended on having connections with somebody already on the force or possessing political influence. As for the priesthood, that required not only the most devout attitude but long years of study. An unquestioning Catholic, young McGraw was nonetheless not an especially devout one or, except for the hours he spent with his baseball guides, at all studious.

Professional sports in that day meant mainly prizefighting and baseball. In the United States, fighting for money had long been dominated by the Irish, from John Morrissey in the 1850s, the first generally recognized American champion, to John L. Sullivan, the indubitable champion of the world in the years when John McGraw was growing up. By the 1880s increasing numbers of Irish youths—from the mill towns of New England, from the slums of the big cities, sometimes even from little places like Truxton, New York—were playing baseball for a living.

At the age of sixteen, John McGraw was a fast runner, a good semiprofessional pitcher, and a sharp left-handed hitter, although he threw right-handed. To avoid further window breakage in the schoolhouse in right field, he'd become expert at slicing hits to his left. He might have starred many years on Saturdays for the Grays and other area teams, until his skills dulled and he was left with his fading notoriety among the locals and a routine of toil ahead of him. Lacking major industrial development and offering land for farming that had little topsoil but plenty of rocks, the Tioughnioga Valley held scant promise for a boy with no family connections and no more than a rough grammar-school education.

John McGraw was one of the millions of youngsters, Irish or whatever, who not only fantasized about playing baseball professionally but practiced endlessly and played as often as they could in the hope that somehow, some kind of opportunity would come along. In a period long before the big-time ball clubs used paid scouts or even held regular tryouts for prospects, getting that opportunity was usually a matter of chance, of knowing somebody who was both interested and able to help. In young McGraw's case that man was Bert Kenney.

A town-ball veteran, Kenney had no illusions about his future as a ballplayer. But he did have a few hundred dollars to spend and a yen to buy into a professional team. In return for putting up some of the money for the Olean, New York, franchise in the newly formed New York–Pennsylvania League, he got himself named player-manager (or "captain," in the parlance of the time), with responsibility for recruiting players for the upcoming 1890 season.

As soon as he heard the news, John McGraw was at Kenney's boardinghouse begging for a chance to play for Kenney's team at Olean. Kenney liked the boy and acknowledged that he was a fine player in the local competition, but he doubted that McGraw's "outcurve" would be enough against professional batters. But he didn't have to pitch, protested the boy; he'd be willing to play any position. Kenney finally agreed to give him a contract. On April 1, 1890, six days before his seventeenth birthday, John J. McGraw signed his first professional baseball contract. It called for a salary of forty dollars per month, provided he stuck with the team.

Olean, New York, located just above the Pennsylvania line in the southwestern part of the state, nearly two hundred miles by rail from Truxton, was the farthest from home the youth had ever traveled. The New York–Pennsylvania League was one of a dozen or so "minor leagues" officially recognized as belonging to "Organized Baseball." When McGraw arrived at Olean early in May to begin the season, he no doubt imagined himself moving quickly up to the "major leagues," of which there were now not two but three, each consisting of eight teams.

Over the winter, in an astonishing turn of events, the Brotherhood of
Professional Players had gone into open revolt against the salary limits
imposed by the National League and the American Association, which
kept even the outstanding performers at a maximum $2,400 per year.
By April 1890, when the new season got under way, nearly all of the
top players in the two older major leagues had joined with a group of
financial backers to form the Players' League. Under a visionary profit-
sharing arrangement, the Brotherhood challenged one or both of the
established leagues in seven of the eight Players' League cities. Besides
adding more than one hundred new roster positions, the "Brotherhood
War" was expected to produce vigorous bidding for the available talent
and big jumps in players' salaries. Suddenly, for players in the minor
leagues and ambitious nonprofessionals as well, prospects in baseball
seemed a lot brighter.

On May 16, 1890, John McGraw started on the bench. Two days
later, for the second game of the season, Kenney put him at third base
against Erie. It was a disastrous debut. The first ball hit to him was a
slow grounder. As McGraw described the moment many years later, "for
the life of me, I could not run in to get it. It seemed like an age before
I had the ball in my hands and then, as I looked over to first, it seemed
like the longest throw I ever had to make. The first baseman was the
tallest in the league, but I threw the ball far over his head."[1] McGraw
had nine more chances in the game and made seven more errors, mostly
on errant throws. One single off the Erie pitcher hardly made up for his
debacle afield.

From his place in center field, Bert Kenney had to admit to himself
that, for all his enthusiasm, the boy just wasn't ready for the New York–
Pennsylvania League. Nor were most of McGraw's teammates, for that
matter. By the time Olean lost its sixth game without a victory, hardly
anybody was coming to the local ballpark. McGraw was the first victim
of the general overhaul Kenney and the other owners decided they had
to make. When Kenney gave McGraw his release, he also lent him
seventy dollars and wished him luck in catching on with another team
somewhere, if he decided not to go home.

The idea of going back to Truxton was intolerable for young John
McGraw. However friendly and comfortable little towns might be for
those who lived there, they could often be insular and unforgiving toward
those who'd left with a hope of finding something better and then failed
to find it. Before McGraw's departure, both Mary Goddard and his father

had urged him to stay at home, take a regular job with the railroad or some other kind of steady work, and forget "this baseball foolishness." In other words, resign himself to being a nobody, going nowhere. The boy was determined to play baseball and to succeed as a professional, to make a name for himself, to get away from Truxton and the poverty and insecurity he'd known there. If he had to start all over again, in another strange town and in another league, then that was what he would do.

Wellsville, New York, was where he started over. Thirty-two miles east of Olean, less than half as large at something over three thousand, Wellsville was a member of the fledgling Western New York League. That was about as minor league as professional ball got. Wellsville proved a refuge for five others cut from Olean, including eventually Bert Kenney, who was bought out as part owner and dismissed as player-manager. Everybody was expected to play everywhere at Wellsville. Appearing in twenty-four games from June until the season ended about October 1, McGraw pitched occasionally and, at one time or another, played all the infield and outfield positions. He still made plenty of errors, but at least he cut down on his wild throws. At bat he was impressive, hitting for a .365 average in 107 times at the plate. Exactly what McGraw had proved at Wellsville, other than that he could hold his own in competition not much better than the semi-pro teams back home, wasn't at all clear. But at least he'd managed to put in a season as a seventeen-year-old professional.

Another wanderer who found his way to Wellsville before the season ended was Alfred W. Lawson. A Britisher by birth who'd grown up in New England, Lawson had started the season as a nominal major-leaguer, pitching (and losing) a total of three games for Boston and Pittsburgh in the talent-depleted National League. Lawson wasn't much of a pitcher, but he had a natural talent for self-promotion and persuading others to follow his lead. Later in his life he would successively lecture on the Chautauqua circuit, publish a religious novel, and, claiming divine inspiration, become a pioneer in American aviation as a flyer, aircraft designer, and magazine publisher. By the 1930s he was promoting "Lawsonomy," one of various short-lived sociotechnocratic movements surfacing in the years of the Great Depression.

In 1890, "Al" Lawson was a twenty-one-year-old journeyman baseball player whose current big idea was to recruit a group of players and lead them to Cuba that winter for a series of games. He liked the braininess of the little McGraw kid, particularly after his minute knowledge of the rules produced a forfeit to Wellsville in a late-August game at Hornell. Lawson asked McGraw if he wanted to join his American All-Stars, who would be playing a few games out of Ocala, Florida, before taking a boat for Cuba about the middle of January. Facing a cold and tedious winter as Mrs. Goddard's hired hand, the boy readily agreed.

After saving as much money as he could out of his wages at the Truxton House, buying Christmas gifts for his brothers and sisters, and visiting briefly with his cheerless and doubting father, McGraw was off for Florida. Traveling the whole thousand miles by day coach because he couldn't afford Pullman accommodations, he reached Ocala in mid-January. A week or so later the dozen All-Stars embarked from Tampa; a couple of days of rough seas brought them into Havana harbor.

In 1891 Cuba was still a colony of Spain, one of only two remaining possessions of consequence in what had once been Spain's glorious New World empire. While the vast majority of Cubans continued to subsist in squalor and ignorance, an affluent class of landowners and sugar producers could afford the time and expense to encourage a variety of sports. Introduced as far back as the 1870s by young Cubans returning from college in the United States and zealously promoted by the wealthy journalist Carlos Ayala, baseball already rivaled cock-fighting and horse racing as the favorite pastimes among the islanders. On the outskirts of Havana, a city of something over 200,000, stood a well-built ballpark seating close to 10,000.

Al Lawson's All-Stars included three men with major league experience besides Lawson, but of the half-dozen games they played against various Cuban teams, they managed only one win. The Cubans played not only with enthusiasm but also, the Americans were surprised to see, with considerable skill. The games drew poorly and provided only enough receipts to cover the All-Stars' expenses. But those who did attend quickly made the hustling, hard-running little shortstop their favorite among the Americans. "*El mono amarillo*" ("the yellow monkey"), they called him because of his size and the bright yellow uniforms in which Lawson had garbed his All-Stars. In fact the Cubans liked McGraw so much that after one game, when, still in uniform, he got separated from his teammates and found himself lost four miles from his hotel, dozens of exuberant *aficionados* surrounded him and made such a commotion that the local police were about to arrest him for creating a public disturbance. Luckily, a famous Havana billiards player named De Oro happened by, rescued the bewildered and frightened youngster, and sent him on his way in a horse-drawn taxi.

Lawson, McGraw, and the others had only enough money to get as far as Key West, where they split into two squads, added some local talent, and played a few games to pay for the boat trip to Tampa. By the end of February, 1891, they were back in central Florida, this time basing themselves at Gainesville. Lawson hoped to arrange games with major league teams training in the area. Half of his players had tired of his schemes and headed north to their homes. McGraw, having no other plans, decided to stay and try to play in the ankle-deep sand that passed for the local ballfield. Lawson had him and four others sign contracts whereby each agreed "to play with the . . . club until further notified, for board, shaving and washing expenses, also a cigar once a week."[2] Inasmuch as McGraw rarely had to shave and would never take up smoking, he obviously expected nothing but the chance to play more baseball.

Billing his team as the champions of Florida after a couple of victories over an outfit from Ocala, Lawson induced the Cleveland National Leaguers, training at Jacksonville, to play. On March 26 a crowd of several hundred filled the pine-boarded bleachers at Gainesville to watch the Clevelands. Reconstituted since the collapse of the Players' League during the off-season, they now included such present or future standouts as captain Oliver "Patsy" Tebeau, infielders Clarence "Cupid" Childs and Ed McKean, and a big rookie pitcher from Ohio named Denton True Young, whose cyclonic fastball had already earned him the nickname "Cy."

John McGraw, hitherto an obscure minor-leaguer, gained a measure of recognition that day. Years later he admitted that Len Viau, Cleveland's pitcher, was still working his arm into condition and didn't really bear down on the Gainesville batters. Nevertheless, McGraw's performance against the major-leaguers—three doubles in five times at bat, three runs (of six Gainesville scored to Cleveland's nine), errorless play at shortstop—made his name widely known when the telegraphed reports of the game appeared in the Cleveland newspapers, were picked up by other dailies, and were also noted in the baseball weeklies *Sporting Life* and *Sporting News*.[3] Within a week or so, McGraw had heard from a score of professional clubs seeking his services for the coming season.

Inasmuch as he and the rest of the players at Wellsville had all received their releases the past October, McGraw was free to go wherever he wanted. With Lawson's advice, McGraw set his price at $125 a month and an advance of $75 against his salary. When Jim Plumb, manager of the Cedar Rapids club in the Illinois-Iowa League, wired him the full $75, he decided that was where he would play. McGraw always maintained that he sent back the money wired by other clubs, but subsequently Davenport and Rockford, also in the Illinois-Iowa League, and Fort Wayne in the Michigan-Indiana League claimed that McGraw had agreed to play for them. The Rockford club went so far as to hire an attorney, promising to "stop his conquettish antics and teach him a needed lesson. At best he is but an experiment and is altogether too gay a young blood who has had but one season out." There was even talk of securing an injunction to keep McGraw from taking the field when Cedar Rapids played at Rockford. McGraw had signed with at least five different clubs, claimed the Rockford officials, and a man who would do that "should not be allowed to play at all."[4] By the time his team made its first trip into the Illinois town, however, such talk had subsided.

By early April 1891, McGraw was in Cedar Rapids, Iowa, a thriving little city of about 18,500. Baseball enthusiasm was running high there, especially when the National League's Chicago White Stockings, led by first-baseman Adrian "Cap" Anson, baseball's first authentic superstar, came into town for an exhibition game. Partly dismantled by principal owner A. G. Spalding and further weakened by the Brotherhood War, the White Stockings were no longer the powerhouse they'd been in the mid-1880s. They were still a good ball club, though, better than any McGraw had seen so far. As an eighteen-year-old veteran of not only American but international competition and as a much-sought-after ballplayer (as his offers from all those minor league clubs proved), McGraw was brash and cocky enough to lead his teammates in razzing the famous big-leaguers. On a field that was deep in mud following a morning of rain, McGraw made a leaping stab at shortstop of a liner off Anson's bat, poked a single to left field off Chicago ace Bill Hutchinson, and yelled for Anson to get out of the way as he rounded first base. His play impressed Anson; at the end of the game (won by Chicago 2–0), he asked the sassy kid if maybe he'd like to play for Chicago some day. McGraw left the field with self-esteem soaring.

For the Canaries, as the Cedar Rapids outfit was called, McGraw played solid all-around ball. The "dandy little shortstop," as a local correspondent described him, handled sixteen chances without an error in a game late in May—a notable achievement in those days. After eighty-five games he was hitting .275, one of the better averages in the league. Around the circuit he was coming to be known for his tough, scrappy style of play.

The league itself, though, was falling apart. The Aurora and Davenport franchises had folded up by the beginning of August, and the remaining six teams were none too steady. McGraw was already thinking about leaving for the Pacific Coast to catch on with a team in the California League when his biggest break so far came along. How it happened gives some indication of the way ballplayers were "discovered" and advanced in those days.

Rockford had a player named Bill Gleason, who'd been the shortstop on the champion St. Louis Browns in the American Association in the mid-Eighties. When Cedar Rapids played at Rockford in mid-August, Gleason told McGraw that Bill Barnie, manager of the Association's Baltimore club, had written to ask about McGraw. Sometimes, Gleason explained, old friends like Barnie wanted him to look over young players. So how good did McGraw think he was? "You can tell Barnie," answered the grizzled eighteen-year-old, "I'm just about as good as they come."[5]

Gleason's report to Barnie must have been a favorable one. When the Canaries reached Ottumwa, Barnie wired Hank Smith, a Baltimorean on the team: "Is there a possible chance for me to get McGraw? Let me know at once. If so, will arrange terms with him on arrival." Late in the evening following the second game in Ottumwa, Smith and outfielder Bill Wittrock went to the hotel room of manager John Godar (who had replaced Plumb midway through the season). They showed Barnie's telegram to Godar, who then asked them what he ought to do. Having often heard McGraw declare that he would do anything to make the big leagues, and convinced that he was already good enough for the Association, Wittrock urged Godar not to hold the kid back. Smith was of like mind.

The three went to McGraw's room and pounded on his door until they woke him up. Godar told him about Barnie's wire. "Sure," said McGraw, "but what do you say about it, John? Will you let me go?" He could leave on the 2:30 A.M. train, Godar told him. McGraw grabbed his little grip and began stuffing collars and socks into it, talking excitedly as he worked. When he finally had everything packed, the foursome went around waking up the others on the team and sharing the news with them. Most of his teammates dressed in the middle of the night and accompanied the boy to the Ottumwa railroad depot. "When the train pulled out," as Wittrock recalled the moment, "Mac was as happy as a schoolboy."[6]

McGraw first returned to Cedar Rapids to gather up the few personal effects he'd left at his hotel, then boarded a Chicago and Burlington coach to start the long trip east. He later argued that inasmuch as he hadn't had a regular contract at Cedar Rapids, he hadn't jumped the club. Some of the locals thought differently, but, according to the *Sporting News* correspondent, McGraw had been such "a great favorite here" that there was little sentiment for trying to get him blacklisted within professional ball.[7]

McGraw's train pulled into Camden Station, Baltimore, on August 24, 1891. An English visitor in those years remarked that Baltimore had a handsome appearance if one arrived from the north via the Pennsylvania system's terminal. But from the western approach on the Baltimore and Ohio into Camden Station, the city seemed at first "a dirty, dreary, ramshackle sort of place." McGraw's view out the window was of "scores of dirty streets with shabby little one- and two-story dwellings, largely inhabited by Negroes, with plentiful supplies of pigs, chicken coops, and swarming children."[8] The great numbers of black people reminded McGraw of Havana and the cities in the American South he'd passed through the previous spring and fall. Baltimore had once been a slave-holding city in a slave-holding state, a place where, only thirty years earlier, pro-Secessionist mobs had assaulted Union troops as they marched through on the way to Washington. It remained a city with a distinctively Southern cultural flavor and powerful Southern economic ties, serving as a conduit for goods manufactured in the interior and shipped to Deep South ports. Baltimore's blacks, nearly a third of its total population, lived and worked in circumstances increasingly segregated, both by the extension of habitual practices and, of late, as mandated by laws and ordinances. Those were mostly the people who lived on the city's three hundred miles of dirt streets. A like amount was cobblestone; only forty-nine miles of street had asphalt or granite paving.

In 1890, only 13.5 percent of Baltimore's residents were foreign-born. In that respect Baltimore was strikingly unlike the country's other major cities. Although something like 600,000 immigrants landed at the port of Baltimore between 1870 and 1900, relatively few of them lingered, mainly because jobs in manufacturing and construction were more plentiful elsewhere. In 1890 nearly 60 percent of Baltimore's foreign-born were of German ancestry, so that besides its strongly Southern orientation, the city also had a marked European influence. Of the remaining foreign-born, the Irish were the most numerous, although by the end of the Nineties Poles and Russians had come to outnumber them.

One of the city's many prosperous German-American families was that of August Mencken, owner of a cigar factory and, for a few years in the 1880s, a major stockholder in the National League's woeful entry in nearby Washington. His son Henry Louis Mencken remembered the area where his family lived on Hollins Street in west Baltimore, only about two miles from the center of the city, as still being almost rural in the 1880s, with plenty of vacant lots and with open country starting nearby. One of the delights of being a Baltimorean then or any other time was eating. At a stand in Hollins Street, Mencken's mother bought eight-inch-long Chesapeake Bay crabs for ten cents a dozen, and peddlers sold the soft-shell variety from door to door at two cents each. Young Mencken had a particular fondness for the German-style sausage properly called *Wecke* but known locally as "weckers" and served in a split bun at the Association baseball field, long before the hot dog was supposedly invented at New York's Polo Grounds.

A city of almost 400,000 people, Baltimore was by far the biggest place John McGraw had ever been. It featured most of the up-to-date amenities of late-nineteenth-century urban life, with electricity having replaced gas lighting throughout the city (leaving a forest of utility poles and a maze of wires drooping over the streets). Horse-drawn trolleys had largely given way to electric street cars. It also offered some urban ills. The Patapsco River, winding northwestward from the bay, was already mostly dead, polluted by the canneries and fertilizer factories situated along its lower reaches. To a greater extent than other major American cities, Baltimore continued to be plagued by almost annual outbreaks of typhoid fever in summer and malaria in the fall. If it was one of the nation's most enjoyable cities—with its ethnic diversity, its marvelous cuisine and flourishing café life, its lovely squares and parks, and such a proliferation of statuary that it was called the Monument City—then it was also not a very healthy one.

McGraw checked in at the Eutaw Hotel, where he had been told several of the ballplayers lived, and found Bill Barnie. Thirty-eight years old, Barnie was bald but sported the luxuriant full mustache favored by nearly every American male who could manage to grow one. Barnie was dismayed by how little the kid was, particularly by his short arms and small hands. Surely this wasn't the ballplayer he'd recruited from Cedar Rapids. His small dark eyes burning, the 5'6½", 121-pound McGraw assured him that he was a ballplayer and a good one. If Barnie didn't think so, then "just get me out there and watch my smoke."[9] Not impressed by such youthful bravado, Barnie told him to report to the ballpark that afternoon, when the Baltimore team would be finishing a series with Washington.

Union Park, on Huntington Avenue near the York Road, due north of the business district, was a new ballpark. Built of wood like the others of that period, it seated about eight thousand. The team that played there, called the Orioles, had been a charter member of the American Association when it started out in 1882 as a rival to the six-year-old National League. In nine seasons, with Barnie the manager in all but the first, Baltimore had never finished higher than fifth place. This year's team was playing pretty good ball, but the turnouts at Union Park had been generally disappointing after an opening-day overflow of 10,500.

If the Baltimore club was losing money, so was nearly everybody else in the league. The Association had come out of the Brotherhood War in considerably worse shape than the National League. In 1891 the National League owners, realizing the weakness of their Association counterparts and seeking to regain their monopoly, had effectively abandoned the 1883 peace agreement with the Association. Now the two circuits were again fighting over rights to players and various other matters.

The Association had never enjoyed the prestige of the National League. For McGraw, though, it was still the big time. At the Orioles clubhouse Barnie gave him a contract for $200 a month for what remained of the season and a uniform worn by Sam Wise, a recently released eleven-year veteran. The uniform was about four sizes too big, but the newcomer gathered and tucked and belted the woolen flannel shirt and pants as best he could. He then pulled on his maroon woolen socks, laced the hightop spiked shoes that would continue to be standard baseball footwear for another fifteen years, carefully set his pillbox-shaped cap (with maroon horizontal stripes), and followed the rest of the Orioles onto the field, across a plank bridge over the ditch running between the clubhouse and the left-field bleachers.

McGraw was only an observer at his first big league game. He concentrated on the action as best he could, despite being jostled by his bigger teammates on the short, uncovered bench that was placed about halfway between the grandstand and the first-base line. Once they pushed him completely off the end of the bench—and then laughed as he scrambled to get up. McGraw threw a couple of wild punches—in full view of the thousand or so spectators—before Barnie calmed him down and had the others give him back his bench space.

The game that McGraw watched on the field was in rapid transition. Practically every winter brought major new rules changes. It had been only seven years since the League-Association joint rules committee lengthened the distance between the rectangular pitcher's "box" and home plate from forty-five to fifty feet, at the same time legalizing overhand pitches (although many still used sidearm or three-quarter-underhand deliveries). After the 1887 season the batter could no longer call for a high or low pitch, and in 1888–89, after experimenting with various combinations, the rulesmakers settled on three strikes for a strikeout and four balls for a base on balls. Padded fielders' gloves, already used by some players, were sanctioned by 1890. Before the start of the present season, substitutions were permitted at any time during the game (whereas previously a player could leave the game only if injured).

Throwing overhand from fifty feet with a ball that was apt to be scuffed and discolored, and didn't carry well off the bat in any case, the pitchers would have completely dominated the game if not for the trouble their fielders had stopping and catching the ball with their little pancake gloves (some still played gloveless) on the rocky infields and even rougher outfield surfaces found in nearly every ballpark. Pitchers had to aim at a home plate that was a diamond-set square only a foot wide (as opposed to the five-sided, seventeen-inch object adopted in 1900), and throw to a catcher who, in the absence of base runners, stood ten or fifteen feet behind the plate. Positioning himself that far back of the batter made it easier for the catcher to grab off foul tips (which if caught retired the batter on any strike). But at a time when catchers wore only a big padded mitt, a wire mask, and a thin chest-crotch pad, self-protection was obviously also a motive.

Despite the superabundance of fielding errors (an average of more than three per team per game in the League and Association in 1891), the pitchers generally held sway. Which is more than could be said for the umpires. Since the elimination of the batter's prerogative to call for his pitch, the umpire had come into his own as the central figure on the baseball diamond. Both the League and the Association normally assigned only one umpire for each game. Working alone, an umpire, no matter how resourceful and experienced, could never have a good view of all or even most of the plays he had to call. Besides resorting to a variety of tricks on their opponents when the umpire wasn't looking (some dirtier than others), players stormed and raged, shoved and shouldered the umpire himself when close calls went against them—and generally came off with little if any punishment from league officials. If the umpiring of the Nineties was the worst in baseball's history, as it no doubt was, then the same can be said for the conduct of the players. In the disorderly, poorly umpired, and loosely governed baseball of the period, John McGraw would flower and flourish as an umpire's nemesis without equal.

That afternoon, the scrawny rookie up from Cedar Rapids watched from the bench as Baltimore won 13–9 to run its record to 57–45, good for third place. Barnie told him he might play the next day against Columbus. It rained all day August 25. As he idled around the hotel, McGraw listened to the players' comments on the biggest baseball news of the day—the jump of Mike "King" Kelly, captain of the Association-leading Boston Reds and one of the game's top stars, over to the Boston Beaneaters, front-runners in the National League.

On Wednesday the twenty-sixth, Barnie put McGraw at shortstop. Hitting sixth in the batting order, he faced Columbus's best pitcher, left-hander Phil Knell, in the second inning. In his first major league time at bat, McGraw struck out with runners on second and third base. He went back out to shortstop and fumbled an easy ground ball, an error that led to Columbus's first run. Then in the sixth inning McGraw hit Knell's fast ball back over second base for a clean single and took second on the center-fielder's misplay. After going to third on a passed ball, he scored on a base hit by Wilbert Robinson, the Orioles' barrel-chested catcher. McGraw's run turned out to be the deciding score in Baltimore's 6–5 victory.

Not a spectacular first outing, but a respectable one. A Baltimore baseball writer described McGraw as "quick on his feet and a swift base-runner." In the field "he runs at the ball, and does not wait until it comes to him," but at least he was "a hard worker and a player willing to learn." "It's nice," McGraw wrote Bill Wittrock about life in the big time. "Just give me a little time and I have got 'em skinned to death."[10]

Yet for all his cockiness, McGraw produced relatively little smoke for Bill Barnie during the remainder of the season. The youth was simply over his head in the American Association, even if baseball men generally agreed that the caliber of play in the Association was inferior to that in the National League. McGraw was out of position on ground balls a good deal of the time, he had trouble making double plays, and he continued to fire the ball over the first baseman's head with discouraging regularity. Barnie tried him at second base, then at third, and finally put him in right field, where presumably his erratic fielding would do less harm. McGraw was one of the young players Barnie blamed for most of the team's losses on a western trip in September.

Late that month Barnie, who had been quarreling all season with Harry and Herman von der Horst, the Baltimore brewers who held most of the stock in the Orioles, finally quit. Outfielder George Van Haltren, a twenty-five-year-old Californian (one of the earliest in the majors) and already one of the top players in either league, took over for the last week of the season.

Baltimore finished in fourth place with a record of 69–65, its best showing ever.[11] McGraw finished with a batting average of .245 in thirty-one games and 106 times at bat. His eighteen errors in eighty-six chances gave him a dreary .842 average afield—close to the worst in the Association. Although Harry von der Horst signed him to a contract for 1892 right after the season ended, Van Haltren, kept on as player-manager, talked of his being at most a substitute on next year's team.

Whether or not McGraw made the team at Baltimore next season, he wouldn't be playing in the American Association. Partly because of National League undermining, partly because of spectator disinterest in the aftermath of the bitter and confusing Brotherhood War, half of the Association franchises were on the verge of collapse by September. In December 1891, in Indianapolis, the two circuits effected a merger whereby one twelve-team organization came into being. Besides the eight National League franchises (New York, Brooklyn, Boston, Philadelphia, Cincinnati, Pittsburgh, Cleveland, and Chicago), the Association's St. Louis, Washington, Louisville, and Baltimore clubs were included in the new amalgamated circuit. Although its official name was "the National League and American Association," only the most diehard Association partisans ever called it anything but the National League. Among the fifteen men assigned to Baltimore under the disposition of Association players worked out at Indianapolis was McGraw, formally listed as a substitute—and the only one so listed.

Meanwhile, he'd grabbed what looked like another good opportunity

to play in Cuba in the off-season for Al Lawson. This year's edition of
Lawson's All-Stars consisted entirely of young major-leaguers except for
Lawson himself, who'd spent another season bouncing around the bush
leagues. According to Lawson's plan, the All-Stars were to play games
in New Orleans, Mobile, and Pensacola, then sail for Cuba—as soon
as Lawson raised enough money. Lawson instructed McGraw and the
others to wait at a New Orleans hotel until he arrived to explain the
travel arrangements. Lawson never showed. He'd found a New Orleans
man willing to put up enough to pay one-way passage to Cuba for the
All-Stars, but nothing more. So Lawson had taken a steamer to Tampa,
leaving the players stranded, some of them nearly penniless. McGraw
was able to pay his train fare back to Truxton, where he renewed acquaintances with friends and relatives and swore never again to follow
one of Al Lawson's schemes.

In 1892 the von der Horst brothers decided that they couldn't stand
the expense of sending their ball club south for spring training. So Van
Haltren held workouts at Union Park when the weather permitted. Most
of the time the Orioles had to content themselves with throwing and
jogging in the Johns Hopkins University gymnasium. McGraw, having
eaten heartily in the off-season, arrived weighing about 130 pounds,
some of which he quickly lost by practicing longer and harder than
anybody else. Twelve hundred dollars for only six months' work was a
lot of money, especially for somebody still in his teens. But McGraw
knew that he stood a good chance of ending up in the minor leagues
again in 1892.

The friendliest of his teammates was Wilbert Robinson, the team's
number-one catcher. A Boston native, twenty-nine years old, only two
inches taller than McGraw but nearly a hundred pounds heavier, "Robbie," as everybody called him, wore the full handlebar mustache that
McGraw would never be able to grow himself. Although now Robinson
was a staunch family man, with four children and a wife he called "Ma,"
as a rookie with the Athletics in the Association he'd been the team's
official measurer of the bosoms on members of the Athletics' "Ladies'
Auxiliary," whose devotion to the well-being of their favorite players
often had known no bounds.

All the other clubs in the new twelve-team alignment had strengthened
themselves with the addition of surplus players from the Association.
The Baltimore club fielded almost the same team that had finished fourth
the year before. The 1892 club proved one of the era's worst. After the

Orioles lost eleven of their first twelve games, Van Haltren turned the manager's job over to club secretary George Waltz. In mid-May, following five straight additional losses, the von der Horsts brought in Edward H. "Ned" Hanlon to run the club.

Hanlon had been a fine center-fielder on the 1887 National League champion Detroit Wolverines and one of the players taken by A. G. Spalding on his famous globe-circling baseball tour in 1888–89. After he broke his leg in 1891, playing for Pittsburgh, his playing career virtually ended. He was thirty-four when he came to the Orioles. Although he'd always been regarded as an exceptionally smart player, not even the most blindly optimistic Baltimoreans could have anticipated that, mainly because of what he accomplished at Baltimore, he would become the most acclaimed manager of his time.

Hanlon was no overnight success. He realized that he'd taken over a dreadful team, one that would have to be patiently and carefully reconstructed. He seems to have seen little future in the players he inherited except maybe Robinson and John "Sadie" McMahon, a hard-throwing and hard-drinking young pitcher. Van Haltren, his best ballplayer but also resentful of Hanlon's authority, went to Pittsburgh late in the season for outfielder Joe Kelley. Numerous others came and went as Hanlon sought to put together a respectable lineup and impose discipline on a club that, according to the *Sporting News* correspondent, "seems to have had more trouble with its players getting drunk than any other club in this league this season."[12]

As for young McGraw, his personal habits may have given Hanlon no trouble, but his ballplaying left the new manager unconvinced. Although McGraw did appear in seventy-six games, more than half of his team's total, Hanlon used him as a fill-in—at second, short, third, or anywhere in the outfield. On three occasions, when the Orioles went on western trips, McGraw stayed behind in Baltimore so the club could economize on travel and lodging costs.

Baltimore finished with a record of 46–101 for the whole season, by far the poorest in the League.[13] That one season should have been enough to demonstrate the fundamental flaws in a twelve-team, top-to-bottom League structure. Even though the "magnates," as the club owners liked to be called in the press, had split the season and provided for a post-season series if different teams won, in each half six or seven teams quickly fell out of the running and local interest faded.[14] Throughout the eight-year history of the unwieldy twelve-team setup, it never seems to have occurred to the magnates even to consider dividing the League into eastern and western divisions of six clubs each and staging a championship series between the two divisional leaders.[15] So year after year, at least half of the National League's franchises piled up deficits after June.

Baltimore's losses had been heavy. Even though the league had instituted austerity measures in mid-year, authorizing the clubs to cut salaries and reduce their rosters to thirteen men, the von der Horsts still lost about $18,000. The official season's attendance at Union Park, for about seventy playing dates, was 93,580.[16] Nicholas E. "Uncle Nick" Young, the National League's ineffectual president, cited in support of his recommendations for even further salary reductions, as well as a shorter season, the fact that for two October games in Baltimore the visiting teams' share of the gate receipts had been $6.37 and $6.87.

Other than his $1,200 salary, as little as any player in the League was paid, McGraw's services had cost the Baltimore franchise very little. He hadn't even been with the team much of the time when it was on the road. As part-time players were expected to do, he'd taken his turns collecting tickets at the Union Park gate, in full uniform, and enthusiastically coached at first or third base when the Orioles were at bat. During a game at Union Park in August, he showed his dedication to the club in an extraordinary manner. Coaching at third, he watched a foul ball bounce over the low fence beyond the grandstand and into the hands of a spectator, who acted as if he intended to keep the ball. The presumption everywhere in that period was that baseballs, which cost $1.25 each, were the property of the club and must be returned to the field when they landed among the spectators. McGraw ran over, snatched the man's hat, and successfully bartered hat for baseball. Maybe to reward the youngster's zeal, Hanlon put him in the lineup the next day— but then left him in Baltimore when the rest of the team took a train that night for Chicago.

At any rate, John McGraw had survived a full season of major league ball, had held on despite the dizzying turnover in players after Hanlon took charge. He'd improved his batting average to .267, in 288 times at bat, and stolen fourteen bases. His defensive skills had also improved markedly; a fielding percentage of .913 wasn't bad, he thought, considering that he'd never been allowed to settle into any one position and stay there. McGraw was still brash, cocky, outwardly still convinced that, as he'd told Bill Gleason, he was "as good as they come." But to himself, at least, he must have admitted that he'd been a marginal player on a sorry ball club, that he wouldn't have been able to hang on with most of the other National League teams. Realistically, his future in baseball was still in doubt.

Yet fortunes were about to brighten for both McGraw and the Baltimore Orioles. McGraw was about to become a better-educated man, at least in the formal sense, and gain his first experience teaching baseball to others. And Ned Hanlon was about to put together one of the most colorful and successful outfits in the game's history.

Two
·
THE OLD ORIOLES

ONE OF THE FEW BENEFITS of John McGraw's short and unhappy trial with the Olean team in the spring of 1890 was his friendship with the Reverend Joseph F. Dolan. Dolan was a young faculty member, a baseball follower, and the person who generally supervised athletics at Allegany College, an institution of about three hundred male students located just east of the village of Allegany and about four miles west of Olean. Founded in 1856, the college was operated by the Order of Franciscan Monks. One evening Dolan brought the downcast McGraw back to the college for dinner. Besides gently admonishing him to keep himself clean, avoid the temptations that awaited a young man on his own far from home, and make regular confession of those transgressions he did commit, Dolan talked to McGraw about the advantages of a college education, even for somebody who might become a big-leaguer.

Dolan's words, at least the part about getting more education, probably made little impression on McGraw at the time. Two and one-half years later, though, he faced spending the off-season either in Baltimore, where things were expensive, or Truxton, where things were dull. Remembering what Dolan had said, he wrote the priest offering a proposition: If the college would let him enroll (despite his bare grammar-school background), let him take some courses, waive his tuition, and provide him room and board, then he would be willing to coach the college baseball team after the first of the new year. With consent from the Reverend Joseph Butler, the college's president, Dolan shortly let McGraw know that he was welcome to come under the arrangement he'd proposed. After paying his bill at the Eutaw, buying a few new clothes, and finally sending Bert Kenney the seventy dollars he'd borrowed when he left Olean, McGraw was off to college.

"John McGraw had no bad habits," according to the recollection of Joe A. Broderick, student manager of the college baseball team when McGraw arrived.[1] He resisted the saloon and the brothel, termed by *Spalding's Guide* (1889) "the two great obstacles in the way of success of the majority of professional ballplayers. . . ."[2] McGraw neither smoked, chewed tobacco, nor even drank beer when he entered Allegany College as a slightly older beginning student and an extraordinarily young baseball coach. He was, moreover, "an earnest student," tackling first-year English grammar and composition, history, and mathematics with an intense determination to make up for what he'd missed—to get the schooling that, as a poor Irish kid, he'd been neither required nor expected to have.[3]

Allegany College in the early 1890s consisted of a dormitory and two classroom buildings, one of which was Alumni Hall. In January the nineteen-year-old coach took his charges down to Alumni Hall's freezing, unfloored basement. After having them level the ground, hang kerosene lanterns around the walls, and put up a chicken-wire batting cage, he started drilling them in baseball fundamentals. Although most of his recruits were older than he was, McGraw insisted on discipline, teamwork, and, when he was able to take them outside for intrasquad games at the end of February, aggressive play. By the time he left for spring training with the Orioles, McGraw had his team ready for its first successful season in years in the only varsity sport played at the college. As for his studies, he'd received full credit (despite enrolling late) for the fall term and, per his understanding with Dolan and Butler, given his full time to the baseball team in the second term.

Over the winter Ned Hanlon had bought 30 percent of the stock in the Baltimore franchise, then pressured the smaller stockholders into electing him club president, with Harry von der Horst becoming treasurer. Hanlon thus acquired the strongest position of any manager at the time, responsible to nobody for the decisions he made on the field or the disposition he made of players' contracts. (Once the season began, von der Horst, in response to customers' complaints about the ball club, would start wearing a badge that said simply, "Ask Hanlon.") Whereas Hanlon had worn a uniform after coming to Baltimore the previous year and even appeared in a few games, he now took to managing in street clothes, often including a silk top hat and spats. That meant staying on the bench, as was required of nonuniformed managers, and leaving the intimate forms of umpire-harassment to his players on the field.

The National League club presidents had decided to reduce the season to 132 games and once again to lengthen the pitching distance by ten feet. Now the pitcher would have to throw from 60' 6". Instead of taking a skip-step within a 5'-by-4'6" box as he delivered the ball, he now had to keep his back foot anchored to a rubber slab twelve inches long and four inches wide (changed to twenty-four inches by six inches two years later).[4] As they'd usually done since the development of full-scale professional baseball in the 1870s, and as they would usually do over succeeding decades, the rulemakers proceeded from the assumption that paying customers preferred lusty hitting over tight pitching. However resourceful they might be, pitchers, having honed their skills moving both feet and throwing from ten feet closer, would be at a severe disadvantage in 1893 and for several years thereafter. Some, especially talented young pitchers like Cy Young of Cleveland, Charles "Kid" Nichols of Boston, and Amos Rusie of New York, would adjust easily to the new distance, to keeping the back foot stationary, and to throwing off the new dirt mounds that would quickly appear in ballparks around the league and indeed throughout the country in 1893. Others—veterans Gus Weyhing, Bill Hutchinson, and Tony Mullane—were never able to regain their effectiveness.[5]

As club president, Hanlon decreed that henceforth the Orioles would train in warm weather. Late in March fourteen players started working out at Charleston, South Carolina. McGraw arrived determined to show Hanlon that he was a ballplayer of major league caliber. That spring, for the first time, he began to display the belligerent, quarrelsome, unprincipled on-field personality that would become basic to his reputation as a player and manager—and to the McGraw legend. In a game with a semi-pro outfit at Savannah, he cursed out the local manager, who proceeded to knock him down. Only Hanlon's cool-headedness prevented a mob fight between the two teams. At Chattanooga a week later, McGraw, playing shortstop, held a runner by the belt to keep him from advancing on a fly ball, spiked the opposition shortstop sliding into second, and slapped a sliding Chattanooga runner in the face with the ball, bloodying his nose. By the time the game ended, a good portion of the crowd was ready to assault the tough kid with the Baltimores.

Hanlon must have liked something in what he saw that spring. On opening day at Washington, "Mac," as his teammates called him, was at shortstop. His error let in two runs in the Orioles' 7–5 loss. It was immediately apparent how much of an edge the new pitching distance had given the batters. Baltimore and Washington combined for twenty-four hits in the opener; over their three-game series, they amassed forty-four runs.

"A very young and promising professional," "a fast base runner and a hard worker" who was "proving himself to be a clever all-around player"—so the New York *Clipper*, a weekly sports and entertainment paper, described McGraw when it printed a lithograph of him in May.[6] By then he'd won a place on the team, although his work at shortstop was still unreliable, often dreadful. So much so that about a third of the way into the season, Hanlon persuaded Bill Barnie, now managing at Louisville, to take infielder-outfielder Tim O'Rourke in exchange for first-baseman Harry Taylor and shortstop Hughey Jennings. The trade would turn out to be a major event in both the history of the Orioles and the life of John McGraw.

Like McGraw and like Ned Hanlon, Joe Kelley, and scores of others (including a string-bean catcher with Pittsburgh who'd changed his name from Cornelius McGillicuddy to Connie Mack), Hugh Ambrose Jennings was part of the great tide of Irish Catholics that came into professional baseball in the Eighties and Nineties. Whereas for McGraw baseball was a way to become something more than a railroad section hand, for Jennings it was a way out of a life of toil in the coal fields of northeastern Pennsylvania. Three years older than McGraw, a couple of inches taller and, in 1893, about thirty pounds heavier, with carrot-colored hair, a densely freckled face, and blue eyes, Jennings was almost equally intense, high-strung, and competitive. Nobody questioned his ability to play shortstop. So far, though, Jennings had been able to do little at bat, even in the midst of that year's hitting surge. When Baltimore acquired him, he was hitting .164.

Jennings became ill right after reporting to Hanlon and wasn't able to start his first game for the Orioles for another ten weeks. McGraw stayed at shortstop. Although he still had trouble playing the position, he'd become a smart and capable hitter. Usually batting leadoff, he'd begun to develop the keen eye and superb bat control that would make him one of the hardest men of his day to keep off the bases. And he knew how to rant at the umpires, block and hold base runners, and intentionally get part of himself in front of pitched balls as well as anybody in the League.

As he became better known around the circuit, some of the writers started referring to him in their columns as "Mickey Face"; others dubbed him "Muggsy." McGraw seems to have had no particular feelings one way or another about "Mickey Face," despite the mild ethnic slur it carried. Being called "Muggsy," though, was something he disliked from the beginning. Over the years he developed a burning hatred for the nickname and anybody who used it, however innocently or good-naturedly. He never explained why he felt so strongly about "Muggsy." For that matter, nobody could ever definitively account for the origin of the term. Some remembered that when McGraw came to Baltimore, a local politician with the same name and an unsavory reputation was called "Muggsy." Fred Lieb, a knowledgeable baseball reporter and historian, maintained that "Muggsy" was "a tough, ungrammatical character of the funny pages of the '90s."[7] Wherever "Muggsy" came from and however suitable the nickname may have seemed for the pugnacious McGraw, it remained to the end of his life one of the surest ways to trigger his wrath.

In 1893 the Orioles finished eighth among the twelve teams, with a record of 60–70. Despite the reduced schedule, attendance at Union Park had nearly doubled, and the franchise showed a profit for the first time since the Eighties. McGraw's batting average jumped to .328, topped on the club only by Robinson's, and he was among the League's leaders in runs scored. Playing shortstop until Jennings took over and then going to left field, he committed sixty-six errors in 127 games, below par even for the error-prone baseball of that period. Still, the *Sporting News* thought him "one of the best young players in the League."[8]

Even though Hughey Jennings had been obtained to displace him at shortstop, McGraw quickly took a liking to the peppery Pennsylvanian. At the end of the season he urged Jennings to join him at Allegany College. Like McGraw, Jennings's formal schooling had been limited to six or seven years; he knew how to read, write, and do basic arithmetic—but little more. McGraw sold Jennings on the value of more education and then convinced the Franciscan monks to give Jennings the same deal they'd given him. By mid-October, McGraw and his "associate coach" were students at what the Franciscans—to end the confusion of their institution with Allegheny College in Pennsylvania—had renamed St. Bonaventure College.

Over the winter McGraw and Jennings solidified what would endure as a warm, deep friendship. While McGraw moved on to algebra, Jennings found his element in history and rhetoric. At night, in their little dormitory room, they talked incessantly about nearly everything: women, their schoolwork, politics, even the hard times that had set in with the collapse of the stock market and many of the country's banks. Mostly, though, they talked baseball, devising new maneuvers, new ways to bend the rules, this or that means of gaining an edge on the opposition. In the poorly lit basement of Alumni Hall, McGraw helped Jennings overcome his fatal tendency to pull away from the ball instead of keeping his head down and stepping directly into it. For weeks McGraw fired high and tight pitches to Jennings while he had him stand with his back against the side of the batting cage. With no room to pull away, Jennings had to learn to step into the ball as he swung.

Whatever position McGraw ended up playing next season, he expected to return to the Orioles and combine his talents with his new pal Jennings. That almost didn't happen. Late in December, Ned Hanlon made one of the most successful trades in baseball history when he sent two journeymen players, Bill Shindle and George Treadway, to Brooklyn for first-baseman Dennis "Dan" Brouthers and outfielder Willie Keeler. Brouthers was one of the game's reigning stars, a big, powerful man who, since entering the majors in 1881, had led the National League in batting four times. Brooklyn's highest-paid player but often injured in 1893, Brouthers had worn out his welcome with manager Dave Foutz. Keeler, despite hitting above .300 in part-time duty in 1892 and the first part of 1893 (including several games as a left-handed shortstop), had ended the past season at Binghampton in the Eastern League. In the judgment of Foutz and a lot of other supposedly sage baseball men, Keeler, at 5'4½" and 140 pounds, was just too small to make it in the National League.

Having traded Shindle, his regular third-baseman, Hanlon dickered with Earl Wagner, president of the Washington club, for Charles "Duke" Farrell, a veteran catcher-infielder. Wagner wanted McGraw in exchange, which was agreeable to Hanlon, but the trade fell through when Wagner refused to pay a few hundred dollars in addition to giving up Farrell. McGraw stayed at Baltimore and barely escaped going to one of the League's most consistently awful teams.

When Hanlon denied him a $600 raise, McGraw grumbled about cheap owners and allowed that he just might stay at St. Bonaventure and pass up the whole season. By mid-March, though, he was at Macon, Georgia, the new spring-training site, along with fourteen other players. Hanlon put him at third base, mainly because there was no other place for him to play. Sensing Keeler's potential greatness, Hanlon announced that he was his right-fielder. Walter Brodie (always called "Steve" after the man who'd become a national celebrity by allegedly jumping off the Brooklyn Bridge some years earlier) was the center-fielder. Purchased from St. Louis during the previous season, Brodie, a Virginian and one of the very few Southerners in the League, was what a later generation of baseball people would call a "flake"—a player who delighted in zany behavior and seemed perpetually in a somewhat different state of consciousness. Yet Brodie was also a good hitter and capable fielder. Joe Kelley, in left field, was one of the finest players of his time, a lifetime .321 batter, fast and aggressive on the base paths—like most of the others Hanlon had assembled. The infield consisted of Brouthers; Henry "Heinie" Reitz, a Californian who in his rookie season in 1893 had quickly become one of the League's top second-basemen; and of course Jennings and McGraw. Wilbert Robinson, jovial, rotund, and rugged, did nearly all the catching in 1894. Sadie McMahon became the ace on what would never be an outstanding pitching staff.

That spring at Macon, Hanlon knew he had the makings of a pennant winner. The task was to turn them into a team. Not only in the daily practices at the local fairgrounds but in after-dinner sessions in the manager's hotel room, Hanlon and his men went over plays and strategy, "baseball as she is played," in one of Hanlon's favorite phrases. Often the dominant figure in those discussions was McGraw, already confident that he knew as much baseball as anybody, including Hanlon. In later years McGraw would freely acknowledge Hanlon's "wonderful faculty of organization," "his really masterful work in building up a team."[9] At the same time, as far as McGraw was concerned, it was his and the other Orioles' imagination and ingenuity that really determined their success. The more successful the Orioles were, the more insolent and overbearing McGraw would become in his relations with his manager.

On the field McGraw was more than ever a disruptive presence. After watching him shove, block, and hold base runners in two games at New Orleans against that city's Southern League team, a local reporter denounced him as "a rough, unruly man, who is constantly playing dirty ball. He has the vilest tongue of any ball-player. . . . On the local grounds he has demonstrated his low training, and his own manager knows that, while he is a fine ball-player, yet he adopts every low and contemptible method that his erratic brain can conceive to win a play by a dirty trick." At the same time, McGraw's work at third base had improved so much that Baltimore's *Sporting News* correspondent was ready to compare him to Boston's Billy Nash, generally regarded as the League's best at that position. McGraw handled ground balls "as a wayfarer swipes the short end of a five-cent cigar out of a gutter."[10]

The Orioles began the season by sweeping three straight from the New York Giants before the biggest crowds in Baltimore history. They went on to win thirty-four of their first forty-seven games, although Boston and New York almost matched them. The tough three-team race continued all sumer, with the spectators who liked plenty of offensive action getting more than their fill of hits, runs, and errors. The season of 1894 brought even lustier batting than the previous one. The 1894 Orioles averaged nine runs per game (Boston did even better) and batted .343 *as a team* (second to Philadelphia's .349). They committed the fewest errors in the League and allowed the second lowest number of runs. But it was their style of play, not the remarkable statistics they compiled, that excited and delighted people in Baltimore and often enraged local partisans around the League.

Before Hanlon came to Baltimore, managers had generally liked to have as many husky, powerful men as possible on their rosters. At 6'2" and more than 200 pounds, Dan Brouthers would have been big at any time in the game's history. But except for Brouthers and some of their pitchers (and the squat Robinson), the Orioles were small men even by the standards of that period.[11] Hanlon put together a lineup that could hit the ball anywhere on the field and run the bases with speed, savvy, and daring.

The foundation of his attack was the hit-and-run play, which the Orioles, especially McGraw and Keeler, brought almost to a state of perfection. McGraw, usually the leadoff man, excelled at getting on base. By 1894 he'd developed extraordinary judgment 'and ability to manipulate the bat, and he made the most of the fact that, before 1901, foul balls didn't count as strikes—unless, in the umpire's judgment, the batter was intentionally hitting the ball foul. Standing upright in the left-hand batter's box, his hands about six inches from the end of the bat, and swinging with a chopping motion, McGraw became expert at fouling off pitch after pitch until the tiring pitcher either threw the ball where he wanted to hit it or gave him a base on balls. Keeler and Jennings were also good at foul-hitting, but, as Keeler later said, "there wasn't any of them that could foul 'em off harder than McGraw. He could slam 'em out on a line so fast that even the umpire couldn't tell he was doing it on purpose." At that particular maneuver, according to Keeler, nobody had McGraw's "aplomb."[12] If a vexed umpire threatened to call McGraw's fouls as strikes, McGraw would just lean on his bat and grin in the umpire's face. And if all else failed, he would stand almost on top of the plate and deliberately take a pitch on his hip, back, or leg.

Once on base, McGraw would flash the hit-and-run sign to Keeler, batting second, and take off with the pitch. More often than not, "Wee Willie" would be able to punch the ball through the space the second-baseman or shortstop, running to cover the base, had just vacated. Turning (or cutting) second at full speed, McGraw would easily pull into third, and an Oriole rally would be in the offing. Once asked the secret of the batting prowess that enabled him to average .345 over a nineteen-year major league career, Keeler answered simply, "I hit 'em where they ain't." Baseball has had no more enduring axiom.

Many years later John B. Sheridan, who'd covered baseball since the 1880s, would remark that while the Orioles may not have invented the hit and run, he'd never heard of it before 1894. Certainly the Orioles' success popularized the play, along with swinging down on the ball and trying to hit toward third to produce such a high hop that a fast batter could beat the third-baseman's throw (what came to be called the "Baltimore chop"), and having the pitcher cover first on balls hit wide of the bag and back up third on throws from the outfield. McGraw and Jennings, who lived at a boardinghouse a block from Union Park and also roomed together on road trips, hit on the idea of having groundskeeper John Murphy contour the foul lines so that bunted balls would be more likely to stay fair, and pack the dirt hard around home plate to effectuate high-bounce base hits. Frequently, before anybody else showed up for the morning practices Hanlon required on home stands, they would be out raking the areas around third and shortstop for lumps and pebbles.

But in McGraw's estimation and that of many others who watched them over the years, the Orioles won because, as McGraw later put it, "We talked, lived and dreamed baseball." That obsession produced close teamwork and team spirit. They all delighted in bedeviling the opposition and bullying umpires. When they needed runs in the late innings, Heinie

Reitz would shout, "Get at 'em," the cue for everybody to grab a bat and start swinging menacingly in the direction of the other team's pitcher. They not only gave the opposition and the umpire a hard time but sometimes one another as well. As McGraw reminisced, "Hanlon didn't have to scold or punish a player for failing to do his part. We attended to that ourselves. . . . Woe betide the player who failed us! His life on the bench was not a pleasant one. He never forgot the roasting and never failed to deliver one if somebody else failed."[13]

Some idea of what Oriole baseball was really like and why they began to encounter hostile crowds everywhere they went can be gained from Tim Murnane, an old ballplayer himself and a highly respected Boston baseball writer. In June, when the Orioles left town after splitting a four-game series with the defending champion Beaneaters, Murnane accused Hanlon's team of "playing the dirtiest ball ever seen in this country." Carried away with visions of a pennant, they were ready "to maim a fellow player for life [in] just retribution for trying to stop them in their temporary flight." As Murnane summarized Oriole tactics: "Diving into the first baseman long after he has caught the ball; throwing masks in front of the runners at home plate; catching them by the clothes at the third base and interfering with the catcher, were only a few tricks performed by these young men from the South."[14] In the second game of the series, reported Murnane, McGraw knocked Kid Nichols off stride when the pitcher tried to score from second, then had the effrontery, later in the game, to howl to umpire Bob Emslie that Nichols was cutting the baseball. When Baltimore's McMahon came back out to pitch, he threw the ball in question over the grandstand so Emslie would have to put a new one into play. His ejection by Emslie occasioned still another protracted wrangle with McGraw and most of the Baltimore team.

By early September, the Orioles had taken over first place for good. Bombarding Cy Young at Cleveland on September 28, with Keeler hitting an inside-the-park home run and McGraw adding two singles and a double, Baltimore clinched its first pennant. Back home at Ford's Opera House, where the play-by-play progress of the game had been received by telegraph and displayed on a big diagram of a playing field, Harry von der Horst took the stage waving a banner that proclaimed the Orioles "Champions of 1894." People spilled out of the theater and spread the news, so that soon the downtown streets were full of celebrating "cranks," as baseball enthusiasts were called in the Nineties. By the light of bonfires, the rejoicing went on long after dark.

The team's return from Chicago four days later became a triumphal procession once the special Baltimore and Ohio train entered the state of Maryland. At Cumberland, Hagerstown, Frederick, and other stops, townspeople turned out by the hundreds to cheer the famous baseball players. When the train finally moved into Camden Station, early in the evening, torpedo fireworks exploded on the track, and the biggest throng in the city's history greeted the victors. Half of Baltimore's population, by some estimates, was in the immediate vicinity of the railroad station. Mounted police cleared a passage for Hanlon and his men and the official welcoming delegation, all of whom entered carriages for a parade through downtown. Preceding them was a platform wagon from which fireworks continued to discharge. At the intersection of Lexington and Howard streets, six horses pulling one of the carriages became frightened and plunged into the crowd, injuring eleven people. The players left their carriages in front of the Fifth Regiment Armory, mounted a platform, and, along with Governor Frank Brown, Mayor Ferdinand Latrobe, and other dignitaries, stood for nearly two hours shaking the hands of their admirers.

They then went to the Hotel Rennert and joined some three hunded others for a six-course banquet amid lavish floral arrangements, one shaped as a huge ball and bat. On team captain Robinson's cue, the players toasted their hosts with empty glasses. "Now turn your glasses down," ordered Robbie. "The boys drank water," an observer reported, "but looked wistfully at the champagne as it sparkled in the glasses of their entertainers."[15]

If they looked wistfully but abstained manfully at the victory banquet, the next day several of the Orioles partook heartily of whatever they wanted in the way of alcoholic beverages, and continued to eat heartily as well. That was only one reason, though, why the team was unprepared to start playing baseball again on October 4, in a best-of-seven series with the runner-up New York Giants for something called the Temple Cup.

Ever since the abandonment of the World Championship Series between the National League and American Association winners in 1889, the baseball magnates had been unable to come up with anything of comparable appeal. The post-season Boston-Cleveland series following the 1892 split season generated little excitement. In the summer of 1894 William H. Temple, a wealthy Pittsburgher, proposed a series between the League's first- and second-place finishers, and offered a large silver loving cup as the winner's prize.

Once Baltimore had clinched the pennant, Hanlon met with John Montgomery Ward, manager–second-baseman for the Giants, who'd barely edged out Boston for second place and finished three games back of Baltimore. Temple had specified a 65 percent–35 percent division between the series' winners and losers, with all gate receipts to go to the players and all expenses to be paid out of those gross receipts. Inasmuch as the series was his idea and he was putting up the cup, Temple was irate when he heard that Hanlon and Ward, supposedly with carte blanche from League president Nick Young, had agreed to a fifty-fifty split.

To appease Temple, Nick Young and Brooklyn president Charles H. Byrne, who with Temple made up the League's Temple Cup Committee, announced that the split would have to be sixty-five–thirty-five. News of that infuriated the Orioles. Already League champions, they felt that they had nothing else to prove. If they were going to play, then they ought to be guaranteed at least half the receipts. McGraw flatly refused to take the field except for even stakes. Hanlon and his players, principally McGraw, argued up to about two hours before the four o'clock starting time for the first game at Union Park. With the whole series on the verge of cancellation, McGraw finally agreed to play. Then the Orioles proceeded to make the whole issue academic: when they went out for practice, each of them found a Giant who was willing to split an individual share fifty-fifty. McGraw, for example, paired with George Davis, the Giants' shortstop, while Kelley paired with Amos Rusie and Keeler arranged his split with first-baseman Jack Doyle.

Hung over, tired, and disgruntled by the financial arrangements, the Orioles nonetheless played hard in the first game, before nearly 12,000. McGraw and Ward almost fought when they collided at second, and Brodie and Doyle did trade punches in the ninth inning. Rusie, who'd posted thirty-six victories that season and allowed 2.78 earned runs per game (against a League average of 5.32), held Baltimore to a single run while McMahon yielded four. It got worse after that. Still sulking, McGraw again declared he wouldn't play, only to be won over again by Hanlon's insistence that the team had a responsibility to Baltimore's loyal cranks. Jouett Meekin, the Giants' other thirty-six-game winner, then outlasted Charles "Kid" Gleason, 9–6. The next day, at New York's Polo Grounds with an overflow crowd approaching 20,000 on hand, Rusie again limited the Orioles to one run, while George Hemming, victimized by six errors, gave up four. On Monday, October 8, about half that many people blew fish-boat horns and made about as much noise watching their favorites rout the Orioles 16–3 behind Meekin. In eight innings, before umpires Bob Emslie and Tim Hurst decided it was too dark to play anymore, the two teams made nine errors and the Giants stole nine bases on Robinson. McGraw almost came to blows with Emslie and remained the special target of the jeering New Yorkers.

Protesting that the Giants' sweep changed nothing, that they were still League champions (a view quickly affirmed by Nick Young), the Orioles enjoyed an evening in New York as guests at a Broadway theater, downed "foaming bumpers" of beer afterward at Nick Engle's saloon, and counted their money. Pairing off with the Giants had saved each of them $175, so that when McGraw left Baltimore a few days later, he was $625 better off than if William Temple hadn't dreamed up his Cup series. Otherwise the whole affair had been an utter debacle. "They could not have beaten Towsontown or Hoboken in those games," a Baltimore newsman was still grumbling ten months afterward. "They were not in condition to beat anybody."[16]

Again McGraw touched base at Truxton before heading across the state to St. Bonaventure. In the following years his visits to his hometown would become increasingly rare, until they stopped altogether. "I find wrestling with the books," he wrote from St. Bonaventure, "much harder than I find wrestling with the umpire." The *Sporting News* hoped that "somebody will slip a book of etiquette between his algebra and geography," adding that "particular instruction upon the swearing commandment would not be out of place." For the second straight off-season, McGraw and Hughey Jennings roomed together, talked and coached baseball, and studied under the tutelage of the Franciscan fathers. "I have gained wonderfully in flesh this winter and weigh 157 pounds now," McGraw wrote in January. "I am going to stick to my college studies," he added, "as I want to be able to do something after I get out of baseball."[17] When he and Jennings left for Macon and spring training, each carried a gold-headed cane as a present from their fellow students.

Neither had signed the contract Hanlon had mailed him, nor had Joe Kelley or Willie Keeler. The "Big Four," as the Baltimore press had started calling them, all wanted more money. Despite the deepening economic depression, close to 300,000 people had passed through the gates at Union Park in 1894. With a salary list of about $35,000, the franchise had turned a handsome profit. McGraw had batted .340 and scored 155 runs; Jennings had batted .335 and led all shortstops in fielding; and Kelley and Keeler had hit .393 and .371, respectively, and tied for second in runs scored with 165. But after all, as Hanlon no doubt pointed out, the League as a whole had averaged .309, and five full-time players had hit above .400 (led by Boston's Hugh Duffy at .438). Besides, officially no player could make more than the $2,400 salary limit reimposed by the owners once the Players' League collapsed. Under the reserve clause in their previous year's contracts (an item that had been basic baseball "law" since 1876), they could either sign with Baltimore for another season or not play at all. So in the end the Big Four settled for modest raises. In McGraw's case, that was about $300, boosting his salary for 1895 to $2,100.

McGraw was in his accustomed leadoff spot in the lineup when the Orioles, wearing the orange-and-black-trimmed uniforms they'd donned for the Temple Cup games, opened the season before a Union Park overflow estimated at 14,000.[18] They lost to Philadelphia that day and didn't really begin to play the kind of baseball their followers expected until half the season was over. By then Hanlon, correctly judging that Brouthers had seen his last good year, had sold Big Dan to Louisville for $700 and installed rookie George "Scoops" Carey, a good fielder if not much else, at first base. Hanlon also kept Kid Gleason, who'd pitched fifteen victories the previous year, as his regular second-baseman when Reitz returned from an injury. Bill Hoffer, who'd played at Cedar Rapids with McGraw, became the bulwark of the pitching staff, with McMahon unable to pitch until August because of a sore arm.

Plagued by a sickness that his Baltimore physicians finally diagnosed as malaria, as well as by a couple of hand injuries, McGraw missed long stretches of the season. In mid-September, when he suffered a recurrence of malaria and again left the lineup, the *Sporting News* remarked that "His constitution is purely one of nerves. . . ." But when he did play, he still had enough stamina to torment the umpires, particularly Tim Keefe, a star pitcher for New York in the late Eighties and a rookie arbiter in 1895. In Pittsburgh, for example, Keefe ordered Jennings out of the game, whereupon McGraw ran up to accuse Keefe of sending out for a bottle of whiskey before the previous day's game. Keefe replied that he'd taken a little whiskey because he'd been sick. "Sick!" yelled McGraw. "Drunk, you mean. You were drunk all last week in Chicago, too."[19]

A few days later Keefe, a first-year umpire, announced his resignation, apparently feeling that $1,250, the maximum salary he could look forward to making, wasn't enough to compensate for the abuse he'd taken from the likes of McGraw. Baseball, he said, had become "absolutely disagreeable. It is the fashion now for every player to froth at the mouth and emit shrieks of anguish whenever a decision is given which is adverse to the interests of his club." Added the *Sporting News* man in Baltimore, "to be aggressive does not mean to make the life of the umpire miserable and to disgust spectators who pay their money to see a base ball game." After an especially strife-ridden series in Cleveland, even Hanlon felt obliged to caution his players against so much "pyrotechnic kicking."[20]

During the second week in September, the Orioles, behind Hoffer and McMahon, won two out of three games from Cleveland at Union Park and virtually killed the Spiders' pennant hopes. Hoffer wrapped up Baltimore's second straight championship on September 30 at New York. McGraw hadn't played for the previous two weeks, but he was able to coach at third and so pester umpire Jim McDonald that McDonald finally called a New York policeman to escort the recovering malaria victim from the field. The next day, after McGraw lined a home run into the right-field bleachers at the Polo Grounds to beat Amos Rusie, Baltimore ended the season with an 87–43 record to Cleveland's 84–46.

The Orioles then went directly to Cleveland to begin another Temple Cup series. The Cleveland cranks, the worst the Orioles had played before that season, were more unruly than ever. In the first game, with only a handful of policemen on duty, Clevelanders came out of the stands, crowded around the Baltimore bench, threw vegetables at the Orioles as they tried to catch fly balls, and stood behind McGraw shouting "Dirty McGraw," "Hoodlum," "Tough." Somehow the game proceeded to a conclusion, Cy Young outlasting McMahon 5–4. More missiles—beer bottles, tin horns, cushions—rained on the Orioles the next day, when the Spiders battered Hoffer and won 7–3. In the third game, the largest Cleveland crowd so far in the series, about 7,500, behaved reasonably well as Young held Baltimore to only one run while his team again scored seven.

Back in Baltimore two days later, with much of the city enraged by the press accounts of the Cleveland spectators' behavior, street thugs pelted the Spiders with rotten fruit as they left their hotel. Harry von der Horst circulated through the Union Park crowd of 7,500 to help keep it under control. On the field, left-hander Charles "Duke" Esper gave the Orioles their first victory in Temple Cup competition, a five-hit shutout. Afterward the police struggled to push back a mass of Baltimoreans so the Spiders could reach their horse-drawn omnibus. As the horses lurched down Huntington Avenue, rocks, bricks, and clods of dirt fell on the Cleveland players, who lay on the floor of the conveyance with their fielder's mitts over their heads. The next day, however, Patsy Tebeau's men appeared unruffled, especially Young. He allowed six hits and two runs while the Orioles committed five errors behind Hoffer and yielded a like number of runs. For the four thousand or so Baltimore spectators, one of the few positive moments came in the third inning, when McGraw slammed the ball into Tebeau's face and split his lip. "Good boy, McGraw!" yelled the bleacher cranks.[21] With a wall of policemen protecting them, the Spiders got away from the park safely and were soon on their way back to Cleveland with $580 each. Unlike the Giants the previous year, the Cleveland players would have nothing to do with a fifty-fifty split of the Cup receipts.

McGraw and Jennings headed for St. Bonaventure with only $385 apiece from the loser's share but still carrying their gold-headed canes and also proudly wearing gold medallions given to them by James Cardinal Gibbons, the first cardinal in the United States. In September, Gibbons had summoned the pair to his Baltimore residence, bestowed the medallions, and also given them small crosses blessed by Pope Leo XIII.

Although batting had moderated somewhat in 1895, as the pitchers adapted to throwing from the 60' 6" distance, to keeping one foot in place, and to working off a mound, the Orioles had continued to pile up runs, again more than a thousand. In ninety-three games, McGraw batted .369, while Jennings, playing in every game, hit .386, second on the ball club only to Keeler. Jennings had become a genuine star, considered even by Oriole-haters to be the game's top shortstop.

Still not fully recovered from his summer-long bout with malaria, McGraw went at his course work—Latin, rhetoric, geometry—more determinedly than ever. His grades were good enough to get him on the college honor roll, listed among those "particularly distinguished for good conduct and application to their studies. . . ." He refused to slacken his hectic pace, even when he had a chance. Knowing almost nothing about football, he nonetheless agreed to organize the college's first team in that sport. A spectator at a St. Bonaventure football game at Olympic Park, Buffalo, pictured him as "a small, slim, nervous little man [who] kept running back and forward on the outside of the painted lines, calling on the St. Bona's . . . , giving them instructions, and in every way proving that he had considerable to do with the game." Afterward, at the team's hotel, McGraw held court for students, priests, and local baseball enthusiasts. Bedecked in jewelry—stickpin, ring, a locket and Gibbons's medallion on his watch chain—and brandishing his cane, he talked "with the speed of ten locomotives, but every word is as distinct, as correct and as plain as an elocutionist's effort." The impression he left was of "a well read and educated man."[22]

By the time the fall term ended in mid-December, McGraw had run himself into a state of physical and nervous exhaustion. Jennings would have to handle the baseball team alone next term, he told Father Dolan; he was returning to Baltimore to rest up. That he did, taking a flat on Twenty-fourth Street near Charles. Twice a day he walked downtown and back. "I study like I play ball, just as hard as I can," he told a reporter. "The strain has proved too much for me."[23]

By early March a rested and restless McGraw had already gone to Macon as Hanlon's advance agent to arrange for lodging and the use of the fairgrounds ball diamond. Reporting with McGraw and seventeen others that spring was Jack Doyle, so notorious for his rough style of play that he'd gained the nickname "Dirty Jack." "Foxy Ned," as the sportswriters liked to call Hanlon, had obtained Doyle from New York in a trade for Kid Gleason to play first base and provide the batting punch that Carey couldn't. Rumors persisted that several of the Orioles held grudges against Doyle, especially Keeler, who was said to be still waiting for his half of the 1894 Temple Cup split he'd made with Doyle. But as the deceptively baby-faced newcomer slammed the ball in practice, showed plenty of speed on the bases, and handled himself deftly around first, it seemed that all was well with the two-time champions. His present ball club, predicted Hanlon, would be "the strongest that ever trod a diamond. . . ."[24]

Hanlon was careful about McGraw's health, excusing him from the daily mile he had the players run around the fairgrounds track. (Brodie liked to run it while holding a bag full of bats.) McGraw seemed in good condition when the team moved up to Atlanta. After playing an intra-squad game there, however, he became ill at the hotel with what was initially presumed to be another round of malaria. When the ball club took a train to Athens for a game with the University of Georgia, McGraw remained behind in the care of Erasmus Arlington "Arlie" Pond, a rookie pitcher who was also well along in his medical studies at Johns Hopkins University. As McGraw's fever continued to rise and he began to vomit, Pond had him admitted to St. Joseph's Infirmary. There he was found to have typhoid fever, one of the scourges of past centuries and still a dreaded malady in the nineteenth.

For the second time in less than a year, McGraw was seriously ill and bedridden. This time he came close to death. Hugh Hogan, the physician who treated him at St. Joseph's, prescribed sponge baths; doses of quinine sulphate and magnesia; and a diet of milk, fruit juices, and meat broths. Week after week his fever persisted, as did his inability to sleep for more than a few minutes at a time. After a month he began to get better, only to relapse with the highest fever yet. Within another week, though, he'd seen the worst. On May 12 his temperature finally registered normal. Said Hogan, "His general condition for one who has suffered as he has is marvelous."[25]

On his back in Atlanta, McGraw missed one of the memorable brawls in Oriole annals. In an exhibition game at Petersburg, Virginia, Jennings got into a fight with a player on the local Virginia League team and much of the crowd poured onto the field. Doyle and Keeler were roughed up before the Orioles could get away to their hotel. There a bloodthirsty mob stormed into the lobby. After a pitched battle that wrecked much of the lobby furnishings, a few policemen and a couple of local citizens who offered their protection spirited the ballplayers to the railroad station and aboard a train to Norfolk. Far down the track, they could still hear curses.

Early in June, praising the nuns at St. Joseph's whose tender care had been "a boon to a stranger in a strange land," McGraw left Atlanta to convalesce at Old Point Comfort, Virginia, a popular seaside resort located about a hundred miles down Chesapeake Bay from Baltimore.[26] When he arrived he weighed 118 pounds and was still so weak he had to use crutches. He spent three weeks at the Hygeia Hotel, abandoning the crutches for a cane and doing lots of walking. He also chatted with hotel guests, went for occasional sails on pilot boats, attended a couple of yacht parties, and even advised the baseball-playing black waiters at the Hygeia and the nearby Chamberlin Hotel. James A. Diffenbaugh, deputy customs collector at Baltimore, made sure that he got daily telegraphed reports on the Orioles' progress, and McGraw received letters of encouragement from people in all the League cities, even Cleveland.

At the beginning of July a revitalized McGraw, weighing 136 pounds and displaying a thin black mustache, came back to Baltimore. Although he donned a uniform and worked on the coaching lines for a few games, he remained at home when the Orioles left on a western trip. By the time they finally returned, late in August, he was ready to play.

The ball club had hardly suffered by his absence. Hanlon had pressed into service Jim Donely, a thirty-year-old veteran of both League and Association, and Donely had played the best ball of his career, hitting well above .300 and handling third base at least as capably as McGraw. Donely helped Keeler, Kelley, Jennings, and Robinson power an attack that again produced more runs than any other team, while Hoffer, Pond, Hemming, and McMahon provided adequate pitching. By the time McGraw got back into the lineup, Baltimore already enjoyed a comfortable lead over Cleveland and the Cincinnati Reds, who were often early contenders in the Nineties but always late faders. The Orioles moved out of reach by trouncing the hapless Louisville Colonels in a triple-header on Labor Day and a double-header the day after that.[27] On September 13 Jerry Nops, a newly acquired left-hander, beat Brooklyn to clinch a third straight Baltimore pennant. The next day, in an intrasquad exhibition at St. Charles College near Ellicott City, Maryland, they gave Cardinal Gibbons his first look at baseball. In the college dining hall that evening, Gibbons called baseball a wholesome game and extolled the Orioles players as "exemplary young men whose moral rectitude of character is above reproach."[28] But then he hadn't watched them in action when a game counted.

Actually the Orioles, with McGraw absent nearly the whole time, had been relatively subdued that season—at least compared to the Cleveland Spiders, who'd outdone everybody in the League in ferocious behavior. The president of the Louisville club went so far as to have Cleveland's starting nine arrested and hustled off to court after a particularly wild display at the Colonels' park. Manager Tebeau, center-fielder Jimmy McAleer, shortstop Ed McKean, and left-fielder Jesse Burkett paid $50–$100 fines for disturbing the peace. Yet for all that, the Spiders had been no match for Baltimore in the last third of the season, finishing ten games back.

McGraw got into only nineteen games during the regular season and contributed almost nothing to what had been the Orioles' easiest pennant drive. His pal Jennings, on the other hand, had again appeared in every game, again led shortstops in fielding, and barely missed batting .400. But McGraw, fit and fresh, and the rest of the Orioles, with pride at stake following two dreary showings, were ready to go all out for the first time in the Temple Cup games.

Both the Orioles and Cleveland played in top form, despite poor crowds in both cities for the second year in a row. The stars for the Orioles were Hoffer and twenty-year-old Joe Corbett, younger brother of heavyweight boxing champion "Gentleman Jim" Corbett. Hoffer outpitched Cy Young in the first and third games, while Corbett, called up from the Tri-State League in September, coasted to victory in game two and closed out the Orioles' sweep with a four-hit shutout and two singles and a double himself, before about two thousand chilled Clevelanders. Although the receipts were the smallest so far, only enough to give each winner about $200 and each loser $117, the Temple Cup games had finally left no doubt about what team was the best in baseball. Tebeau and catcher Jack O'Connor were in such foul spirits that the night after the last game they went to their favorite saloon, encountered Elmer Pasco, a Cleveland reporter who had written unfavorably about the Spiders, and proceeded to beat up the journalist.

For the first autumn since 1892, McGraw didn't resume his work at St. Bonaventure, nor for that matter did Jennings. Jennings would later enroll at Cornell University, coach the baseball team there, and eventually learn enough law to pass the bar exams in both New York State and Maryland. McGraw's education, at least the classroom kind, had come to an end. He was still far short of having enough credits for a degree, but he'd achieved his foremost objective: self-improvement. He'd learned how to behave in the company of educated people, how to organize his thoughts and express himself clearly; in short, he'd learned a great deal besides baseball.

For now, though, he intended to have some fun. As soon as the Cup series ended, McGraw, Jennings, Willie Keeler, Joe Kelley, and Arlie Pond, bachelors all, headed for Europe aboard the steamship *St. Paul*, bound for Liverpool. On October 26 they landed and registered at a hotel "in very large letters," Jennings wrote Robinson, "for fear they would not know where we came from."[29] After Liverpool and London, they'd seen enough of the country their Irish forebears had despised. Crossing to the Continent, they took in the international exposition at Brussels and then Paris. After that they booked passage from London on the *Majestic*, which steamed into New York harbor on December 9. All four arrived home wearing Prince Albert coats, silk top hats, and London-made boots.

McGraw's dandy apparel must have caused quite a stir in Truxton, where he went directly from New York. He had an important reason— and a happy one—for returning to the place that had once been his home: to look up his father and brothers and sisters and tell them that he was going to get married. That was all he had time for; by December 13 he was back in Baltimore, calling on his fiancée.

Her name was Minnie R. Doyle and she was the daughter of Michael H. Doyle, a widower who, until his recent retirement, had made a decent if modest living as a clerk for the Appeals Tax Court in the city. Minnie Doyle was dark-haired, about twenty years old, and lived with her father at 1815 Guilford Avenue in the northern part of town. She had, of course, been raised a Roman Catholic. That much is known about her. But when and how she first made McGraw's acquaintance can only be guessed at. Conceivably she was the young woman who enclosed pressed wild flowers in one of the many letters McGraw received while he was convalescing at Old Point Comfort. If so, then he may have made it a point, when he returned to Baltimore, to arrange for an introduction.

The couple were married on the evening of February 3, 1897, at St. Vincent's Church on Front Street. A notable event of the winter social season, the wedding drew a huge turnout despite the cold weather. People filled the seats and jammed the aisles of the church, and several women stood on pews to have a better view until one of the young priests admonished them to get down. Outside, while baseball enthusiasts jostled each other to see Wilbert Robinson, Arlie Pond, and other ballplayers as they arrived in their carriages, several sassy boys kept yelling, "Get your rain checks!"[30] Jennings served as best man, Keeler and Kelley as groomsmen. One of the assisting priests was Father Joe Dolan, now vice president at St. Bonaventure. Among the guests were the Reverend Joseph Butler, pastor at St. Patrick's in Truxton, and Bert Kenney and his wife. Nobody from McGraw's family was present.

McGraw and his bride did stop over at Truxton on their honeymoon trip to Niagara Falls. On their way back they spent several days enjoying the night life in New York City and the sights in Washington. Because they didn't want to leave Michael Doyle alone, McGraw agreed that he and Minnie would live in Baltimore at his father-in-law's house.

Meanwhile McGraw and Robinson had decided to go into partnership and invest some of their accumulated baseball earnings in a business enterprise that would provide them with a comfortable living once they gave up playing. Late in February they purchased a saloon and restaurant at 519 North Howard, close to the central business district and directly across the street from the Academy of Music, one of Baltimore's top theaters. They then spent $10,000–$15,000 on the place, installing steel-lane bowling alleys on the street floor and the finest tables they could find for the "billiard parlor" upstairs. The Diamond Café, as they sedately named the establishment, turned out to be one of the few good investments McGraw ever made. By the time the baseball season was in full swing, the Diamond had become a popular and profitable gathering place for Baltimore's sporting crowd.

Spring training at Macon in 1897 was an enjoyable time for McGraw, marred only by a telegram from St. Bonaventure reporting the sudden death of Joseph F. Dolan, O.F.M. He'd brought Minnie south with him, and he didn't have to worry about competition at third base from Jim Donely. The previous fall Hanlon had concluded a big trade with Pittsburgh, sending Donely and Steve Brodie to Connie Mack's Pirates for outfielder Jake Stenzel and three other players. Stenzel was one of the best hitters in the League, while Brodie had slumped to .297 the previous year and, according to von der Horst, was "excitable and caused considerable friction in our team." Donely's solid play in 1896 had made him so popular that some of the customers at Union Park hooted McGraw when he returned to the lineup and sent Donely to the bench. Hanlon had realized, the Baltimore *Sun* reported, that McGraw wouldn't be happy as long as Donely was on the club, so Donely had had to go. At any rate, Hanlon was satisfied that he again had the best outfit in baseball. "I cannot see how we can lose," he said before the season started.[31]

Baltimore got off to its usual good start, even though McGraw was out nearly three weeks after spraining his ankle in the season's opener and for another two weeks with an injured arm in late May–early June. On June 11, when Arlie Pond outpitched Cleveland's Cy Young at Union Park, the Orioles improved their record to 27–9, two and one-half games better than Boston's. Elmer Horton, a pitcher included in the Stenzel deal, could hardly believe the new ball club he found himself on. "They play more with their heads than their hands," he enthused. "It is like going through college to watch them work. . . . It is . . . the unexpected all the time and it is a wonderful game."[32]

Soon, though, injuries and illnesses began to wear away at the three-time pennant winners. Sprains, sore arms, split fingers, beanings, spikings, malaria, and bronchitis were among the disabilities that caused every regular except Kelley, Stenzel, and Keeler to miss a good portion

of the season. Meanwhile Boston's taciturn Frank Selee had built a team
that was even better than his 1891–93 National League champions. Late
in June the Orioles found themselves in second place after dropping two
out of three games in the cramped confines of South End Grounds, home
of the Beaneaters.

Before long the Baltimore writers traveling with the team were reporting "personal antagonisms" that had already reached the point where
"every man is looking out for himself and his record." Jack Doyle, by
McGraw's account, was the reason for much of the trouble. The next
year, after Doyle had left the Orioles, McGraw would claim that Doyle's
"heart was not in the game when he was with us. He didn't want to play
in Baltimore." On one occasion during the 1897 season, McGraw said,
Doyle had taken a punch at him "in a cowardly manner. . . . I got a
bat and would have broken his jaw if Manager Hanlon had not stopped
me."[33] By August, Doyle was telling anybody who'd listen that he wanted
to go back to New York.

Yet according to another source, McGraw himself was a major cause
of discord on the 1897 Orioles. "He had a mean way of nagging a man
that worked against the success of the team," one of his teammates that
year related sometime afterward. Game after game McGraw picked on
Keeler. After one defeat, McGraw cursed out the little right-fielder for
failing to throw home to prevent a run that started the opposition's winning
rally. On his way into the shower, Keeler asked McGraw, "What did
you mean by cursing me like that today?" McGraw's only answer was
"Play ball!" Keeler jumped on him and, both naked, they struggled on
the dressing-room floor. Doyle, also naked, grabbed a bat, threatened
to break the head of anybody who interfered, and offered 5–4 odds that
Keeler wouldn't be the first to give up. In fact McGraw was the first to
"squeal."[34]

Evidently even Ned Hanlon didn't escape McGraw's verbal blasts.
The same source for the McGraw-Keeler scrap (who was almost certainly
Joe Quinn, a utility infielder traded to St. Louis with Stenzel in 1898)
remembered McGraw's shouting at the manager, "We made you what
you are and here you are putting on airs. It don't go with me. You were
a stiff until we boosted you and your head's swelled by newspaper praise
you don't deserve." The ex-Oriole couldn't understand how Hanlon tolerated McGraw's insubordination. "I often wonder," he said, "how McGraw
got away with some of the plays he made on and off the field."[35]

Between injuries and illnesses, dissension, and the splendid play of

Selee's Bostons, the Orioles found themselves in a grueling fight for the pennant. If they turned on each other more frequently, they also continued to make the umpire's life one of pain and suffering. In August, Tom Lynch declared that he would never work another game involving the Orioles—"a vile lot of blackguards" who'd called him names that would "bring a response in the shape of a bullet if they were off the field. . . ."[36]

Decades later the aging men who'd played in the 1890s would laugh and swap stories about the depredations visited on the umpires in those days. Invariably most of the stories revolved around the Orioles. John Heydler, who'd been a young umpire in the Nineties and subsequently rose to the presidency of the National League, would have none of it. For Heydler there was nothing funny about what he and others had endured at the hands of the Baltimore rowdies. "The Orioles," as he remembered them, "were mean, vicious, ready at any time to maim a rival player or an umpire, if it helped their cause. The things they would say to an umpire were unbelievably vile, and they broke the spirits of some fine men. I've seen umpires bathe their feet by the hour after McGraw and others spiked them through their shoes. . . . I feel the lot of the umpires never was worse than in the years that the Orioles were flying high."[37]

On September 22, when the Orioles lost at New York while Boston won its game over in Brooklyn, the pennant race came down to a three-game series with the Beaneaters at Union Park, beginning two days later. Those three games marked the high point in Baltimore's history as a National League city. On Friday the twenty-fourth, nearly 13,000 were on hand to watch Boston's 6–4 victory behind Kid Nichols. Saturday's attendance, officially given as 18,123, broke all Baltimore records. Standing and sitting everywhere, the throng saw Hoffer hold on until the Orioles rallied in the seventh and eighth innings to beat Bill Klobedanz. After an idle Sunday (baseball was illegal on the Christian Sabbath in all the eastern cities), an even greater turnout, some 25,000, stood in the aisles, sat on the grandstand roof and the outfield fences, overflowed the playing field, climbed utility poles, and found a variety of other vantage points. To their dismay, the Beaneaters knocked out Corbett and continued to pound three other pitchers—Hanlon's whole staff except for Pond. Nichols struggled to a 19–10 win. Boston left town in first place by one and one-half games, a circumstance that delighted, among others, the septuagenarian Henry Chadwick, dean of baseball journalists. As far as Chadwick was concerned, the Orioles had "forfeited the respect of every lover of manly ball playing."[38] Three days later Baltimore lost to Washington, Boston won at Brooklyn, and the National League had a new champion.

After the high drama and frenzied crowds in the showdown series at Baltimore, the annual competition for William H. Temple's loving cup was even more of an anticlimax than in past years. In five games, with Baltimore winning all but the first, the two teams scored ninety-nine runs, made numerous errors, and played listless, helter-skelter baseball before small turnouts. To fatten the receipts, the Beaneaters and Orioles slipped in a couple of exhibition games in Worcester and Springfield before leaving Massachusetts after the third game. The Orioles supposedly ended up with $357 apiece, the Beaneaters $254, although rumors were plentiful that the players had split fifty-fifty again. For the fourth time in the five years of the Cup games, the runner-up team had beaten the pennant winner, which, except to the most rabid cranks in the victorious runner-up cities, had proved absolutely nothing. When the National League presidents met in Philadelphia the next month, only Hanlon opposed a motion to bring the Temple Cup series mercifully to an end.

McGraw's batting average had slipped to .328 in 1897, whereas Keeler's had soared to .432 (on a record-setting 243 base hits), Kelley had hit .390, and Jennings, Doyle, and Stenzel had all batted around .350. McGraw's average was only three points better than what the team as a whole had done. And he still had trouble around third, still tended to hurry his throws and send the ball sailing beyond the first-baseman's reach. McGraw was an established major-leaguer, to be sure. But he wasn't happy with Doyle, or with Hanlon for that matter, and they weren't happy with him. Again somebody would have to go.

Although they were still a tough, exciting ball club—a relatively young one, too—the "old Orioles," as baseball nostalgists would come to call them, had already seen their most successful times. So had the twelve-team National League, which every season had proved its impracticability and unprofitability for two-thirds of its franchises. Not far ahead were momentous changes—in the structure of the League, the ownership of franchises, the makeup of the Baltimore Orioles. Those changes would shape the future of John McGraw.

Three

TWO CITIES, TWO LEAGUES, AND THREE JOBS

McGRAW WASN'T TRADED, but Dirty Jack Doyle was. Early in December 1897, Hanlon got J. Earl Wagner of the Washington club to take Doyle, Heinie Reitz, and pitcher Morris Amole in exchange for pitcher Jim McJames, first-baseman Dennis "Dan" McGann, and Gene De-Montreville, a young second-baseman who'd hit .348 in 1897 and led Washington to a seventh-place finish, the best ever for the nation's capital in either the American Association or the National League. De-Montreville was a valuable addition, but Hanlon expected the departure of the cantankerous Doyle to help his team even more.

McGraw spent most of his off-season time with Robinson at the Diamond Café, visiting with customers, sharpening his own skills with a cue stick, and generally promoting what was already a profitable enterprise. McGraw and his rotund partner also paid about $7,000 each for two newly finished row houses on fashionable St. Paul Street. Robinson moved his large family into 2738; for the first time since their marriage a year earlier, McGraw and his young wife occupied a place of their own, next door to the Robinsons at 2740. Occasionally that winter McGraw heard from Hughey Jennings, who'd married shortly after the season ended and then returned to St. Bonaventure for still another fall term.

For Americans in general, the biggest news of the new year was the explosion and sinking of the battleship U.S.S. *Maine* in Havana harbor, on February 15, 1898, with the loss of 260 crew members. The immediate and overwhelming presumption across the United States was that the *Maine* disaster was, as Assistant Secretary of the Navy Theodore Roosevelt put it, "an act of dirty treachery on the part of the Spaniards."[1]

Congress quickly voted $50 million in military appropriations, and despite the cautious behavior of President William McKinley, the country moved steadily toward war with Imperial Spain—in the name of justice and humanity for the oppressed Cubans and revenge for the *Maine.*

A fairly well-educated young man, McGraw no doubt read something besides the sports pages in the Baltimore newspapers. But what interested him as much as the prospect of war with Spain was the adoption by the National League owners of something called "A Measure for the Suppression of Obscene, Indecent and Vulgar Language upon the Ball Field." The Brush Rule, so called because its principal proponent had been president John T. Brush of the Cincinnati club, proclaimed that henceforth any player who addressed an umpire or a fellow player in a "villainously filthy" manner would be brought before a three-man board of discipline and, if found guilty, banished for life.[2]

Everybody assumed that the Brush Rule was aimed primarily at the Orioles. He'd always tried to discourage rowdyism on the Baltimore club, Ned Hanlon said, but because his players complained that other teams were winning with such methods, he'd "winked at the evil. . . ." From now on, though, "the Baltimore Club can be counted on as one of the reformers. . . ." McGraw wasn't so sure. He would try to live with the Brush Rule, he said, but he intended to continue playing as he always had, "for all there is in me to help my club win games." It might be that he would have to "abandon the profession entirely." Anyway, the owners ought to do something about the umpires, who "used as much foul language as any player who ever walked. A man is at [their] mercy."[3]

Assigning two umpires for each game in 1898 would also help keep the players in check, the baseball moguls hoped. To cover that additional expense, and because room no longer had to be made in October for the Temple Cup series, the owners extended the season from 132 to 154 games. Doing well with the Diamond Café, McGraw had no salary demands that spring, but others on the Orioles and around the League complained bitterly over the perpetuation of the $2,400 salary cap at the same time that the season was lengthened by nearly a month. Willie Keeler, the game's premier batsman in the late Nineties, voiced sentiments that were common to the ballplayers of his as well as succeeding generations: "We can count on our fingers the number of years that we'll be able to play. . . . That makes it plain that we must make all the money we can during the short period we may be said to be star players."

Hanlon's reply was that he and Harry von der Horst already had the biggest payroll in the League, paid the players' expenses in spring training (unlike most clubs), and had given them an $1,800 bonus pool for finishing second the previous year. "The trouble," Hanlon thought, "is they have been treated too well."[4]

The Orioles' training at Macon and subsequently Savannah featured something less than harmony. But then the whole eastern United States was on edge that spring. Early in April, as their steamer passed Old Point Comfort on the way from Norfolk to Baltimore, the Orioles saw several U.S. warships lying offshore, guarding the approach to Chesapeake Bay. Three weeks later Congress authorized McKinley to make war on Spain.

The "splendid little war," as Secretary of State John Hay termed it, was over by mid-summer, with U.S. forces in control of Cuba and much of the Spanish Philippines, as well as Puerto Rico and Guam. But the unsettled conditions associated with the war were blamed for a substantial falling off in attendance around the National League that season. Only about 6,500 showed up for the opener at newly refurbished and enlarged Union Park, and that was the biggest home crowd the Orioles played before all year. By June, Hanlon had already arranged for several choice home dates to be moved to Philadelphia, on the assumption that the visitor's share there would be greater than what he could make at Union Park. He also unloaded Jake Stenzel's salary, along with that of utilityman Joe Quinn, to St. Louis, taking on instead the more modest contract of Bill "Ducky" Holmes, a 5'6" outfielder.

The Orioles still offered their followers good baseball. Twice during the season they put together twelve-game winning streaks. With both pitching and fielding in the National League improving each year, they still topped .300 in team batting (the only team that did). Keeler again led the League and was outstanding in nearly every other facet of the game. At Washington in June, he made a catch that McGraw would always refer to as the greatest he ever saw. Diving in foul territory off the right-field line for Jack Doyle's low liner, Keeler speared the ball with his bare (left) hand, then plunged into a barbed-wire fence separating the spectators from the playing field. He ended up suspended in the wire, his uniform caught on the barbs. After getting his arm bandaged, Wee Willie was ready to finish a game in which the Orioles were already hopelessly behind.

McGraw hit .342 and DeMontreville, Jennings, Kelley, and McGann all had good years at the plate. Arlie Pond finished his M.D., entered the Army Medical Corps, and began a long career in the Philippines. Joe Corbett quit baseball altogether to help his adored older brother regain the heavyweight boxing title he'd lost in 1897 to Bob Fitzsimmons. But Jim McJames, Jerry Nops, the veteran Al Maul, and rookie Jim Hughes gave Hanlon the most solid pitching staff he'd had so far.

Still, the Orioles couldn't overcome the 1898 Boston Beaneaters, possibly the finest baseball team of the nineteenth century. Undoubtedly Frank Selee had the strongest infield up to that time: Fred Tenney at first; Bobby Lowe at second; Herman Long at shortstop; and the brilliant Jimmy Collins captaining the team at third. The outfield consisted of Hugh Duffy, Billy Hamilton, and Charles "Chick" Stahl, all strong hitters and fast on the bases, especially Hamilton. Marty Bergen was probably the best defensive catcher of his day, despite being so emotionally disturbed that in the off-season of 1899–1900 he would murder his wife and two children and then take his own life. Boston's pitching was superb, particularly that of Kid Nichols (who averaged thirty-one victories in the years 1891–99), Ted Lewis, and a tall rookie named Vic Willis. Finally, the Beaneaters took maximum advantage of their home ballpark, where Collins and Duffy excelled at lifting pop flies against or over a left-field fence that was only 235 feet down the foul line. In 1898 Boston won 80 percent of the games it played at friendly South End Grounds.

All season long Hanlon complained that his players were abiding by the Brush Rule while other teams ignored it. Whatever the cause, the 1898 Orioles had fewer explosive encounters with the umpires and opposition than in previous years. In fact the most memorable unpleasantness of the summer involved not an old Oriole but a new one, who found himself embroiled not with an umpire or another player but another club's owner.

In July, during the second game of a double-header at the Polo Grounds in New York, Ducky Holmes struck out, and one of the New York cranks, having watched Holmes in a Giants uniform last year, yelled, "Oh, Ducky, you're a lobster. That's what you left here for." Holmes looked in the direction of the gibe and yelled back, "Well, I'm glad I'm not working for a Sheeny anymore."[5] At that, Andrew Freedman, majority stockholder and president of the New York club, jumped up from his box near home plate, ran onto the field, and demanded that umpire Tom Lynch throw Holmes out of the game. When Lynch denied having heard

Holmes say anything, Freedman had Giants manager Bill Joyce take the team off the field. Lynch then declared a forfeit to Baltimore, whereupon many of the thousand or so spectators crowded around Freedman, demanding their money back. Freedman agreed to that, but then Hanlon hustled over to insist on Baltimore's share of the day's receipts.

While Hanlon demanded that the National League's four-man board of directors make the New York club pay Baltimore $100 in lost receipts and fine the Giants $1,000 for leaving the field, Freedman demanded that the directors suspend Holmes for the rest of the season for his "insulting language at the Polo Grounds . . . to the Jewish race and the Hebrew patrons of the game."[6] With customary irresolution, Nick Young and the club owners tried to satisfy everybody, initially both suspending Holmes and fining Freedman, then, with Freedman in Europe, reinstating Holmes and rescinding Freedman's fine. By September, Holmes was again playing for the Orioles at the Polo Grounds.

By 1898 Andrew Freedman had become the storm center of the National League. A handsome bachelor of German-Jewish ancestry, in his late thirties, Freedman had made himself rich in real estate speculation and become an influential confidant to Richard Croker, boss of Tammany Hall. In various ways Freedman was the prototypical sports franchise owner of that and later times: wealthy from other sources, volatile, overbearing, a man who insisted on operating his team as an extension of his own huge ego. Besides barring from the Polo Grounds sportswriters who criticized him, Freedman effectively forced John Heydler off the League's umpiring staff. From 1895, when he bought a controlling interest in the Giants, until the end of the 1898 season, Freedman ordered nine managerial changes. Even the venerable Cap Anson could last only twenty-two games working for Freedman. By 1902 he would have changed managers seven more times, at which point his ambitions and those of John McGraw would fatefully converge.

In 1898, though, McGraw was still just a ballplayer, albeit a very good one—and a fairly well-off young man as well. He was well enough off to concern himself closely with the well-being of Billy Earle, a former catcher in the Association and the National League, whom McGraw had first got to know in New Orleans in 1891, at the time of Al Lawson's aborted second Cuban expedition. Since then Earle, succumbing to morphine addiction, had become a derelict wandering the streets of Washington. McGraw had heard about Earle's plight, brought him to Baltimore, had him admitted to City Hospital, and paid the costs of his six-week treatment. By the end of September, pronounced cured by his physicians, Earle was an outpatient and able to attend a game at Union Park, where he seemed "like a new man" to a local reporter. McGraw as a good Samaritan struck a Washington writer as "a sort of Jekyll-and-Hyde transformation. . . ."[7] In later years that would become a favorite way of describing the contrast between McGraw's belligerent behavior on the baseball field and the growing number of people he helped in one way or another off the field.

During the first week in October, the Orioles went to Boston, lost two straight games, had a third rained out, and went home with their pennant chances all but dead. They finished six games behind the Beaneaters, whose 102 victories were the most in the game's history up to then. The Orioles' ninety-six wins were also their most ever, but Hanlon griped about "a spirit of indifference to the success and welfare of the team among some of the older players." His pitchers had done well, he granted, and McGraw had "worked earnestly and effectively for the team's success."[8] But the ball club's general lack of enthusiasm had made for a lot of empty seats. Baltimore had drawn only 123,416 customers, less than half the turnouts in the Orioles' pennant years. Already Frederick A. Abell, president of the Brooklyn club, was talking about the prospect of Hanlon's buying into that franchise and moving all or some of the Baltimore players there.

Such talk went on throughout the winter, acquiring more substance week by week. Early in February 1899, drawn-out negotiations between representatives of the Baltimore and Brooklyn clubs resulted in their outright merger. Hanlon and Harry von der Horst bought half of the stock in Brooklyn; Abell and Charles Ebbets became half-owners of the Orioles.

That was one of two such amalgamations in the off-season of 1898–99 that brought to full flower what was known as "syndicate baseball." While Hanlon and von der Horst were merging with Brooklyn, Frank and Stanley Robison, owners of the Cleveland Spiders, acquired control of the St. Louis franchise. Angry because local authorities wouldn't allow Sunday games in Cleveland and convinced that baseball would never make much money there anyway, the Robisons had closed their ballpark and sent the Spiders on the road for the last half of the 1898 season.

Although syndicate baseball wasn't really new—Cincinnati's John T. Brush, Chicago's A. G. Spalding, and Boston's Arthur Soden all owned substantial stock in the New York Giants—bringing two different ball clubs under one management was an innovation. Besides moving their offices to St. Louis, the Robisons stripped Cleveland of its best players— including player-manager Patsy Tebeau, two-time batting champion Jesse Burkett, and the great Cy Young—and left behind almost nobody of major league caliber.

Things worked out rather differently for Baltimore. Aware of what was happening, McGraw and Wilbert Robinson were determined one way or another to stay in Baltimore, where they had a thriving business. Asked if he would go to Brooklyn if transferred there, McGraw answered, "I have gotten all the glory I can out of baseball and am not looking after any more. I'm more interested in getting money. . . . Baltimore is good enough for me."[9] For a time the pair tried to persuade a group of local capitalists to buy the Baltimore franchise for $35,000, which von der Horst considered a reasonable price. But with rumors circulating that after one more season the National League would trim down to eight teams and leave Baltimore adrift, nobody was willing to take the plunge.

Permanently soured on Baltimore as a baseball town, Hanlon looked to Brooklyn as his opportunity for continuing fame and greater fortune. Until its incorporation into Greater New York under the charter that became effective on January 1, 1898, the borough of Brooklyn had been an independent city, the second largest in the nation. With a tenth-place ball club in 1898, Brooklyn had still drawn some 300,000 at home. With a winner, Brooklyn would probably be a gold mine. And with the cream of the talent he inherited there and would transfer from Baltimore, Hanlon intended to give Brooklyn cranks a winner.

Hanlon wasn't expected to leave much in Baltimore except Robinson and McGraw, who remained adamant about staying. Finally, early in March at the League's scheduling meeting in New York, Hanlon asked McGraw whether he wanted to manage the Orioles. Next day, still a month shy of his twenty-sixth birthday, McGraw returned to a big welcome at the Diamond Café as the new boss at Baltimore.

Pledging not to transfer any additional players from Baltimore once the season formally began, manager Hanlon took his Trolley Dodgers to Augusta, Georgia, for spring training.[10] His roster already included ex-Orioles Willie Keeler, Joe Kelley, Dan McGann, Jim McJames, Jim Hughes, and Hugh Jennings, although Jennings, his throwing arm gone bad, would spend most of the rest of his playing career as a part-time first-baseman. At Macon, McGraw had Steve Brodie (reacquired from Pittsburgh the previous season) and Ducky Holmes as outfielders, Robinson as assistant manager and regular catcher, Jerry Nops as a pitcher, and otherwise a cast of unknowns.

McGraw soon had his men hustling through morning and afternoon practices. A Cincinnati scribe had quipped that "McGraw as a disciplinarian is likely to achieve as much success as a man on roller skates trying to walk on eggs."[11] From the beginning, though, McGraw seems to have had the confidence and respect of his players. John Ryan, a catcher who'd played for several different managers in the National League, remarked that he'd never seen anybody get such enthusiasm out of his men. People around the League took notice when the Baltimores won two out of three practice games from Hanlon's club at Augusta. Dan McFarlan, a pitcher being given a tryout by McGraw, looked so good in his stint against Brooklyn that Hanlon decided to take him, and McGraw was barely able to talk Hanlon into letting him keep another pitcher, a barrel-chested twenty-eight-year-old rookie out of the Indian Territory named Joe McGinnity.

Assuring the Baltimore faithful that "We're going to be strictly 'in it' this year," McGraw began his first season as a major league manager on April 15, 1899. Hanlon and von der Horst wouldn't authorize the hiring of a brass band, so there was no parade from downtown to Union Park, but otherwise it was a festive day. About 4,000 spectators cheered McGraw's every move and delighted in the Orioles' 5–3 victory over New York behind right-hander Frank Kitson. The Orioles also took the next two from the Giants, and although they lost two in a row in their first official encounter with Brooklyn, in brand-new Washington Park, they salvaged the finale when McGraw stalled umpire Jim Gaffney into calling the game on account of darkness with Baltimore ahead 12–11. The Brooklyn *Eagle*'s Al Yager described McGraw as being "all over the lot, hustling his youngsters to do their best; he was next to Gaffney one minute and doing a song and dance around [umpire] Andrews the next. . . ."[12]

Young and energetic, long convinced that he knew more baseball than anybody else, and getting good work from his mostly nondescript players, McGraw found managing to be fun. He liked his players, liked to joke around with them, occasionally liked to turn a harmless prank on one of them. On a night train from Cleveland to Cincinnati, for instance, he came through the Orioles' sleeping car with a lantern and persuaded Pat Chrisham, a rookie catcher from rural New England, that on such trains, somebody always had to volunteer to stand on the rear platform of the sleeper and wave a lantern to prevent a locomotive from coming up too fast and colliding with the sleeper. Crisham dutifully took the "10–2 shift," standing at his post and waving his lantern until an incredulous brakeman happened along and told him to get off the platform and into bed.

McGraw showed that he knew how to impose discipline when he suspended Jerry Nops for being hung over and getting battered at Union Park by the once-fierce but now usually pathetic Cleveland Spiders. That, incidentally, was one of only twenty games the Spiders won that season, all but the first few weeks of which they spent on the road, trying their best most of the time but compiling a record for futility unparalleled in major league annals. McGraw also showed that he could outfox Foxy Ned, trading shortstop Billy Magoon to Chicago for Gene DeMontreville, whom Hanlon had traded away the previous winter. Once McGraw had DeMontreville, Hanlon wanted him back and offered to exchange a lame-armed Jennings for DeMontreville as well as the suspended Nops. When McGraw refused, von der Horst blustered that McGraw had no authority to make trades anyway. With the baseball press generally siding with Baltimore, the Brooklyn empire-builders finally backed down.

The Orioles' surprisingly strong showing was the talk of the League for most of the season. On August 8 McGraw's team was in fourth place with a 55–38 record but only five and one-half games behind Brooklyn, which, as everybody expected, had been in first since the early going. McGinnity, already dubbed "Iron Man" because he'd worked in his father's foundry at South McAlester, Indian Territory, became the mainstay of McGraw's staff. Throwing with an easy three-quarter-underhand motion that put minimal strain on his arm, the twenty-eight-year-old McGinnity pitched 380 innings and posted twenty-eight victories. Holmes hit .320, shortstop Billy Keister hit .329, and McGraw played the best ball of his career. In 118 games he batted .390, scored 140 runs, drew 124 walks, stole seventy-three bases, and made only twenty-five errors at third. One way or another, he was on base more than 70 percent of the time. In a double-header with Brooklyn in June, he made five hits in six official times at bat and, all told, reached base nine straight times.

Asked how he managed so many walks, McGraw contrasted his hitting style with those who took "the cigar sign pose": "I shift about, I step from one corner of the box to the other, and I crowd the plate. Again, I stand at the edge of the box and walk into the ball. . . . I swing and jerk my bat, and all these little feints rattle the average pitcher." Said

Chicago's Clark Griffith, one of the League's premier pitchers, "He simply worries the life out of you. . . . He stays there fouling the balls off one after another. . . . When he has had enough fun he gives the ball a dinky little push and it lands safe, you can bet on that." "All things considered," thought Frank Selee, "there is no one in his class."[13]

McGraw's Orioles were every bit as contentious and disorderly as Hanlon's Orioles had been. By 1899 the Brush Rule, never really enforced and unenforceable anyway, was a dead letter. "For five hours," reported Hugh Fullerton, a young Chicago sportswriter who accompanied that city's ball club into Baltimore for an August double-header, "the Baltimore park reeked with obscenity and profanity." While the crowd howled its approval, McGraw engaged in what Fullerton, with some partisan exaggeration, described as "the worst species of abuse and ruffianism ever witnessed on a ballfield," thoroughly intimidating umpires Al Mannassau and Jim McGarr.[14]

Following a tough series in St. Louis, in which McGraw and Patsy Tebeau had a shoving match and the spectators pelted his men with rotten eggs, the Orioles came into Louisville on Sunday, August 27, for a double-header. When McGraw returned to the bench at the end of the second inning, he was handed a telegram reporting that his wife was "desperately ill" back in Baltimore. He finished out the game (won by the Orioles), then left matters in Robinson's hands and caught the six o'clock train for the East.

All summer Minnie McGraw had experienced periodic abdominal discomfort. On August 26 the pain became severe. Two physicians, called to the McGraw home on St. Paul Street, agreed that she was suffering from acute appendicitis. Deciding that it would be better not to try moving her to a hospital, they operated on Sunday night, while McGraw was worrying his way through the long ride from Louisville. They found the appendix ruptured and a massive infection in the abdominal cavity. All they could do was remove the appendix, clean up as much of the infection as they could, administer morphine to lessen the pain, and hope that Minnie might be strong enough to fight off the malady. By the time McGraw reached his wife in the early daylight hours, she was running a high fever and unable to keep down nourishment. With the onset of peritonitis and then blood poisoning, it became a matter of waiting for the end. Minnie Doyle McGraw died at the age of twenty-two just after noon on Thursday, August 31.

The next Sunday, after a Solemn Requiem Mass at Saints Phillip and

James Church on North Charles Street, she was buried in her bridal dress in Bonnie Brae cemetery. Joe Kelley, Hugh Jennings, and Willie Keeler were among the pallbearers, with Nick Young, Ned Hanlon, and Harry von der Horst part of the crush of people that forced the bereaved to struggle to reach the graveside.

Losing his young wife of two and one-half years was the worst thing that had happened to McGraw since his mother's death. Preferring to bear his grief alone, he went into semi-seclusion at the row house on St. Paul Street. To well-wishers who brought the immemorial advice that the best thing for him would be to get back to work, he answered, "I wouldn't be of any use to the team at present. I feel exhausted physically and mentally, and am in no condition to play ball. . . . It seems to me just now as if the last thing I could interest myself in would be baseball." "He bears up bravely," noted the *Sun*'s Frank Patterson, "but it is pitiful to see how terribly it has hurt him. He has aged much, and I saw gray hairs in his head today."[15]

In his absence the Orioles played only slightly better than .500 ball. McGraw rejoined them on September 11 for a game with Louisville at Union Park, although he didn't put himself back in the lineup for another week and a half. Sleeplessness and depression (what he called "nervousness") had worn him down, he said.

Near the end of the month his spirits brightened somewhat when John T. Brush offered him the manager's job at Cincinnati for the following year at a salary of $5,000, about $1,500 more than he was now making at Baltimore. Although McGraw told Ted Sullivan, Brush's agent, that the amount was much too little in light of his Baltimore business interests, it gave him a lift to be wanted someplace else, especially by the president of one of the most consistently profitable franchises in the League.

Even more of a tonic was taking three straight from Brooklyn at Union Park a few days later. McGraw showed that his concentration was again fully on baseball when he caused a Brooklyn error in a unique manner: Coaching at third with Keister standing on first, he called to pitcher Bill "Brickyard" Kennedy to let him see the ball. The unthinking Kennedy threw over to McGraw, who smilingly stepped aside and watched the ball roll to the grandstand fence. Keister ran to second and then scored on George LaChance's single.

The season ended on October 14 at Brooklyn, accompanied by enough confusion and disorder to prove that things were pretty much back to normal for McGraw's outfit. When Oriole Jimmy Sheckard was called out on a steal attempt in the second inning, he went into such a rage that umpire George Hunt ordered him out of the game. Instead Sheckard headed for right field, picked up his glove, and took his position. Hunt made a futile appeal to McGraw, then turned to Hanlon, who was, after all, Sheckard's employer. With Hanlon's approval, Hunt declared a forfeit to Brooklyn. To appease the angry crowd of about 2,500, McGraw and Hanlon agreed to play another game and thereby make up for one postponed earlier in the season. Umpires Hunt and Tom Connally called it because of darkness at the end of five with Brooklyn comfortably ahead.

That double defeat left Baltimore in fourth place with a record of 86–62, three and one-half games better than St. Louis. Everything considered, it was a remarkable showing, one that established McGraw's reputation as the finest young managerial talent in the game. Hanlon's Brooklyn powerhouse, led by Hughes's twenty-eight wins (which tied McGinnity) and Keeler's .377 at bat, cruised to the pennant, finishing eight games ahead of Boston. Even so, the home attendance hadn't been up to Hanlon's expectations. About 270,000 had paid to get into Washington Park, fewer than had seen the dreary 1898 ball club and far less than Chicago and Philadelphia had drawn. Baltimore's home attendance almost matched the previous year's. With an outlay of only about $35,000 for players' salaries, the club lost less money—but still lost.

As soon as the season was over, the baseball press began to buzz with rumors that over the winter the National League would drop some of its weaker franchises. In that case, so other rumors had it, McGraw would either play for Brooklyn next year, go to New York as a player, sign to manage New York, or even join with a new ownership at Washington to try to revive that club's fortunes. It was early March 1900, before the National League voted officially to eliminate four franchises: Washington, Louisville, Cleveland, and Baltimore. Yet for just about everybody connected with baseball, it had been common knowledge for months that those four were doomed. And for months McGraw and his friend and business partner Robinson had been hustling to ensure some kind of future for professional baseball in Baltimore.

That future, they hoped, would take the form of a Baltimore franchise in a revived American Association. Among those promoting such a project were Alfred H. Spink, sports editor of the St. Louis *Post-Dispatch* and co-editor of the *Sporting News*; Francis C. Richter of Philadelphia, editor of the weekly *Sporting Life* and the annual *Reach's Baseball Guide*;

Harry D. Quin, a Milwaukee entrepreneur; and Cap Anson of Chicago. Working with those men, McGraw and Robinson tried to line up financial backing in eight cities, namely Baltimore, Chicago, Boston, Milwaukee, Louisville, Providence, Detroit, and Philadelphia. The Association formally organized in Chicago on February 12–13, 1900, with Anson chosen president. By that time McGraw and Robinson had joined with Philip Peterson, Police Court judge Harry Goldman, and John J. Mahon (Joe Kelley's father-in-law) to form the Baltimore Baseball Club of the American Association.

Hanlon's lease on Union Park having expired, McGraw obtained its use for the Association. When he found out that McGraw had the lease, Hanlon put armed guards at the gates to the park. The exuberant Peterson clambered over a fence, jumped and pummeled one of the guards, and left in his pocket a court order restraining Hanlon and von der Horst from removing any property from the grounds. Later several constables and policemen, acting under court instructions, rigged a sleeping tent in the bleachers in left field. Meanwhile, Hanlon's men occupied the clubhouse and groundskeeper's cottage.

The *opéra bouffe* in Baltimore ceased to have any purpose after the middle of February. The Association promoters had barely left the Chicago organization meeting when Cap Anson announced the Association's disbandment. All along, the critical factor in the scheme had been Philadelphia's participation. On his way home from Chicago, McGraw stopped off to see W. J. Gilmore, the principal Philadelphia financial backer, who told him that no ball grounds were available and the Philadelphians would need another three weeks before they'd know for sure whether they could come in. At that McGraw threw up his hands and wired Anson that Philadelphia couldn't be counted on, whereupon Anson made his announcement. McGraw came back to Baltimore grumbling about "the entire lack of business sagacity in the men promoting the deal [in Philadelphia]" and protesting, "I am going to stay here if I have to play on a town lot."[16]

Within three weeks the National League officially lopped off Baltimore and the other three franchises, as had long been expected. Automatically all Baltimore player contracts passed to Brooklyn, but Hanlon almost immediately sold the contracts of McGraw, Robinson, and Billy Keister to St. Louis for an aggregate $15,000. McGraw talked about putting a Baltimore team in the Eastern League or maybe even organizing a strong semi-pro outfit to play up and down the East Coast. If he played major

league ball in 1900, though, he and the others, bound by the reserve
clause in the contracts first transferred from Baltimore to Brooklyn and
now to St. Louis, would have to play for the Robison brothers or nobody.
Frank de Haas Robison came all the way from St. Louis to talk to his
three acquisitions. Keister alone pronounced himself ready to play for
St. Louis. Hanlon and von der Horst even visited the Diamond Café to
try to convince McGraw and Robinson to go, but the partners were
unyielding. Said McGraw, "Business reasons alone is what keeps us.
We have no objection to Robison or to St. Louis, nor even to Tebeau,
but we can't afford it."[17]

In fact, McGraw and Robinson were angling for a situation in New
York or some other eastern National League city whereby they could
remain in baseball and still look after their affairs in Baltimore. According to Hanlon, New York owner Andrew Freedman, given first choice
on players from the four severed clubs, had declared that he wouldn't
take McGraw and Robinson as a gift. Nonetheless, they kept trying to
make some kind of deal. On the pretext of taking in the Joe Gans–Frank
Erne prizefight in New York, McGraw talked with William "Buck" Ewing,
once the game's premier catcher and Freedman's latest managerial choice.
A couple of weeks later, accompanied by Robinson, McGraw visited
Freedman at his Manhattan office. Did Freedman have a personal grudge
that kept him from being interested in their services? No, replied Freedman, but then he had no intention of buying them, either. At that,
according to one report, Freedman "advised them to go to St. Louis,
ordered drinks, and bade them good-bye."[18]

Having hawked themselves in various places without success, "the
redoubtable ex-Oriole and his avoirdupois partner," as they were described in St. Louis, had little alternative but to play baseball for a team
located more than eight hundred miles away, in the League's westernmost
city.[19] The season was three weeks old when they capitulated, wiring
Frank Robison that they accepted the terms he'd offered and were on
their way. Those terms, McGraw later disclosed, were the most generous
in the history of professional baseball. McGraw's contract specified a
season's salary of $10,000—of which, because of reporting late, he
would actually receive $9,500. Robinson, nearly thirty-six and clearly
on the down side of his career, would be paid about $5,000. The most
remarkable feature of their contracts, though, was that to get them to
come to St. Louis, the Robisons had to strike out the reserve clause in
both their contracts—an unheard-of concession in that day.

On Saturday, May 12, 1900, despite a bitter transit-workers' strike that had shut down the city's streetcar system, some 7,500 St. Louisians reached the ballpark on Natural Bridge Road to see McGraw and Robinson debut with the team once called the Browns and now variously known as the Perfectos, Red Caps, or Cardinals. Ironically, the opposition that day was Brooklyn. McGraw singled, walked twice, and managed to get himself in front of one of McGinnity's pitches; but his throwing error in the ninth inning gave Brooklyn an opening for a rally climaxed by Willie Keeler's game-winning hit.

It proved to be a difficult and uncertain season for McGraw. He soon discovered that he'd stepped into something of a minefield. Patsy Tebeau named McGraw team captain, as instructed by the Robisons but against the wishes of Jesse Burkett and several others, who wanted their pal Jack O'Connor to have the honor and the extra $600 that went with it. O'Connor was sold to Pittsburgh shortly before McGraw's arrival, but resentment lingered among his new teammates. McGraw never really knew where to fit in, although he praised St. Louis as a great baseball town and said Tebeau, often his violent enemy in the past, had treated him well and told him "to go right ahead and do what you think best."[20] McGraw decided early on that his best course was to hustle and give his employers their money's worth but also to mind his own business. At the end of the season, no longer bound by the reserve clause, he could look for something better.

In general McGraw did earn his pay—what time he was in the lineup. In ninety-eight games, he batted .337, drew eighty-five walks, scored eighty-four times, and continued to have the highest on-base percentage of anybody in the League. But he was disabled for two lengthy stretches, once after being spiked by Dirty Jack Doyle in New York in June, and again in August because of a case of boils. Often during both periods, instead of going to the ballpark, he spent the afternoons at the horse races. All too conveniently, the best track in St. Louis was situated right across the street from the baseball grounds.

By 1900 gambling, mainly on the horses but really on anything from prizefights to pool games, had become a fairly important part of McGraw's life. He was never what might be called a compulsive gambler, never so addicted that he got himself into any serious financial difficulty. But he did enjoy immensely what gamblers call "the action"—the ambience, the gambling confederates, the thrill of putting money on an unpredictable outcome. McGraw didn't bet more than he could afford to lose, although his fondness for making wagers undoubtedly helped keep him from becoming a rich man. He'd started going to Pimlico and other tracks around Baltimore in his early years with the Orioles, as soon as he had enough money to spare for the races. Playing the horses was a widespread indulgence among ballplayers in the 1890s and would remain so long thereafter. Fred Lieb recalled that even Connie Mack, who later, as a manager and owner, would project such an image of high-collar propriety, liked to put an occasional bet on a horse's nose during his playing days.

After St. Louis, with a talent-loaded ball club, finished in a tie for fifth place, some of the local sportswriters complained that McGraw had had his mind more on the horses than on baseball. Even if true (which it wasn't), that hardly explained the team's failure. Patsy Tebeau was no longer the fiery spirit he'd been when he and his Clevelands terrorized the League. With Tebeau unable to enforce discipline, his players became apathetic, discontented, and more than a little dissipated. Tebeau's ten years as manager at Cleveland and St. Louis came to an end when he quit on August 18, after a loss to Cincinnati. Recovering in his rooms at the Southern Hotel from boils and various hurts and bruises, McGraw declared, "Under no circumstances will I accept the management of the St. Louis team, and there is the end of it."[21] Actually, though, when club secretary Louis Heilbronner moved to the bench as nominal manager, McGraw agreed to name the starting pitchers and generally be in charge of the team on the field. But he despaired of ever getting his teammates to play "Oriole baseball."

Wilbert Robinson's morale and patience both became so frayed that on September 19, at Brooklyn, he threw the ball at the legs of umpire Gaffney and, joined by McGraw and others, behaved so abusively that Gaffney first swung his mask at Robinson's head and then ordered him off the field. When McGraw refused to put anybody else behind the plate, Gaffney forfeited the game to Brooklyn, which at the time needed every win it could get to fight off Pittsburgh's rush and grab another pennant.

The season finally ended in St. Louis on October 14. That evening McGraw had a long talk with John T. Brush, who again sought his services as manager at Cincinnati. For the second October in a row, McGraw turned him down. He and Robinson had another scheme cooking for a second major league. This time, though, they were associated with a man who could command the wherewithal and who had the intelligence, imagination, and determination to put it over.

As far back as the previous April, Judge Harry Goldman had told McGraw that if he would just be patient, go to St. Louis for the present season, and then return to Baltimore free of commitments, then he could be assured of managing a major league team there in 1901. In a series of meetings held in various cities over the summer, McGraw and Robinson gave their all-out support to a plan for upgrading the former Western League into a full-fledged major circuit, stocked with as many National Leaguers as could be lured away from their teams, and including Baltimore as a charter member.

The driving force behind the American League, as the new organization was called, was Byron Bancroft "Ban" Johnson. Thirty-six years old in 1900, much overweight but tireless, Johnson was a college dropout who'd started out as a sportswriter on the Cincinnati *Commercial-Gazette* and then become president of the Western League. Under Johnson's firm hand, that circuit became the best-run baseball operation in the country. In 1900 he changed its name to the American League, put franchises in Cleveland and Chicago, and prepared to move into other territory vacated by the Nationals in Baltimore and Washington and challenge the older league head-on in Boston.

Johnson intended to inaugurate a new era in baseball history with a tightly run, orderly league in which players and owners would give the customers good baseball and abandon the rowdyism and infighting that had always featured the National League's history. "My determination," Johnson said not long before his death in 1931, "was to pattern baseball in this new league along the lines of scholastic contests, to make ability and brains and clean, honorable play, not the swinging of clenched fists, coarse oaths, riots or assaults upon the umpires, decide the issue."[22]

How McGraw ever thought he could work amiably for very long with a man who held such exotic views and seemed determined to enforce them will always be something of a puzzle. In the winter of 1900–1901, though, McGraw was full of enthusiasm and praise for the dynamic Johnson. On November 12 McGraw and Robinson signed papers with Johnson giving them exclusive rights to form an American League franchise in Baltimore, and afterward supped on pheasant and champagne with Johnson and Charles W. Somers of Cleveland, the league's chief financial backer. The Baltimore franchise was incorporated a week later with a capitalization of $40,000. Among the major stockholders were McGraw and Robinson; Judge Goldman; the Reverend John Boland (who'd married John and Minnie McGraw); Judge Conway Sams of the appellate tax court; and James P. Shannon, owner of the Eutaw House.

For the next four months McGraw was on the go most of the time, traveling all over the eastern half of the country wooing unattached ballplayers. Johnson had ruled that the American League would sign no National Leaguer already under contract, but anybody unsigned was fair game.[23] In reply to rumors that his reason for being in New York was to talk with Andrew Freedman about managing the Giants, McGraw declared, "I am with each passing day more than ever with the American League and have the fullest faith in its success." Commented Freedman, "There is no more chance on my part of engaging McGraw for the New York team than there has been of annexing the moon to the New York map."[24] Later, pressed by Baltimore sportswriter Frank Patterson, McGraw finally admitted that on January 13, 1901, he had met with Freedman, who'd urged him to come back to the National League but hadn't directly offered him the New York managership. Johnson knew all about it, he added.

Meanwhile, the new Baltimore club secured a five-year lease on the old baseball grounds on York Road between Twenty-eighth and Twenty-ninth streets, where the Baltimore Association team had played until 1891. On a cold and windy Lincoln's Birthday, Johnson came to Baltimore to help break ground for what McGraw and his associates had decided to call Oriole Park. Soon steamrollers, lumber wagons, carpenters, bricklayers, painters, and groundskeepers swarmed over the site. Within seven weeks they had Oriole Park—a single-decked facility with a brick grandstand and wooden bleachers that seated about 8,500— ready for occupancy by Baltimore's American League entry.

Right after the ground-breaking, McGraw left for Hot Springs, Arkansas. Located in the foothills of the Ozarks, Hot Springs was in its glory as a popular health resort, a place where people came to drink mineral water and soak themselves in warm mineral baths, both of which were thought to have curative or at least ameliorative effects. Quite a few ballplayers in McGraw's time made annual pre-season visits to purge and boil out a winter's overload of food and drink, as well as to enjoy the plush hotel pool rooms and Hot Springs' year-round horse races.

On his way to Hot Springs, McGraw met in the St. Louis railroad station with Joe McGinnity, who came up from South McAlester, Indian Territory. When they parted, McGraw had the Iron Man's signature on a contract obligating him to Baltimore for a salary of $2,800. At Hot Springs itself, he signed Jimmy Williams, Pittsburgh's fine second-baseman, and Mike Donlin, a gifted young substitute outfielder who'd been one of McGraw's free-living teammates at St. Louis. Losing Williams was an especially bitter pill for Pittsburgh president Barney Dreyfuss, who was expecting Williams to arrive any day from his home in Denver and sign for another year with Dreyfuss's Pirates. Lamented Dreyfuss, "I not only lose Williams, but I pay his fare east for McGraw to steal him from me."[25]

McGraw's most publicized acquisition from his stay at Hot Springs was a dark-skinned infielder billed as a full-blooded Cherokee Indian and called "Chief Tokahoma." McGraw noticed the young man taking infield practice on a diamond near McGraw's hotel. He looked to McGraw like an already polished ballplayer. Which indeed he was, inasmuch as the man McGraw watched was Charley Grant, second-baseman for the Columbia Giants, a strong black professional team in Chicago. That winter Grant was working as a bellhop at the Eastland Hotel, where McGraw was staying.

Like many other white Americans who'd grown up in small towns in the northern states, McGraw had no particularly strong racial views one way or another. He'd rarely seen any black people until he traveled south for the first time in the fall of 1890. Certainly he was no crusader for racial justice, not one to challenge the national consensus that presumed the innate superiority of white over black. He was, though, a baseball manager always on the lookout for new talent. So he concocted an impossible scheme for selling Charley Grant, a black American from Cincinnati who happened to have straight hair and sharp features, as Chief Tokahoma, complete with a fake ancestry in the Indian Territory and a fake mother said to be living in Lawrence, Kansas.

The whole thing never had a chance, although McGraw evidently intended to take it as far as he could. Under an unwritten but scrupulously observed gentleman's agreement among baseball owners, no black player had worn a major league uniform since 1884, when brothers Moses Fleetwood Walker and Welday Walker had appeared in forty-seven games between them for Toledo in the American Association. Frank Grant, a minor league infielder, had played his last game in the Interstate League in the early Nineties. After that, so-called Organized Baseball had remained lily-white.

Despite McGraw's efforts, it would remain so in 1901 and for another forty-five years after that. Charles Comiskey, president of the American League's Chicago entry and Ban Johnson's close friend, torpedoed McGraw's project as soon as he heard about it. Proclaiming that "this Cherokee of McGraw's is really Grant, the crack Negro second-baseman, fixed up with war paint and a bunch of feathers," Comiskey threatened to "get a Chinaman of my acquaintance and put him on third" if McGraw tried to keep "this Indian."[26]

That did it. McGraw never actually signed Grant to a Baltimore contract, but left him in Hot Springs with the assurance that he would send for him later. Grant never got the call. Within a few weeks he was back in Cincinnati; then it was on to Chicago for another season with the Columbia Giants. McGraw had come closer than he ever would again to breaking baseball's color line.

Nobody, wrote an observer from Hot Springs, had "cut a wider swath . . . than . . . the little Pooh-Bah of the American League."[27] In truth, McGraw was a power in the new circuit. So far he'd had a hand in just about every facet of League operations. As a member of the League's three-man rules committee, for example, he was able to convince Comiskey and Connie Mack, slated to manage at Philadelphia, that "unintentional" foul balls still shouldn't count as strikes. The National League, on the other hand, had just decided that the first two fouls a batter hit, intentional or not, would be strikes.[28]

By the time the American League was ready to start its first season as a major league, 111 of the 185 players under contract to its eight clubs had experience in the National League. It hadn't taken a great deal of money to lure most of the league-switchers; a few hundred dollars above the decade-old salary cap had usually been sufficient. So even though McGraw had induced McGinnity, Williams, Donlin, Billy Keister, and Jerry Nops to join him in the new league, as well as pitcher Harry Howell from Brooklyn, utility man Roger Bresnahan from Chicago, and pitcher-turned-outfielder J. Bentley "Cy" Seymour from New York, the whole Baltimore player payroll wasn't supposed to be much in excess of $20,000. McGraw and Robinson would take their pay out of whatever profits the club made.[29]

After training his players for three weeks at a diamond in one of the city's public parks, McGraw had his team in reasonably good shape to open the season by hosting Boston, which had attracted most of the talent from that city's National Leaguers. Ban Johnson and everybody else had to wait through a rainout and another postponement for wet grounds for the debut of the American League in Baltimore. On April 26, 1901, an officially reported overflow of 10,371 watched Johnson toss out the ceremonial first ball, then cheered a 10–6 Oriole victory behind McGinnity, who was struggling with an attack of malaria. McGraw twice doubled into the roped-off spectators, as did Keister, and "Turkey Mike" Donlin (so called because of his swaggering walk) hit two triples. The next day, before a smaller overflow, the Orioles defeated Cy Young, one of the Johnson circuit's biggest catches; and the day after that, with Johnson again presiding, they helped open Washington's new park, losing to the "Senators" 5–2.

McGraw made it through nearly two weeks before he had his first serious run-in with one of Johnson's umpires. After actually bullying Jim Haskell into reversing a decision at Philadelphia on May 6, he protested so protractedly over a call the next day that Haskell ordered him out of the game. That evening McGraw wired Johnson's office in Chicago to complain about Haskell's incompetence. Johnson remarked to newsmen that "those who I hear are getting to be rather boisterous and rowdy" might "have their wings clipped right off."[30] The next week he suspended McGraw for five days after he received umpire Joe Cantillon's report on McGraw's repeated outbursts during a series at Baltimore with Mack's Athletics. Inasmuch as the Orioles were rained out for the next week, the suspension was of no practical consequence. But it was an ominous portent for McGraw's relations with the American League umpires and their boss.

At the end of May, in Detroit, Harry Howell cursed out Jack Sheridan for calling Ducky Holmes safe at home on a play that tied the score. Sheridan ejected Howell as well as Donlin, who'd picked up the ball and thrown it at Sheridan's back. When McGraw told Howell to go back to the mound, Sheridan announced a forfeit to Detroit. That episode and others in Baltimore's first western trip prompted McGraw to write home that Haskell, Sheridan, and Al Mannassau were all incompetent; National League veterans Sheridan and Mannassau, "having grown cunning in the business," were also "notorious home umpires." If Johnson wanted discipline on the ballfield, he added, then give the teams competent umpires.[31]

About a week later McGraw and Johnson clashed bitterly over the disposition of Hughey Jennings. According to McGraw, the previous winter, when Jennings had been a student and baseball coach at Cornell University, his old friend had agreed to play with Baltimore in 1901 if he played anywhere. According to Johnson, only Connie Mack had put in an official claim to Jennings, and Mack had come to terms with

Jennings before McGraw ever thought of negotiating with him. Infuriated, McGraw insisted that Jennings would play in the upcoming series against Milwaukee at Oriole Park. In that case, countered Johnson, he would instruct Milwaukee not to take the field with Jennings on it. "I am not going to tolerate any such interference by one manager with another manager's plans," Johnson declared. "McGraw hasn't a leg to stand upon in this matter."[32]

First Jennings, from Ithaca, New York, pronounced himself ready to play at Philadelphia for what Mack had offered him, $3,500 for the rest of 1901. But then he came down to Baltimore, had a long talk with McGraw, and said he'd either play for Mac or return to the National League. When club secretary Harry Goldman was unsuccessful in getting Mack and Benjamin Shibe, president of the Athletics, to sell their claim on Jennings, Hughey left for Philadelphia. There he signed not with Mack and Shibe but with Colonel John S. Rogers, owner of the National League Phillies, for a reported $3,360.

Johnson blamed McGraw and only McGraw for his league's failure to secure a ballplayer whose skills might have slipped, but who was still one of the game's biggest names. "I cannot see what McGraw can be thinking about," fumed Johnson. "McGraw's actions lost Jennings for the American League and I'm sorry for Mack's sake."[33]

In the midst of the Jennings affair, the Orioles won eleven straight games and took over third place with a 28–21 record. It should have been twelve in a row, McGraw contended, because Johnson should have awarded a forfeit to Baltimore when Boston manager Jimmy Collins got mixed up on the schedule and took his team to Philadelphia while 2,500 people waited vainly for the Bostons to show up at Oriole Park. No, said Johnson, the game should be made up at a later date.

McGraw must have wondered what else could happen when, at Philadelphia in mid-July, he hit a slow roller to second base and, as he ran to first, the pet collie of first-baseman Harry Davis darted from the Athletics' bench and nipped at McGraw's heels all the way down the line. McGraw beat the throw, then had to endure the dog's harassment until Davis finally called him off and had him tied.

It would get worse, though. McGraw dislocated his right kneecap in a collision at third in Washington and had to give way to Jack Dunn, another converted pitcher. Two weeks later, Johnson charged that a Baltimore newsman acting as McGraw's agent had approached managers and part-owners Jim Manning of Washington and George Stallings of

Detroit with a proposal for those two clubs to join with Baltimore in deserting the American League and becoming members of a new twelve-team National League. "We don't want any Benedict Arnolds in our camp," roared Johnson. "The accusations are mean, cruel, malicious lies," shot back McGraw. The real threat to the American League, as McGraw saw things, was in Johnson's intention to abandon Baltimore for one of the National League cities. Johnson, added *Sporting Life*, had insisted on "going off half-cocked and rushing into print" with his charges.[34] Maybe so, but then quite a number of baseball followers, remembering the "Tokahoma" episode, must have wondered just how much McGraw could be believed.

McGraw limped to the plate to pinch-hit on August 1, but it was another week before he returned to third base full-time. By then the Orioles, having climbed to within a game and a half of second-place Boston and six and one-half games of front-running Chicago, were beginning to stir pennant talk in the city. On August 20, though, he tore cartilage in the same knee he'd hurt earlier. This time his physicians encased the knee in plaster and ordered him to stay off his feet for three weeks. He was through for the season as a player.

The next day, August 21, he was at home, disabled, when the Orioles took on Detroit at Union Park. It was the sixth straight game that Tom Connally, another of Johnson's National League recruits, had umpired at Oriole Park, and plenty of ill feeling on the part of players and spectators had built up against him. In the fourth inning Connally called out Jack Dunn on a close play at first base. McGinnity charged over from the coaching box to stamp on the umpire's toes and spit tobacco juice in his face. Detroit's Norman "Kid" Elberfeld ran in from second to try to protect Connally, only to be knocked down by Donlin. Players, spectators, and police jammed the area between first and the grandstand. When the police tried to leave the park with Elberfeld under arrest, McGinnity and Keister went to the Kid's aid, apparently believing that it was all right for ballplayers to battle each other as long as outsiders kept out. All three were arrested, along with a spectator named Allen, and hustled off to Judge Harry Goldman's police court. Goldman quickly discharged the players but fined Allen twenty dollars. Meanwhile, at the ballpark, Connally forfeited the game to Detroit and got away in a closed carriage under mounted police escort.

Johnson was furious when he heard about the brawl in Baltimore, especially inasmuch as he'd recently had to lay an indefinite suspension on Oriole first-baseman Bill Hart for punching umpire Haskell and had banned for life Chicago shortstop Frank Shugart for still another assault on Haskell. Now he announced McGinnity's permanent suspension as well. The trouble, he said, was that such ex–National Leaguers as McGraw and Clark Griffith (Shugart's manager) had brought their disruptive habits into his league.

After losing to lowly Milwaukee in a game in which they committed seven errors and lost a run when Steve Brodie absentmindedly stopped ten feet from home plate to cheer Bresnahan's triple and was tagged out by the catcher, the Orioles went west accompanied by McGraw, who hobbled aboard the train on crutches in defiance of his physicians. Grumbling about injuries and mistreatment by Johnson and threatening retirement, he explained that he would go with the team only as far as Chicago, where he'd arranged to see Johnson on the McGinnity matter.

Carrying testimonial letters from Judges Goldman and Sams and accompanied by a penitent McGinnity, McGraw pleaded the Iron Man's case in Johnson's office. Johnson finally agreed to set McGinnity's term of suspension at twelve days, retroactive to the day of his original suspension, provided he apologized personally to Connally. Said McGinnity afterward, "Mr. Johnson is a much better man than I had been led to believe." McGraw ventured that Johnson would deal fairly with Baltimore in the future. "We did not fall on each other's necks," Johnson told reporters, "but we came to a perfect understanding. . . . I think the trouble is all past now."[35]

Under Robinson's direction, the Orioles could do no better than 2–12 in the west. Back at home, with McGraw managing from the bench, they won eight straight games before losing to Detroit to close out the season. Their final record, 68–65, left them in fifth place, thirteen and one-half games behind Griffith's Chicago pennant-winners. The Orioles had played above .500 after May except for the September slump in the western cities with McGraw laid up in Baltimore. McGraw himself had had a good all-around season until it was cut short in his seventy-third game. Up to then he'd batted .352, tops on the club, and averaged a run scored per game. Yet the injury to his knee was a bad one, bad enough to put in doubt his future as a player.

Over the past four years McGraw had been a player and playermanager at Baltimore, the highest-paid player in history at St. Louis, and then, back at Baltimore, a franchise organizer, part owner, and player-manager. He'd also taken a prominent role in promoting the abortive American Association enterprise. Through it all he'd remained the focus of controversy on and off the field. And he'd endured and surmounted a terrible personal loss.

In the fall of 1901 McGraw seemed outwardly confident about the future of the American League and his own future in it. Total attendance in the new circuit, by Francis Richter's calculations, was, 1,658,000, less than 200,000 below what the National League had drawn. Yet at Oriole Park the attendance of 142,000 had exceeded only that of Milwaukee and Cleveland, the League's last and next-to-last clubs. The Baltimore franchise may have barely broken even, but little if anything remained with which to compensate McGraw and Robinson.

Still, McGraw thought Johnson's transfer of the flagging Milwaukee franchise to St. Louis ought to strengthen the whole league; in most matters Johnson was "manifestly trying to do the right thing. . . ." On the subject of his battles with Johnson's umpires, McGraw sounded positively mellow. Some of the umpires had been good, some bad, but then, "Good umpires are born, not made, and the born variety is remarkably scarce."[36]

The mellowness, if that's what it was, would disappear quickly once another season was under way and McGraw and Johnson again found their horns locked. They were two men with massive egos—both of them young, brilliant, hot-headed, and insatiably ambitious. So far they'd managed to coexist within the confines of one league, but more strife was ahead—and a drastic alteration in the course of McGraw's career in baseball. For now, though, the main thing on widower John McGraw's mind was a young woman named Blanche Sindall.

Four
·
THE MAIN CHANCE

BLANCHE SINDALL WAS NINETEEN when she met McGraw. At that time she was a student at Mount St. Agnes College for Young Women, located just inside Baltimore's northern city limits. She was about 5′ 1″ tall, had dark eyes and a great deal of jet-black hair, and was appropriately plump for turn-of-the-century tastes in the female form. She lived with her parents in a handsome row house at 1353 York Road in the Waverly section, one of the city's most fashionable. Her father, James Sindall, was, like John McGraw, a self-made man. Starting out as a stove sales-man, he'd moved on to become a highly successful building contractor, erecting lines of brick row houses with neat wooden trim and gleaming white-marble steps all over the northern part of Baltimore. Like many contractors, he liked to build a house, live in it for a while, sell it, and build another. His wife finally persuaded him to settle his family in the best of his most recently built row houses in Waverly. By that time the Sindalls had five children, of whom Blanche was the oldest. Although the Sindalls and the Smicks, Blanche's mother's family, were both of Dutch ancestry, somewhere along the line their Protestant forebears had converted to Roman Catholicism.

In the fall of 1900, at a time when he was busy helping get the American League started, McGraw, along with Hughey Jennings and a number of other young people, came for a social evening at the Sindall house. Like McGraw, Jennings was a widower, his wife having died a year earlier, a few months after Minnie McGraw's death. The two ball-players were there at the invitation of Charles Schryver, Blanche Sindall's cousin and also her more-or-less boyfriend. A baseball enthusiast, he'd met them through his acquaintance with the booking agent for the Baltimore and Ohio railroad. McGraw was eight years older than Blanche Sindall. Although she knew nothing about baseball or his world, he impressed her as a man of affairs.

When he spoke to her, she would remember a half-century later, "His voice was light and pitched rather high, but it was hatpin sharp. . . ." At that time he was still slightly built, weighing about 150 pounds. He wore his black hair parted in the middle and swirled on the sides of his forehead in the "fish-hook effect" then favored among young men. His black eyes were small and intense, and his skin, no longer tanned as it had been at the close of the ball season, was white, even pasty. He wasn't handsome, but he was well dressed in his dark-blue suit, high starched collar, and light-blue tie with gem-studded stickpin. His manner was courteous and self-assured. When he told her that he was a professional baseball player, all she could think to say was that he must be "one of the batters."[1]

Over the winter months McGraw became a frequent caller at the Sindall house. Blanche enjoyed his company; he'd had an interesting life so far (even if she didn't understand much of what he told her about it), and he talked easily and confidently. She'd seen almost nothing of the world outside of Baltimore and environs, and he'd been to Cuba and other faraway places. His shirts and shoes were made in Cuba, he explained, because he wanted to encourage the country's economy, especially now that it was an independent republic—under the protection of the United States, of course.

She first saw him in a baseball uniform on the opening day of the American League season in 1901, when the whole Sindall family plus Charlie Schryver and a couple of his pals filled the grandstand box McGraw had bought for them. That summer McGraw came to the Sindall house practically every night when the Orioles were in town. Often Blanche drove the family's carriage through the Johns Hopkins University campus and Druid Hill Park. McGraw never drove; throughout his life he seems to have preferred being driven to driving, whether the conveyance was horse-drawn or motorized. On other nights they had dinner downtown at the Northampton Hotel, took in a light-comedy production or a vaudeville show at one of the city's half-dozen theaters, or simply stayed at home with Blanche's parents and her baseball-inquisitive younger brothers. His fondness for just sitting quietly and watching her family struck Blanche "as a sort of gnawing hunger."[2] Later he would explain to her about his own broken and scattered family.

On Sundays, when he was in town, McGraw joined the Sindalls for Mass at St. Ann's Church, a few blocks south on York Road (or Greenmount Avenue, as it became at that stretch). He invariably brought a bouquet of violets for Blanche or had flowers sent when the Orioles were away from Baltimore. "He was always kind, considerate, and affectionate, but never demonstrative," she later remarked.[3] But if McGraw wasn't a passionate suitor, he was a very earnest one. A successful and busy but lonely young man, he found Blanche Sindall to be everything he wanted and needed. She was intelligent, sweet, pretty, even-tempered, and the daughter of a good Catholic family—a well-to-do one, besides. Late in the summer, still walking on crutches with his knee in a cast, he asked James Sindall's consent to marry his daughter. The engagement was formally announced on October 24.

The wedding, at St. Ann's Church on Wednesday evening, January 8, 1902, was an even bigger occasion than McGraw's marriage to Minnie Doyle five years earlier. It wasn't entirely free of trouble on the groom's side. James Doyle objected to McGraw's remarrying and talked for a time about suing if McGraw went ahead with his intention to sell the house on St. Paul Street (probably because some of the money that had gone toward its purchase had been Doyle's). The wedding itself went smoothly enough, even though the Reverend Cornelius F. Thomas of St. Ann's provoked giggles among the group gathered at the altar and mystification in the pews by whispering such baseball-influenced homilies as "You know it is the 'sacrifice hit' that adds to the number of runs and wins the game," "Make her 'steal' her way . . . until she reaches the 'home plate' of happiness," and "Make her 'score' many bright and happy days, that the 'pennant' of prosperity may continually wave over your heads."[4]

The Reverend John Boland, who'd performed the ceremony for McGraw's first marriage, and six other priests assisted Thomas. The luminaries in the church and at the reception at the Sindall house included Joe Kelley, Willie Keeler, Wilbert Robinson, Joe McGinnity, and Steve Brodie. McGraw's younger brother James was also on hand.

At eleven o'clock that night the newlyweds left for the South on their honeymoon trip. After a stopover in Washington, they boarded a sleeper for Savannah. There McGraw booked them into the seedy Hotel Pulaski because, as he explained it to his bride, he'd obtained a good discount at the Pulaski for spring training, and it wouldn't be fair if he took his business someplace else. In Florida, at St. Augustine and Palm Beach, as well as in Charleston, South Carolina, on their way home, the accommodations were better. Back home, they took a suite at the Northampton Hotel, Baltimore's finest, and McGraw went to bed with influenza. By the end of January, though, he was again up to his neck in complex baseball business.

Despite McGraw's quarrels with Ban Johnson, the two stayed in touch during the off-season about a variety of matters, most of all prospects for gaining an American League foothold in New York City. Convinced that his league would never be really solid and secure unless it had a prosperous New York club, Johnson intended to relocate one of his franchises after the 1902 season. If the Baltimore operation were moved, then presumably McGraw would be the manager in New York. During the fall and winter of 1901–1902, McGraw as well as Clark Griffith made mystery-shrouded trips into New York to talk with prospective financial backers and scout out possible playing sites. Andrew Freedman of the Giants could be expected to do everything possible to keep the American Leaguers out, but the recent election defeat of the Tammany Hall forces by a reform slate headed by Mayor-elect Seth Low had supposedly undercut Freedman's ability to stop the extension of transit lines and otherwise frustrate Johnson's plans.

McGraw repeatedly denied being in New York for any reason except to visit the racetracks and generally enjoy himself. No, he said, the Baltimore club wasn't going anywhere and neither was he. The American League, in Baltimore and all its cities, was "firmly established, with splendid financial backing. . . . If the National League is waiting for the death of the American League, they are likely to have a long, lonesome wait of it." Johnson wouldn't comment publicly on any machinations involving Baltimore or any other club, only affirm that "we shall be in New York next year without doubt."[5]

In February, John K. Mahon, who two years earlier had been one of the leading backers of an American Association franchise for Baltimore, bought a big block of stock in the Orioles, so big that the other dozen or so stockholders elected him president. His son-in-law Joe Kelley also bought into the club and announced that he was leaving Ned Hanlon and Brooklyn to play for McGraw. Meanwhile, Dan McGann, who'd remained in the National League at St. Louis, and Albert "Kip" Selbach, a steady outfielder with the New York Giants in 1901, signed with the Orioles. Jimmy Sheckard, who'd jumped from Brooklyn to Baltimore and back to Brooklyn the previous spring, jumped again, promising to stay with the American League this time. With those additions and holdovers Donlin, Brodie, Seymour, Robinson, Williams, Bresnahan, McGinnity, and Howell, the Orioles looked like sure-fire pennant contenders.

Taking Blanche and her younger sister Jeannette Sindall with him, McGraw left for Hot Springs on February 22, his main purpose being to soak his damaged knee in the resort's healing mineral waters. He'd been there about three weeks when he received news that blunted his pennant hopes. It was the first but by no means the last time that Mike Donlin's mercurial disposition and erratic behavior would have that effect on McGraw.

At the age of twenty-three, "Turkey Mike" Donlin was on the verge of stardom. In 1901, his first season as a full-time player, he'd hit .341. A slashing left-handed hitter and a fast, aggressive base runner, he was a muscular 5' 9" and 170 pounds, a dark-featured, handsome Pennsylvanian whose likable ways made him a favorite on every team he ever played for. But Donlin lacked self-discipline and professional commitment, and he enjoyed saloons, showgirls, and high living more than he did baseball.

On the evening of March 12 he showed up drunk at the Academy of Music, where an actress named Mamie Fields, who'd evidently caught his fancy, was appearing in the stage version of Lew Wallace's enormously popular novel *Ben Hur*. The ushers threw Donlin out on that occasion, but the next night he waited until Fields came out of the theater, accompanied by another actress and Ernest B. Slayton, who lived at the nearby lodging where Fields was staying. Donlin first took a swing at Slayton, then hit Fields in the face with his fist and knocked her down. When onlookers yelled for the police, Donlin ran across Howard Street and hid in the Diamond Café, then made it to the train station and fled to Washington. The next day a quarrel with a Washington streetcar conductor resulted in his arrest and return to Baltimore.

Under the speedier if not necessarily surer justice of that day, Donlin stood trial less than a week later in criminal court. His only defense was that he'd been drunk and wasn't responsible for hitting Mamie Fields. She appeared in court with a face still bruised and swollen and swore that she hadn't even known Donlin. Donlin's plea for mercy—on the ground that the Orioles had already released him and he'd thus lost $2,800 in salary for the coming season—was unavailing. Judge Ritchie fined him $250 and sentenced him to six months in the Baltimore County jail.

Actually the Orioles hadn't released Donlin. As soon as he'd heard about the affray in Baltimore, Ban Johnson had wired McGraw in Hot Springs that Donlin was expelled from the American League. When McGraw returned to the city on March 21, he snapped that he didn't know any particulars about Donlin's trouble and didn't want to know any.

Not even bothering to unpack their trunks, the McGraws left the next day on the steamship *Hudson* for Savannah, in the company of fifteen players and various club officials, wives, and reporters. McGraw was so pleased with how his knee had come along that he released Jack Dunn and announced that he expected to play most of the time in 1902. Despite losing Donlin, he was in good spirits; so was the rest of the team. Blanche McGraw proved that she already knew how to handle her responsibilities in the delicate area of wifely relations. She made a big hit by hosting the wives of Mahon, Robinson, and stockholder Miles Brinkley at a "box party" at the Savannah Opera House, where the celebrated May Irwin was appearing in a play.

Once the season began, though, McGraw's mood darkened quickly. The Orioles opened at Boston, where so many people wanted to get into Huntington Avenue Grounds that they battered down the fence behind the third-base bleachers. Players struggled alongside policemen to push the crowd back so the game could start. McGraw didn't play, but he gave Tom Connally enough trouble from the bench and the coaching lines that Connally ejected him after a few innings. Boston's ninth-inning rally won it before an estimated 16,000 partisans.

Four days later Baltimore also lost its home opener, before about a third more people—an official 12,726—than Oriole Park had seats for. Philadelphia's Bill Bernhard held the Orioles to a single run; the Athletics piled up eight on rookie Charlie Shields. In only one respect was it a notable game. After seven innings an officer from the state supreme court in Pennsylvania served injunctions on Bernhard, pitcher Charles "Chick" Fraser, and second-baseman Napoleon "Larry" Lajoie, permanently prohibiting them from appearing for the Athletics. The previous year their desertion from the National League Philadelphia Phillies for Connie Mack's team had prompted a legal battle in the Pennsylvania courts. In the meantime, Fraser had won twenty games for Mack, Bernhard seventeen, and Lajoie had batted a stunning .422.

Although Ban Johnson cleverly circumvented the Pennsylvania judges by transferring the contracts of Lajoie and Bernhard to Cleveland, neither he, McGraw, nor anybody else could do much about National League counter-raids on their league.[6] McGraw went so far as to punch an agent for Ned Hanlon who came to Baltimore to try to talk Jimmy Sheckard into returning to Brooklyn. Early in May, for the second year in a row, Sheckard did just that, this time leaving behind a debt of $1,000 the Baltimore club had loaned him so he could square accounts with Hanlon.

McGraw put himself into the lineup for the first time on April 28. Two days later he disputed long and bitterly with Jack Sheridan when the umpire signaled a Boston runner home after McGraw bumped him on the base path, and then when Sheridan ruled that McGraw hadn't tried to get out of the way of a pitch that hit him. The next day pitches from Boston's Bill Dineen hit McGraw five times; not once would Sheridan allow him to take his base. After the last denial, in the ninth inning, McGraw simply sat down in the batter's box and refused to move until Sheridan ordered him off the field. When Dineen retired the side to end the game, Sheridan was almost mobbed leaving the park.

Johnson hit McGraw with a five-day suspension, while the Baltimore *Sun*'s Frank Patterson complained that "the umpires are making a mark on McGraw." Certainly it looked as if Johnson had instructed his arbiters to take no abuse from McGraw, and some observers even suspected that Johnson was trying to run him out of the American League. Others thought McGraw was actually inviting Johnson to run him out of the League—and into the eager embrace of Andrew Freedman in New York. In the view of the Pittsburgh *Press*, it had to be more than coincidence that McGraw had released first Dunn and then Brodie, and both had immediately signed to play for Freedman. "Freedman and McGraw," said the *Press*, "seem to be working upon the 'community of interest' plan. . . . Perhaps he will move to New York himself one of these days. Stranger things have happened."[7]

On May 24 a fair Saturday crowd of about 3,600, including Blanche McGraw, was on hand at Oriole Park for a game with Detroit. In the first inning, with runners on first and third, the Tigers faked a double steal. Instead of throwing to second, catcher Bresnahan fired the ball to McGraw at third and caught outfielder Dick Harley several feet off the bag. Harley leaped feet first into McGraw, his spikes ripping open McGraw's left knee. As the umpire yelled "Out!" McGraw hurled himself on top of Harley. His young wife was horrified at the sight of her husband grappling in the dirt with another man. "It was the first outburst of his rage that I had seen," she would remember, "and it wasn't easy to watch."[8] Finally pulled away from Harley, McGraw limped off the field with his black wool stocking soaked with blood. With Blanche, he took a hack to the Northampton and called Standish McCleary, the club's physician. McCleary cleaned up the knee as best he could, applied disinfectant, and put seven stitches in the three separate wounds McGraw had sustained.

In that period a bad spiking usually meant at least infection, and ballplayers lived in dread of something worse—gangrene, lockjaw, or blood poisoning. McGraw's knee became nastily infected; it was nearly two weeks before he was able to leave his rooms for a short walk around the hotel. When he'd come back from being suspended, he lamented, he'd had "a time lock on my lips," only to have Harley put him out of action again.[9]

Unable to play or even to go with his team when it left on its first western swing, McGraw had plenty of time to think about his situation. The people had come out in respectable numbers so far; in the Orioles' eleven home games, they'd averaged close to four thousand, fourth best in the League. Yet just about everybody—from club officials and managers to ballplayers and reporters—seemed to agree that when the League moved into New York next year, Baltimore would be abandoned. McGraw fully understood what a supreme opportunity it would be to manage an American League club in New York, maybe even be a part owner. But he'd also become convinced that Johnson would never let that happen. Johnson, he said many years later, planned "to ditch me at the end of the 1902 season. So I acted fast. . . . Someone would be left holding the bag, and I made up my mind it wouldn't be me."[10]

On June 18, while the Orioles, under Robinson, were floundering in the West, McGraw slipped into New York to see Andrew Freedman, the first of several conferences they would have over the next two weeks. Two years earlier the mercurial Freedman had supposedly had no interest at all in McGraw, even as a gift. Now he wanted him very much, enough to pay him a record salary and give him complete authority over the acquisition and disposition of players. For McGraw's part, he'd had enough of Ban Johnson's league and wanted the money and acclaim that would be his if he could make a winner out of the sleeping Giants. But neither he nor Freedman was content for him simply to jump his contract, as so many others had done in the past year or so. Instead they conceived a complicated plot to destroy the Baltimore franchise and cripple the American League.

When McGraw returned to the lineup, at Oriole Park on June 28, both he and Joe Kelley seemed to go out of their way to antagonize umpires Tom Connally and Jimmy Johnstone. In the eighth inning Connally had enough and ordered McGraw to the clubhouse. McGraw raged and fumed and refused to leave the field, and Kelley ran up to shoulder and curse Connally. Having seen and heard it all before, Connally did what he'd done before. The game was forfeited to Boston, he announced through his megaphone.

The forfeit left Baltimore in seventh place with a record of 26–31. It also produced indefinite suspensions for McGraw and Kelley, as they were informed by wire two days later from Chicago. Added Johnson, "I am glad [Connally] maintained his position and humiliated Mc-Graw. . . . Rowdyism will not be tolerated in the American League . . . and the men who disregard the organization rules must suffer the consequences." In Philadelphia with his team but forbidden to appear in a uniform or even sit on the bench, McGraw claimed that he'd only spoken to Connally "in a kidding way." Then he warmed to the subject: "No man likes to be ordered off the earth like a dog in the presence of his friends. Ballplayers are not a lot of cattle to have the whip cracked over them." He'd already put a lot of his own money into the American League, "but there is an end to self-sacrifice. A man must look out for himself."[11]

"I'm disgusted," he said when he returned to Baltimore. Johnson was "down on the town and would like to see it off the map."[12] By that time a New York newspaper had already disclosed that he was dickering with Freedman, although McGraw wouldn't comment on that or on growing talk along the same lines in Baltimore. On the evening of July 2 he was seen outside the Northampton in intense conversation with Kelley and John K. Mahon. Next day he was off again to New York.

On Monday night, July 7, he met at the Northampton with the Baltimore club directors: Mahon, vice president Sidney Frank, Harry Goldman, Miles Brinkley, Kelley, and Robinson. He demanded that they either pay him the $7,000 he calculated the club owed him or give him his outright release. The directors adjourned without taking any action but agreed to reconvene the following morning. At that meeting McGraw received his release in exchange for his stock holdings, which Mahon bought for $6,500. McGraw then told local reporters that he would leave that night for New York to take up his duties as manager of the New York Giants. He would be paid "as much as any ballplayer ever drew" and have "practically unlimited funds" for buying players. "I certainly will not draw on the Baltimore team for players," he promised. Then a parting shot at Ban Johnson: ". . . I would be a fool to stay here and have a dog made of myself by a man who makes no pretence of investigating or giving a hearing to both sides."[13]

The next morning, at the New York ball club's offices in Manhattan, McGraw officially signed to manage the Giants, although he'd already secretly signed a contract brought to Baltimore three days earlier by Giants secretary Fred M. Knowles. Most estimates put the amount he would be paid at $10,000 a year or less. Actually his contract called for a salary of $11,000 a year for four years, which made him the highest-paid ballplayer or manager (on a straight salary basis) up to that time.

When he met the New York newsmen, McGraw said he was happy to be in the city, "the cornerstone of baseball." The American League, dominated by "Czar Johnson" and the Chicago-Philadelphia-Boston clique, "is a loser and has been from the start." Baltimore hadn't made a penny in the American League, and in Philadelphia as well Johnson "has a big white elephant on [his] hands." Asked about the Giants' prospects, he'd only say that "it will be my aim to secure desirable players wherever I can find them."[14] That particular statement must have seemed ominous in Baltimore.

McGraw always insisted that he didn't jump his contract at Baltimore, that he'd obtained his release in regular form and been free to do whatever he wanted. Technically, that was true, but most of the baseball press treated him as a turncoat and deserter. Wrote Frank Patterson of the Baltimore *Sun*, "Loyalty and gratitude are words without any meaning to ballplayers and especially to McGraw." The final row with Tom Connally on June 28, Patterson charged, was contrived by McGraw so he wouldn't have to play anymore and would look like a martyr when he jumped to New York. The Baltimore *News* blamed McGraw for the club's disappointing showing. Once a fine hitter and baserunner, he'd "degenerated into an ordinary player, discontented, soured, full of vain imaginings that every man's hand was against him and that his hand had necessarily to be against every man." "The language of twelve-year-old back-lot boys," added the *News*, "won't do on a professional diamond today. . . ." McGraw's course all season, thought the *Sporting News*, had been "offensively dictatorial." The Freedman-McGraw alliance wouldn't

last, though, because "one is as arbitrary as the other is anarchistic. . . ."15

Now McGraw and Freedman, along with John T. Brush of Cincinnati
and their co-conspirators in Baltimore, Mahon and Kelley, went forward
with the rest of their scheme for sabotaging the Baltimore Orioles. On
July 16 Joseph C. France, acting as Freedman's agent, came to Baltimore
and, with McGraw as go-between, acquired 201 of the four hundred
shares in the franchise, for a total cost of $50,000. The stock bought
by Freedman consisted principally of Mahon's original holdings (including what he'd recently bought from McGraw) and that transferred
by Robinson to McGraw in exchange for McGraw's half-interest in the
Diamond Café, and then transferred again to Mahon. Mahon also gathered in Kelley's and the Reverend John Boland's stocks for sale to
Freedman.

As the new controlling stockholder, Freedman directed the releases
of Joe McGinnity, Dan McGann, Roger Bresnahan, and pitcher Jack
Cronin. John and Blanche McGraw accompanied the four players to the
Pennsylvania Railroad Station in Baltimore, where McGraw told them
they'd all been unconditionally released and he would see them later in
New York to sign them to Giants contracts. Meanwhile Joe Kelley also
received his release and headed for the Stafford Hotel, where Brush,
registered as "J. T. Brown," signed him to manage the Cincinnati Reds.
Shortly afterward, Cy Seymour was off to Cincinnati to join Kelley.

Left with only five players, Baltimore obviously couldn't field a team
on July 17, against St. Louis at Oriole Park, and had to forfeit. McGraw
and his new National League associates might well have succeeded in
mortally wounding the American League if Johnson hadn't acted quickly
and masterfully. Declaring the Baltimore franchise vacant, he assumed
control for the League and borrowed enough players from the other seven
clubs to reconstitute a team. With Robinson as their manager, the new
Orioles beat St. Louis on July 18. Somehow they would manage to hold
together and play out the season, finishing on the bottom with a record
of 50–88.

"Muggsy McGraw is the Aguinaldo of base ball," cried the *Sporting
News*, comparing McGraw to the leader of the insurrection against American forces occupying the Philippines. "He was and is in the game for
loot. . . ." How that particular trait distinguished McGraw from anybody
else in professional sports the St. Louis editors didn't explain. McGraw
had seen the main chance and taken it. "If [Johnson] planned to ditch

me, I ditched him first," McGraw said long afterward. Inasmuch as Johnson probably had no intention of bringing him along when he moved the American League into New York, McGraw did face a crisis in his professional life. His way of dealing with that crisis was totally ruthless and unscrupulous. Subsequently he would develop warm friendships with Connie Mack and Charles Comiskey, but with Ban Johnson his relations remained at best distant. "Johnson's enmity was carried to the grave," wrote Fred Lieb, who knew both of them well. "The pair never spoke again."[16]

On July 17, while Robinson and four other Orioles gathered at the ballpark and forfeited to St. Louis and while Johnson scrambled to find replacements for those who'd taken flight, John and Blanche McGraw arrived in New York for good. He was twenty-nine years old; she was twenty-one.

Five

THE TOAST OF NEW YORK

THE McGRAWS MOVED their several trunkfuls of possessions into an upper-floor parlor of the Victoria Hotel. Standing at Fifth Avenue and Twenty-seventh Street, the Victoria was in the heart of what was then the city's main business district and only two blocks from the St. James Building, where both the National Exhibition Company, the corporate name for the New York Giants, and the National League had their offices. As Blanche McGraw recalled, "We practically tiptoed into town. . . . I was cautioned against talking to anyone about baseball, especially newspapermen."[1] Not talking to members of the press was fairly difficult in turn-of-the-century New York, inasmuch as the city of close to four and one-half million people had a dozen dailies, appearing morning and evening, ranging from Adolph S. Ochs's staid and sober *Times* to William Randolph Hearst's breezy and sensationalistic *American*.

In 1902 what would become Times Square, Forty-second Street and Broadway, was still relatively tranquil Longacre Square, and a structure called the Pabst Building stood at the convergence of Broadway and Seventh Avenue. It would be another six years before the *New York Times* erected its headquarters building there and gave the square its unique identity. The transformation of that section of midtown Manhattan was part of an unprecedented building boom that had been going on for the past ten or fifteen years and produced such landmarks as the Flatiron, Singer, and Woolworth buildings, structures that heralded the age of the commercial skyscraper. Two years after the McGraws arrived, the city's first subway line, long delayed by opposition from streetcar and elevated-railway interests, would finally go into operation.

Leaving Blanche to unpack at the Victoria, McGraw went directly to

94

see Andrew Freedman at the National Exhibition Company offices, then took a hack up through Central Park and Harlem to the Polo Grounds, the Giants' ballpark. At that time Harlem, named after a seventeenth-century Dutch settlement on that part of upper Manhattan Island, was mostly an area of middle-class residences occupied by Jewish New Yorkers. Within a few years, though, overbuilding and a sharp decline in real estate values in Harlem would leave a great number of unoccupied residences. For the first time black realtors, often as agents for white owners and developers, would be able to open up Harlem to black buyers and renters. The racial transformation of the area would be well under way.

The Polo Grounds was situated on the northern fringe of Harlem, at 157th Street and Eighth Avenue. Those two streets were the southern and eastern boundaries of the site; the Eighth Avenue elevated railroad tracks curved north between the ballpark fence and the Harlem River, and to the west the boulders and trees of Coogan's Bluff loomed over the grandstand roof. The name "Polo Grounds" had a tortuous lineage. Nobody had ever played polo there, but a few matches had been held on the site of the original National League ballpark, just north of Central Park. In 1889 the Giants had moved to Manhattan Field, on 155th Street. The next year the Players' League club built its ballpark next door, and when that experiment in baseball socialism collapsed, the Giants leased the superior Brotherhood Field from the Coogan estate. Long-standing Giants fans were so fond of the old designation "Polo Grounds" that they quickly made that the name for the Giants' new home.

The Polo Grounds had a double-decked wooden grandstand running from first base around to third, wooden bleachers that extended into left- and right-center fields, and a big carriage park separated from the spacious outfield only by an arc of rope-linked hitching posts. Its seating capacity was about 18,000, although four or five thousand more people could crowd into the carriage park and stand, squat, or sit in various other places in and around the ballpark, including the rocks on Coogan's Bluff and the precarious grandstand roof.

Such overflows had been rare in the years since John Montgomery Ward's Giants demolished Baltimore in the first Temple Cup series back in 1894. Potentially the richest in all baseball, the New York franchise had become the sick man of the National League. After Ward left to pursue legal studies at Columbia University (and later become a successful New York attorney), twelve men, representing fifteen different changes, had managed the Giants—or at least tried to in the face of repeated interference from the front office. Freedman's pinch-penny practices and arrogance toward the paying customers had made him possibly the most hated man in the city of New York.

Despite Freedman's refusal to send the team south, so that the Giants had to do spring training at the Polo Grounds, the present season had started off well. An overflow of ever-hopeful New Yorkers had turned out to see the Giants beat Philadelphia in the season opener, with young Christy Mathewson throwing a shutout. Managed from the bench by Horace Fogel, formerly a Philadelphia sportswriter, they'd won ten of their first fifteen games. After that, though, they reverted to form, losing thirty-eight of forty-nine and falling into last place. Fogel turned over direction of the team to captain and second-baseman George "Heinie" Smith and left on a scouting expedition. When the Giants concluded a road trip by winning at Cincinnati on July 17, behind Mathewson, their record improved to 23–50.

That afternoon McGraw found the four players he'd brought with him from Baltimore in uniform and working out at the Polo Grounds. He signed them to contracts and told a couple of reporters hanging around the park, "Of course, the pennant is out of our reach as this season's playing goes, but look out for us next year."[2]

The ball club McGraw took over was not only listless and defeatist but, according to some reports, split into Protestant and Catholic factions as well. However that may have been, one of his first actions was to get off a wire to Cincinnati informing four Giants players of their outright releases. When the team got back to New York the next day, he released two more. To Freedman's protests about the money he'd invested in those players, McGraw reminded him that he'd given his new manager complete authority to hire and fire and do whatever was necessary to build a winning ball club. Freedman acquiesced, maybe because he was planning to sell his interests in the Giants anyway.

After an off-day on Friday, the Giants played their first game under McGraw on Saturday, July 19, before a curious crowd of about 10,000, the biggest since opening day. Many showed up long before the four o'clock starting time to get a good look at the newcomers. As the Giants went through pre-game practice with uncharacteristic dash, one delighted spectator yelled in a voice that was audible throughout the park, "They're awake!"[3]

The opposition was the Philadelphia Phillies, whose first-baseman, ironically, was Hughey Jennings. McGraw's damaged knees had made him an ordinary ballplayer, but partly to please the crowd and partly because he had nobody else with experience at the position, he put himself at shortstop. The Phillies scored four runs in the third inning off Joe McGinnity; Herman "Ham" Iburg let the Giants have only three. McGraw punched a single in three official at-bats, plus a walk and a sacrifice bunt. It wasn't what the New York cranks would have preferred, but the Giants' hustling play pleased them nonetheless. After the game several hundred people gathered outside the clubhouse behind the right-field fence to greet the New York players as they left the ballpark. No doubt some of the faithful noted that McGraw had even induced John Murphy, the Baltimore groundskeeper, to jump to the Giants.

McGraw's men won their first game on July 23 at Brooklyn's Washington Park, with Luther Taylor beating Ned Hanlon's club 4–1. Taylor, who'd pitched for two years at New York, then jumped to Cleveland, and then returned to the Giants early in the present season, had lost a staggering twenty-seven games in 1901. But he was a smart right-hander who in the years to come would make the most of his limited abilities and end up with 117 major league victories. He would, moreover, become both a source of amusement and an object of affectionate regard among the Giants, because "Dummy" Taylor, as he was almost invariably called in that less delicately sensible time, had been a deaf-mute from birth.[4]

Besides the foursome from Baltimore, McGraw had former Orioles Steve Brodie in the outfield and Frank Bowerman behind the plate. McGraw's old enemy Jack Doyle was also on the team, but McGraw gave Doyle's job at first base to Dan McGann and released him before the end of the season. Within a week after arriving in New York, McGraw also signed outfielder George Browne, released by the Phillies, and pitcher Roscoe Miller, who jumped over from Detroit. His pitching ace was Mathewson, who'd won twenty games with a seventh-place team in 1901.

Thus overhauled, the Giants won twenty-five and lost thirty-eight over the remainder of the season, ending up seven and one-half games behind seventh-place Philadelphia and fifty-three and one-half behind the Pittsburgh Pirates, who coasted to their second pennant in a row. Under McGraw the club had made something of an improvement, hardly a major reversal of fortunes. Actually McGraw was away much of the time in August and September. He popped up in various American League cities with offers of more money for such players as Jesse Burkett (now with the St. Louis Americans), Detroit's Kid Elberfeld, and Washington's Ed Delahanty, maybe the greatest natural hitter of his time. Besides buying a winner for New York as quickly as possible, McGraw obviously took pleasure in spreading as much consternation as he could in Ban Johnson's league.

He also found himself again acting as intermediary in one of Freedman's complex schemes. This time, though, Freedman was not buying but selling, and John T. Brush was doing the buying. Brush had been privy to the Baltimore sabotage operation and had come out of the affair with Joe Kelley to manage and Cy Seymour to play the outfield for his Cincinnati Reds. Now Freedman gave him an opportunity to take full control of the most valuable baseball market in the country, and Brush was prepared to act quickly. Brush had owned part of the Giants since 1891, when he and various other National League club owners had gone to the aid of the nearly bankrupt John B. Day, then owner of the Giants. In the years since Freedman had become majority stockholder, most of the rest of the stock had continued to be held in Boston and Cincinnati.

Early in August, Brush sold his majority holdings in the Reds to the brothers Julius and Max Fleischmann, heirs to the yeast fortune; George Cox, Cincinnati's political boss; and Cox's close associate, August "Garry" Herrmann. On August 12 Brush came to New York, announced that Freedman had agreed to his becoming "managing director" of the Giants, had a long meeting with McGraw, and came out pledging to obtain the best players money could buy.

Already talking as if he owned the Giants, Brush proceeded to leave no doubt in the matter. In a series of conferences with McGraw at Brush's home in Indianapolis and between McGraw and Freedman at Freedman's Red Bank, New Jersey, estate, the arrangements were worked out whereby controlling interest in the National Exhibition Company passed from Freedman to Brush. McGraw came home one night in September to report that all the shares had been disposed of but four. His young wife said she'd buy those four herself, out of her own money, at $250 per share. Thereby Blanche McGraw became a stockholder in a corporation in which, as yet, her husband was only a salaried employee.

At the end of September, Freedman formally announced his resignation as Giants president in favor of Brush, and shortly he was off to Europe for a lengthy stay. Said Brush when asked about McGraw's status, "He is a fixture."[5] For the next ten years the two men would make up one of the most successful president-manager combinations in the game's history.

The foundation of John Tomlinson Brush's fortune was his big Indianapolis department store, one of the earliest establishments of its kind outside of Chicago and the major eastern cities. Brush had first gotten into baseball in the late 1880s as owner of the short-lived Indianapolis National League franchise. He'd then bought a controlling interest in the Cincinnati club, at the same time maintaining his holdings in Indianapolis after that city entered Ban Johnson's Western League. Brush had often clashed with Johnson in Western League councils, while in the National League he became an increasingly powerful and controversial figure. Once bitter foes, especially at the time of the notorious Brush Resolution in 1897, Brush and Freedman had subsequently become close allies (if never good friends).

Fifty-seven years old in 1902, gaunt, even ascetic-looking, Brush lacked the bombastic personality of some of his fellow magnates. He preferred to avoid publicity and work in quiet (some said sinister) ways to achieve his ends. "Chicanery is the ozone which keeps his old frame from snapping," wrote one critic, "and dark-lantern methods the food which vitalizes his bodily tissues."[6] The remarkable thing is that Brush could be as active and influential as he was, and as much an object of suspicion and fear, while suffering intense pain most of the time. For some fifteen years before his death he struggled against locomotor ataxia, a progressive disease of the nervous system usually (though not always) associated with syphilis. The condition had already forced him to walk with two canes at the time he took over the Giants; in later years he would be wheelchair-bound.

Events in the off-season caused both Brush and McGraw intense pain of another sort. First they learned that Mathewson and Bowerman had accepted $500 signing bonuses from president Robert L. Hedges of the St. Louis American League club, and that Jesse Burkett had decided to remain in St. Louis. McGraw thought he had Elberfeld, Delahanty, and shortstop George Davis (who'd jumped to the Chicago Americans after an unhappy year in 1901 as Freedman's manager) all neatly packaged for delivery to the Giants next spring. It turned out that he didn't.

In December, when the National League's annual meeting was held downstairs in the Victoria, the club owners chose Henry Clay "Harry" Pulliam, the thirty-three-year-old secretary of Barney Dreyfuss's Pittsburgh club, as League president. Brush cast one of the two votes against

Pulliam. Then, over Brush's bitter opposition, the rest of the National Leaguers agreed to make a peace overture to Ban Johnson and his associates. With the Americans going forward with plans to open next season with a team in New York, the Nationals were finally ready to accept the reality of a second major league and bring the costly baseball war to an end.

Their American League counterparts were just as ready for peace, and early in 1903 Pulliam, Johnson, Garry Herrmann, and Charles Comiskey held a series of meetings. The result was a peace pact called the National Agreement, which recognized the two leagues as separate and equal entities with common playing rules and player contracts and complementary schedules. Overall governance for the two major leagues and the various minor leagues recognized as belonging to Organized Baseball would be in the hands of a three-man National Commission, consisting of Pulliam and Johnson as league presidents and a chairman elected by the club owners. Cincinnati's Herrmann, who'd remained Johnson's good friend despite the strife of the past two years, was the owners' choice.

Under the assignments of disputed players directed by the National Commission, the Giants lost Davis, Delahanty, and Elberfeld. Mathewson and Bowerman gave their bonuses back to Hedges and remained Giants property, but McGraw, again taking the mineral baths at Hot Springs, insisted that the three American Leaguers were his as well, and that Fielder Jones, center-fielder for the American League Chicago White Sox, had signed to play with the Giants in 1904–1905. None of those men could play for McGraw, Harry Pulliam declared, unless their American League clubs granted them their releases. Henry Chadwick, who, like most followers of the game, had applauded the National Agreement, was again dismayed by McGraw's behavior. "What is it this fellow won't do," asked the aging and revered Brooklynite, "that is not in direct conflict with honorable work in the business?"[7]

So McGraw took his Giants—a rebuilt ball club but not nearly as much so as he'd intended—to spring training at Savannah. His major catch before the peace agreement had been Sam Mertes, an outfielder signed away from Comiskey's White Sox. He'd also picked up Billy Gilbert, his shortstop at Baltimore in 1902. And he still had Mathewson, already hailed by a local sportswriter as "the greatest drawing card the New York club has had since the days of Amos Rusie."[8]

Christopher Mathewson was twenty-two years old when he went to

Savannah that spring to begin his fourth major league season. If he was already the favorite of New Yorkers, he wasn't yet the superstar and superhero he would become within a few years. In fact, if one is to judge from occasional comments in the baseball press, Mathewson was then an aloof, rather swell-headed young man, fully cognizant that he was the big attraction on a bad ball club. A native of Factoryville, Pennsylvania, Mathewson had had a solid Protestant, middle-class upbringing by parents whose family roots in the area were deep. Unlike the great majority of ballplayers of his time, he was a college man, a graduate of Bucknell, where he'd dominated the athletic scene as a star in both football and baseball. If McGraw's fiery, combative managerial style seemed appropriate in years when President Theodore Roosevelt was thrilling the country with his strong-arm policies in Latin America and his blasts at the business trusts, Mathewson seemed to have other qualities that suited the period.

A couple of inches over six feet tall, a broad-shouldered (if knock-kneed) two hundred pounds, the blond and blue-eyed Mathewson was uncommonly handsome in just the right way for old-stock Americans. Projecting an image of sportsmanship and fair play in a rowdy, win-at-all-costs professional environment, he seemed to have stepped right out of one of Burt L. Standish's college novels featuring the exploits of Frank Merriwell. Over the years "Matty," as he was universally called, became something of a paragon, really the first professional athlete to function as a role model for America's youth.

No other baseball player of Mathewson's time served that function so well. The brilliant Ty Cobb, who would come into the American League in 1905, proved to be volatile, mean-spirited, and generally unlikable. John "Honus" Wagner, Pittsburgh's great shortstop, was likable enough, but he was also a homely, ungainly, beer-bellied "Dutchman," while Larry Lajoie was a swarthy French-Canadian, popular among his peers, but poorly educated and uninspiring. Matty, on the other hand, was just about everything that clean-cut young American manhood was supposed to be.

The real Mathewson fit the image fairly well but not completely. True, he wouldn't pitch on Sundays because, it was understood, he'd so promised his mother. But inasmuch as Sunday ball was legal only in Chicago, Cincinnati, and St. Louis, that was no real hardship on either his own career or his team's fortunes. Certainly Mathewson was no prig. He sometimes bawled out umpires, threw at batters' chins, or even traded a punch or two in the heat of combat. He smoked cigars and pipes, liked poker, and, if feeling gregarious, would have a few beers with teammates. He could command enough four-letter words to hold his own in dressing-room repartee. And he liked money, which meant that he liked to win. McGraw would never manage a fiercer competitor.

Mathewson's abilities were equal to his competitive drive. Possessing a good (though not overpowering) fastball, an excellent curve and change of pace, and a reverse-breaking "fadeaway" ("screwball" to a later generation), Matty also usually had masterful control. In seventeen years of pitching in the National League, he averaged slightly more than a walk and a half per nine innings. Another of his assets was a remarkable memory for hitters' weaknesses—a facility that he also put to use playing checkers against as many as eight opponents simultaneously.

McGraw knew that his ball club's fortunes and his own depended to a great extent on Christy Mathewson's right arm. So in the spring of 1903 he went out of his way to cultivate the pitcher's friendship and trust. Spring training served as a honeymoon for Mathewson and his new wife, Jane, who'd been a Sunday school teacher in Lewisburg, Pennsylvania, when Matty had been a student at Bucknell. Blanche McGraw made friends with the bride, and when the ball club returned to New York, the McGraws and Mathewsons agreed to share a ground-floor apartment at Eighty-fifth Street and Columbus Avenue, near Central Park and the elevated line to the Polo Grounds. For seven rooms they paid $50 a month.

McGraw's right knee had given way during a workout at Savannah, and he knew that his playing career was virtually over. He wasn't prepared, though, for any more on-field mishaps. Before the season's third game, McGraw was hitting practice grounders to the infielders when a ball errantly thrown from the outfield by Dummy Taylor hit him flush in the face. The blow not only knocked him down and smashed his nose but broke a blood vessel inside his throat, so that a torrent of blood gushed from his nostrils and mouth. Physicians at a nearby hospital finally stopped the bleeding. With bandaged nose, McGraw returned to the Polo Grounds and, from the clubhouse porch, watched the final innings of a 5–5 tie with Brooklyn. A few days later, though, he had to leave the team in Philadelphia because his nose had again begun hemorrhaging. Under Blanche's care in New York, the bleeding stopped for good, but the broken cartilage inside his nose never healed right.

For the rest of his life he would be tormented by improper drainage from his sinuses and periodic upper-respiratory infections.

If he had to watch in physical discomfort, he still liked what he saw on the field during the early part of the season. At the end of May, after taking two out of three from Chicago, now managed by Frank Selee and called the Cubs, New York moved into first place, barely ahead of Chicago and Pittsburgh. The crowds at the Polo Grounds, though exaggerated in the figures club secretary Knowles gave reporters, were still the biggest in nearly a decade. Brush hurriedly directed the installation of more gates and turnstiles.

Toward the end of June, McGraw's team began to slump. Still in a three-way battle for the League lead, he decided to go ahead and put George Davis at shortstop. Since the National Commission's ruling on player disposition, Davis had refused to return to Chicago, instead spending much of his time at New York–area racetracks. Those rulings weren't binding, Brush and McGraw argued, because Johnson himself had abrogated them by arranging a trade that sent Kid Elberfeld from Detroit to the American League's New York team.

Davis appeared in four games at the Polo Grounds early in July, whereupon Charles Comiskey, his erstwhile owner, secured an injunction in federal district court in New York City to keep him off the field. Davis stayed behind when the Giants left on a western trip. Meanwhile Brush sued in state supreme (district) court to keep Elberfeld from playing with the New York Highlanders (so-called because their hurriedly built ballpark stood on the highest point on Manhattan Island, at 165th Street and Broadway).

In the midst of all the confusion over which player belonged where, Ed Delahanty made a tragic misjudgment. He'd started the season back with Washington, owing that ball club $3,000. That was the amount of advance money he'd received from McGraw the previous fall, money then paid back to New York by the Washington club when the National Commission reassigned Delahanty to the Senators. On July 2, as soon as he learned that Davis was playing with the Giants, Delahanty took the first train he could get out of Detroit, bound for New York and the big money. En route he got into some kind of altercation, and at Niagara Falls, Canada, the conductors put him off the train. Probably drunk, he tried to walk across the International Bridge, slipped off or through the bridge, and fell into the swift waters below the falls. It was days before searchers far downriver found the body of the man whose career batting average of .346, compiled over sixteen years in the majors, was then the highest in the game's history.

By the end of July the Giants had lost eleven of their last thirteen games and tumbled into third place. Three straight defeats at Pittsburgh put them six games behind the Pirates, a margin they could never make up. That series and all the games with the two-time pennant winners were tough, often disorderly encounters. After a game at the Polo Grounds, for example, the Giants' rugged Frank Bowerman lured Pirates manager-outfielder Fred Clarke into the business office in the clubhouse and gave him a thorough beating. The 1903 New York–Pittsburgh clashes left a lot of bad blood between the two teams and between McGraw and Barney Dreyfuss. For the next twenty years and more, the clubs would sustain a bitter rivalry.

The Pirates were better in 1903, despite the extraordinary pitching of the Giants' Joe McGinnity and Christy Mathewson. Thirty-two years old and at the peak of his strength and effectiveness, McGinnity pitched and won three double-headers in the month of August: at Boston, at Brooklyn, and at the Polo Grounds versus Philadelphia.[9] Over the season he won thirty-one times and pitched an astonishing 434 innings. Mathewson matched him in victories and toiled 367 innings. Yet the Pirates had superior overall pitching, and they had Honus Wagner, who that year won the second of his six National League batting titles, besides stealing forty-six bases and driving in 101 runs. Wagner was an everyday star of a magnitude such as McGraw wouldn't have on one of his ball clubs for another twenty-five years.

The Giants kept second place after regaining it from Chicago early in August, but when the season closed, they still trailed Pittsburgh by six and one-half games. McGraw had been thrown out for the first time as Giants manager in May, by his old foe Bob Emslie. At the end of August, Pulliam suspended him for two days after a run-in with Tim Hurst at Boston. Although he was chased five other times during the season, that was his sole suspension. Those who'd watched his antics since old Oriole days agreed that he'd held himself pretty well in check.

At the end of the season Barney Dreyfuss and the owners of the Boston American League champions arranged a "World Championship Series," which the American Leaguers unexpectedly won five games to three. Clark Griffith, who'd managed the New York Highlanders to a fourth-place finish, proposed an intracity series with the Giants, in line with what the Chicago, Philadelphia, and St. Louis clubs had agreed to do. Still unreconciled to the intrusion of the American League into Manhattan and angry over the Elberfeld matter, Brush and McGraw haughtily rejected the offer.

Denied the chance to pick up extra money from what would undoubtedly have been a popular matchup with the Highlanders, McGinnity and various other Giants left town unhappy. The Iron Man threatened to play next season for an independent team in California, while Roger Bresnahan, according to *Sporting Life*'s New York contributor, said flatly that he didn't want to play for McGraw anymore. All that, however, hadn't kept McGraw from "his profitable onslaught on the bookmakers at Brighton Beach track."[10]

At its winter meeting at the Victoria, the National League officials voted to extend the season from 140 to 154 games for 1904. The American League shortly followed suit. Doubtful that he would ever see George Davis in a Giants uniform again, McGraw struck a deal with Ned Hanlon, who was retrenching at Brooklyn, for Bill Dahlen, a thirteen-year veteran who was generally considered the League's best shortstop behind Wagner. All McGraw had to give Hanlon was Charley Babb, a mediocre infielder, and Jack Cronin, who'd pitched poorly since coming with McGraw from Baltimore.

The most exciting thing that happened to McGraw that winter was being arrested at Hot Springs, along with a local citizen named C. T. Buckley, for unlicensed public gambling. For several days they'd taken on all challengers in pitching silver dollars at a basket on the Eastman Hotel grounds. McGraw and Buckley had reportedly hustled about $2,300 before the police closed them down. They had to post bond of $200 each, but a couple of days later the local municipal judge dismissed the charges against them.

As McGraw had expected, the official disposition of George Davis went against him. A committee of Dreyfuss, Herrmann, and Jim Hart, president of the Chicago Cubs, found for Charles Comiskey in the Davis case and also ruled out whatever pre-peace deal Fielder Jones, Comiskey's center-fielder, may have made with McGraw for 1904–1905. Brush had, moreover, decided that there was no point in pursuing his litigation in the Elberfeld case.

So at the beginning of March 1904, with Dahlen to anchor his infield but with the situation at third base unresolved, McGraw, along with Blanche, the Mathewsons, and eight or nine others, boarded the steamer

City of Memphis at New York for the coastal voyage to Savannah. That spring McGraw so much liked the third-base work of Art Devlin, a Georgetown University product by way of the New England League, that he stopped talking about playing third himself. George Wiltse, a left-hander up from the Eastern League and called "Hooks" because of his curve ball, the shape of his nose, or both, and right-hander Leon "Red" Ames, who'd joined the team late in the past season, looked as if they might take some of the load off McGinnity and Mathewson.

After a week at Savannah, McGraw moved the team to Birmingham. The local Athletic Club invited the Giants to use its facilities in their leisure hours, only to have McGraw and his players take over the club for their dressing quarters before and after their twice-a-day workouts. The New York reporters with the team wrote unflatteringly of what was, in truth, a dingy, smoke-enshrouded industrial city, mentioning, among other items of local color, Birmingham's large population of prostitutes. Besides having available that particular form of southern hospitality, the ballplayers also accepted the sheriff's invitation to watch the hanging at the Jefferson County jail of a black man convicted of murder.

In addition to several games with the Birmingham Southern League team, the Giants traveled to Little Rock to meet that city's Southern Leaguers and back by way of Nashville for more competition from the same circuit. McGraw always took exhibition games seriously, whether they were played in the spring or on off-days during the season, and whether he had regulars or substitutes on the field. He wanted his men to hustle at all times, and whatever kind of game it was, he wanted to win. For one thing, he believed that paying customers were entitled to good baseball regardless of the circumstances. Beyond that, he always feared that losing when it didn't count would make for losing habits when it did. Baseball was never a game to McGraw, never just practice, never without meaning. Once the contest began, even an old Baltimore teammate like Tony Mullane, struggling to make a living as a minor league umpire, was fair game if McGraw didn't like his work. At Nashville, when Mullane ordered Bresnahan off the coaching line and McGraw off the bench, they nearly assaulted him. Police finally had to come on the field to clear the moiling players and spectators and enforce Mullane's wishes.

When the Giants returned to the Polo Grounds, they discovered that Brush had had the bleachers extended to raise its seating capacity by about six thousand and, as further indication of the club's prosperity, had fitted out the business offices and dressing rooms with steam heat and electrical lighting. Remarked McGraw on the eve of the season opener at Brooklyn, "I have the strongest team I've ever led into a pennant race. I ought to come in first. . . ."[11]

The 1904 New York Giants numbered seventeen players, including McGraw. They averaged twenty-eight years of age, 5' 10½", and 171 pounds. It was an almost entirely veteran ball club, with an infield of McGann, Gilbert, Dahlen, and eventually Devlin, and with Mertes, Browne, and the versatile Bresnahan making up the outfield most of the time. Bowerman and Jack Warner, two tough men if weak batters, shared the catching, while Mathewson, McGinnity, Taylor, and young Wiltse would do nearly all the pitching.

McGraw appeared in only five games that year. One of those appearances, on May 7 at St. Louis, prompted manager Kid Nichols of the Cardinals, as they were now called, to file a protest with Harry Pulliam. Although eyewitness accounts weren't entirely clear, apparently McGraw, running for Warner with New York down 1–0 in the ninth, took off on Bresnahan's drive between the outfielders with Gilbert, the coach at first, running after him. When he rounded third, nearly all of the rest of the Giants skipped and bounded toward home in his wake. Mistaking one of the trailing Giants for Bresnahan, who intended to stop at third, outfielder Jake Beckley pegged the ball over an uncovered home plate, whereupon Bresnahan trotted in with the winning run. Umpires Jimmy Johnstone and Charlie Moran found nothing wrong with the scene, nor could Pulliam find any justification for Nichols's protest.

That kind of wild exuberance wasn't unusual on the 1904 Giants. They won and won and kept on winning—eighteen games in a row in June-July, fifty-three of their first seventy-one. By the beginning of September they'd opened up a fifteen-game lead over Chicago. By then, moreover, McGraw had reacquired Mike Donlin, who'd signed with Cincinnati after getting out of jail two years earlier and hit .351 in 1903. At the time New York dealt for him, Donlin was sitting out a month-long suspension imposed by Joe Kelley for drunken behavior in Chicago. McGraw, convinced that he could get the troublesome Turkey Mike to quit carousing and play ball, wanted him back.[12]

The key to the Giants' success in 1904 was their ability to play evenly with the stronger western clubs while they dominated Brooklyn, Boston, and Philadelphia, the League's weakest. Against those three, New York's aggregate record was 56–9. As with the old Orioles, McGraw based his attack on the hit and run and rarely had anybody but a pitcher sacrifice bunt. "What's the use of having hitters," he asked rhetorically a few years later, "if they can't advance the base runner in that way?" Most of the time McGraw stayed off the coaching lines and managed from the bench. Because so many of his players were new to one another, he later explained, he'd decided to call every play from the bench. His favorite signal was to blow his nose. "Honestly," he recalled, "before I got through that year my nose was red."[13]

He also hit on the idea of having everybody learn the signing technique used by deaf-mutes. That not only made Dummy Taylor happy but gave McGraw a backup set of signs. If somebody missed his regular signal, he would yell to get their attention, then spell out "take" or "steal" or "hit-and-run" on his fingers. Whatever his method for communicating his wishes, his basic dictum continued to be "Do what I tell you, and I'll take the blame if it goes wrong."[14]

For all his concentration on the pennant race, he still found time for the horses. Early in July at Covington, Kentucky, just across the Ohio River from Cincinnati, he won several hundred dollars on a tip from a local tout. After they clinched the pennant on September 22 at the Polo Grounds, beating Cincinnati for their hundredth win, he started taking in the early races at any of various tracks around the city, then rushing to get to the Polo Grounds by four o'clock for that afternoon's game. The Giants played so poorly after they clinched that as far as Henry Chadwick was concerned, "they forgot all about their contractual obligations to give the club their very best at all times. . . ."[15] The crowds at the Polo Grounds had dwindled into the hundreds by the time the season dragged to a close.

It dragged because there was nothing to look forward to in the way of post-season play. As early as July both Brush and McGraw had declared that under no circumstances would the Giants take part in post-season competition against an American League representative. As the ball club kept extending its lead and as the New York Highlanders battled for the top in the other league, pressure mounted on Brush and McGraw to relent. Ban Johnson wrote Harry Pulliam, proposing that they arrange a championship series between the two pennant winners that, unlike last year's Boston-Pittsburgh series, would have official sanction and supervision from the National Commission. Asked about the possibility of a matchup with Boston, which won again by beating off the Highlanders on the last day of the season, Brush was contemptuous and adamant: "There is nothing in the constitution or playing rules of the National League which requires its victorious club to submit its championship honors to a contest with a victorious club in a minor league."[16]

In later years McGraw invariably explained the failure to play what would have been the second World Series in terms of Brush's concern over the absence of previously established rules on the distribution of receipts, assignments of umpires, and the like. Of course Pulliam and Johnson could have made the necessary arrangements within a matter of days if Brush had let them go ahead. The truth is that for both Brush and McGraw, disdain for the American League upstarts was mixed with fear of losing to them, as Pittsburgh had done in 1903. Those feelings outweighed the opportunity for big profits in a New York–Boston matchup.

In McGraw's case, personal hatred for Ban Johnson probably counted for more than anything else. On October 10, with the matter already decided, McGraw gave his particular reasons for refusing to play Boston. "I know the American League and its methods," he said caustically. "I ought to, for I paid for my knowledge. . . . they still have my money." He wouldn't consent to "a haphazard box-office game with Ban Johnson & Company. No one, not even my bitterest enemy, ever accused me of being a fool."[17]

Maybe not, but plenty of accusations of cowardice rained on the Giants' management. "All this ran off Mr. Brush like water off a duck's back," McGraw said much later. "He was a man of great determination, firm as a stone wall." The Giants players were unhappy, too. A couple of theater benefits, proceeds from an exhibition game between present and former Giants (preceded by field events and a boxing match), and even Brush's personal gift of $5,000 didn't make up for what the players thought might have been theirs if they'd been allowed to take on Boston. Joe McGinnity, upset because his contract prohibited him from pitching in California that winter, claimed that he and his teammates, having realized less than $400 apiece in extra money, were "sore to the core." In Cleveland on his way home to Erie, Pennsylvania, Mike Donlin assured a local newsman that "there was a sore bunch of ballplayers around the club house when McGraw refused to stand for the post-season games." Brush had made "a barrel of money" the past season, then had "let McGraw con him" into turning down the chance to make even more.[18]

In truth, Brush had made a lot of money, something like $100,000 in clear profits. About half a million people had passed through the Polo

Grounds turnstiles that season, a new club record. Despite the sour notes at the end, it had been a splendid season for the New York Giants, one in which they set a new major league record for victories (106) and John McGraw came into his own as a manager. Although they boasted not one .300 hitter, the Giants stole 283 bases and led the League in both scoring and fielding. McGinnity (thirty-five), Mathewson (thirty-three), and Taylor (twenty-seven) were the League's winningest pitchers.

Looking over the statistics for both leagues, McGraw and other veteran baseball men couldn't help but perceive the transformation under way. The lusty hitting and big scores of the Nineties had given way to a style of baseball featuring tight pitching, improved defense, lots of strategy or "inside" baseball, and generally low-scoring games. The ball hadn't changed; it was still the rubber-centered, yarn-wrapped, horsehide-covered Spalding "dead ball" in use since the Eighties (though manufactured for the American League under a different label). Fielders' gloves had improved only slightly, and with a few exceptions the playing surfaces were as bad as ever. What made the difference, then?

Of various factors that contributed to the reduction in team batting averages in the National League by thirty points from 1900 to 1904 (and by another ten points by 1908), three are especially significant. The adoption of the foul-strike rule in 1901 by the National League—and by the American League as well in the peace agreement of 1902–1903— tipped baseball's delicate balance of skills clearly toward the pitchers. They also benefited from having a bigger home plate to throw at after 1901, when both leagues scrapped the old diamond-shaped, twelve-inch-wide plate in favor of a five-sided object seventeen inches wide. The last and most recent edge for the pitchers was the advent of the "spitball," a generic term for pitchers' application of any of a variety of substances—tobacco, slippery elm, or licorice juice; paraffin; talcum powder; even plain sweat or saliva—to make the ball break in unusual ways. Introduced early in 1903, the spitball had been put to most effective use by Jack Chesbro, who'd won forty-one games the past season and almost pitched the New York American Leaguers to a pennant.

Intermittently during the past season, McGraw had griped about the foul-strike rule, which had originally been aimed more at him than any other particular ballplayer. At the December league meeting in New York, he returned to the subject for the benefit of reporters. The rule took too much away from the batters and too much excitement out of the game, he contended. "People do not care for ten- and eleven-inning games with a 1 to 0 score. They want action produced by clean, hard hitting . . . and . . . plenty of action in the shape of steals and runs."[19] Yet whatever the merit of McGraw's argument, what impressed the club owners more was Pulliam's report that total league attendance had fallen just short of two million, a new record. Baseball had become a more popular spectator sport than ever, even as its style of play continued to change.

At the beginning of March the McGraws went directly from Hot Springs to Savannah, where the talk of spring training was the new spitball. McGinnity and Mathewson, among others, had begun experimenting with it. Again the ball club was berthed at the Hotel Pulaski, which by Blanche McGraw's estimation hadn't improved any since she spent part of her honeymoon there. Bozeman Bulger of the New York *Evening World* met McGraw for the first time that spring. His most vivid memory of the team's stay at Savannah was watching McGraw devour a whole pound box of candy as they strolled from the Pulaski to the ballpark on Bolton Avenue. "That's probably the last candy I'll have for a month," rationalized the Giants manager. "But I always believe in shooting the works. Can't stop, once I start."[20] McGraw's sweet tooth and his tendency to "shoot the works" with any kind of food in front of him explained why he'd already thickened considerably around the middle, and why within a few years he would have a full-fledged Edwardian paunch.

Opening-day festivities in New York featured a parade of sixteen automobiles carrying Brush, McGraw, Boston manager Fred Tenney, and the players of the two teams from the Polo Grounds down to Washington Square and back. At the ballpark, heavyweight boxing champion Jim Jeffries rode onto the field in an automobile to help the Giants hoist the 1904 pennant, while a U.S. Coast Guard patrol boat in the Harlem River fired a twenty-one-gun salute. A crowd of 24,000 (which Knowles gave out as 40,000) watched as Mike Donlin hit the ball into the right-field bleachers and McGinnity toyed with Boston en route to a 10–1 victory.

McGraw always said that his 1905 Giants were the best team he ever managed. It was basically the same as the 1904 champions, the notable changes being that Donlin played every day in center field (and hit .356) and Bresnahan was behind the plate most of the time. Switch-hitting Sammy Strang, acquired from Brooklyn, filled in capably anywhere in the infield or outfield, and McGraw's willingness to use him fourteen times to bat for somebody else "in a pinch" prompted the baseball writers

to coin the term "pinch-hitter." Some of his later teams would have more
speed or more natural talent, but the 1905 outfit was McGraw's favorite
"for its smartness. We did not have a really slow-thinking player on the
team."[21]

The Giants were never really threatened in their drive toward another
pennant, even though McGinnity's work wasn't up to his 1903–1904
heroics. But Mathewson posted a sparkling 31–9 record, and twenty-
one-year-old Red Ames won twenty-two games. New York's main competition was a resurgent Pittsburgh team, which had faded to fourth in
1904 after three League titles. But when McGraw's club swept the Pirates
three straight at Exposition Park in Allegheny City (then a Pittsburgh
industrial suburb), it was all over. New York won 105 games, one less
than the previous year, and finished a comfortable nine games ahead of
Fred Clarke's team.

Yet it was a turbulent season, much more so than 1904. It was only
eight days old when a fight broke out in Philadelphia between Dan
McGann and Phillies catcher Fred Abbott after McGann was tagged out
trying to score. Umpire George Bausewine ordered McGann out of the
game, whereupon McGraw stormed at Bausewine and 20,000 Phillies
rooters howled for his banishment. Meanwhile, Mathewson, "just to show
that his association with the old Baltimore crowd had also made a hoodlum of him," in the words of one Philadelphia observer, knocked down
a boy selling lemonade who happened by the Giants' bench, splitting
the youth's lip and loosening several teeth.[22] After the game a mob of
angry and disappointed Philadelphians (New York had won 10–2) pelted
the Giants' carriages with rocks and bricks until a squad of policemen
got things reasonably under control.

A week later, during an exhibition game at Newark, McGraw nearly
fought with an umpire. He'd also recently encountered Allen Sangree
of the New York *Evening World* in a hotel lobby, cursed the reporter
out, and ended by twisting his nose. Bill Klem, who joined the National
League's umpiring staff that season at the age of thirty-one, had the first
of his numerous run-ins with McGraw on May 5. Before a New York–
Chicago game at the Polo Grounds, McGraw graciously presented to
Klem a silver ball-strike indicator on behalf of friends from his native
Rochester, New York. Three innings later McGraw unleashed such a
barrage of vituperation on the rookie umpire that Klem thumbed him off
the field. The next day, after Klem called a Giant out on a close play
at second, McGraw trotted past him on his way to the bench and snarled,

"I can lick any umpire in baseball, you know." The day after that, in the midst of another argument with Klem, McGraw threatened, "I'm going to get your job, you busher."[23]

What appeared to be (and no doubt was) a deliberate campaign of intimidation being waged against the umpires by McGraw and his players, with the full acquiescence if not encouragement of John T. Brush, drew wide condemnation. Joe Vila of the New York *Morning Sun,* who'd despised Freedman and never had any use for McGraw and Brush, either, thought New York's terrorism had already had its effect: "The umpire has no chance for his life. . . . the umpires have been afraid to decide against McGraw's men, threatened as they are with physical violence and certainly subjected to foul language that the roughest rowdies in the Bowery would not make use of. . . ."[24] Vila and plenty of others around the League were prepared to believe estimates that the Giants' bullying tactics had won twenty-five games for them in 1904.

Riding high atop the League, McGraw wasn't content with harassing umpires and opposing players. Other club owners were fair game, too. On Thursday, May 18, at the Polo Grounds, he almost came to blows with Fred Clarke over his razzing of Pirates pitcher Mike Lynch. Umpire Jimmy Johnstone finally tired of the taunts back and forth and ordered McGraw as well as Mathewson and Bill Clarke, an old Oriole now serving as McGraw's assistant, to leave the playing field. As he'd sometimes done in the past, McGraw headed for the clubhouse, then doubled back under the grandstand and sneaked inside the groundskeeper's shed near the New York bench. From that position he had a clear view of the field and could make himself heard to his players. Manager Clarke's remonstrances eventually prompted Johnstone to chase McGraw out of the shed.

Before the next day's game, McGraw greeted Barney Dreyfuss contemptuously when he entered the box reserved for visiting-team officials behind third base, then went to the grandstand upper deck, leaned over the railing, and directed more insults at the president of the Pirates. Repeatedly shouting, "Hey, Barney," McGraw made what Dreyfuss later termed "false and malicious statements," namely that Dreyfuss welched on his gambling debts and controlled the umpires through his onetime protégé Harry Pulliam.[25]

Dreyfuss quickly lodged a formal protest with Pulliam, who referred the matter to the League's board of directors, a quasi-judicial body. Of the four men constituting the board of directors, Dreyfuss and Brush were directly involved in the controversy and Boston's Arthur Soden owned part of the Giants. Only Chicago's Jim Hart had any legitimate pretensions to neutrality. Meanwhile, McGraw, unable to keep quiet, telephoned Pulliam at the League offices in the St. James Building to denounce him as "Dreyfuss's employee" and his "hand-picked president," whereupon Pulliam told McGraw that he was fined $150 and suspended for fifteen days.[26]

The directors met on June 1 in Boston, where Pulliam had stipulated that they should convene rather than New York. Brush still brought along half a dozen alleged witnesses to the "Hey, Barney" episode, all prepared to swear that McGraw had said nothing offensive. The Broadway actor Louis Mann carried a petition with 12,000 names on it, every one of which supposedly belonged to a real person who'd been at the Polo Grounds that day and seen nothing untoward in McGraw's behavior.

Brush, Soden, and Hart combined against Dreyfuss to exonerate McGraw and formally disapprove of the Pittsburgh president's "undignified conduct in indulging in an open controversy with a ball player."[27] Then Soden and Hart voted with Dreyfuss to commend Pulliam's action in fining and suspending McGraw for his telephone outburst.

Exoneration of Dreyfuss's charges wasn't enough for McGraw or for Brush, either. They both wanted McGraw's absolution from any wrongdoing of any kind against anybody. On June 5 attorneys for McGraw and the National Exhibition Company went into superior court in Boston and quickly secured an injunction against Pulliam and his umpires, preventing enforcement of the suspension or collection of the fine Pulliam had imposed. In granting the injunction, Judge Sheldon held that Pulliam had violated due process of law by penalizing McGraw without "proper proof."[28] In view of Sheldon's ruling, a frustrated Pulliam told newsmen, he intended to return all the fines he'd collected so far this season above ten dollars.

McGraw had remained in uniform throughout the controversy with Dreyfuss and Pulliam, except for a couple of days at the end of May when he'd hurried to Fulton County, New York, to be at the bedside and then attend the funeral of his father. Residing in his last years with one of his daughters near Gloversville, the elder John McGraw had rarely seen his illustrious son over the past decade. He was in his early sixties at the time of his death.

The "Hey, Barney" affair was a pretty tawdry business all around. Yet its outcome left little doubt about how much influence John T. Brush

wielded in League councils, how much John McGraw could get away
with on the ballfield, or how little Harry Pulliam could do about the
Brush-McGraw combine. When, for example, McGraw and Charles Ebbets, president of the Brooklyn club, had a lengthy exchange of bil-
lingsgate at Washington Park, and Ebbets sought McGraw's suspension,
Pulliam sat on his hands.

Not surprisingly, the New York Giants became the most hated and
reviled baseball team in the country. All over the League they were the
targets of street thugs and ballpark hoodlums. It got so bad in Philadelphia that Bresnahan, Donlin, and Browne loaded with rocks the
barouche they'd hired and, when a jeering crowd showed up outside
their hotel, started throwing their missiles with uncommon accuracy.
Several bicycle police hustled the barouche to a local stationhouse, where
the three ballplayers were held until McGraw arrived and got them
released. Brooklyn partisans became equally hostile—especially after
the Ebbets-McGraw encounter—so much so that Giants followers mostly
stopped making the trip over to the "Ginny Flats" where Washington
Park was located. Brooklynites on the rooftops outside the fences liked
to fashion spears from umbrella tips and fire them at the Giants outfielders.

At Pittsburgh in August, McGraw and his whole infield bawled so
loudly and lengthily over a call at third that umpire Bausewine pulled
his watch, waited a couple of minutes for the Giants to get ready to
resume play, and then declared a forfeit when they kept arguing. Umpire
Emslie managed to slap Art Devlin's face before he and Bausewine ran
off the field. Much of the capacity crowd of 18,000 swarmed out of the
bleachers and grandstand and surrounded the Giants, who huddled in
fear near their bench. With help from manager Fred Clarke and several
other Pirates, the police were able to hold the mob back long enough
for the Giants to get to their waiting carriages. Stones rained on players
and horses all the way down General Robinson Street to the Allegheny
River bridge. Although several Giants came out of the fray with bumps
and bruises, nobody was seriously hurt.

So it went for much of the rest of the season. McGraw was ejected
from three straight games later that same month. Each time he sent his
ten dollars into Pulliam's office without complaint, even when Pulliam
insisted that he stop using the term "thief" in addressing the umpires.
In Chicago in September, McGraw nearly came to blows with a man
outside the Cubs' West Side Park. McGraw's behavior, wrote a New

York observer, "would have provoked serious results if the crowd outside had not been in good humor over the victory [for Chicago]."[29] Six days later, when the Giants left Pittsburgh, McGraw was the manager of the National League pennant winner for the second year in a row.

Back in New York they sang songs about him (or least one song, a ditty called "John McG" offered by the comedian Nat Willis at a benefit for the Giants at the Majestic Theater). This year there would be no repeat of the silliness on Brush's and McGraw's part that had prevented a meeting between the league champions in the fall of 1904. Early in the present season Ban Johnson, Harry Pulliam, and Garry Herrmann had agreed on arrangements for the World Championship Series, specifying a four-of-seven-game format and a 75–25 split of receipts from the first four games only. The Giants players were anxious for the extra money; McGraw was anxious to prove his team the best in baseball; Brush, for all his animosity toward the other league, was happy to add to the year's already substantial profits; and people everywhere looked forward to what would undoubtedly be the biggest and most glamorous event in the game's history thus far.

The American League opposition was Connie Mack's Philadelphia Athletics, who'd barely beaten out Chicago's White Sox. Already the "tall tactician" (as the sportswriters would later dub Mack) had established himself as one of the game's foremost managers. Born Cornelius Alexander McGillicuddy in 1862 in East Brookline, Massachusetts, Mack (the name he adopted for the benefit of the scorekeepers) had played eight years in the National and Players' leagues before becoming player-manager at Pittsburgh in the mid-Nineties. After two years of middling success with the Pirates, Mack moved into Ban Johnson's Western League as manager and part owner at Milwaukee. In 1901 he took over at Philadelphia when Johnson's new American League challenged the Nationals' supremacy, and the next year, despite losing Napoleon Lajoie (as well as pitchers Bill Bernhard and Chick Fraser), he brought his Athletics in first.

Once he gave up playing (in his second season at Milwaukee), Mack had managed from the bench in street clothes. His high starched collar was basic male apparel at the turn of the century, but many years later, long after it had become unfashionable, he would still be wearing one. Tall and thin, nearly always careful to keep his emotions under control, Mack projected a managerial image directly opposite to McGraw's. Generally easygoing with his players, he preferred quiet, private lectures, as opposed to McGraw's penchant for sarcasm and angry outbursts. Once the game started, Mack mostly relied on his players to know what to do; McGraw sought to command their every movement.

In their first World Series encounter and their two subsequent meetings, McGraw and Mack would offer knowledgeable baseball followers a fascinating study in contrasts. As they became the game's two most successful field leaders, partisans of the McGraw versus Mack school of managing would argue endlessly over which man possessed the greater portion of genius.

Mack's ball club went into the 1905 World Series at a severe disadvantage. G. Edward "Rube" Waddell, his big left-hander and one of the most irresponsible, irrepressible, and vastly talented men who ever put on a baseball uniform, wouldn't be available. The official explanation for Waddell's absence was that he'd injured his left shoulder horsing around with teammates aboard a train, but Joe Vila, among others, thought there just might be something to the widely circulating rumor that big-time gamblers had reached Waddell. In any case, Mack had to rely on his three young stalwarts, the right-handers Charles "Chief" Bender and Andy Coakley and lefty Eddie Plank.

Always the showman, McGraw ordered new uniforms for the Series. On October 9 the Giants took the field at Philadelphia's Columbia Park, before a capacity-plus 18,000, wearing black flannels with white stockings. Before the first pitch, McGraw was called to home plate and given a statue of a white elephant as a reminder of his mildly insulting reference to the Athletics franchise at the time he left Baltimore in 1902. He doffed his cap and made a deep bow to the hooting spectators.

Then Plank delivered the first pitch to George Browne, and a World Series that would be unmatched for pitching brilliance was under way. That game and the four others it took for the Giants to dispose of the American Leaguers were all shutouts: three by Mathewson, one by McGinnity, and the Athletics' sole victory, Bender's over McGinnity in game two. Mathewson's performance in blanking the Athletics in the first, third, and fifth games was the finest of his career. For the three games, he allowed fourteen hits, struck out eighteen, and walked a solitary batter. He and McGinnity held the Athletics to twenty-five hits and a team batting average for the five games of .161.

McGraw won about $400 betting at even money with Philadelphia rooters. Each of his ballplayers received $1,142 in winners' shares; the Athletics came away with only $382 apiece. Some of the Giants still weren't satisfied. For three years they'd seen Fred Knowles's inflated attendance figures, and now, with the National Commission certifying the numbers, they learned that the biggest turnout of the Series, for game two at the Polo Grounds, was not the 35,000 or 40,000 that Knowles had often claimed, but 24,992, with much of that crowd standing in the carriage park and down the foul lines. Again the Giants had something to grumble about as they headed for their off-season homes.

Not Brush and McGraw, though. At a post-Series banquet honoring the Athletics in Philadelphia, Brush startled everybody by toasting the lasting friendship of the two leagues. "There is room for two major leagues," he was willing to proclaim at long last.[30] McGraw was on top of the baseball world. He'd accomplished everything he came to New York to do. The franchise was the fattest in baseball, his Giants had erased any doubts about their claims to supremacy, and he'd become a celebrity of the first order. He was the toast of New York. Politicians, show business people, and Wall Street operators sought his friendship and favor, while sportswriters praised his genius on the ballfield and tried not to say anything that might offend him. Not really wealthy, McGraw nonetheless made plenty of money, enough to keep himself and his young wife living in high style. He'd come a long way since that May afternoon in Olean when he started out as a professional by erring eight times. Soon, though, he would discover just how hard it was to stay on top.

Six

REBUILDING AND BARELY MISSING

A MONTH AFTER THE END of the season, Brush signed McGraw to a new three-year contract. The amount wasn't made public, but it was around $15,000 per year. Inasmuch as he owned almost nothing beyond his immediate personal possessions, McGraw again decided to put some of his money into a pool hall. His partners were Jack Doyle, a young gambler and prominent member of the local sporting crowd, and the internationally celebrated jockey Tod Sloan, whom McGraw had first met in the summer of 1900 when Sloan was visiting the tracks in his native St. Louis and McGraw was a ballplayer there. Located on Herald Square, at the intersection of Thirty-fourth Street, Broadway, and Sixth Avenue, the establishment had fifteen tables that were "works of art and the highest-priced ever placed in a billiard-room in the world"—or so its proprietors claimed.[1] It opened in mid-February 1906 with the young billiards champ Willie Hoppe among the guests.

That winter John and Blanche McGraw spent most of their time at the Victoria, while the Mathewsons, with a baby on the way, took an apartment of their own. Before the season started, the McGraws would move into the Washington Inn, a residential hotel at 155th Street and Amsterdam Avenue near the Polo Grounds. One of the residents they would get to know was Harold Chase, a well-mannered, pleasant twenty-two-year-old Californian, playing his rookie season with the Highlanders.

Mike Donlin again made off-season news by getting thrown into jail, this time for being drunk and disorderly and brandishing a pistol aboard a train from New York City to Troy, New York. Donlin spent one night behind bars in Albany, paid his fine, and managed to get to Memphis on time for spring training. He was far from a reformed man, though.

At Memphis he would say good night to everybody in the hotel lobby about eleven, take the passenger elevator up to his floor, then sneak back down in the freight elevator and hit the streets. When he showed up at five o'clock one morning far under the influence, McGraw suspended him and barred him from the hotel. Within two days, though, Turkey Mike had apologized and won his way back into McGraw's good graces.

That was only the beginning of McGraw's troubles. Mathewson fell ill with what was first thought to be only a cold but turned out to be diphtheria. Having lost half his family to that scourge, McGraw no doubt feared for the life of the man who'd become not only baseball's outstanding pitcher but his personal friend as well. Mathewson fought off the illness, but he wasn't able to take the mound until the season was three weeks old. On May 15, at Cincinnati, Donlin broke his ankle sliding into third base and virtually ended his season. At the time he was leading the League with a .349 average. McGinnity pitched 340 innings and won twenty-seven games, but neither his efforts nor those of Wiltse, Taylor, or Ames could compensate for Mathewson's inability to regain his full strength and effectiveness. Matty took the worst pounding of his career on June 7, yielding nine runs in the first inning in what became a 19–0 rout by Chicago at the Polo Grounds.

By winning three games out of four in that series, the Cubs opened up a two-and-one-half-game lead over New York. The Giants never got any closer. McGraw's 1906 team, for all its misfortunes, was still a good one, especially after Brush paid $10,000 in July for Cy Seymour, who'd led the League in batting for Cincinnati the previous year but hadn't been able to get along with Ned Hanlon, Joe Kelley's successor as manager of the Reds. McGraw further improved his outfield situation— and maybe avoided some strife on his ball club—by acquiring William "Spike" Shannon from St. Louis in exchange for Sam Mertes, who subsequently maintained that being a member of the Masonic order had made him unpopular with the Catholics on the New York team.

The main difficulty the Giants had in 1906 was simply the blazing play of the Chicago Cubs. Manager–first-baseman Frank Chance's team left New York on June 8 with a record of 34–15. From that point they won eighty-two games and lost twenty-one, surpassing the Giants' 1904 victory total by ten games and finishing a full twenty ahead of the New Yorkers. The 1906 Cubs were the first ball club in major league history to record fewer than two hundred errors in a season, and their pitching staff allowed an average of 1.76 runs per nine innings.

Nobody could have overtaken the Cubs that year (although the cross-town White Sox would score an astonishing upset in the World Series). For McGraw, though, it wasn't that simple. Early in the season he began insisting that sinister forces were arrayed against him and his Giants. "Everybody in the National League," he said, "is out to do us. The seven rival clubs, the League president and his umpires want to see New York lose the flag." To be sure, the Giants had plenty of enemies wherever they went. The fact that they were the first major league team to wear collarless shirts (McGraw's personal innovation) occasioned no particular reaction one way or another in opposition cities. But "Champions of the World" lettered on their shirt fronts made hostile crowds even more so, and the big yellow blankets bearing the same legend worn by the horses that drew their carriages to and from enemy ballparks made the Giants easier targets than ever for local hoodlums armed with rocks, bricks, vegetables, and rotten eggs. As Mike Donlin recalled some years later, "I got so I could feel a brick coming when I couldn't see it."[2]

Yet for those who remembered McGraw's claims in his American League days at Baltimore that Ban Johnson and the umpires had conspired against him, and who could recall how much the Giants had gotten away with in recent years, his present plaints neither impressed nor amused. Nor did a particularly shabby maneuver he pulled at the Polo Grounds in August.

On August 6 the Giants lost to Chicago 3–1 in a game that was probably decided when Jimmy Johnstone called out Art Devlin on a play at home plate late in the game. In the ensuing row, Johnstone ejected both Devlin and McGraw, artfully dodging several pop bottles hurled from the grandstand as he did so. That night, when he heard Johnstone's report on the episode, Pulliam quickly notified McGraw and Devlin that they were suspended.

The next day Johnstone and Bob Emslie, his umpiring partner, arrived as usual at the Polo Grounds, only to be told by a gatekeeper that Johnstone couldn't enter the park because the management feared for his safety. If Johnstone couldn't go in, said Emslie, then he wouldn't either. At game time, with about eight thousand people in the stands, McGraw put his team on the field; told Frank Chance that under League rules they were obliged to choose a player to do the umpiring; and, when Chance refused to go along with the farce, sent Sammy Strang to the plate carrying two baseballs to pronounce himself acting umpire and declare a forfeit to New York. At that Chance disgustedly led his team to the clubhouse, while Joe Humphreys, the Giants' public-address announcer, stood in front of the grandstand and bellowed through his megaphone that Johnstone had been refused admittance at the request of police inspector James Sweeney—a claim that Sweeney later denied vigorously.

Pulliam interrupted his vacation at Saratoga Springs and returned to the city in a highly agitated state. He would put the matter before the League, he said, and see whether the owners "are a lot of poltroons and dogs and eke out their existence through the receipts on the New York grounds. . . ." Denouncing "black-guardism, jobbery, and bulldozing tactics," he threatened to resign if the owners didn't support him in resisting New York's power.[3] On August 8, with McGraw and Devlin not in uniform, the Polo Grounds crowd actually cheered Johnstone and Emslie when they appeared to work a game that proceeded without incident, Chicago winning 3–2.

Next week Pulliam dismissed what he termed "the silly and unsportsmanlike protest of the New York club" when he refused to certify a forfeit to the Giants. His description pretty much fit the reactions of people around the League, including New York. Joe Vila's stern condemnation was to be expected, but not that of W. H. Rankin, the *Sporting News* New York correspondent, who'd loyally supported McGraw and Brush up to now. Editorially the St. Louis weekly denounced "the anarchistic club owner and manager" and predicted that "McGraw is making his baseball grave by persisting in rowdyism." Ned Hanlon had become convinced that "the only way to get along with the New York team is to regard them as bitter enemies and treat them as such."[4]

The Cubs didn't need the game in New York they hadn't played. They won three of the four games that were played and all but wrapped up the pennant. Pulliam kept McGraw's indefinite suspension in force for twenty days, the longest of his career. Later in the month, he wasn't in uniform but in the visitors' box at West Side Park to see the Chicago rooters wave thousands of yellow megaphones at him and the distinguished members of the Board of Trade unfurl a huge yellow banner with a caricature of a yellow-streaked McGraw, captioned "Muggsy."

McGraw took it all more good-naturedly than he might have if the Cubs hadn't already been out of reach.

The Giants ended the season at home by losing to Joe Kelley's tail-end Boston club before about four hundred people. Having agreed to a tryout for nineteen-year-old Henry Mathewson, Matty's brother, McGraw let the kid pitch the full nine innings, walk fourteen batters, hit one, and lose 7–1. Although "young Matty," as the sportswriters were quick to call him, would come to spring training in 1907, he failed to demonstrate to McGraw that he would ever have the makings of a major league pitcher.

The Chicago Cubs set a new National League record by playing before 654,300 customers at West Side Park, whereas the Giants' home attendance was a little over 400,000, down about 100,000 from 1905 and 20,000 less than the Highlanders drew. "The success of the Cubs was a triumph for clean ball," proclaimed the *Sporting News*, "and the failure of the Giants a fitting rebuke for the methods of their manager."[5]

As soon as the season ended, the McGraws returned to Baltimore to visit, and John McGraw sought to replenish his spirits at Pimlico racetrack, in the company of Joe Kelley and Jack Dunn. Dunn, who'd played for McGraw at Baltimore and in his first years at New York, was about to take the reins of the Baltimore Eastern League club from Hugh Jennings. In turn Jennings, now combining dual careers in baseball half the year and the law in the off-season, had just been hired to manage the Detroit Tigers (which meant that he would try to manage Ty Cobb).

In December, Harry Pulliam, pledging to fight "the brand of sportsmanship known as 'McGrawism,' " won reelection to the League presidency, with Brush casting the only negative vote.[6] Brush did make a positive contribution to the League's business by getting the rules committee to require that all National League ballparks have dressing facilities for the visiting teams, as had long been provided at the Polo Grounds. Brush was tired of his players' having to dress at their hotels, then ride in uniform through the hostile and often dangerous streets of League cities.

Right after New Year's, McGraw left the pool hall in the care of his partners (who now included Fred C. Knowles) and with Blanche made the four-day trip across the continent to Los Angeles. There he made arrangements to hold spring practice at Chute Park, the home of the Los Angeles Pacific Coast League club. He'd sold the Los Angeles venture to Brush partly as a publicity stunt but mainly as a moneymaker. No big league team had ever traveled that far from its home city for spring training. The Santa Fe Railroad was willing to offer special rates from Chicago (where most of the players would gather) and would even publish a booklet advertising the New York team as well as Albuquerque, the Grand Canyon, and other stops along the way. Once in California, the Giants could command good crowds for exhibition games in Los Angeles, San Francisco, and Oakland, cities where baseball interest ran high but the chance to see big-leaguers in action was rare. Then the New York team could play its way east by way of San Antonio, New Orleans, and other baseball-hungry stops.

It didn't work out as planned. Foul weather for most of the three-week period in California made for poor turnouts. When the Giants arrived at San Antonio in the middle of the night, after a long, hot trip across desert country, they found that no hotel rooms had been reserved for them. They rested as best they could on pool tables, cots, and lobby furniture before going out to play the St. Louis Browns.

At New Orleans, McGraw finally made contact with Mike Donlin. Although he'd settled down somewhat following his marriage to the actress Mabel Hite the previous year, Donlin was no more dedicated to the profession of baseball than he'd ever been. In fact, his wife had already filled his head with notions about becoming an actor, and instead of going to Los Angeles, he'd remained in Chicago as assistant manager of a theater where Mabel Hite was appearing. Donlin wired McGraw that for a $600 raise, he would sign a contract with a no-alcohol clause. That amounted to blackmail, as far as Brush was concerned. At last McGraw wired Donlin a promise that he would pay the $600 out of his own pocket if Turkey Mike met the team in New Orleans.

In that city McGraw provided another entry for anybody who might be logging the number of times he'd made a fool of himself. The Giants defeated the Philadelphia Athletics in the first of what was supposed to be a four-game exhibition series. The next day, with a good Sunday crowd on hand, umpire Charles "Chief" Zimmer, an old adversary from Cleveland Spider days, refused to call a balk on Eddie Plank, despite McGraw's and Bresnahan's protestations. Zimmer finally summoned the police to escort Bresnahan from the field. When McGraw wouldn't leave, Zimmer announced a forfeit to Philadelphia. Inasmuch as it was still only the first inning, the New Orleans club management had to refund the customers' money.

On Monday McGraw wouldn't put his team on the field with Zimmer umpiring. After a player with the local Southern League team agreed to do the officiating, McGraw let the game proceed. But then the next day he took his team north without playing the remaining game of the series. The New Orleans club filed an appeal with the National Commission, seeking compensation for its lost gate receipts. Under a National Commission directive, Brush eventually paid president Charles Frank $1,000.

McGraw's hopes for having Mike Donlin in his outfield for 1907 vanished at Louisville, where they quarreled over whether Donlin would get his $600 now or at the end of the season and the ballplayer jumped the team to rejoin Mabel Hite in Chicago. The Giants proceeded to New York by way of Ohio, finally concluding their eight-thousand-mile odyssey on April 9. They were worn out, the club had lost money, and McGraw was having one of the numerous attacks of sinusitis that would bedevil him over the years.

He was too sick to be part of the unruly scene at the Polo Grounds when the season opened two days later. It had snowed in New York the previous day, and the 16,000 or so people on hand shivered as the game moved into the late innings. With the Philadelphia Phillies' Frank Corridon shutting out McGinnity and the Giants, spectators began jumping out of the stands and running through and around players to the sunny area in right field. Because of an edict by police commissioner Theodore H. Bingham, regular police were no longer available for duty at the ballparks. With the crowd completely out of hand, Bill Klem called a forfeit to the Phillies.

A sidelight to all the opening-day commotion in New York, barely noted in the press accounts, was that Roger Bresnahan had worn a pair of modified cricket-style leg guards, the first time a catcher in the major leagues—or anywhere else as far as was known—had used such protective equipment. Bresnahan's innovation caught on with the younger catchers in the majors and minors, but veterans generally resisted it. Some played out their careers without ever donning "shinguards."

Managing strictly from the bench in the early part of the season, McGraw watched his team surge to seventeen straight victories following the opening-day forfeit. The Cubs, though, almost matched them win for win; at the end of May, New York and Chicago were tied for first place with 24–5 records. Then the Giants lost three straight games at West Side Park and fell five back. By mid-July McGraw's men were fifteen games behind the Cubs and barely ahead of Pittsburgh.

The team that had no apparent weaknesses in 1904–1905 had several by 1907. Donlin was gone, Billy Gilbert had been released before the season, and seventeen-year veteran Tommy Corcoran, picked up from Cincinnati, hadn't been able to do the job at second. In July the Giants paid Springfield, Illinois, of the Three-I League $4,500, a record price for a minor-leaguer, for second-baseman Larry Doyle. Found by "Sinister Dick" Kinsella, the Giants' full-time scout and the first of his kind, Doyle showed a great deal of promise but was shaky afield. At shortstop Bill Dahlen no longer covered much ground and barely hit .200. After slumping in 1906, Dan McGann hit well until he broke his arm and had to sit out most of the second half of the season. Aside from Cy Seymour, McGraw's outfielders were undistinguished. Bresnahan was a fine catcher, but he resented sharing the catching with Frank Bowerman and was as much convinced of his own managerial abilities as McGraw had been playing under Ned Hanlon. And while Mathewson was again the League's top pitcher, McGinnity, at the age of thirty-six, had started to "go back," as was said of fading ballplayers in those days.

Stuck with an aging, basically mediocre team, McGraw seems to have lost much of his interest in baseball matters rather early in the season. He talked about maybe retiring after the present campaign, complaining that he'd reached the point that "the very sight of a railroad train appalls me. . . . I am a slave to the Pullman sleeper and the tender mercies of the hotel in the next city."[7]

He also spent more time at the racetracks than he had in any summer since 1900 in St. Louis. The season was less than two months old when Joe Vila reported seeing McGraw and Joe McGinnity at Belmont Park, with a game scheduled at the Polo Grounds three hours later. By July, Sam Crane of the New York *Evening Journal*, a former ballplayer and McGraw's good friend, was chiding the Giants manager for spending so much of his time at the races.

Apparently oblivious to such criticism, McGraw sent two of his players up to Yonkers to the Empire City track to get down bets on a horse named Confessor. While McGraw won $500 at 10–1 odds and other bettors on the team won lesser sums, Pittsburgh was slaughtering the Giants 20–5. A few days later, when the Giants played an exhibition game at New Bedford, Massachusetts, McGraw spent his time at Yonkers with the racing set. And according to Vila, for four straight days, while his team performed at Washington Park in Brooklyn, McGraw and Fred Knowles had been at the Sheepshead track on Long Island. Not only

Vila but several other writers reported angry words between Brush and McGraw over the manager's absences.

In August, McGraw drew a three-day suspension after a fracas with Bill Klem in Chicago. Six weeks later, in Pittsburgh, the two renewed their quarrel, this time disputing whether Bresnahan could be in the lineup, inasmuch as he faced a possible suspension for his behavior toward Bob Emslie in Cincinnati the previous day. When Klem wouldn't relent, McGraw dashed a cup of water in his face. The young umpire let that pass, but six innings later he chased McGraw for arguing over his ruling on a fair ball, then ordered him out of a hiding place under the Exposition Park grandstand. Still later Klem also ejected Art Devlin; the next day he banished four more Giants; and in the third game of the series in Pittsburgh, he sent two more to the dressing room—a total of eight New Yorkers in three days.

Such outbursts were relatively uncommon that year, though. All in all it was a rather bland season, at least by McGravian standards. Much of the time McGraw sat quietly on the bench (no doubt mulling over his racing selections, his detractors suggested). He seemed more at odds with his players than with the umpires. Before leaving for the final western swing, he fined McGann for lackadaisical play and left him at home, and also fined Bresnahan for the same offense and Seymour for taking off after the first game of a double-header. The Giants lost the last seven games of the season, including a last-day double-header at Philadelphia that enabled the Phillies to slip past them into third place. New York finished at 82–71.

In the aftermath of McGraw's worst full season in New York, rumors abounded that Brush was unhappy with his showing on and off the field. According to Vila, McGraw had received an ultimatum: It was either the ball club or the racetrack. The New York *American* even reported that McGraw would be fired in favor of Roger Bresnahan.

McGraw's situation in the fall of 1907 wasn't nearly as precarious as some made it out to be. Brush never really lost confidence in him; besides, the frugal Giants owner wasn't about to hire another manager at the same time that he paid off McGraw for the remaining two years of his contract, at $15,000 a year.

Yet McGraw had come to something of a crossroads. At the age of thirty-four, he may have questioned whether he wanted to go on indefinitely in baseball, wanted to put up with being on the road half the time, sleeping in Pullman berths and hotel beds, worrying about his players, about their health, their dispositions, their drinking habits, the degree of their commitment to the game. He may have gotten tired of the team's fickle followers at home, the frequently ugly crowds on the road, the inconsistent umpires, the second-guessing sportswriters. Conceivably Blanche McGraw may have tired of it all as well. "It was not in my province or my mind," she once said, "to ask for facts or explanations. He needed understanding and silence, and obedience to his needs was a sacred mission in itself." She was always staunchly loyal, remembered Fred Lieb, "with no criticism or nagging in the sanctity of their house and no discussion of . . . incidents with friends."[8] Still, she may have raised enough questions about what kind of future they had that he may have started to wonder himself.

If he (or she) had any such misgivings, they were a passing phase, an aberration. For the next twenty-five years neither of them would look back. For one thing, they needed money in 1907, and given their living style, they always would. The Herald Square pool hall, after a promising start, hadn't been able to turn a profit, and McGraw had sold out the previous May. In mid-summer he'd invested in a brokerage with a Californian named R. E. Whitcomb to handle mostly western mining stocks, one of the great speculative lures of those years. Although he told a reporter that his business and his baseball affairs weren't interfering with each other, by the fall he'd also pulled out of that venture. McGraw was the kind of person who could always make plenty of money, but he never seemed to have much of a plan for doing anything with it—except to spend it.

Spend it he did, often at the tracks but also often on people who seemed to need his money more than he did. One of McGraw's major accomplishments that off-season was to invite Joe Vila to accompany him to Aqueduct racetrack; to convince him that, contrary to what Vila had insisted, Andrew Freedman's connection with the Giants had ended in 1902; and at least partly to win the friendship of the waspish sportswriter. A long time afterward, Vila told how that day at Aqueduct, they'd encountered an elderly former horse trainer who said he'd like to get to New Orleans for the winter. McGraw took out his money roll, peeled off five $100 bills, and gave them to the old man. After he'd blessed his benefactor and departed, McGraw warned Vila not to print anything about what he'd just seen. "It's all private stuff and doesn't interest the public," he said. Besides, he'd won a lot more money on the old fellow's tips than he'd "loaned" him.[9]

Another accomplishment was signing Mike Donlin for 1908 for a salary of $4,000, with a no-alcohol clause and a $500 bonus for serving as team captain. At the December National League meeting, held at the opulent Waldorf-Astoria, McGraw pulled off the biggest trade of his managerial career thus far. By letting Boston have McGann, Dahlen, Browne, Bowerman, and a rarely used pitcher named George Ferguson, he obtained Al Bridwell, an acrobatic shortstop; Fred Tenney, a fourteen-year veteran first-baseman; and, as a throw-in, substitute catcher Tom Needham. McGraw, as Branch Rickey once put it, "would give whatever it took to make his club right now."[10] McGraw never had a long-range plan for the Giants. For him rebuilding was always a matter of building for the present, putting together a winner for next season. He would worry about an aging player like Tenney, for example, when he had to; next year Tenney ought to be able to stabilize an otherwise young infield, and that was why McGraw had wanted him.

The McGraws had enjoyed Los Angeles so much, despite the rain, that in January 1908 they returned for a vacation. Spring training, though, was scheduled for a very different place, a little town 1,500 miles to the east, in central Texas. Marlin, Texas, was no stranger to big league baseball teams; the Cincinnati Reds had trained there a few years earlier but had given it up as being too remote from major population centers. A town of slightly less than four thousand, situated approximately one hundred miles south of Dallas, Marlin depended for its livelihood on the prosperity of the surrounding agricultural country and the popularity of the mineral baths fed by its underground springs. Hot Springs, Arkansas, it would never be, but it did draw a steady regional clientele seeking the regenerative effects of its waters.

Marlin's relatively out-of-the-way location was attractive to McGraw because he intended, he said, to enforce strict discipline for the coming season. It was time for his players to "get wise to the fact that I am not going to be imposed on any longer. . . . I'm going to put my heel down good and hard." Yet at the same time that it was well removed from the fleshpots of Dallas, San Antonio, or Houston, Marlin also provided adequate rail service to those and other places for exhibition games. Sid Mercer of the New York *Globe* described Marlin as "a pretty little city . . . situated on a broad prairie." Mostly things were quiet, although there were occasional excitements. "Tuesday night," Mercer reported, "a Texan used his artillery on three colored persons. The white went on his way unharmed and the colored gentlemen were taken to the hospital for repairs."[11]

The baseball field at Marlin, with its falling-down fence and ramshackle little bleachers, was about a mile south of town, down a railroad track. "It's lucky they sent me down ahead," said groundskeeper John Murphy, "for the grounds had been given up to steers, stray pigs and horses, so I had my work laid out to fix things right."[12]

McGraw arrived at Marlin on February 22 in the company of Fred Snodgrass, whom he'd watched play for St. Vincent's College in a game against the Giants in Los Angeles the previous spring. He had the rookies report early and gave a great deal of personal attention to Snodgrass, formerly a pitcher and catcher but assigned to the outfield by McGraw, as well as Larry Doyle and Charles "Buck" Herzog, a hard-bitten twenty-two-year-old infielder from Maryland's Eastern Shore.

The weeks at Marlin went so smoothly and the Giants were so well received when they played the local Texas Leaguers in Dallas, Fort Worth, and Waco that McGraw decided he would bring his men back to Marlin next year. Mike Donlin had behaved himself; Bresnahan was in excellent spirits with Frank Bowerman gone and the catching job indisputably his; and about the only troublesome aspects of the spring had been the uninviting meals served at Marlin's Hotel Arlington, a split finger suffered by McGraw from a line drive he tried to spear while throwing batting practice, and McGinnity's recurrent malaria, which necessitated leaving him at his home when the Giants passed through what was now the state of Oklahoma.

The season began auspiciously, Mathewson pitching the Giants to victory in the opening game, at Philadelphia, and Donlin proving his worth by homering to give Matty a 3–2 win over Brooklyn in the home inaugural. For the first two months, though, McGraw's club barely played .500 baseball. McGinnity didn't pitch until May 30; when he did, he was far from the Iron Man of old. McGraw first asked waivers on him, then, when nobody put in a claim, decided to keep him on the roster rather than send him to the minors. Used as an occasional starter and often in relief, McGinnity finished out his major league career with a creditable 11–7 record.

Early in the season the Giants won a game 7–6 at Boston when Dan McGann grounded into a double play to kill a ninth-inning rally. Late that night the ex-Giant went to the Copley Square Hotel looking for McGraw, who'd yelled "Ice wagon!" at McGann and then announced to everybody in the vicinity of the New York bench: "That's how the Giants lost a lot of games last season. . . . There isn't a regular on my team now who wouldn't have beaten the ball that cut McGann off at first and ended the game."[13] When McGann found his nemesis in the hotel's billiard room, the two immediately began to grapple and flail at each other. They were quickly pulled apart, but when McGraw went upstairs, McGann followed him and threw another punch, hitting the manager on the shoulder. At that point McGraw ducked into his room and locked the door.[14]

In the last part of June the Giants took two games in a three-game set with Chicago at the Polo Grounds and suddenly found themselves very much in a race that baseball pundits had assumed would be confined to the Cubs and Pittsburgh. From that point on, the three teams would stage the most closely fought and nerve-wracking competition in National League history. The season of 1908 would leave the "fans" (as they were now being called) exhausted not only by the National League race but by an almost equally frantic three-way struggle in the American League among Chicago, Cleveland, and Detroit. People who'd followed baseball since its emergence as the nation's favorite spectator sport many years earlier shook their heads and said they'd never seen anything like the events of 1908.

Mathewson had the finest season of his career, appearing in fifty-six games, winning thirty-seven, saving five, striking out 259 batters, and pitching twelve shutouts. He did whatever McGraw asked of him, although on one notable occasion he wasn't ready when the manager called. In Chicago in July, he'd warmed up for a while in the late innings; then, with the Giants ahead 4–1 and rookie right-hander Otis Crandall apparently in command, Matty went in to shower and dress. When Crandall walked the bases full in the ninth, McGraw sent McGinnity in to stall and frantically sent word for Matty. Still wet, Mathewson pulled on his baseball pants, shirt, and stockings; jammed on his street shoes because he couldn't get his damp feet into his baseball spikes; and, bareheaded, raced out to the mound. By that time McGinnity had walked in a run. Matty took over, got the next man to ground out while another run scored, then struck out Del Howard to end the game.

Hooks Wiltse also pitched better than he ever had or ever would again, including a ten-inning no-hit game against Philadelphia on July 4. Roger Bresnahan's play behind the plate made fans around the League—except in Chicago, of course—question whether the Cubs'

Johnny Kling was really baseball's top catcher. McGraw's infield was quicker than what he'd had the previous year, even if Bridwell and Doyle both led the League in errors at their positions. But Doyle also batted .308 and Bridwell hit a solid .285. Spike Shannon and Harry "Moose" McCormick, two journeymen, alternated in left field; Cy Seymour, the center-fielder, batted a disappointing .267 and fielded erratically. The team's real stalwart was Mike Donlin, who played in every game, batted .334, drove in 106 runs (to Honus Wagner's 109), and stole thirty bases.

With all that, Donlin's dedication to his ballplaying remained less than total. On July 30 he became probably the only batter ever ejected for protesting when he drew a walk. With the Giants ahead of St. Louis 11–0 at the Polo Grounds, Donlin sought escape to more pressing concerns. After taking ball four, he started jumping around and yelling to Jimmy Johnstone that the Cardinals' pitcher had taken more than the allotted twenty seconds between pitches. Johnstone obligingly ordered him out of the game, and Donlin ran to the clubhouse, changed into his street clothes, and hurried off to a dinner date with wife Mabel.

Measured by overall ability, McGraw's 1908 Giants shouldn't have been able to contend with Chicago and Pittsburgh. The Cubs were almost exactly the same ball club that had won 223 regular-season games over the past two years and swept Hugh Jennings's Detroit Tigers in the previous fall's World Series. Besides having a superb pitching staff, the Cubs played the best defense in baseball. The infield of Frank Chance at first, ferocious little Johnny Evers at second, handsome and agile Joe Tinker at short, and underrated Harry Steinfeldt at third was probably the finest the game had seen. Basically Pittsburgh was a team with pitching that was almost as strong and deep as Chicago's, a cast of unspectacular but reliable everyday performers, plus the great Wagner. That year the Dutchman led the League in batting, hits, runs batted in, doubles, triples, and stolen bases.

The persistence of McGraw's team brought new acclaim for his managerial ability from observers around the League and even from Joe Vila at home. On August 24 New York won a double-header at Pittsburgh and moved into the lead for the first time. A month later, after winning eleven straight (until the Pirates' Al "Lefty" Leifeld stopped them), they still held first. With all but three of their remaining nineteen games scheduled at the Polo Grounds, they'd become the gamblers' favorites for the pennant. President Brush had had the grandstand extended to the foul lines and the bleachers built into the carriage park, thereby adding about six thousand seating spaces to his ballpark. Looking at the record numbers of people going to the Polo Grounds, the police commissioner had decided that it was a good idea for New York's finest to resume responsibility for keeping order.

Then Chicago came into town, swept a double-header, and moved to within a game of New York. The meeting between the two teams the next day, Wednesday, September 23, would become the single most famous baseball game ever played—and the most controversial. Roughly speaking, it happened this way: The score was tied 1–1 in the bottom of the ninth in a duel between Mathewson and left-hander John "Jake" Pfiester. With two out, Harry McCormick on third base, and Fred Merkle, a nineteen-year-old rookie subbing for the sore-legged Tenney, on first, Al Bridwell lined the ball over second base into right center field. As McCormick trotted home and center-fielder Art "Solly" Hofman moved over to intercept the bounding ball, Merkle, following the usual practice of the time, veered off the baseline and headed toward the clubhouse behind the bleachers in right center. Meanwhile the spectators—20,000 or so—poured onto the field, all of them believing the Giants had won on Bridwell's base hit, many hurrying toward the Eighth Avenue "L" entrance behind the left-field bleachers.

Johnny Evers had another thought. Nineteen days earlier, in Pittsburgh, the Pirates' Warren Gill hadn't run down to second when the next batter hit the ball through the infield and a Pittsburgh runner came home. Evers had called for Jimmy Slagle to throw him the ball, had touched second, and thereby, under the rule book, had registered a force-out and invalidated the run, which, again by the rules, couldn't score with a force play in process. Evers appealed to Hank O'Day, the only umpire working that day, but O'Day had been running off the field (like everybody else but Evers and Slagle) and hadn't seen the play. Harry Pulliam disallowed Chicago's subsequent protest on the grounds that the run had scored before Evers made his force-out. A commonsensical and logical decision, maybe, but not one that strictly accorded with the rule book.

Two umpires were on duty in New York on September 23, O'Day behind the plate and Bob Emslie on the bases. Again both were on their way to their dressing cubbyhole as soon as Bridwell's smash struck the ground in the outfield. Evers tried again, though, yelling for Hofman to return the ball to him. Joe McGinnity, maybe aware of what was happening or maybe acting instinctively, intercepted the ball and threw it in the direction of the left-field bleachers, into the surging crowd. Somehow (and nobody will ever really know how) Evers retrieved the ball, stepped on second, and looked around for an umpire—any umpire. But neither of them had seen the play.

That evening, at his hotel, umpire-in-chief O'Day finally ruled the game a tie, on the grounds that whatever had happened, it had been too dark to continue the game another inning. President Charles W. Murphy of Chicago claimed that the game belonged to the Cubs because of McGinnity's interference with Evers's efforts to complete a force-out. McGraw said, "There is no set of fair-minded men in the country who would decide the game against us."[15]

McGraw was wrong. While the season progressed, Pulliam took the easy way out (as O'Day had), ruling the game a tie on account of darkness. At one-thirty on September 24, with Pulliam still mulling over what to do, Frank Chance brought his team to the Polo Grounds, put them on the field ready to resume the previous day's game, and, in a scene reminiscent of McGraw's umpire-barring maneuver two years earlier, claimed a forfeit with no opposition on hand. Hardly anybody paid attention to Chance's ploy, and at four o'clock the real business of the day commenced. In the seventh inning Mathewson came on to save a 5–4 victory. By then the mist and fog off the Harlem River was so thick that Matty had to walk up close to the plate to see Bresnahan's signs. Bob Emslie, who'd seconded O'Day in calling yesterday's game for darkness, wouldn't call this one for fog.

More than three decades later, Bill Klem, who warred with McGraw longer than any umpire, nevertheless would agree that the game of September 23 should have been New York's. The refusal of first O'Day and then Pulliam to rule in favor of the Giants was, in Klem's words, "the rottenest decision in the history of baseball. . . . it was bad umpiring and gutless thinking at League headquarters."[16] Ironically McGraw, who since boyhood had prided himself on his mastery of baseball rules, had run afoul of a technicality and was reduced to arguing from customary, extra–rule book practice.

Of course none of it would have really amounted to much if the Giants had outplayed the Cubs the rest of the way, or if Pittsburgh had managed to win one more game than either New York or Chicago. What happened, though, was that Chicago and Pittsburgh finished their seasons on October 4, with the Cubs beating the Pirates at Chicago to eliminate Fred Clarke's team. The Giants still had three games to play against Boston at the Polo Grounds. Four 1907 Giants played in each of the three games, which New York swept by scores of 8–1, 4–1, and 7–2. The Giants thereby finished their schedule with a record of ninety-eight wins and fifty-five losses, identical to that of Chicago. The pennant would have been safely New York's if McGraw's men hadn't stumbled against Philadelphia, losing three times within five days to Harry Coveleski, the Phillies' Polish-American rookie left-hander from the Pennsylvania coal fields. Coveleski's undoing of the Giants, W. W. Aulick of the *New York Times* wrote facetiously, proved the "dangers of unrestricted immigration."[17]

In the immediate aftermath of the Boston sweep, Chicago partisans and Giants-haters in various other places charged that George Browne and other ex-Giants, with the approval of McGraw's old pal Joe Kelley, hadn't played their best against their former teammates. Nothing ever came of those accusations, which were predictable enough, given the circumstances, and impossible to prove anyway. More serious was the charge that New York interests had tried to bribe the Philadelphia pitchers. Although no specifics came to light at the time, sixteen years later Charles "Red" Dooin, the Phillies' regular catcher in 1908, would corroborate the bribery allegation. It hadn't been just the pitchers, either. Dooin said that he, along with infielders William "Kitty" Bransfield, Mickey Doolan, and Otto Knabe, outfielder Sherwood Magee, and other players were offered $40,000 to throw the games with the Giants in New York and Philadelphia, September 28–October 3. "In fact," Dooin added, "the money was placed in my lap by a noted catcher of the New York Giants while I was in a railroad station." Asked why he hadn't reported the matter at the time, Dooin explained that "the other players and myself believed it would be in the best interest of baseball not to say anything, as none of us accepted the bribes."[18]

Worse was yet to come. On October 6, while Wiltse was beating Boston in the next-to-last game of the season, the National League board of directors—Garry Herrmann of Cincinnati, Charles Ebbets of Brooklyn, and George B. Dovey of Boston—upheld Pulliam and O'Day in ruling the September 23 game a tie, and ordered that the game be played over at the Polo Grounds on Thursday, October 8. Grumbled Charley Murphy, "The Giants were given as much as possible the best of it without giving them the game direct."[19]

The Giants and their followers, on the other hand, were convinced that by all rights they'd already won the pennant. McGraw, according to Mathewson's account, told his players, "I don't care whether you play this game or not. You can take a vote."[20] A vote was taken, with several Giants voting no. Finally the players agreed to send Mathewson, Bresnahan, Devlin, Donlin, and Tenney as a committee to call on John T. Brush. The Giants president was bedridden at the Lambs' Club, which he'd made his residence. Like McGraw, Brush left the matter in the hands of the players, although he added that he didn't suppose they would want to quit after coming this far. Matty and the others left Brush and talked among themselves, then returned to tell him that they'd decided to play. Win or lose, Brush said, he would give the team a $10,000 bonus to distribute.

Early in the afternoon of the eighth, after a fourteen-hour trip, the Cubs arrived at Penn Station on the Twentieth Century Limited. Thousands of hostile New Yorkers jeered as, under police escort, they entered a line of waiting automobiles and went directly to the Polo Grounds. There the wildest spectacle in the sport's history greeted them. The gates to the ballpark had been locked at two o'clock, closing out thousands who held tickets but hadn't been able to get through the jammed streets. As many as 40,000 may have seen part of the game, including an overflow inside the park and thousands gathered on the grandstand roof, the cliffs behind, and the "L" viaduct beyond left field. People were everywhere, filling the air with the din of cowbells, fog horns, and trumpets. A mass of fans, unable to get in, charged across the old Manhattan Field and knocked down a section of the park's back fence before being repulsed by mounted police. One man fell to his death from the viaduct pillar to which he'd been clinging.

The Cubs had to shove their way through the crush of people to get into the ballpark. There wasn't enough time for batting practice, and they'd had only about fifteen minutes to throw the ball around when Joe McGinnity rang a bell by the Giants bench and came out to tell them they had to clear the field. As players from both teams milled around home plate, McGinnity and Frank Chance almost came to blows; McGraw and Johnny Evers cursed each other at a distance. "From the stands there was a steady roar of abuse," remembered Mordecai Brown, Chicago's pitching ace. "I never heard anybody or any set of men called as many foul names as the Giant fans called us that day from the time we showed up till it was over."[21]

Umpires Bill Klem and Jimmy Johnstone also had been late getting to the park and working their way inside. As they were about to go onto the field, a man they both recognized approached them carrying an envelope. He was Joseph M. Creamer, M.D., who at McGraw's instigation had been with the Giants all season as team physician. Creamer showed the umpires the contents of the envelope—$5,000, $2,500 for each of them—and said, according to Klem, "You know who is behind me and you needn't be afraid of anything."[22] Klem ordered Creamer to get away from them, and that was the last they saw of him.

A few minutes before game time, Mathewson, wearing a long linen duster over his uniform, slowly walked across the field to the Giants bench—"making his lordly entrance," as Brown described it. Cries of "Fadeaway, Matty, fadeaway!" rose from the grandstand. Then he went out to face Jimmy Sheckard, the Cubs' leadoff man, and begin what was probably the most publicized and closely followed athletic contest the nation had known. "Perhaps never in the history of a great city, since the days of Rome and its arena contests," enthused the *New York Times* in its first-ever page-one coverage of a sporting event, "has a people been pitched to such a key of excitement as was New York 'fandom.' . . ."[23] Matty turned excitement into delirium by striking out Sheckard and Frank "Wildfire" Schulte and getting Evers to ground out.

What many people later thought was the game's critical moment came in the Giants' first at-bat. Jake Pfiester's first delivery hit Tenney on the arm, and Buck Herzog walked on four pitches. As Bresnahan missed a third strike, the rookie danced too far off first, and Kling's snap throw to Chance beat him back to the bag. Donlin then lined a double down the right-field line, but only Tenney was still aboard to score. After Pfiester walked Seymour, Chance brought on Mordecai Brown, nicknamed "Three Finger" because a boyhood farm accident had cost him the index finger on his right hand and left the middle digit mangled. But Brown had turned that handicap into an asset, perfecting a marvelous curve ball that snapped off his finger stub. Already in 1908 he'd won twenty-eight games. Now he calmly struck out Art Devlin to retire the side.

Herzog's poor base-running had cost the Giants an opportunity for a big rally, and Mathewson would need more than a single run. When Joe Tinker led off the third inning, Matty motioned for his outfielders to play deeper. Seymour in center field didn't move, so that Tinker's drive over his head fell just out of his reach for a triple. Tinker came home on

Kling's single. After Brown bunted Kling to second and Sheckard flied out, Evers walked and Schulte and Chance hit back-to-back doubles to send in three more runs.

That decided the outcome. Mathewson stayed in until the seventh inning, when McGraw sent up Larry Doyle, injured the last part of the season, to bat for him with the bases loaded. Doyle lifted a foul to Kling, and although Devlin scored on Tenney's sacrifice fly, Brown got Herzog to ground out, Tinker to Chance.

Wiltse held Chicago scoreless in the eighth and ninth innings, but Brown remained in control as well. It took him only four pitches to dispose of Devlin, McCormick, and Bridwell in the ninth and win Chicago a third straight pennant. "The Cubs beat me because I never had less on the ball in my life," Mathewson said a few years later. "What I can't understand to this day is why it took them so long to hit me."[24]

Having to cross the field through swarms of angry New Yorkers to get to the clubhouse, Chance and his men were quite fortunate to escape without fatal injury. "It was as near a lunatic asylum as I ever saw," Brown recalled. One enraged fan punched Chance and broke a cartilage in his neck, while another inflicted a superficial knife wound on Pfiester's shoulder. A cordon of police, revolvers drawn, pushed the players through the clubhouse door and then guarded it against what had become a truly frightening mob. On the advice of the police, the Cubs dressed and left singly or in pairs to attract as little notice as possible. Among the last to leave was the triumphant Three-Finger Brown, who was offered an escort by two policemen as he strolled up the board walkway toward the "L" station at 155th Street. "You fellows get away from me!" yelled Brown, who judged correctly that anonymity was his best protection.[25]

Barely able to swallow, Chance led his Cubs back west the next day, to Detroit. There, on October 10, they began their third-straight World Series and their second in a row with Detroit. Hugh Jennings's Tigers finally managed to win a game from the Cubs, but only one.

John McGraw would go to his grave still believing what he told newsmen soon after the game: "My team merely lost something it had already won three weeks ago."[26] Nor did he ever stop believing that it wasn't poor Fred Merkle who'd blundered and lost the September 23 game but the umpires on the scene and the League officials afterward. Roundly denounced as a "bonehead," the youngster lost his appetite and had trouble sleeping. After dropping fifteen pounds from an already lean frame, he took on a haggard, almost emaciated appearance. "I wished that a large, roomy and comfortable hole would open up and swallow me," was the way he described his feelings. After the final loss to Chicago, he asked McGraw to release him. McGraw's response, as recalled by Mathewson, was to praise Merkle's "gameness . . . through all this abuse" and to assure him, "I could use a carload like you. Forget this season and come around next spring."[27] A few weeks later, when Merkle, back home in Toledo, received his 1909 contract, he found that McGraw had written in a $300 raise.

McGraw could afford to be generous with John T. Brush's money, inasmuch as the Giants had just set a new attendance record of some 764,000 and cleared at least $200,000. Brush kept his promise and gave the whole proceeds from the playoff game, about $10,000, to the players, who also collected $3,700 from a theatrical benefit. Brush's bonus to McGraw was a new automobile, said to have cost $5,000. It was the McGraws' first motor vehicle. They hired a chauffeur to operate and maintain it for them; neither would ever learn how to drive.

It appeared that McGraw could look forward to a long future with the New York Giants, if he wanted it. The talk about Boston's "laying down" in the concluding series at New York and about bribery money being tendered members of the Philadelphia team was virtually forgotten. But then, in November, Bill Klem and Jimmy Johnstone reported to Harry Pulliam on the bribe they'd been offered just before the Chicago–New York playoff game.

Incredibly, ludicrously, the committee that Harry Pulliam appointed to look into the umpires' story consisted of Garry Herrmann and Charles Ebbets—with John T. Brush as chairman. Those three held secret hearings, which involved little more than listening to what Klem and Johnstone had already told Pulliam. In the end they commended the umpires for their integrity and forthrightness and passed along what they'd learned to the National Commission. On April 19, 1909, that ruling body (Herrmann, Ban Johnson, and League secretary John Heydler, sitting in for Pulliam) voted to bar Creamer for life from all major league ballparks. Lacking additional powers and testimony to corroborate what Klem and Johnstone had said, the National Commission could only proscribe "the person who attempted the offense."[28]

The fact that the League was investigating an attempt to bribe the playoff-game umpires received full publicity in the last weeks of 1908.

Yet even though Klem and Johnstone unhesitatingly named Creamer in their private testimony, the committee never released that information. It was left to Harry Woodruff of the Chicago *Tribune* to bring to light Creamer as the man who'd offered the bribe, as well as the fact that he'd been hired by McGraw a year earlier without Brush's knowledge. Brush had paid Creamer $2,834 at the end of the season, but only after ascertaining that he'd been serving under McGraw's authority. With Creamer's name now public, in May 1909 the New York *Evening Journal* started asking the same question each day on its sports page: "Who were the men behind Doctor Creamer?"[29] After a week or so, however, the newspaper dropped its query. Nobody had anything further to say, at least not for public consumption. With the pennant races again heating up, the whole business just seemed to evaporate.

Indeed, who was behind Creamer? Professional gamblers? Had the gamblers shifted their attention from horse racing to baseball, as various sportswriters had predicted they would do now that the New York legislature, under prodding from Governor Charles Evans Hughes, had outlawed wagering at the tracks? Or was it possible that McGraw himself, believing his team was rightfully entitled to the pennant anyway, had put Creamer up to the deed? Would McGraw risk his whole career, his whole reputation as a baseball man, on such a shabby venture? Would he do literally anything to win, as his enemies had often said? And would he or somebody else then pay Creamer to keep quiet and take whatever mild punishment the baseball authorities settled upon?

Brush seemed personally above suspicion, inasmuch as he'd been too sick during most of 1908 to watch the New York club's affairs closely and hadn't even known that Creamer was his employee until the physician insouciantly submitted his bill. But what possessed Harry Pulliam to constitute a committee to investigate a bribery attempt involving the Giants' team physician and then make the president of the New York franchise its chairman? Was Pulliam so cowed by New York's influence in League affairs that he thought he had to appease Brush and McGraw? Whatever his reason, it would be hard for most people to believe that such a committee had probed into the Creamer business as far as it should have.

Not for the last time, John McGraw emerged from a set of highly questionable circumstances with his prestige and reputation little affected. McGraw's greatest success and fame were still ahead of him.

Official baseball—that is, the owners and executives, the vain, often arrogant men who ran things—would continue to stumble along believing that they could operate their burgeoning sport like a private society, giving minimal attention to the situation of their highly skilled employees or the presence of big-time gamblers. Neither McGraw nor the magnates of his day had learned much from the stormy events of 1908.

Seven

THE LITTLE NAPOLEON

CERTAINLY MCGRAW HAD NO INTENTION of changing the way he chose his friends and business partners. It never seemed to occur to him that there might be anything wrong with the manager of the most famous sports team in the country having close ties to men who operated on the edge of criminality. In October 1908, for example, McGraw invested in still another pool hall, this one also located on Herald Square but in the Marbridge Building, diagonally across from the place he'd partly owned in 1906–1907. His principal known partners were Fred C. Knowles and later young Willie Hoppe, whose fame as a player was growing rapidly. Subsequently he also took on a silent partner. Arnold Rothstein, as a cigar salesman and pool hustler, had frequented McGraw's earlier establishment. Twenty-six years old in 1908, Rothstein was still a small-time gambler whose greatest ambition was to have a $100,000 roll in his pocket. Within a couple of years, though, he would have become so successful at poker that he was "bankrolling" other gamblers and acquiring a piece of McGraw's pool hall. And he would also have become a high-stakes man with the cue stick, once playing an epic match with Jack Conway of Philadelphia that lasted thirty-four hours, until McGraw stopped it.

McGraw's second New York pool-room venture would prove somewhat more profitable than the first, even if every month he and his partners, along with operators of the city's other four hundred or so rooms, had to pay the police an average of $300 in "protection" money. New York was an expensive town to do business in, but it could also be a very rewarding one. John T. Brush had baseball's most lucrative franchise; McGraw was its best-paid manager; the Giants had the biggest payroll in the sport. But the pressure to win and keep winning was intense, especially in New York.

In complete charge of player acquisition and disposition, McGraw was never one to let sentiment interfere with his constant reevaluation and rearrangement of his personnel. Joe McGinnity and Dummy Taylor, two men who'd been largely responsible for his early success in New York, received their releases late in 1908. McGraw traded Roger Bresnahan to St. Louis so the catcher could satisfy his managerial cravings, getting in return outfielder John "Red" Murray, a solid all-around ballplayer, and pitcher Arthur "Bugs" Raymond. In 1908 Raymond's record with the last-place Cardinals had been 14–25, but McGraw believed the spitballing right-hander had a lot of ability and promise. Raymond was also, at the age of twenty-six, a thoroughgoing alcoholic, already the subject of jokes and anecdotes around the League, such as that he didn't actually spit on the ball but blew on it, so that it came up to the plate drunk. Or that, when told that he might try an antiseptic to reduce his hair loss, he replied, "None of that for mine; those mixed drinks will kill you." Or his observation, when somebody said that Fred Tenney was nearly ambidextrous, "Yeah, he'd shoot you in a minute."[1]

Like many drunks, Raymond was unintentionally funny a good deal of the time and generally well liked. But he was also a pathetic young man who would never be able to make much of his life. With Raymond, as with various other problem ballplayers he acquired during his managerial career, McGraw thought he could work a transformation where others had failed. Trying to reform Raymond would severely test and eventually exhaust his patience, determination, and forbearance. "I believe that worrying over Bugs Raymond took five years off my life," he later said.[2]

When he greeted the ballplayers at Marlin that spring, though, he had high hopes for Raymond and everybody else. Everybody, that is, but Mike Donlin, who was still touring the vaudeville circuit with Mabel Hite and had decided that his future was on the stage. (With half the season gone, Donlin would offer to play the rest of the way for $4,000, but Brush wouldn't hear of it.) Wilbert Robinson, McGraw's friend and teammate from the old Orioles, had traveled from Baltimore to coach the pitchers and catchers that spring, and Walter Arlington "Arlie" Latham, former major league third-baseman and sometime umpire, was McGraw's new full-time assistant. Besides being, in Fred Snodgrass's estimation, "probably the worst third-base coach who ever lived," Latham liked to play practical jokes and otherwise kid around in ways that not everybody appreciated.[3] Cy Seymour had barely got settled at the Hotel Arlington when he took offense at something Latham said or did and proceeded to beat up the little coach in the hallway. Initially McGraw barred Seymour from the hotel, chased him away from the next day's workout, and vowed that he was through as a Giant. Seymour returned to New York, where, just before the season opened, he persuaded McGraw to take him back.

Doubts and suspicions regarding the Creamer affair still hung over the Polo Grounds when Richard Croker, boss of the Tammany Hall organization that was again in control of the city's government, threw out the first ball to inaugurate the season of 1909. The ballpark had a new look. The grandstand was painted a bright yellow (to bother opposing outfielders, some said), and box seats had been suspended from the upper deck. The bleachers now enclosed the outfield, raising the capacity of the park, still constructed predominantly of wood, to some 30,000. The only bigger sports facility in the country was Harvard University's stadium.

McGraw wasn't present for the opener. Again a spring-practice line drive had split a finger. This time the finger—the index member on his left hand—had become so badly infected that for a time McGraw's physicians considered amputating part of it. Although he rejoined the team for the season's second game, he had to remain home for part of May, and it was mid-June before he was able to take the bandages off his hand.

McGraw's ball club was never really in the pennant race, which was fought out between Pittsburgh and Chicago, with the Pirates pulling away at the end. To overcome the three-time League and two-time world champions, Pittsburgh had to win 110 games to the Cubs' 104. The Giants finished at 92–61, eighteen and one-half games out of first place. Injuries had something to do with their lackluster season, but the main reason was the loss of Donlin and Bresnahan, which turned a ball club that shouldn't have done as well as it had the previous year into one that was no longer capable of contending. With the exception of Mathewson, who recorded twenty-five victories and (statisticians would later calculate) a microscopic 1.14 earned-run average, and Wiltse, who won twenty, McGraw's older players were slipping.[4] He had five or six very promising youngsters, but besides Larry Doyle, they weren't ready to become big league regulars.

And of course he had Bugs Raymond. Raymond pitched well in the first and last parts of the season and ended up with an 18–12 record. In between he ran into trouble with himself and with McGraw. In June, after pitching a fine 2–1 victory at Cincinnati, Raymond celebrated in a hurry and boarded the Pullman car for the trip to Pittsburgh quite drunk. McGraw confronted him. In McGraw's version of what happened, Raymond "gave his usual ribald reply, 'You are a —— liar.' He got a clout in return and an invitation to settle the dispute any place he liked." Players who were there, however, reported that McGraw lost his temper and began swinging wildly. Thinking that his manager was being playful, Raymond simply fended him off. Told later that McGraw's attack had been for real, Raymond said, "Why, if I'd known the little bastard was serious, I'd have killed him."[5]

McGraw didn't suspend Raymond on that occasion, but he did fine him so severely that the pitcher threatened to jump the team when he found his next bi-weekly pay envelope virtually empty. "Great pitcher," McGraw lamented to a Pittsburgh sportswriter, "but you know a man cannot pour thirty-five drinks of beer a day and stay long at baseball. Have pleaded with him to cut it out and get down to work. . . . Won't behave."[6] Late in August, Raymond went on another binge, and McGraw showed his disgust by letting him take a ten-run pounding in front of the New York fans. A month later he suspended the spitballer for the balance of the season. Raymond's losses from fines and suspension amounted to $1,700 out of his $4,200 salary, although, according to some reports, McGraw sent most of the money to Raymond's wife, without his knowledge.

McGraw spatted with various other players over their late hours and fondness for dice games on road trips. He had an exchange of curses with Otis Crandall during a game in New York. That night Crandall received notification that he was fined $100 and suspended thirty days for what McGraw termed "your abuse of me today. . . ."[7] Although McGraw lifted the suspension after a few days, he made Crandall pay the fine.

Brush and McGraw agreed to a post-season best-of-seven series with the Boston Red Sox, third-place counterparts to the Giants in the American League. The series held little appeal for either players or fans. After Mathewson won the opener, the Red Sox took four straight games, the fifth of which, played on a cold day in New York, attracted only 789 customers. The twenty Giants came away with only $125 apiece. The best part of an otherwise desultory five games, the New York writers agreed, was watching the sparkling play of Tristram Speaker, Boston's rookie center-fielder.

The National League ended the 1909 season without an elected president. At the beginning of the year Harry Pulliam, reduced to physical and nervous exhaustion by six years of combat with and between owners, managers, players, and umpires, took a six-month leave of absence. When he returned in mid-summer, he seemed as depressed and distracted as ever. On the evening of July 28 he returned to his apartment at the New York Athletic Club; stripped to his shoes, socks, and underwear; and shot himself in the right temple with a small-caliber revolver. As a suicide, Pulliam was as inept as he'd often been as League president. Entering at an angle, the bullet barely passed through the skull but tore out both eyes. The partly conscious Pulliam must have tried to call for help, because the mouthpiece of his telephone was off its cradle when he was found, still barely alive, about dawn. A couple of hours later he died at the age of thirty-nine.

All National League games were canceled on August 3, the day Pulliam was buried in Louisville. Neither Brush nor McGraw was among the many baseball people who attended the funeral; Brush was bedridden and McGraw was supposedly too busy with club business in New York. Some critics were tactless enough to suggest that Pulliam's repeated troubles with the New York leadership had helped drive him over the edge.

To succeed Pulliam, McGraw personally favored League secretary John Heydler, who'd handled things in Pulliam's absence and "seems level-headed and . . . doesn't play favorites."[8] Ban Johnson used his influence with Garry Herrmann to block the candidacy of John Montgomery Ward, now a thriving New York attorney, and the club owners' eventual choice was Thomas J. Lynch. Husky and blunt, Lynch was a former major league outfielder and umpire who was running a theatrical booking agency in Hartford at the time of his election.

After a stay in Baltimore, visiting Blanche's family, old friends from Oriole days, and people and horses at Pimlico, McGraw returned to New York to serve as the main attraction at his pool room. Bugs Raymond, he now said, was "just a big, good-natured kid. He means no harm and will soon steady himself."[9]

When Raymond reported at Marlin late in February, he claimed to have just set a personal record by not taking a drink since leaving his home in Chicago a week earlier. McGraw greeted him in the Arlington lobby and told him to be in uniform by nine the following morning. McGraw's spring routine included two weeks of early work with the pitchers, catchers, and rookies. Pitchers tended to get more out of shape in the off-season than other players, he believed, and he wanted them to run and field bunts and sweat until they shed their winter fat and were ready to pitch when the regulars arrived. Robinson was again on hand to work with the pitchers, but McGraw always liked to take personal charge of the rookies. After the second week he'd usually made up his mind whom he would keep, assign to a minor league team, or send home with a handshake and best wishes.

That spring of 1910 the town of Marlin deeded the ballpark, with its recently sodded field and rebuilt stands and fences, to the Giants for as long as they continued to train there. Each morning the players, some in old Giants uniforms, some in uniforms they'd worn on their previous clubs, followed McGraw down the mile of railroad track to Emerson Field, named after the local postmaster who'd raised the money for its improvements. They walked, as a visitor from New York described the scene, "in the caressing morning sunlight, 'joshing' each other amicably, taking great draughts of the pure air, stopping at the negro cabins to tease some mammy or snapshot her pickaninny."[10]

McGraw regularly pitched batting practice. At eleven o'clock he led everybody in a jog around the field and back to the hotel for a hot shower in the common bathhouse (there were no private bathrooms at the Arlington) and then lunch—or "dinner," as the Texans called it. As Mathewson noted, it was hard to get used to sitting down to the day's biggest meal at noon, with afternoon practice still ahead, and then making do with a leftover "supper" in the evening when the players were hungriest.[11]

McGraw insisted that everybody—rookies and veterans alike—spend a portion of every day at sliding practice. He stood by and personally supervised each man's effort in a ten-foot-long pit. Only feet-first slides were permitted, because McGraw believed that sliding headfirst simply ran a man directly into the tag, whereas doing it feet first, especially with a "hook" or "fadeaway" maneuver, got the runner to the base just as fast and with more chance of evading the tag.

Once the regulars were on hand, McGraw organized intrasquad games between them and the "Yanigans" (rookies), usually umpiring himself from behind the pitcher. By mid-March the two squads were traveling to Waco, Austin, San Antonio, Fort Worth, and Dallas for games; and at the end of the month the Giants "broke camp" and, usually still split up, began playing their way meanderingly toward New York.

For six weeks of every year for eleven years—1908–1918—the New York Giants were part of the cycle of life in Marlin. The men who made up the country's best-known baseball team became familiar faces to the residents of the little town on the central Texas prairie. Fish fries at the nearby falls of the Brazos River, benefit intrasquad games for local charities, the annual community dance at the Arlington organized by Art Devlin just before the Giants left town—such events became a part of Marlin's existence that was taken for granted. As were McGraw's losses at poker and his winnings at bridge (with Mathewson as his partner), Mathewson's multiple checker games with the town experts, the manager's fondness for late-night visits to hear local black musicians play ragtime, and Larry Doyle's penchant for throwing firecrackers under the lobby chairs of napping sportswriters. There was occasional friction as well, such as the time pitcher Richard "Rube" Marquard decided to break the tedium by discharging his pistol out the window of his room. McGraw had to threaten to abandon the town before the Marlin police chief would agree to forget that particular disturbance.

During the team's stay at Marlin in 1910, McGraw wouldn't permit Raymond to have any spending money beyond the dimes and quarters he gave him for occasional soft drinks or candy. Raymond stayed sober until the Giants played at Dallas on their way out of the state and were the guests of local civic leaders at a banquet in the Oriental Hotel. Before everybody sat down, Raymond happened to wander back to the kitchen annex, where he discovered paradise: a long tableful of cocktails set out for the banqueteers but not yet picked up by the waiters. By the time somebody came looking for him, the pitcher had downed at least a dozen drinks. "Raymond, after imbibing nothing stronger than ice cream soda for six weeks, fell off the water wagon with a dull thud last week," reported Ernest J. Lanigan, one of the New York writers with the ball club.[12]

Although he sobered up and traveled east with the team, Raymond pitched erratically on the exhibition route. Once the season began, he hurled one outstanding game, going all the way in a thirteen-inning victory over Philadelphia, before a disastrous appearance at the Polo Grounds in mid-June. Called in to relieve Louis Drucke in the top of the ninth inning, with New York ahead 3–2, he hit two batters, gave up two hits, and made a wild throw to first. The Pirates scored four times and won the game. As McGraw learned afterward, when Raymond had gone to warm up behind the right-field bleachers (out of the manager's sight), he'd headed for an all-too-familiar saloon across Eighth Avenue and traded the warmup ball for several shots of cheap whiskey. Then he returned to the ballpark just in time but in no condition to take the mound.

Again McGraw put Raymond under suspension; again, after a few weeks, he relented. But when Raymond walked in the winning run at Pittsburgh (for the Giants' fourth straight defeat there) and then went to the St. Louis ballpark obviously inebriated and refused to take off his uniform when McGraw ordered him to, the manager had reached the limits of his patience. Suspended for the rest of the season but not released, the ne'er-do-well spitballer returned to Chicago and, under an assumed name, began pitching for a local semi-pro team.

Up to that series in Pittsburgh, the Giants had stayed within a few games of Chicago. McGraw had released Fred Tenney and installed Fred Merkle as his regular first-baseman. Doyle, Bridwell, and Devlin still made up the rest of his infield; but Red Murray was now ensconced in right field, Fred Snodgrass had supplanted Seymour in center, and little Josh Devore, who like Snodgrass had spent last year watching and learning, was the regular in left. Another second-year man who'd become a regular was catcher John Tortes, a Mission Indian from California who'd adopted the surname Meyers when he dropped out of Dartmouth College to play professionally. Like practically every other Indian in American sports, he bore the nickname "Chief." Mathewson was still Mathewson, leading both major leagues with twenty-seven victories; Wiltse, Ames, Crandall, and Drucke carried most of the rest of the pitching load. At the time of his banishment, Raymond's record was a dreary 4–9.

Dropping that four-game set in Pittsburgh pretty much killed whatever pennant chances the Giants may have had in 1910. McGraw, carefully working in his youngsters, had put together a fairly solid team, but he needed another strong pitcher and tighter infield play. Although Pittsburgh faded in the second half of the season, Frank Chance's Cubs, with the same everyday players but a largely rebuilt pitching staff, were too powerful for the Giants. Chicago finished thirteen games ahead of New York, then went into the World Series and won only one game against Connie Mack's Athletics.

The Giants also played a post-season series, one that generated a great deal more interest than the previous year's games with the Boston Red Sox. At last New York fans got their wish for a confrontation between the Giants and the city's American League team. The Yankees, as they were now generally known, had finished a distant second under the management of first George Stallings and then star first-baseman Hal Chase, who late in the season had persuaded club president Frank Farrell to dump Stallings and give him the job.

The series for the mythical championship of Manhattan was a considerable success. Mathewson pitched three complete-game wins and saved a victory for Drucke, while the Yankees were able to win only two games and hold the Giants to a tie in another. Despite poor weather, more than 100,000 turned out for the seven games, so that each Giant picked up an extra $1,110, each Yankee $706.

Fresh from vanquishing the local American Leaguers, McGraw met with Brush and signed a new contract—this time for five years at a salary of $18,000 per year. Concerned about talk from various quarters that an attempt to form a third major league was in the offing, Brush secured Mathewson's services through 1913 for $9,000 annually.

Again McGraw spent most of the winter in New York, tending to paperwork at his National Exhibition Company office and making himself available at his pool hall for out-of-towners brought in to shake his hand, nonprofessionals who challenged him to friendly games, or anybody else who happened in. Fred Knowles, fatally ill with tuberculosis, sold out to Willie Hoppe, whose name, McGraw hoped, would make the place even more popular. Occasionally he held forth for sportswriters badly needing off-season copy. After noting that Bugs Raymond had entered a clinic at Dwight, Illinois, to be treated for his addiction to drink, McGraw went on to inveigh against both the old evil of alcohol and the new evil of cigarette-smoking among ballplayers. "You'll find cigarette stubs on the guideposts on the path to base ball oblivion," he said with eloquence and conviction. If they wanted to be successful in the game, youngsters had to "shake booze and cigarettes." Beyond that, they should learn from the smart veterans on their team but pay no attention to what the fans or newspapers said, take care of their eyesight, keep away from shady women, and "remember they're hired to play ball and not to play hell."[13]

That was the gospel McGraw had been preaching to his younger athletes for two or three years now. And by 1911 those players had come to regard him with an abiding respect if not with reverence. He might be "Mac" to veterans such as Mathewson, Wiltse, Ames, Devlin, even a latecomer such as Red Murray. For Snodgrass, Meyers, Devore, Merkle, or Marquard, however, he was and always would be "Mr. McGraw." Although he was still only thirty-eight after his birthday that spring, he'd added a great deal of weight and his hair had turned almost completely gray in the last few years, so that he'd acquired a kind of fatherly presence for the younger Giants.

Many years later, those men were still full of their affection for him. "Take Mr. McGraw," said Rube Marquard. "What a great man he was! The finest and grandest man I ever met. He loved his players and his players loved him. Of course he wouldn't stand for any nonsense. . . . when he laid down the law you'd better abide by it." "He was a fighter, but he was always the kindest, best-hearted fellow you ever saw," was the way Al Bridwell remembered McGraw. "I liked him and I liked playing for him." Even when McGraw shunted them off to other clubs in the expectation of getting something better, as he did with most of his players sooner or later, a remarkable number remained loyal to him. As Chief Meyers put it, "once a Giant, always a Giant. That's the truth. It was because of Mr. McGraw. . . . Oh, we held him in high esteem. We respected him in every way." For Fred Snodgrass, "it was an education to play under McGraw. He was a great man, really a wonderful fellow, and a great manager to play for."[14]

Of course not everybody felt that way about McGraw. Snodgrass granted that "he had the most vicious tongue of any man who ever lived. Absolutely! Sometimes that wasn't very easy to take, you know."[15] Buck Herzog, for one, gave back about as much as he took in a succession of disputes with McGraw going back to mid-season, 1908, when Herzog had refused to play in an exhibition game and gone home for six weeks. After the 1909 season McGraw had sent Herzog to Boston for infielder Beals Becker, but in 1911 he would reacquire the Marylander and make him his regular third-baseman.

Bugs Raymond, McGraw's biggest headache for the past two years, was the model of proper deportment that spring. Supposedly cured of his alcoholism, Raymond emerged from the clinic in Illinois weighing 220 pounds, forty above his playing weight. But he worked hard, trimmed down, stayed sober, and seemed actually to have reformed. Maybe he was finally ready to become the second strongman of the pitching staff, working in tandem with Mathewson as McGinnity had done a few years earlier. In stints at Greensboro, North Carolina, and Baltimore on the exhibition trail, he looked so good that, for at least one New York writer, he'd "effectively put a quietus on the dissipation charges brought against him."[16]

Fred Lieb, a young man who'd just been hired to write sports for the New York *Press*, would always remember vividly the scene at the Polo Grounds on opening day, Thursday, April 13, 1911. Close to 30,000 were on hand. The big grandstand was decorated in red, white, and blue bunting; John Murphy's playing surface was green and lush; and in right field and near second base, where Red Murray and Larry Doyle held forth, Murphy had stuck in the ground little Irish flags—green with a gold harp. In the box seats, the Lambs' and Friars' clubs were well represented by such entertainers as George M. Cohan, Eddie Foy, and DeWolf Hopper. Trains from lower Manhattan brought the usual big contingent of baseball lovers from Wall Street. A brass band played "East Side, West Side" as McGraw accepted the obligatory floral horseshoe from announcer Joe Humphreys. Red Ames pitched for New York, with McGraw, as usual, holding back Mathewson for Saturday, when another big crowd could be expected. Ames was good that day but Philadelphia's Earl Moore was even better, throwing a 2–0 shutout.

That was Fred Lieb's first game at the Polo Grounds and the last ever played in its wooden incarnation. Fire broke out in the middle of that night and within twenty minutes destroyed the grandstand and everything else except part of the left-field bleachers. Friday's game was canceled, but on Saturday, Brush, McGraw, and company reopened for business at Hilltop Park, which Frank Farrell graciously invited them to use until the Polo Grounds could be rebuilt. Before 15,000 people, as many as could find seats in the Yankees' cramped little wooden park, the Giants beat Brooklyn 6–3.

It may have begun ominously, but 1911 was a season of resurgence for the Giants. Playing their home games at the Hilltop for the first half of the season, they battled for the League lead with Chicago, Pittsburgh, and a Philadelphia team sparked by the brilliant pitching of rookie Grover Cleveland Alexander.

Raymond, as matters turned out, was of little help to McGraw. He did win six games over the first two months of the season, but then in June he fell from grace for good. When the team got off the train in Pittsburgh, Raymond was nowhere to be found. He soon materialized with the story that he'd ridden all the way from Philadelphia with the locomotive engineer, an old friend. McGraw didn't know what to make of that but to accept it. What he couldn't accept, though, was Raymond's floundering mound work throughout the road trip. When Louis Drucke tired in St. Louis and left the game in Raymond's care, Bugs yielded all of the Cardinals' runs in their 8–4 victory. Convinced that the pitcher had been swiping tip money in hotel dining rooms and imbibing as much and as often as he could manage, McGraw hit him with a $200 fine and again suspended him. Again Raymond's sentence was indeterminate.

Besides getting rid of Raymond, McGraw made another move to strengthen his team's pennant chances. Late in July he sent Al Bridwell and Henry Gowdy, a towering rookie catcher, to Boston for Herzog, whom he installed at third. Art Fletcher, who'd caught McGraw's attention at Dallas in the spring of 1909 and come up to the Giants late that year, took over at shortstop. Fletcher was so self-conscious about his jutting chin that he had a collar sewn on his uniform and wore the collar turned up, but he was a wide-ranging fielder who hit .319 in 112 games.

More than anything else, though, it was the emergence of Rube Marquard that made the Giants a substantially stronger team than they'd been in 1910. Back in 1908, after Marquard had won twenty-eight games at Indianapolis in the American Association (a strong mid-continent minor circuit organized in 1901), McGraw had paid $11,000 for his contract, a phenomenal sum for that period. Marquard was hardly a rube; his father was a city engineer in Cleveland and his origins were distinctly urban middle class. He acquired the nickname because his hopping fastball was reminiscent of Rube Waddell's. The tall, lean left-hander also had a wicked curve, but his inability to put the ball where he wanted had made him a persistent disappointment—"McGraw's $11,000 lemon," as he was often called. His three-year major league record up to 1911 was 9–17.

That spring, though, Wilbert Robinson made Marquard his special project, finally getting him to concentrate on throwing a first-pitch strike and then mixing his pitches as to location, fastball, or curve. On April 28 Marquard signaled what was to come that season by pitching a four-hitter against Brooklyn and striking out eight. He would go on to win twenty-three more games, lose only seven, and lead the major leagues in strikeouts. Between them, Marquard and Mathewson would account for fifty New York victories.

Meanwhile reconstruction work at Coogan's Bluff went forward with remarkable speed, so that by late June the Giants could move back in, despite having only the bleachers and grandstand lower deck ready for occupancy. The new Polo Grounds, on which work would continue for the rest of the summer, would have an all-steel-and-concrete grandstand, in the fashion of Forbes Field in Pittsburgh, opened in 1909, and the new American League ballparks inaugurated last year in Philadelphia and Chicago. But while its double-decked grandstand would be thoroughly modernized, the Polo Grounds' bleachers would still be of wooden construction. When finished, the new facility would seat about 35,000, making it again the biggest in baseball.

By August, Philadelphia had fallen off the pennant .pace, and it seemed that the Giants—a game and a half behind Pittsburgh, five behind Chicago, not much ahead of Roger Bresnahan's surprising Cardinals—might be about to do the same thing. All season long McGraw had harassed Tom Lynch's umpires, especially first-year man Bill Finneran and Jimmy Johnstone, McGraw's longtime adversary. An old umpire himself, Lynch sought to protect his men as best he could. At the end of July, when McGraw shook his fists in Johnstone's face and accused him of being drunk, the League president suspended the manager for three days. Said McGraw afterward, "I am tired of having the Giants being put in a hole by such umpiring as has been done against the New York club by Johnstone. . . . Johnstone is not a fit man to be on the staff."[17] All told, McGraw sat out seven games under suspension in 1911. It was a modest showing by the standards of five or ten years earlier, but respectable enough for a man who was thought to have mellowed in the last few seasons.

Then, in the latter part of August before big crowds at the Polo Grounds, McGraw's team won five out of seven games from Chicago and Pittsburgh—and took first place. Remarked Johnny Evers as the Cubs left town, "The Giants are a second-division team with a first-division manager. Without McGraw they wouldn't be heard of."[18] By the time they went west for the last time, the Giants had a four-game lead. On that trip they won ten straight, eighteen out of twenty-two, and virtually tucked away the pennant. They clinched it at home on October 4 when Mathewson shut out Brooklyn.

Besides Marquard's emergence as the League's top left-hander, Merkle, Fletcher, Herzog, Snodgrass, Devore, and Meyers had ripened into first-rate major-leaguers. They were all fast men and good base runners, even Meyers, a broad-shouldered two-hundred-pounder, who stole thirty-three bases while hitting .332 and narrowly losing the batting title to

Honus Wagner. Devore led the team in steals with sixty-one; all told the young Giants stole 347 times, a record for the twentieth century. McGraw, often irked by the charge that he'd bought his earlier championships, could take credit for developing nearly all of his 1911 winners. "Now if this present club doesn't come close to being one which I selected and brought up myself," he exulted, "I'm willing to get out of baseball."[19]

Yet it was also a period in which almost all ballplayers had some kind of superstition. Besides the usual business about rabbits' feet, black cats, and numbers, many of them also believed in the magical effects of being blessed by somebody cross-eyed or rubbing a hunchback's hump or a black man's head. By the time they'd clinched the pennant in 1911, most of the Giants and even McGraw himself were quite ready to believe that the supernatural had figured at least partly in their success. They believed in Charles Victor Faust.

Faust had grown up on a farm outside Marion, Kansas. Thirty years old, tall and husky but possessing virtually no athletic ability, Faust had nonetheless convinced himself that his destiny was to be a star pitcher for the New York Giants. He was, in fact, quite mad.

McGraw received a wire from Faust, offering the Giants his services in the pennant drive. Of course McGraw threw it away and forgot all about somebody named Faust until he showed up late in July at the Planter's Hotel in St. Louis, where the Giants were staying while they played a series with the Cardinals. McGraw and a few of his players decided to go along with the idea, and the next day they, as well as manager Bresnahan and some of the Cardinals, put Faust through an exhausting but ludicrous workout. The Giants won that day and, with Faust sitting on the New York bench in uniform, swept the four games in St. Louis.

Having tired of Faust and the whole joke, McGraw sent him back to the hotel on the pretext of picking up a train ticket and contract, jumped aboard a Pullman with his players, and left the trusting Kansan behind in St. Louis. In Chicago, though, the Giants lost a series, and when they returned to New York and found Faust waiting for them, a number of the players wanted him back on the bench. So once again, Faust thought, he was a member of the team. He sometimes assisted Dick Hennessey, the Giants' regular batboy; sometimes put his nonskills on display during batting practice; sometimes warmed up as if he genuinely expected McGraw to call on him in the late innings. Mostly he just hung around, serving as an increasingly credible good-luck charm. Because

with "Victory," as the Giants started calling him, in uniform and ex-
horting his "teammates," they won nearly all the time. "This peculiar
character has worked wonders as a mascot in McGraw's camp," reported
Sporting News writer Ernest J. Lanigan in mid-September. Connie Mack
ventured that Faust had become a real asset to the Giants, as much as
the little hunchbacked mascot, Louis Van Zeldt, had been for Mack's
Athletics. All McGraw would say was that he would rather lose anybody
on his club before Faust.[20]

Charley Faust actually appeared in two ballgames. On October 7,
with the pennant clinched, McGraw let him pitch the top of the ninth
inning in a game with Boston at the Polo Grounds. The Braves, as the
Boston National Leaguers were now called, cooperated in the burlesque,
intentionally making three outs, giving Faust a turn at bat in the bottom
of the inning even though the Giants' third out had already been made,
and, when he tapped the ball back to the pitcher, throwing it around
the field until Faust, lumbering home, was tagged out by catcher Bill
Rariden. Five days later, in the nightcap of a season-ending double-
header loss to Brooklyn, Faust again came on in the ninth inning. Again
the opposition went along with the fun. Hit by a pitch and allowed to
steal second and third, Faust scored on Herzog's infield out as eight
thousand Polo Grounders laughed and cheered.

Faust was also on hand to help out however he was needed during
the 1911 World Series with the Philadelphia Athletics. Although the
Series had been the top national sports event since its inception in 1903,
the annual inter-league showdown truly came into its own in 1911. For
the first time, for example, the National Commission ruled that the
playing field must be kept clear; fans without seats wouldn't be allowed
to overflow and constrict the playing area. The 1911 Series was also the
first to be played at both ends in new steel-and-concrete ballparks. It
was the first to receive comprehensive national and substantial international press coverage. As many as fifty telegraphers sent play-by-play
reports directly into cities all over the United States as well as Havana.
After each game a two-hundred-word summary of the day's action went
by trans-Pacific cable to Tokyo. Finally, it was the first Series in which
daily accounts were ghostwritten by journalists and syndicated under
participants' names to different newspapers. The most enterprising ghost
was John N. Wheeler of the New York *Herald*, who paid Mathewson
$500, published a column under Matty's name, and used his early

syndication arrangements as the basis for what later became the North American Newspaper Alliance.

McGraw was extraordinarily intense as he led the Giants against the world-champion Athletics. Once the two teams left New York, Blanche McGraw recalled, "I never saw him, and I doubt that he knew I existed. He remained close to the players."[21] Seeking to repeat the magic of 1905, McGraw again dressed the Giants in black uniforms trimmed in white. But the 1911 Athletics were a much stronger outfit than the one the Giants had beaten six years earlier. They had outstanding pitchers in Jack Coombs (who'd won fifty-nine games in the past two seasons), Eddie Plank, and Chief Bender; baseball's preeminent second-baseman in Eddie Collins; a hard-hitting third-baseman in J. Franklin Baker; and a highly capable supporting cast.

Before a record crowd of 38,281 at the Polo Grounds, Mathewson needed only ninety-two pitches to overcome Bender 2–1. Because baseball on the Christian Sabbath was legal in neither city, the teams traveled to Philadelphia the next day. On Monday, Marquard and Coombs had each given up only one run when, in the bottom of the sixth, the Rube threw a high fastball and Frank Baker lined it over the Shibe Park right-field fence for a two-run home run. That was the ballgame.

In Mathewson's ghosted post-game column, he criticized Marquard for throwing a pitch that, in the clubhouse meeting, McGraw had warned him not to give Baker. Then the next day, at the Polo Grounds, Mathewson served up the same pitch with the Giants ahead 1–0 in the top of the ninth, and Baker hit the ball into the right-field bleachers to tie the game. Philadelphia eventually won in eleven innings. Frank G. Menke, "a breezy kid," as Fred Lieb remembered him, stirred up a minor controversy by ghosting Marquard's equally critical comments on Matty's choice of pitches.[22] But the major consequence of Baker's two clouts in that period of dead-ball place-hitting and pitching preeminence was that he'd become and would always remain "Homerun" Baker.

That third game was an especially bitterly fought contest. In the tenth inning Snodgrass slid hard into third, ripped Baker's pants from crotch to knee, and inflicted a minor spike wound. Baker held his ground and tagged Snodgrass out. Moments later Merkle, seeking to put the game-winning run in scoring position, was called out on a steal attempt at second by Tom Connally. McGraw and Merkle jostled and jawed at Connally for several minutes; then, on his way back into the New York dugout, McGraw looked in the direction of the National Commission box, caught Ban Johnson's eye, and growled, "This is a sure-thing game. Old American League methods. . . . You've got it all framed up to rob us."[23]

For that outburst McGraw received an official reprimand from the National Commission, while Merkle had to pay a $100 fine for abusing Connally. Relations between the two teams, between Johnson and McGraw, maybe even between Mathewson and Marquard might have taken an ugly turn if the rains hadn't set in and interrupted the Series for six days. When play resumed on October 24, at Philadelphia, a well-rested Mathewson yielded three runs in the fourth inning, and the Giants went down to defeat 4–2. Merkle's tenth-inning sacrifice fly scored Doyle and won game five for New York, but the next day the Athletics battered Ames, Wiltse, and Marquard for thirteen runs. Bender gave up two in the first, then coasted to his second victory in three starts. After the Athletics' four-run fourth inning, McGraw disappeared from the coaching lines, no longer willing to expose himself to the howls and gibes of the 20,000 or so increasingly festive Philadelphians.

Having scorched the base paths during the regular season, the Giants could manage only four stolen bases over the six games of the Series. In game three catcher Jack Lapp threw out five New York runners. It was, of course, hard to do much base-stealing without base runners. As a team the Giants batted .175. But they did go home with $2,436 for each of the twenty-one men on the club; the victorious Athletics pocketed $3,655 each. Those figures set records, as did the total attendance of nearly 180,000.

Exactly three weeks after the final out was made at Philadelphia, John and Blanche McGraw, Christy and Jane Mathewson, sixteen other Giants, five other wives, several writers, and National League umpire Cy Rigler left New York by train for Jacksonville, Florida. Playing their way down to Key West, the Giants then took a boat to Havana, where they were scheduled to play a series of twelve games over four weeks with the two top Cuban baseball teams, the Havana Reds and Almendares. Each New York player was guaranteed $500. For one reason or another, Marquard, Merkle, Meyers, Murray, Ames, and Snodgrass elected not to make the trip; but McGraw added Mike Donlin, whom he'd had on the Giants for a few weeks the past summer, when Donlin came out of retirement. In August Donlin had been sold to Boston.

The Giants were the fifth major league team to come to Cuba since

1908. The driving force behind the annual off-season visits of the North American *peloteros* was Jose Massaguer, sports editor of the Havana daily *El Mundo*. Usually coming in under strength and having to play against several top black ballplayers from the United States who signed on for the winter with the Havana Reds (Almendares was always all Cuban), the big-leaguers had found the going tough at Tropical Stadium, the big ballpark near the Almendares River. Even the Athletics, fresh from disposing of the Chicago Cubs in the 1910 World Series, had lost most of their games against the Cuban teams. That same year the Detroit Tigers had made the best showing so far among the big-league teams, coming out with a 7–4–1 record. This year the Philadelphia Phillies, preceding the Giants, had won five games and lost three.

For McGraw the Cuban excursion was partly a matter of nostalgia, of returning to the scene of vivid youthful adventure. The thirteen-year-old Republic of Cuba looked to be generally better off than the old colonial Cuba. A native elite had replaced the Spaniards as the ruling element in the country. Havana seemed more prosperous, certainly a gayer place than he'd found it in 1890; at least in the city, misery and squalor were somewhat less visible. Baseball, just catching on at the time of McGraw's first visit, had become almost as much of a national obsession as in the United States. An abundance of native talent was available. Although most of the outstanding Cuban players were black or racially mixed, two certifiably Caucasian Cubans—outfielder Armando Marsans and infielder Rafael Almeida—had already put in a season with Cincinnati.

No black North Americans were on hand in 1911, but the Cubans were plenty good on their own. The Giants lost their first two games, one each to Almendares and Havana. Havana's victory was pitched by a little right-hander named Adolfo Luque, who, as a white Cuban, would begin a twenty-year career in the majors in 1914. McGraw was furious over the two defeats, especially put out with Josh Devore, who'd partaken freely of the city's pleasures at night and then failed to hit with men on base in the daytime. When McGraw fined him twenty-five dollars and Devore protested that he wasn't under any contract, the manager proclaimed to him and everybody else: "Then you take the next boat home. I didn't come down here to let a lot of coffee-colored Cubans show me up. You've got to either play ball or go home."[24]

The third game, on Thanksgiving, was a long-awaited duel between Mathewson and Almendares's Jose Mendez. Twenty-four years old, Mendez was 5' 10" tall, weighed only about 150 pounds, and was very black. Having consistently beaten National and American League teams since 1908 (and even struck out Ty Cobb), Mendez had become a national hero. "We can't help thinking," wrote the Cincinnati baseball pundit W. A. Phelon, "what a sensation Mendez would be if it was not for his color. But, alas, that is a handicap he can't outgrow."[25]

Still remembered as *el mono amarillo* by many older Cubans, McGraw angered the younger ones by yelling, "Who's that guy?" as loudly and irreverently as possible when Mendez started out to the mound and the big crowd in Tropical Stadium fell silent, as was the custom when the great pitcher began his work. That inning Mendez gave up a two-run triple to Beals Becker, one of only five hits he yielded but more than enough runs for Matty, who threw a three-hit shutout.

With the Giants $800 richer from the bets they'd made on the game, McGraw relaxed a bit and threw a party for the New York delegation at a restaurant in the city. By three in the morning, everybody had gone to bed but McGraw, Cy Rigler, and a couple of writers. They were about to close the festivities when several tough-looking Cubans, still smoldering over McGraw's rudeness toward Mendez, as well as a call Rigler had made in game one and a run-in between McGraw and Almendares catcher Miguel Gonzalez in the same game, surrounded McGraw's table. When one pulled a knife, the 240-pound Rigler grabbed it and held the Cubans at bay until the police arrived. The police court judge wasn't interested in McGraw's and Rigler's explanations. Not only did he fine them twenty dollars each; he also had them publish a statement in the Havana *Post*, an English-language daily, apologizing for any disrespect they may have appeared to show toward Cuban baseball or the Cuban people.

Meanwhile, the series continued, with the Giants winning six straight and seven of the remaining eight games with the Cuban teams. Mendez struck out eleven New Yorkers in his second outing but lost to Otis Crandall in the eleventh inning when Herzog clouted a three-run homer. On December 14 Mendez and Eustaquio Pedrosa combined to give Mathewson his only loss on the Cuban trip. Credit for the victory went to Mendez, his eighth against seven losses and a tie in competition against major league teams. If he could play him, McGraw remarked, he'd be willing to pay $50,000 for Mendez. Mathewson called him "a great pitcher," and Larry Doyle added that he had "wonderful speed, a tantalizing slow ball and perfect control. I've never seen a pitcher with better control."[26]

No doubt thankful that they would never confront the likes of Mendez or Pedrosa within the all-white world of Organized Baseball, the Giants returned home just before Christmas, 1911. While her husband tended to the usual off-season paperwork at the National Exhibition Company offices and spent part of most days at the pool room, Blanche McGraw finished decorating and furnishing the six-room apartment at Broadway and West 109th Street they'd moved into about fourteen months earlier. That apartment, which would be their residence for eleven years, was the first real home they'd had since their marriage.

It was enough of a home that McGraw felt obliged to include among its accoutrements a Boston bull terrier, given to him by an acquaintance in Massachusetts who bred such dogs. "Truxton" was the name McGraw unhesitatingly bestowed on the darting, leaping, tirelessly busy little fellow. And Truxton remained the name for one after another bull terrier, as well as an Airedale and a fox terrier, that joined the McGraw household over the years. Like nearly everybody else in that day, the McGraws paid little attention to veterinary medicine, which in any case was only just beginning to concern itself with the health of pets—as opposed to livestock. Nor were they as attentive as they might have been to their dogs' whereabouts. The result was that the life expectancy of a particular McGraw canine was never more than a few years. Even so, for more than two decades, when he was at home in New York, McGraw's cry, "It's Truxton against the world!" signaled the day's beginning for him and for a long succession of Truxtons.[27]

Truxton I made the long trip with the McGraws to Marlin for the Giants' fifth spring training there. Almost every day telegrams arrived from Charley Faust, who was killing time at Hot Springs, where Bill Dahlen had gathered his Brooklyn players. After spending the winter in New York and doing a couple of weeks at a Harlem vaudeville theater, Faust reported that he was in fine condition and ready to pitch for the Giants. Unless McGraw gave him a contract, though, he might offer his services to Brooklyn. McGraw finally wired back for Faust to report to Marlin on March 27—the day after the Giants started for home.

Maybe because of the intervention of some kind-hearted Brooklyn player, Faust didn't make that quixotic journey. Instead he headed for New York, where he greeted the Giants when they arrived to start the season. As far as McGraw was concerned, the Giants' World Series defeat proved that Faust had lost whatever magical influence he may once have had, and he'd become more annoying than amusing. McGraw did agree, though, to let Faust sit in the new home dugout at the Polo Grounds in his street clothes—as long as he stayed out of the way.

For the first half of the season the Faustian charm seemed to be working again. A loss to Brooklyn in the first game of a July 4 doubleheader broke a sixteen-game winning streak and left the Giants' record at 54–12, far better than Chicago or Pittsburgh. The previous day Marquard had beaten Brooklyn for his nineteenth victory without a loss in 1912 and his twenty-first in a row in regular season play. Again the Giants relied on the hit-and-run play and derring-do on the base paths to overwhelm the opposition. As a team they stole 319 bases, batted .286, and scored 823 runs, the most in the National League since 1899. McGraw had no outstanding everyday players, but his ball club, seasoned but still relatively young, had become a well-tuned machine.

McGraw marked his tenth anniversary as manager of the Giants on July 15 at a dinner given for him at the Hotel Schenley in Pittsburgh. "My admiration for you has grown to love," wired the bedridden Brush from New York, "because of your honor, loyalty, genius and indomitable determination to succeed."[28]

Yet once again McGraw's honor—or at least his honesty—was about to be called into question. In August president Charles W. Murphy of the Chicago Cubs hinted at an excessively cozy relationship between McGraw and manager Bresnahan of St. Louis, adding that New York wouldn't win so many games "without undue assistance from other teams." Late the next month Horace Fogel, McGraw's predecessor as Giants manager and president of the Philadelphia Phillies since 1909, joined the attack. In a signed statement in Chicago (which some suspected Murphy had actually written), Fogel bluntly accused Bresnahan of having his players "take it easy" against the Giants, and also charged certain umpires with favoring New York throughout the season in hopes of getting to work the World Series after New York won another pennant. Tom Lynch, said Fogel, was "a figurehead president," unwilling to do anything about the umpires in his league.[29]

While the Murphy-Fogel accusations no doubt bothered McGraw some, he was a great deal more concerned about his team's slump beginning in July. On the tenth of that month, in Chicago, the Cubs knocked out Marquard and, behind rookie Jimmy Lavender, ended the Rube's phenomenal run. From that point on, the tall left-hander lost ten games and won only seven. Mathewson won twenty-three but was generally less effective than in previous seasons. If it hadn't been for Charles "Jeff" Tesreau, a burly Missourian bought in the off-season from Toronto, the Giants would have found themselves in deep trouble indeed. Tesreau won sixteen games, nearly all of them after mid-July, including a no-hit game against Philadelphia.

By early September the Cubs had crept to within three and one-half games of the League leaders, and some observers wondered whether the Giants might be worn out after a year and a half of almost continuous baseball in the United States and Cuba. But by taking seven of nine games at Boston and Philadelphia, New York moved out to an eight-game lead. A double-header sweep of the Braves at the Polo Grounds on September 26 clinched McGraw's fourth pennant.

In the triumphant Giants team photograph, Charley Faust, given a uniform for the day, stood proudly alongside Larry Doyle. Believing that "Lulu," his imaginary sweetheart, was calling him home, Faust decided to skip the World Series and head back to Kansas. Later, after migrating to the Pacific Northwest, he would become so deranged that his brother would have him committed to the Western Hospital for the Insane at Fort Steilacoom, Washington. There he would die of tuberculosis in June 1915 at the age of thirty-four.

Missing from the 1912 team photo, of course, was Bugs Raymond, who might have become one of the top pitchers of his time. McGraw hadn't asked Raymond to come to spring training or otherwise made any disposition of his contract, so that while he remained on New York's reserve list, the only money he received for playing baseball was what he was paid by local semi-pro teams in Chicago. One day early in September, Raymond went as a spectator to a ballpark on the city's northwest side, where he quickly got into a disagreement with several local toughs. Knocked down and repeatedly kicked in the head, he suffered a skull fracture. Two days later he died at the little rundown hotel where he'd been staying with his wife and two children.

It's not likely that anybody with the Giants shed a tear or lit a candle over the violent, pathetic death of a man who'd been their teammate only a year earlier. Professional baseball left little room for genuine sentiment, as opposed to the heavy sentimentalism in which its promoters, then and later, liked to engage when they talked about baseball's wholesome, uplifting qualities and its vital place in the life of the nation.

As the Giants readied themselves for another World Series, Bugs Raymond was all but forgotten.

The ninth "modern" World Series matched the Giants, winners of 103 games, against the Boston Red Sox, who'd won 105 games and finished fourteen ahead of Washington. Led by center-fielder Tris Speaker, as brilliant defensively as he was potent at bat, and Joe Wood, a young right-hander who'd won thirty-four games, the Red Sox were at least as strong as the Athletics, last year's adversaries.

Against Boston, though, the Giants made a considerably better showing. On October 7 nearly 38,000 jammed the Polo Grounds as Tesreau and his teammates took the field in their new violet-trimmed uniforms, which McGraw had chosen out of his fondness for the colors of New York University's athletic teams. Wood outpitched Tesreau in that game as well as game four, also played in New York. In between, at Boston's new Fenway Park, Mathewson battled three Red Sox hurlers to an eleven-inning, 6–6 tie, and Marquard regained form to win the third game. Mathewson didn't allow a base runner over the last five innings in game five, but Boston's two runs in the third were enough for Hugh Bedient. Marquard had another good outing on October 14, at the Polo Grounds, holding Boston to two runs while his team scored five. The next day Wood lasted only an inning, yielding six runs, an ample cushion for Tesreau. The Giants had tied the Series.

Inasmuch as seven games (one a tie) had already been played, a coin toss determined the site of the deciding game, which turned out to be one of the most notable in Series history. The turnout at Fenway Park was a disappointing 17,000, the result of a boycott by the numerous and well-organized Royal Rooters, furious because the previous day they'd been denied their seats in the temporary bleachers in left field through a mixup in ticket allocations. Those who were there saw Mathewson pitch heroically, holding the Red Sox to a single run for nine innings. But Bedient and Wood, who relieved him after seven innings, would let the Giants have no more. Then in the top half of the tenth, New York got to Wood for one run on Red Murray's second double of the day and Fred Merkle's single. Mathewson needed only three more outs to give the Giants the Series.

Leading off, pinch-hitter Clyde Engle sent a routine fly ball to center field, which Snodgrass camped under and then dropped for a two-base error. But then "Snow," as his teammates called him, made a fine running catch of Harry Hooper's long fly, Engle holding second. Inexplicably, Mathewson walked Steve Yerkes, Boston's light-hitting second-baseman. Speaker, batting with runners on first and second and one out, lifted a foul near the first-base coach's box. Although it was clearly Merkle's play, for some reason he failed to make it. At the last second Chief Meyers lunged for the ball, but it fell out of his reach. Given another life, Speaker lined Mathewson's next pitch past first, scoring Engle and sending Yerkes to third. McGraw had Mathewson intentionally walk Duffy Lewis to set up a force play anywhere. But Larry Gardner's long fly to Josh Devore in right field sent home Yerkes to win it for Boston.

It was a heart-rending loss, the toughest of Matty's long and illustrious career. Fred Lieb remembered that Sid Mercer of the New York *Globe* sat in the press section with tears streaming down his face, dictating his account of the fateful tenth inning to a telegraph operator. Like Merkle's failure to touch second in 1908, "Snodgrass's muff" would become part of baseball folklore. The Californian would forever bear the blame for the Giants' defeat. McGraw, though, always came to his defense. "It could happen to anyone," he said shortly after the game. "If it hadn't been for a lot that Snodgrass did, we wouldn't have been playing in that game at all."[30] Besides, he would point out on numerous occasions in the years to come, Merkle, Meyers, or somebody should have grabbed Speaker's foul fly. As he'd done for Merkle in 1908, McGraw wrote a nice raise into Snodgrass's contract for 1913.

The day after the Series ended, the National League owners met in New York in special session to consider the nagging matter of charges of favoritism toward the Giants. By this time Charley Murphy had hushed up and removed himself from the controversy, so that attention centered on what Horace Fogel, widely regarded as Murphy's stooge, had said. Besides the charges published in Chicago under his name, Fogel had declared—in the presence of reporters and spectators at the Philadelphia ballpark, during the Phillies' last series with the Giants late in September—that the pennant race had been fixed for New York to win, and that Tom Lynch knew about it. Fogel went so far as to name Bill Brennan as one of the umpires who consistently called close plays for New York.

The owners convened themselves as a "court of inquiry" to investigate Fogel's charges. Fogel had little standing with the other magnates. It was fairly common knowledge around the league that Murphy had arranged for Charles P. Taft of Cincinnati, half-brother of President William Howard Taft, to loan Fogel the money to buy the Phillies. Fogel had put little of his own money into the venture and was in fact the kind of figurehead executive he accused Lynch of being.

For those who were always prepared to believe the worst about McGraw and the Giants, the disposition of the Fogel matter looked like a case of killing the bearer of bad tidings. Actually, as Fogel himself admitted in his testimony before the other executives, he had no specific evidence to support his charges. In the end his peers turned on him, finding him guilty of having slandered the League's president, its umpires, and the League itself. Fogel was "barred forever from the councils of the National League."[31]

Mainly because of his accuser's personal lack of credibility, McGraw again emerged unscathed from what might have become a very messy set of circumstances. Fogel was gone and so, within a short time, was Roger Bresnahan. Although Bresnahan's four St. Louis teams had played respectable baseball, especially when compared to the dreadful outfits that had represented the city in the years before his arrival, the Cardinals owners let him go and gave the job to Miller Huggins, their fiery little second-baseman.

On November 11 John T. Brush died in his private railroad car near Louisiana, Missouri. He'd been en route to San Antonio, where he'd spent much of the past two winters taking the waters at Hot Wells, just south of the Texas city. An invalid for years, Brush had watched games at the Polo Grounds the past two seasons from his automobile, parked in deep center field. A broken hip, suffered when he was thrown from his auto during a collision in Harlem the past September, had speeded his decline. McGraw served as an honorary pallbearer at Brush's funeral in Indianapolis and also gave one of the eulogies. He spoke feelingly of Brush's physical suffering and courage. "He was as tender as a dear girl," said McGraw, "as resourceful as a man in the fullest of grand health. . . . What a wonderful—what a beautiful character—was John T. Brush."[32]

Then McGraw hurried back to New York to become one of the numerous baseball personages who'd taken to the vaudeville stage in recent years. McGraw's contract with the B. F. Keith circuit called for a salary of $3,000 per week for fifteen weeks, which made him the highest-paid performer in vaudeville at the time. Bozeman Bulger of the New York *Evening World* wrote most of his material, which consisted mainly of anecdotes and reminiscences about players and events and a little monologue on "the hitherto carefully guarded secrets of inside baseball as perfected by the Giants."[33]

Despite Bulger's entreaties, McGraw put off rehearsing his act. Finally, two nights before his opening at the Colonial Theatre, he and Bulger rode in a taxicab around Central Park until McGraw had memorized his lines. Arriving for his debut only five minutes before he was to go on, he managed to get through the performance without a flub. "As he progressed," according to Bulger, "he became a delightful speaker." Yet as he played other theaters in the New York area and then moved on to the other major league cities, McGraw never got accustomed to the stresses of his new public environment. "I'll admit I cannot get used to this life," he told a reporter in his dressing room at the Bronx Theatre. "It's a daily reminder that I have nerves."[34]

Shunning makeup, wearing a black coat with tails, gray trousers, and a black-and-white-striped vest, McGraw did his act six days a week, matinees and evenings, from New York and Boston to St. Louis and Chicago. He closed in the last city in mid-January, having, he felt, given honest effort for the money he'd been paid. Then it was back to New York.

With Brush's death, majority ownership in the Giants passed to his second wife and her young daughter, Brush's daughter by his deceased first wife, and his son-in-law Harry Hempstead, who'd been managing Brush's department store in Indianapolis. As the new president of the Giants, the forty-three-year-old Hempstead moved quickly to cement relations with his renowned manager. In February 1913 he tore up McGraw's contract and signed him to another one, for five years at $30,000 a year. With that new arrangement and the money from the vaudeville tour, McGraw no longer saw any reason to hold onto the pool room that he now owned in partnership with Willie Hoppe (and Arnold Rothstein). When their lease on the space in the Marbridge Building expired at the beginning of February, McGraw and Hoppe closed the place and sold the tables and other equipment.

That same February, McGraw again demostrated his flair for showmanship when he signed Jim Thorpe, the celebrated college football player and Olympic track-and-field champion, to a Giants contract. Recent revelations that Thorpe had played professional baseball two summers in North Carolina had prompted indignant Olympic officials to take back the gold medals Thorpe had won in the decathlon and pentathlon competition at the 1912 Games in Stockholm. Nominally still a

student at Carlisle Institute, a training school for young Indians where
he'd had a sensational football season in 1912, Thorpe had no particular
plans and grabbed the chance to make $5,000 a year with the Giants.
Although signing Thorpe, who'd never played baseball above the college
and low-minors level, was more a publicity stunt than anything else,
McGraw seems to have hoped that, given Thorpe's all-around athletic
ability, he might some day develop into a major league–caliber player.

Later in February, Thorpe reported at Marlin along with the other
rookies and the pitchers and catchers. McGraw tried him at first base
and played first himself in the early intrasquad games. Despite the two
hundred pounds he now carried on his short frame, McGraw could still
handle himself fairly well afield and at bat. One of the youngsters McGraw
especially liked that spring was George L. Burns, who'd appeared in
only twenty-nine games the previous year but was now, McGraw believed,
ready to take Josh Devore's outfield place. As McGraw's new leadoff
hitter, Burns would bat a solid .286 in 1913 and establish title to a job
that would remain his for nine seasons.

Rube Marquard reported late, joining the team at Houston after a
stormy vaudeville tour with Blossom Seeley that ended with their marriage in San Francisco. The previous fall, in New York, Seeley's estranged husband had accused her of sleeping with Marquard, threatened
to shoot her onstage, and filed (and then withdrawn) a $25,000 damage
suit against the pitcher, charging alienation of affections. Seeley didn't
contest his subsequent divorce action, so that by March the way was
clear for her marriage to Marquard. A little more than five months later,
to the embarrassment of everybody who supposed that their baseball
favorites' behavior should be exemplary, Blossom would present Rube
with a healthy baby boy.

Wearing their violet-trimmed uniforms (which delighted NYU boosters
but left baseball traditionalists cold), the Giants had trouble getting
started in the early part of the season. In an effort to bolster his pitching,
McGraw made one of his poorest trades, exchanging Devore, Red Ames,
and utility infielder Henry "Heinie" Groh for Cincinnati pitcher Art
Fromme. As the season progressed, though, the team's pitching proved
more than adequate. Mathewson won twenty-five games and put to rest
notions that he might be slipping. Troubled by tonsillitis and domestic
stress, Marquard still won twenty-three, and big Jeff Tesreau won twenty-
two. Rookie Al Demaree posted a 13–4 mark, proving that, besides
being a talented baseball cartoonist, he was a major league pitcher.

The Philadelphia Phillies led the League for nearly half the season. Late in June, with his team still four and one-half games behind, McGraw remarked contemptuously, "If a team like the Phillies can win a pennant in the National League, then the League is a joke."[35] At the end of the month, by beating the Phillies 11–10 at their Huntingdon Avenue home grounds, New York finally took over first place—for good, as it happened. Throughout that game, coaching at third base, McGraw exchanged barbs with the enemy players in their nearby dugout. The insults he offered to pitcher Ad Brennan were particularly vile, and when, at the end of the game, McGraw headed for the center-field clubhouse along with fans and players, Brennan ran up, hit him with both fists and knocked him down, and added a few kicks before he was hustled away by teammates. Treated for cuts on his chin and cheek, McGraw wasn't badly hurt and would have been content to let the matter drop. Tom Lynch, though, blew into town that night from New York; interviewed McGraw, Brennan, and various witnesses; and assessed a $100 fine and five-day suspension on both manager and pitcher. From the stands, McGraw watched his team sweep the remaining three games at Philadelphia. New York went home with a lead of three and one-half.

On their home stand, the Giants won fourteen of seventeen and all but wrapped up the pennant. A broken thumb disabled Chief Meyers for the last two months of the season, but Art Wilson, Meyers's backup, and tall, hard-drinking Larry McLean, acquired from Cincinnati, handled the catching capably. Meyers was the only Giant to bat above .300, but pitching and speed (296 stolen bases) made what was otherwise a very ordinary ball club into a pennant-winner for the third year in a row. New York finished with a record of 101–51, twelve and one-half games better than the Phillies.

Echoes of Horace Fogel's charges a year earlier that the umpires, notably Bill Brennan, called them the Giants' way were distinctly audible after an incident at Philadelphia on August 30. With the Phillies ahead 8–6 in the top of the ninth, a couple of hundred fans moved into the bleachers in deep center field (usually kept vacant as a hitter's backdrop) and began waving newspapers and programs to distract the Giants at bat. McGraw calmly went to home plate and asked Brennan to clear the section. After appealing to manager Red Dooin and then the park police and getting no cooperation, Brennan declared the game forfeited to New York. The Giants ran to the clubhouse ahead of the angry fans, dressed quickly, and then had to push and punch their way through a mob gathered outside the Broad Street train station. Buck Herzog suffered a cut cheek, and another rowdy waved a pistol in Red Murray's face until a policeman disarmed him.

The Phillies protested to League president Lynch, who overruled Brennan and gave the game to Philadelphia. Then the League's board of directors, acting on the Giants' appeal, overruled Lynch and stipulated that the game had to be played to a conclusion from the point at which it had been stopped. By the time it was resumed, on October 2 as a preliminary to a double-header at the Polo Grounds, the pennant race had been over for a week. Nobody cared much whether the game that had caused such a furor a few weeks earlier was ever finished. (For the record, the Phillies retired two more Giants and won the game.)

For New York fans and the legions of people who'd become convinced that John McGraw was the game's supreme genius, the 1913 World Series was another disappointment. It was even more of a letdown than the previous two, because the Philadelphia Athletics, having won the American League championship for the third time in four years, disposed of the Giants so easily.

New York won only one game. Larry Doyle and Fred Merkle made critical errors and Frank Baker homered and drove in three runs behind Chief Bender to defeat Marquard in the opener at the Polo Grounds. Mathewson, in one of his finest performances, pitched a ten-inning shutout in game two at Philadelphia, the Giants finally scoring three times in the top of the tenth on Eddie Plank. In the third game Leslie Ambrose "Bullet Joe" Bush, only twenty years old, throttled the Giants while the Athletics pounded Tesreau. They did the same thing to Demaree the next day, and Bender withstood a late Giants rally to win 6–5. On October 11, at the Polo Grounds before 36,682, the biggest crowd of the Series, Mathewson pitched well but received poor support afield. Plank was masterful, throwing a two-hitter and facing only twenty-nine batters. The final score was 3–1, Philadelphia. Like Hugh Jennings, McGraw had managed three straight World Series losers.

That didn't keep him from going through with a riotous reunion he'd organized for Jennings and the rest of the old Orioles, held at a New York saloon the night after the Giants' fourth Series loss that afternoon. McGraw even invited umpire Bill Klem, who'd been one of the four officials working the Series. McGraw had become a drinking man in recent years. Generally he knew his limit; the trouble was that on those

occasions when he exceeded it, he tended to become surly and belligerent. That night, having imbibed too much, he told Wilbert Robinson,
his faithful aide for the past five years, that Robinson had looked bad
several times on the coaching lines that afternoon. McGraw, Robbie
retorted, had made more mistakes during the Series than everybody else
on the team put together. McGraw fired his old friend and Orioles
teammate on the spot. "This is my party," he barked. "Get the hell out
of here." Robbie left but only, according to Klem, after dousing McGraw
with a glass of beer.[36] The two men wouldn't speak to each other again
for seventeen years.

Besides Robinson, a few others questioned elements of McGraw's
managerial style. For example, they pointed out that several times in
the three Series the Giants had lost, McGraw's attachment to the hit and
run and aversion to the sacrifice bunt had kept his team from advancing
runners into scoring position. His fondness for base-stealing, moreover,
had taken the Giants out of potential rallies. Some also noted that he'd
shown little interest in scouting his Series opponents, relying instead on
snap judgments, intuitive moves when critical situations arose.

Yet such mild criticism left undamaged McGraw's popular image—
an image promoted in the daily newspapers, the mass-circulation magazines, and the endless baseball talk of people everywhere. For many
millions of Americans he'd become the master manager, the archetypal
baseball field general, the "little Napoleon." Most of them could never
expect to see him in the flesh. But they could imagine him—his craf-
tiness, his strictness with his players, his infuriation with the umpires,
his manipulation of the emotions of the Polo Grounds spectators. They
could visualize him as Mathewson described him (in a piece probably
written by John Wheeler), crouching in the third-base coaching box,
pounding his fist into the fielder's glove he liked to wear. The first Giants
batter might draw a base on balls, whereupon, in Mathewson's rendering,
"McGraw leaps in the air, kicks his heels together, claps his mitt, shouts
at the umpire, runs in and pats the next batter on the back, and says
something to the pitcher. . . . The whole atmosphere inside the park is
changed in a minute. . . . the little, silent actor on the third-base coaching line is the cause of the change." "McGraw," another admirer wrote
in 1913, "combines in a rare degree the ability to . . . take advantage
of an opportunity, to see into the future, and to plan for what may happen
as well as what is happening."[37]

Lavish praise, maybe, but typical of what was being said and written about McGraw in those years. The immediate future into which he looked and for which he'd already carefully planned held an adventure for himself, Blanche, and several dozen others that would be vastly more exciting than anything any of them had ever known. So far McGraw had played for and managed baseball teams all over the United States as well as in Cuba. Now he was about to manage around the world.

Eight

AROUND THE WORLD, INTO THE CELLAR, BACK ON TOP

In December 1912 McGraw's tour on the Keith vaudeville circuit took him to Chicago, where the American League's annual mid-winter meeting was being held. One evening Charles Comiskey, president of the Chicago White Sox, and Joe Farrell of the Chicago *Tribune* encountered McGraw and Garry Herrmann in Smiley Corbett's bar. Once rivals as National League players and then as pioneers in the American League, McGraw and Comiskey had put aside their differences and become if not good friends, then at least warm acquaintances. After a round or two of drinks, the four men began to talk about the around-the-world baseball tour that Albert G. Spalding, then president of the Chicago National League franchise and emerging sporting goods tycoon, had organized in the off-season of 1888–89. Matching his Chicagos against players picked from the rest of the League and leading the expedition from Shanghai to Cairo to London, Spalding had achieved a major publicity coup for himself, even if his venture made few converts to the game in foreign lands and thus did little to promote Spalding-made sporting goods.

Farrell suggested that Comiskey and McGraw might do the same thing. As they became more lubricated and convivial, the two baseball leaders liked the idea more and more. By the time the get-together broke up, they'd agreed in principle to take two ball clubs around the world, show off the game to people who would probably never have a chance to see it otherwise, and have the time of their lives besides.

During the next six or eight months, the idea born in Corbett's bar took firm shape. Comiskey and Jimmy Callahan, his manager, put together a team made up mainly of White Sox but including Tris Speaker of Boston; Sam Crawford, Detroit's slugging outfielder; Herman "Germany" Schaefer, Washington's zany infielder; and a couple of others. McGraw could only entice six of his Giants and had to add two Philadelphia and four St. Louis National Leaguers. (In fact, McGraw was walking toward the Philadelphia clubhouse and talking to Phillies shortstop Mickey Doolan about joining the tour, in June 1913, when Ad Brennan came up and socked him.) McGraw also invited Mike Donlin, who'd spent the 1913 season at Jersey City in the International League and recently lost his beloved Mabel to cancer. By September, Comiskey and McGraw had their teams put together; each player had posted a $300 deposit to guarantee his presence on the trip. Bill Klem from the National League and Jack Sheridan from the American would do the umpiring.

The basic plan was for the so-called White Sox and Giants to play a series of games in the United States before embarking for Japan. Receipts from those games, it was hoped, would cover expenses for the overseas part of the trip. Beginning in Cincinnati on October 18, a week after Eddie Plank retired the last Giant to close out the World Series, the two teams had played thirty-one games by the time they reached Seattle at the end of November.

Mathewson went with the group from New York as far as Cincinnati, where he pitched and won the first game of the cross-continental series. He then headed back east. Marquard and Tesreau also stayed at home, so that McGraw ended up borrowing Urban "Red" Faber, just purchased by the White Sox from Des Moines of the Western League. Faber would pitch so well for McGraw that at the end of the trip he tried, without success, to buy the right-hander from Comiskey.

About halfway through the zigzag rail journey across the country, in Texas, Blanche McGraw received word of her mother's death. Because McGraw refused to go ahead without her, the two of them made an arduous trip back to Baltimore for the funeral, then traversed the continent to rejoin the tour at San Francisco. McGraw arrived in time to have a nasty spat with Klem in a game that others may have taken to be an exhibition, but never McGraw. Reminding Klem that he was paying the umpire's expenses out of his own pocket (as Comiskey was doing for Sheridan), McGraw threatened to leave Klem at home. Comiskey managed to soothe the feelings of both men on the way up to Seattle.

From Seattle the baseball tourists took a coastal steamer on up to Vancouver, where they boarded the *Empress of China*, a small oceangoing Canadian Pacific liner. The whole party consisted of sixty-seven people, including sixteen wives. Larry Doyle and Jim Thorpe were newlyweds. Thorpe, unlike Chief Meyers, seemed determined to live up to the prevailing stereotype of the unruly and irresponsible Indian. At various times on the trip, McGraw took it upon himself to lecture Thorpe about drinking and playing cards to the point that he neglected his bride.

Besides being Thorpe's boss, McGraw could also offer himself as, in most respects, a successful husband. On January 8, 1914, in Australia, the McGraws would celebrate their twelfth wedding anniversary. At the time McGraw was forty years old, Blanche thirty-two. Their marriage had produced no children and never would. No doubt they'd hoped and expected to become parents, as their religious faith and the mores of their time taught them they should do. But Blanche McGraw never became pregnant, nor, for that matter, in two and a half years of marriage, had Minnie Doyle McGraw. Inasmuch as both were young, healthy women at the time they married, it seems unlikely that both were incapable of conceiving, although in Blanche McGraw's case that was probably the common presumption after a few years. There's no way of knowing to what extent—if at all—the McGraws may have sought medical answers to their situation. Male infertility research was still in its infancy anyway. All in all, it seems a fair inference that sterility on John McGraw's part accounted for their childlessness through thirty-two years of marriage.

By the notions of the time, though, they were a well-matched, contented, generally happy couple. They enjoyed travel and meeting new people—even if the grind of road trips in the summer months sometimes got to McGraw. The globe-circling expedition of 1913–14 would be one of the high points of their life together.

Of course the travelers brought along tons of luggage, with the McGraws by themselves accounting for several big trunks. Blanche McGraw possessed a great number of outfits and a substantial quantity of jewelry. In fact, Blanche's first impression of Jane Mathewson, when they'd met in Savannah in the spring of 1903, was that the Sunday-school teacher from Lewisburg, Pennsylvania, didn't approve of the amount of jewelry the manager's wife was wearing.

For all her chic apparel, Blanche McGraw brought no cosmetics for what would be a three-month journey. John McGraw had strong opinions about women who wore makeup and smoked cigarettes; both practices, he was inclined to think, made them not quite respectable. Once, he discovered a hidden lipstick in his wife's dresser drawer. "It's bold to wear this stuff," he scolded. "It makes you conspicuous. . . . this rouge and stuff make a girl look cheap." Being around women smokers always made him uncomfortable, Blanche McGraw believed. Basically a nineteenth-century man, McGraw "idealized femininity as it was" and could never reconcile himself to the "new woman" emerging in this century's early decades.[1]

The Pacific crossing, a little more than seven thousand miles, was cold, rough, and forlorn; only three other vessels were sighted in the twenty-three days it took to complete the voyage. By the time the *Empress of China* steamed into the harbor at Yokohama, everybody was bored and tired. The Japanese welcomed them enthusiastically and turned out in large numbers for four games between the amalgamated American squads and Japanese university teams. Several years earlier, such teams had begun coming to the United States to play against eastern colleges, and by 1913 baseball already had a strong appeal for athletically minded Japanese.

From Japan the tourists took an Australian ship, the *St. Alban*, to Shanghai, Hong Kong, Manila, and then Sydney and Melbourne. The Americans in the Philippines were delighted to see them, particularly army surgeon Arlie Pond, an old Oriole, whom McGraw had last seen twelve years earlier. The British colonial officials at Hong Kong and the Australian hosts were polite and accommodating but unimpressed by the game the talented Americans put on display. Cricket, they remained convinced, was a superior pastime.

After crossing the Indian Ocean, which McGraw, in his cable to New York, described as "almost as smooth as a mill pond," the party stopped for a few days at Colombo, the capital of the British colony of Ceylon.[2] Then they steamed through the Suez Canal to Cairo. Reenacting what Spalding's group had done in 1889, the two teams played at Giza, in the sight of the pyramids and in the shadow of the Sphinx. A few Egyptian and British officials, Americans wives and newsmen, and bewildered locals watched what may have been the second strangest baseball exhibition ever staged.

At Rome rain prevented any baseball, so the ballplayers spent their time as they wished. The Roman Catholics in the party—men in white tie and tails, women in black formals—received the blessing of Pope Pius X in a private audience at the Vatican. After that Comiskey, stricken with an intestinal ailment, left the tour and started home ahead of schedule. The teams did manage to get in a game at Nice, and that evening McGraw and twenty or so others took in the casinos at Monte Carlo. Enjoying the most elegant "action" he'd yet encountered, McGraw dropped $250.

Rain in Paris again kept the players off the field and in search of amusement. McGraw had reunions with Tod Sloan, his jockey friend and former pool-hall associate, now living as an expatriate, and Sammy Strang, who, under the name Strang Nicklin, was studying with a singing teacher and hoping for a career in musical theater.[3] The McGraws also visited the tomb of Napoleon. Proud of being called the little Napoleon of baseball, McGraw peered up at the bronze figure and quipped, "I, too, met the Duke of Wellington, only his name was Connie Mack instead of Arthur Wellesley."[4]

The climax to the trip was a game at the Chelsea Football Grounds at Stamford Bridge, outside London, on February 26. Thirty thousand people, by far the biggest crowd the Americans had seen since Japan, turned out, some of them because they were curious about baseball, most because King George V had decided to attend. His Royal Majesty and his subjects saw a dandy baseball game, whether they fully appreciated it or not. The "White Sox" won 5–4 when little Tommy Daly, a part-time outfielder with the Philadelphia Athletics the past season, lined one of Faber's pitches into the short right-field stand in the last of the ninth inning. Comiskey's team finished the tour with twenty-four wins, the "Giants" with twenty.

At Liverpool the travelers boarded the British liner *Lusitania* for home. Snow was falling on the morning of March 6, 1914, when the big ship pulled into New York harbor. John and Blanche McGraw had completely circled the world, New York to New York, in 139 days.

After attending lavish welcome-home banquets in New York and Chicago for the global tourists, McGraw, in the company of Doyle, Thorpe, and Fred Merkle, was off to Marlin for spring training. In his absence the National League owners had voted not to renew Tom Lynch's contract and given the League presidency to Governor John Tener of Pennsylvania, who'd pitched in the major leagues for a few seasons before going into law and politics. Although the League's central offices remained in New York, Tener's duties as governor kept him in Harrisburg most of the time.

McGraw knew little about Tener but expected that at least he would be an improvement over Lynch, whom McGraw had never liked. On another matter, though, his feelings were considerably more pronounced.

In December, with McGraw somewhere in the Pacific, Harry Hempstead and club secretary John B. Foster had traded Buck Herzog and Grover Hartley, a young catcher, to Cincinnati for outfielder Bob Bescher. Garry Hermann then had named Herzog to manage the Reds for 1914.

Though only twenty-eight, Herzog had long wanted to become a manager. At the same time, Bescher was a player on whom McGraw had had his eye for some time. Although he'd had a poor season in 1913, over the four years prior to that Bescher had amassed 281 stolen bases. Apparently Herzog had obtained Hempstead's consent to dicker with Herrmann about the manager's job at Cincinnati. Herrmann had been willing to give up Bescher but insisted that Herzog had to bring somebody else from New York with him. So in effect Herzog traded himself and Hartley, too. It was a slipshod deal, in McGraw's estimation, and it hadn't had his specific approval. He was glad to get Bescher, but he also liked Herzog as a ballplayer, for all the personal antagonism that had passed between them. Besides, McGraw had handled player transactions on his own ever since coming to the Giants. The episode caused no permanent rift in his relations with Hempstead, but when he arrived at Marlin, the little Napoleon's feathers were still ruffled.

One matter that worried many other managers that spring was of little concern to McGraw. In the past nine months or so ambitious and well-heeled baseball enterpreneurs in Chicago, St. Louis, Pittsburgh, Indianapolis, Buffalo, Kansas City, Baltimore, and Brooklyn had banded together to form the Federal League and challenge the Nationals' and Americans' shared monopoly in major league baseball. In the off-season of 1913–14 the Federal Leaguers had assiduously wooed players in the two established leagues. They were successful mainly with younger players and substitutes, plus a few aging stars like Chief Bender and Mordecai Brown. By 1915, 172 players who'd previously appeared in the National or American League had signed Federal League contracts; but the only outstanding player still in his prime going over to the new circuit was Hal Chase, who left the Chicago White Sox in mid-season 1914 to join the Buffalo Federals.

Late in the 1913 season, McGraw and Hempstead had moved to forestall desertions to the Federals by signing virtually all the Giants to new two- or three-year contracts at substantial pay boosts. Otis Crandall, who'd done no better than a 4–4 record in 1913, and backup catcher Art Wilson were the only Giants to sign with the "invaders," as hostile baseball writers often termed the Federals. Mathewson, making around

$12,000 a year under his new contract, would have nothing to do with the new outfit, nor would any of the other Giants mainstays. The New York club had long been the best paying in baseball, not to mention the three straight World Series checks most of McGraw's players had picked up. So what came to be known in baseball history as the "Federal League war" hurt the Giants little if at all.

One last time, McGraw signed Mike Donlin, who was still bereft over his wife's death as well as in financial straits. McGraw had no particular use for the veteran, but he felt sorry for him and hoped he might help out as a pinch-hitter. Donlin's once superb skills were about gone. In thirty-one times at bat during the coming season, Turkey Mike would manage only five hits.

The two most notable happenings that spring were a fight in Houston between McGraw and player-manager Pat Newnam of that city's Texas League team (with McGraw ending up on his back with a split lip) and McGraw's first look at a big, swarthy, moon-faced pitcher named George Herman Ruth, who'd just signed with owner-manager Jack Dunn of the Baltimore International League club. "Dunn's baby" or "Babe," as the local writers had already nicknamed the nineteen-year-old left-hander, so impressed McGraw in his exhibition-game stint against New York that he made Dunn, an old Oriole, promise to give him the first chance to buy the young pitcher. Three months later, for reasons of his own, Dunn would offer Ruth first to Connie Mack, who would refer him to owner Joseph Lannin of the Red Sox. So it would be Boston where Ruth ended up, and McGraw would never forgive Dunn for what he considered a broken promise.

The Giants were the bookmakers' heavy favorites to win a fourth straight pennant. The season didn't start off well. Brooklyn defeated the Giants at Ebbets Field, the fine modern ballpark the cross-river rivals had occupied since 1912. Wilbert Robinson, summarily dismissed by McGraw after the World Series, had landed on his feet, signing to manage a Brooklyn team that the writers and fans would soon start calling the "Robins." Robinson's presence apparently made a difference in what had been one of the League's poorest entries for more than a decade. In 1914 Brooklyn, sparked by first-baseman Jake Daubert and outfielder Zack Wheat, two of the premier ballplayers of the period, would rise to fifth place, only four games below .500.

It was the end of May before the Giants moved into first place ahead of Pittsburgh and Cincinnati—both of which would quickly start to fade, ultimately to seventh and eighth, respectively. Buck Herzog's maiden season as a manager was something less than thumpingly successful. McGraw made things as tough as possible for his ex-third-baseman. Early in June, when Herzog brought his ball club into New York for the first time, his local admirers wanted to honor him at home plate. McGraw spitefully vetoed the idea, and used his influence to prevent a similar affair planned for a Manhattan theater. The Giants manager freely voiced his contempt for Herzog to Reds catcher Bill Clarke, who passed McGraw's remarks along to Herzog. Although the ill treatment of their young manager served to fire up the Reds, successive defeats at the hands of Marquard, Tesreau, and Mathewson quickly cooled them off.

Nobody really seemed capable of challenging the Giants, despite increasingly evident weaknesses. Bescher, it turned out, had slowed down considerably and seen his best years in the majors. Neither Milton Stock nor Fred Snodgrass could hold down third as capably as Herzog; George Burns, Art Fletcher, and Chief Meyers were the only men who hit the ball with any consistency; and Marquard was maddeningly erratic. Still, at nightfall following the July 4 double-headers, New York, with a record of 40–24, held first by two games over Chicago, the latest team to behave like a serious contender. At the bottom of the League that night were the Boston Braves, a surprising sixth-place finisher under George Stallings in 1913 but apparently holding no surprises this year.

Two weeks later, at Pittsburgh, Marquard and the Pirates' Charles "Babe" Adams both went all the way in the longest game ever played in the National League up to then. The Giants scored twice in the top of the twenty-first inning to win 3–1. Their hold on first seemed secure; few baseball followers outside of Boston noticed that the Braves had climbed out of the cellar and by July 19 had jumped all the way to fourth place.

At the end of July and the beginning of August, New York lost four out of five games at Cincinnati, with McGraw getting the thumb from umpire Bill Byron three times during the series. After the last expulsion McGraw received word from League president Tener that he was suspended for three days. The next day (August 4) the sports pages reported that particular bit of baseball strife, while the front pages reported that Great Britain, in the final act of the falling-dominoes sequence of the past month, had declared war on Imperial Germany.

The greatest war in human history was under way, but all that was far away in Europe and seemed to have little bearing on the United

States, least of all on the rapidly heating National League pennant race. By August 10 Boston had taken a firm grip on second place, though still six and a half games behind the Giants. McGraw had become petulant, believing that all the other teams had ganged up on the Giants, maybe even the umpires, too. "It's the league against New York," he complained. "I feel like the Kaiser."[5]

On September 2, after Boston swept a double-header at Philadelphia and Brooklyn beat Marquard and the Giants at Ebbets Field, the Braves found themselves in first place by a game. Five days later Boston and New York split a morning-afternoon Labor Day double-header, played at the Red Sox' Fenway Park rather than the Braves' rickety little South End Grounds. Both games attracted big overflows; more than 70,000 saw the two contests, an astonishing circumstance for a club that had trailed the League in attendance for most of the past decade.

In the afternoon game the crowd nearly rioted when George "Lefty" Tyler hit Snodgrass with a pitch, Snodgrass made an obscene gesture as he stood at first, and Tyler then pantomimed Snodgrass's already legendary muff in the 1912 World Series. Pop bottles rained on Snodgrass as he took his position in center field near the standees, and several Giants ran to his aid. Boston's Mayor James Curley stormed onto the field to demand that Bill Klem remove Snodgrass. The umpire refused, the game continued, and Tesreau throttled the Braves to move the Giants back into a tie for the lead.

Yet the Braves' torrid winning pace was too much for the Giants. Nearly McGraw's whole team was in a batting slump. Of the twelve straight losses Marquard suffered after that twenty-one-inning epic, the Giants couldn't score in five. By September 15 they trailed Stallings's club by two and one-half games; in another week Boston's lead had grown to eight. On October 1, at the Polo Grounds, George Davis barely held onto a big early lead to give the Braves a 7–6 victory and Boston's first National League pennant since 1898. Klem stopped the game in the top of the seventh inning, walked over to the unruly Giants bench, and ordered twenty-four Giants—regulars and rookies just called up from the minors, everybody except McGraw and the players in the field— to head for the clubhouse. Led by an uncharacteristically puckish Mathewson, they marched in step, single file, across the green expanse and through the gate in the right-center-field fence.

By winning sixty-eight times in the eighty-seven games they played after July 4, the Boston Braves astounded the sports world. They not only overtook the Giants but finished ten and a half games ahead of the second-place New Yorkers. Stallings, a dark-featured Georgian who managed from the bench in street clothes and sometimes shocked even veteran ballplayers with his torrents of vile language, was hailed everywhere as the "Miracle Man." At least as miraculous as the Braves' rise from last place on July 4 was their four-game World Series sweep of Connie Mack's mighty Athletics, American League champions four of the last five years, Series winners in three of the last four. The National League's first in the Series since 1909, the Braves' triumph also convinced Mack to begin dismantling his great ball club. In 1915 the Athletics would fall all the way to last place. There they would remain for another six seasons.

While the Braves were dispatching the Athletics, the Giants and the New York Yankees, seventh-place finishers in the American League, went through the motions of their second (and last) city series. All the games took place at the Polo Grounds, which the Yankees had leased from the National Exhibition Company since 1913. According to Billy Evans, one of the umpires working the series, most of the fans who watched the Giants win four games to the Yankees' one cheered for the American Leaguers and jeered McGraw on those few occasions in game one when he stuck his head out of the dugout. For the rest of the games he sat in the Giants' bullpen in far right center field. Not many fans of any allegiance, though, bothered to take in the series. The five games drew only a little more than 40,000, which left a $353 share for each victorious Giant.

As he sat in the faraway bullpen watching the listless intracity series, McGraw may have contemplated a recent offer he'd had from the multimillionaire oilman Harry Sinclair. One of the Federal League's strongest backers, Sinclair was moving the champion Indianapolis team to Newark for the coming season. By some accounts, Sinclair offered McGraw $100,000 to manage the Newark Federals; by others he simply gave McGraw a blank check and told him to write in his own figure. Whatever Sinclair was willing to pay the Giants' manager, it wasn't enough to get him. Like Ty Cobb, Tris Speaker, and Walter Johnson, nearly all the top names in baseball, McGraw was unwilling to stake his future on an unknown and unpredictable quantity. McGraw did feel a genuine loyalty to the New York Giants, the National League, and the entire established structure of baseball, even including Ban Johnson and the American League. Asked after the season about prospects for an accommodation

Seventeen-year-old
John McGraw during
his brief stay at Olean,
New York, spring
1890. (NATIONAL
BASEBALL LIBRARY)

The 1894 St. Bonaventure College team,
coached by John McGraw (*standing, extreme right*) and Hugh Jennings (*standing, extreme left*). The Reverend Joseph Dolan,
O.F.M., sits in the middle, second row.
(ST. BONAVENTURE UNIVERSITY ARCHIVES)

The 1896 Baltimore Orioles, three-time National League champions. *Front row, left to right:* Jack Doyle, John McGraw, Willie Keeler, Arlie Pond. *Middle row, left to right:* Steve Brodie, Bill Hoffer, Joe Kelley, Ned Hanlon, Wilbert Robinson, Hugh Jennings, Heinie Reitz. *Back row, left to right:* Joe Quinn, Sadie McMahon, Duke Esper, George Hemming, Frank Bowerman, Bill Clarke, Jimmy Donely. (NATIONAL BASEBALL LIBRARY)

Union Park, Baltimore, during the climactic game of the 1897 season, on September 27, the Boston Beaneaters defeating the Orioles 19–10. Note spectators atop the outfield fence. (NATIONAL BASEBALL LIBRARY)

John McGraw, 1899.
(NATIONAL BASEBALL LIBRARY)

The 1899 Baltimore Orioles, fourth-place finishers (out of twelve teams) in John McGraw's managerial debut. *Front row, left to right:* Dave Fultz, Gene DeMontreville, Billy Keister. *Middle row, left to right:* Ducky Holmes, Billy Magoon, Steve Brodie, John McGraw, Wilbert Robinson, Charlie Harris, Kit McKenna. *Back row, left to right:* Jerry Nops, Joe McGinnity, Pat Chrisham, George LaChance, Harry Howell, Frank Kitson. Missing: Jimmy Sheckard. (NATIONAL BASEBALL LIBRARY)

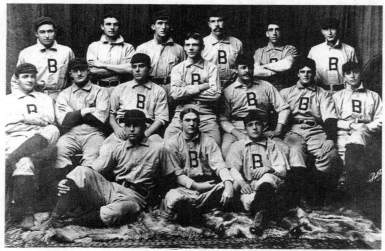

National League
and World Series
winners, 1905,
from the front page
of *Sporting Life*,
October 15, 1905,
issue. (NATIONAL
BASEBALL LIBRARY)

The Polo Grounds grandstand
and left-field bleachers, from
the center-field carriage park,
about 1902. (NATIONAL
BASEBALL LIBRARY)

John McGraw at the time
he became manager of the
New York Giants, 1902.
(NATIONAL BASEBALL
LIBRARY)

John T. Brush at about the time
he bought a controlling interest in
the New York Giants, 1902.
(NATIONAL BASEBALL LIBRARY)

Christy Mathewson, 1906.
(NATIONAL BASEBALL LIBRARY)

A pregame moment at the Polo Grounds, 1907. As the Giants take infield practice, Joe McGinnity starts to warm up (pausing to exchange a look, maybe a few words, with a spectator), and John McGraw, wearing his fielder's glove, watches his pitcher intently. Note the "L" train beyond the left-field bleachers. (NATIONAL BASEBALL LIBRARY)

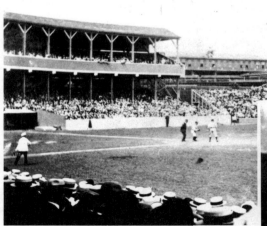

Game action at the Polo Grounds, about 1906. Note the concessionaire on the playing field, at left. (NATIONAL BASEBALL LIBRARY)

John McGraw, 1912.
(NATIONAL BASEBALL LIBRARY)

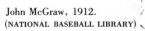

McGraw and the
mainstays of the
1913 National
League champions.
Note the misspelling
of "Mathewson."
(NATIONAL BASEBALL
LIBRARY)

John McGraw,
1912. (NATIONAL
BASEBALL LIBRARY)

John McGraw and manager Hal
Chase of the New York Yankees before the opening game of the 1910
city series, at the Polo Grounds.
(NATIONAL BASEBALL LIBRARY)

Mathewson, 1913.
(NATIONAL BASEBALL LIBRARY)

Ross Youngs.
(NATIONAL BASEBALL LIBRARY)

World's champions, 1921. *Front row, left to right:* Wally Kopf, Bill Ritter, (?) Kelly, Bill Heine, Ed Mackall (trainer), (?) Clancy, Casey Stengel, Frank Frisch. *Middle row, left to right:* Bill Cunningham, Dave Bancroft, Art Nehf, Johnny Rawlings, George Burns, Hugh Jennings, Irish Meusel, Alex Gaston, Earl Smith, Jesse Burkett. *Back row, left to right:* George Kelly, Ross Youngs, Slim Sallee, Cecil Causey, Bill Ryan, Pat Shea, Eddie Brown, Phil Douglas, Fred Toney, Jess Barnes, Frank Snyder. (NATIONAL BASEBALL LIBRARY)

Left to right: Christy Mathewson, Blanche McGraw, John McGraw, Jane Mathewson, at the McGraws' home in Pelham, N.Y., 1923. (NATIONAL BASEBALL LIBRARY)

National League champions, 1923. *Front row, left to right:* Erwin (trainer), Moses Solomon, Walter Huntzinger, Dennis Gearin, Claude Jonnard, Frank Frisch, Ross Youngs, Heinie Groh, Red McQuillan, (?) Gross. *Middle row, left to right:* Hack Wilson, Casey Stengel, Jack Scott, Art Nehf, Hugh Jennings, John McGraw, Cozy Dolan, Dave Bancroft, Alex Gaston, Irish Meusel, Parker (trainer). *Back row, left to right:* George Kelly, Jimmy O'Connell, John Watson, Travis Jackson, Bill Ryan, Jack Bentley, (?) McGuire, Hank Gowdy, Virgil Barnes, (?) Leete, Bill Cunningham, Kent Greenfield, Bill Terry, Frank Snyder. (NATIONAL BASEBALL LIBRARY)

Interior of the "modern" Polo Grounds (probably late 1940s). Note the center-field clubhouse and offices, and the bullpen shed in far left-center. (UNITED PRESS INTERNATIONAL AND NATIONAL BASEBALL LIBRARY)

McGraw greeting Rogers Hornsby, spring training, Sarasota, Florida, 1927. (NATIONAL BASEBALL LIBRARY)

John McGraw, 1925.
(NATIONAL BASEBALL
LIBRARY)

Charles A. Stone-
ham, about 1930.
(NATIONAL BASE-
BALL LIBRARY AND
ASSOCIATED PRESS)

Bill Terry at spring training, San
Antonio, 1930. (NATIONAL
BASEBALL LIBRARY)

Mel Ott, 1927. (NATIONAL BASEBALL LIBRARY)

John McGraw at Saratoga Springs race-
track, August 1932. (NATIONAL BASE-
BALL LIBRARY AND UNITED PRESS
INTERNATIONAL)

with the Federals, McGraw was unforgiving: "The Feds tried to wreck base ball. . . . If I had my way, those fellows would be left to die a natural death."[6]

McGraw's disposition toward the Federals didn't improve when he learned early in December that Marquard, still obligated for a season (at $8,000) under his two-year contract, had signed an affidavit for president Robert B. Ward of the Brooklyn Tip Tops swearing that he wasn't under contract to the Giants, and then had accepted a $1,500 advance against $10,000 the Federals would pay him for jumping. The Rube had pitched considerably better the past season than his 12–22 record, and McGraw still counted on him for 1915. Wrangling over Marquard's status continued all winter, until McGraw finally telephoned Ward his personal promise that the Giants would return the $1,500 he'd advanced to Marquard if the Tip Tops would give up their claim to the pitcher. Ward agreed to that, and the Rube found himself with nothing better to do than report to McGraw at Marlin.

The Marquard business clouded the off-season, but at least the first part of it was spent enjoyably. Along with the Mathewsons and John "Hans" Lobert, who'd been one of the "Giants" on the global trip and recently been obtained from Philadelphia for Al Demaree and Milton Stock, the McGraws were the guests in Havana of Tillinghast L'Hommedieu Huston. Coming to Cuba right after the war with Spain, Huston had served as an army engineer and then, as a civilian contractor, had made a fortune building roads, bridges, dams, and the like. He and McGraw had struck up a friendship during the Giants' 1911 Cuban visit. Two years later McGraw had helped bring Huston together with Jacob Ruppert, a wealthy New York brewer and sportsman, and then direct them to Frank Farrell when they sought to buy a major league franchise. By the start of the 1914 season, Ruppert and Huston owned the New York Yankees.

Besides wagering on the races at the Marinao track outside Havana and vainly trying to sign Armando Marsans away from the St. Louis Federals, McGraw took golf instruction from Mathewson at the Marinao country club. For the next ten years or so, McGraw would occasionally take to the links, but unlike numerous baseball people, he would never develop a passion for the new and rapidly growing pastime.

At Marlin in the spring of 1915, McGraw worked in the knowledge that, like the other National and American League managers, he would have to get along with four fewer players between the May cutdown and

September (when rookies could be brought up for trial). With overall attendance substantially down in both leagues in 1914, mainly because of competition from the Federals in Chicago, St. Louis, Brooklyn, and Pittsburgh, the National and American owners had voted to trim the regular rosters from twenty-five to twenty-one.

McGraw expected much from Bill Perritt (inevitably nicknamed "Pol"), a lanky right-hander who'd jumped from the St. Louis Cardinals to the Pittsburgh Feds, then decided he'd made a mistake. On the way to Marlin, between St. Louis and Texarkana, McGraw made a deal for Perritt with Cardinals manager Miller Huggins. At Texarkana, McGraw took another train south forty miles, still another one nine miles due east, then hired an automobile to transport him nine more miles over muddy roads to Perritt's house at Brice, Louisiana. After waiting in vain until nightfall for Perritt to show up, he instructed Perritt's wife to make sure he signed the contract St. Louis had mailed him (so McGraw's deal with Huggins could go through), and then got back in his hired car to resume his tortuous journey to Marlin. When he finally arrived there, he immediately dispatched Dick Kinsella to Louisiana to get Perritt. Two days later the scout materialized with Perritt in tow. Within a few weeks Bob Bescher went to the Cardinals to complete the deal for Perritt.

The whole episode, of little significance in itself, nonetheless illustrates a couple of salient facts about baseball in that day. First, it shows the lengths to which McGraw would go when he saw a chance to acquire needed talent. Second, despite being the most celebrated and highest-paid manager in baseball, indeed one of the most famous men in America, McGraw still had to do most of the important things himself. The Giants employed a club secretary and a treasurer, but in 1915 neither the Giants nor anybody else had what would later be called a general manager. McGraw was field manager and general manager rolled into one, as well as coach on the bases, scout, and just about anything else he needed to be. The baseball business of his time was a comparatively bare-bones operation.

One of McGraw's less onerous annual tasks was deciding how he wanted his team to look in the coming season. In 1915 he abandoned NYU violet and chose Philadelphia Athletics—style conical white caps with dark blue horizontal stripes, and also dark blue stockings. McGraw decided he would switch from vertical to horizontal pinstripes on the shirts and pants as well. The result was a uniform that reminded spectators of nothing so much as convict garb.

If, as McGraw always believed, a well-dressed baseball team played better, then the Giants' apparel may have had something to do with what happened to them that year. McGraw's 1915 club was the worst he ever managed, the only one to finish in last place. It was still a relatively young team, mostly the same players who'd won a pennant only two years earlier. But several key men—Mathewson, Marquard, Meyers, Snodgrass—had started to fade much faster than even McGraw had suspected. Matty's decline was the severest. At age thirty-four he'd finished the previous season with twenty-four wins. In 1915, though, troubled by back and shoulder pains, he would manage only eight victories against fourteen losses. For all practical purposes, his career had played itself out. (As had McGraw's hopes for Jim Thorpe, whom he sent to Jersey City early in the season.)

The season started promisingly enough, Tesreau easily handling Brooklyn before 25,000 at the Polo Grounds. The next day Marquard pitched a no-hitter against the Robins. Two days later, though, Philadelphia knocked around Mathewson, and on April 19 the Phillies' Al Demaree threw a shutout at the Giants, the first of several fine performances he would turn in against his old team over the coming two seasons.

New York quickly took possession of last place, and showed little inclination to vacate. With Red Murray no longer able to do the job and Fred Snodgrass in a woeful slump, McGraw needed outfield help. Dave Robertson, a broad-shouldered Virginian brought up in 1915, took over in right. For his new center-fielder, McGraw wanted little Benny Kauff, who the previous year, at the age of twenty-three, had led the Federal League with a .370 average and seventy-five stolen bases. Over the winter Kauff had gone to the Brooklyn Tip Tops. McGraw always maintained that both Ban Johnson and John Tener had encouraged him to go after Kauff, despite a National Commission rule against signing Federal Leaguers already under contract. When, on April 30, Kauff trotted out to center field at the Polo Grounds to start a game with the Boston Braves, Braves president James E. Gaffney ordered George Stallings to take his team off the field. At that moment umpire Mal Eason was on the telephone with Governor Tener, who agreed that Kauff, still under the three-year contract he'd signed at Indianapolis, was ineligible to play for the Giants. But by the time Eason got back to the field, Ernie Quigley, the other umpire, had announced a forfeit to New York. The next day Tener reaffirmed the National Commission's ruling on Federal contract-jumpers and not only overruled Quigley's forfeit but declared that what both Stallings and McGraw had agreed would be an exhibition game, following the forfeit, should be recorded as a 13–6 Braves victory.

McGraw was furious with just about everybody: Tener, Gaffney, the umpires, maybe most of all Ban Johnson, whom he blamed for instigating the abortive Kauff coup. With the forces arrayed against him, he protested, he had "no hope of success." But then "I got the worst of it back in 1908"; things hadn't changed in the National League.[7] Kauff, given a $2,000 raise (to $6,000) by Ward, returned to the Brooklyn Federals and again led the League in hitting and stolen bases.

When the cellar-bound Giants left for the West at the end of May, McGraw told his players to leave their wives at home and forbade them to drink even one glass of beer on the trip. Neither proscription made much difference in the team's lackluster play, but the ban on beer worked an especial hardship on Larry McLean. Called "Long Larry" because, at 6′ 5″, he was the tallest catcher in major league history, McLean had come to the Giants from St. Louis in the last part of the 1913 season when Chief Meyers was injured. Although he'd played with several different clubs and had a reputation as a "bad actor" (baseballese for problem player), McGraw had liked his work early on, especially in the 1913 World Series. After watching him catch four games and bat .500 in the Series, McGraw said that "McLean behaved like a man from the moment we got him. . . . He took a drink whenever he needed one, but that wasn't often. I found him easy to handle."[8]

Except for a few troubled moments, McLean and McGraw had gotten along all right since then—up to the present road trip. One warm evening in St. Louis, McGraw, Dick Kinsella, and a couple of players were sitting on the lawn of the elegant Buckingham Hotel when McLean, escorted by two "rough companions" and obviously drunk, walked up. Kinsella immediately rose and announced that he was going to bed. "Not unless you're carried there," roared McLean, who went on to accuse McGraw of welching on his promise to pay the big catcher a $1,000 bonus for good behavior, and Kinsella of tattling on him. McGraw told McLean to quiet down and go on up to bed, whereupon McLean lunged at the manager. Others tried to restrain him; Kinsella threatened to brain him with the thick leg of a chair broken in the melee. His courage suddenly gone, McLean ran into the street, jumped on the running board of a passing automobile, and disappeared.

When he reappeared at the Buckingham the next day, McLean found his luggage in the lobby, his name stricken from the hotel register, and a notice from McGraw that he was suspended indefinitely. Said McGraw, "I'm done with Larry McLean. He will never play with New York again."[9] McGraw was as good as his word. Willing to give Bugs Raymond, Mike Donlin, and other bad actors another chance, McGraw wouldn't forgive McLean, despite Long Larry's tearful entreaties. After going on another bender, McLean wandered back East and joined a Philadelphia semi-pro ball club. He would drop out of sight for the next six years, until brief notices in the sporting press that, at the age of thirty-nine, he'd been shot and killed in a brawl with a Boston saloon-keeper.

Late in June the Giants finally climbed out of the cellar. On July 17 they reached .500, and the next day, by beating St. Louis, they took over fourth place. That day Ernie Quigley chased McGraw for the third time in four days. Then Pittsburgh came into the Polo Grounds, swept a double-header, and pretty well squelched whatever hopes the Giants may have had for a strong finish. They did rise as high as fourth again, on August 3, when their record stood at 49–47 after they'd played thirteen games in seven days.

That stretch seemed to exhaust McGraw's club, maybe even McGraw as well. No matter how much he might tongue-lash his players, they didn't give him what he wanted. "McGraw has never been an easy boss," commented the *Sporting News*, "but now he is more severe than ever before." McGraw fined team captain Larry Doyle for cutting off a throw from the outfield that might have beaten a runner to home plate, benched and then peddled to Boston Fred Snodgrass after he loafed running out a ground ball, and gave Red Murray his outright release. At the same time, McGraw seemed to lapse into the kind of apathy he'd shown on previous occasions when he wasn't winning. "The aggressiveness has departed from McGraw," observed *Sporting Life* in August, "and . . . the Giants haven't the fighting spirit to get up and win out this season." Sid Keener, a young St. Louis reporter, noted that McGraw had deserted the coaching lines and seemed generally subdued. "The Giants don't look like the Giants," wrote Keener, "without McGraw fussing at every close decision that goes against the Giants and the Giants of today don't look like the Giants that won pennants and played in World Series."[10]

In mid-August four straight losses at Pittsburgh and Brooklyn dropped the Giants into sixth place. Later that month, after four defeats in a row at St. Louis, they were back in the cellar. When Marquard, struggling with a 9–8 record, asked McGraw to trade him, the manager replied contemptuously, "Who would take you? . . . You couldn't lick a postage stamp."[11] McGraw did put the left-hander on waivers, but he went unclaimed. Scheduled to spend the rest of the season at Newark in the International League, Marquard called up Wilbert Robinson in Brooklyn and arranged his own sale to the Robins for $7,500, the figure McGraw had named.

Waiting out the end of his most dismal season in baseball, McGraw was in a surly mood. Umpire Cy Rigler chased him and nineteen others from the dugout in the nightcap of a double-header defeat at Pittsburgh, and after another twin loss at brand-new Braves Field in Boston, McGraw tripped a particularly rowdy fan who was leaving the ballpark, called him "a yellow cur," and drew his pocketknife. Others stepped in to break up what might have become a truly ugly incident.[12]

New York ended the season by pummeling the Braves 15–8, with Larry Doyle making four hits to win the National League batting title with a .320 average. Having a batting champion on his team for the first time was small solace for McGraw. At 69–83 the Giants trailed seventh-place Cincinnati by one game. They'd finished only three and one-half games behind fourth-place Chicago, twenty-one behind the pennant-winning Philadelphia Phillies. For McGraw, though, a strong last-place finish was still last place—an intolerable circumstance.

Saying he'd seen enough baseball for one year, McGraw stayed in and around New York during the World Series, in which the Boston Red Sox easily defeated the Phillies. At the Series and elsewhere, there was much talk of a settlement with the Federal League and of the possible sale of the Giants to Harry Sinclair and James Gaffney, who'd recently sold his interest in the Boston Braves.

The settlement with the Federals did materialize. After two years of financial losses, the Federal League owners were ready to capitulate and recoup as much as they could by selling ballplayers to the National and American clubs. Charles Weeghman, president of the Chicago Whales, and Philip de Catesby Ball, who'd operated the St. Louis Terriers, gained permission to buy the Chicago Cubs and St. Louis Browns, respectively. Weeghman then moved his new ball club out of wooden West Side Park and into the steel-and-concrete facility he'd had built for the Whales, on the city's Near North Side.

Harry Hempstead's reported price tag for the 62 percent of the Giants stock held by John T. Brush's heirs was $390,000. Whether Sinclair and Gaffney ever actively sought control of the Giants is questionable; the whole idea may have been mostly a product of the overactive imagination of various sportswriters, particularly Joe Vila. At any rate, rumors of the ball club's sale pointed up what a valuable property it had become since the days of Andrew Freedman (who died that winter in New York at the age of fifty-five).

Even though he didn't buy into the Giants, Sinclair did well in the disposition of former Federal League players. Seeking new talent wherever he could find it, McGraw was only too happy to pay Sinclair $50,000 for the contracts of catcher Bill Rariden, infielder Bill McKechnie, and outfielder Edd Roush, who'd all played at Newark in 1915, as well as pitcher Fred Anderson and at last Benny Kauff. Sinclair had shrewdly acquired the rights to Anderson, a nineteen-game winner with the Buffalo Federals, and Kauff, the star of Brooklyn's seventh-place finishers in the now-defunct league. Meanwhile McGraw sent Chief Meyers to join Marquard on the Brooklyn Robins. After all that, and after two attacks of influenza, McGraw took Blanche to Cuba for a couple of weeks of sun, golf, and gambling.

Benny Kauff, a brash young man from the southeastern Ohio coal fields, was delighted to be a Giant and play for John McGraw. He intended, he said, to become the Ty Cobb of the National League. McGraw liked Kauff, too, liked his cocksureness, his honest conviction that he was the best ballplayer going. Kauff, said McGraw, was "a player of the old school. He thinks and lives baseball. That's the way I did when I was a youngster. That's the way all the old Orioles felt toward the game. There aren't many players like that today."[13] It didn't even bother McGraw a great deal that, besides the $6,000 a year for the next two years the Giants would pay Kauff, he insisted on getting $5,000 out of what Sinclair had received for his contract. McGraw ended up giving him that amount in lump sum, out of the Giants treasury.

Kauff descended on Marlin, Texas, with a trunkload of bats (fifty-two in all), a pocketful of money, and a hearty greeting for everybody. Edd Roush, on the other hand, wasn't at all happy. A small-town Indiana boy, he didn't like New York, didn't like what he'd heard about McGraw, and, when he got to know his manager, still didn't like him. An extraordinarily independent-minded young man, Roush at first refused to sign the contract McGraw had sent him, then gave in and went to spring training. But he remained unhappy.

One of the pleasant features of that spring for McGraw was the chance to get together with Hughey Jennings, whose Detroit Tigers were training about seventy-five miles north, at Waxahachie, Texas. The people at

Marlin were sadly disappointed when the Tigers came down for a game minus Ty Cobb, who as usual hadn't yet arrived for spring training. Cobb did appear in Houston in time to play against the Giants and Benny Kauff. An overflow crowd turned out for what had been touted as a confrontation between baseball's reigning star and the man who claimed to be just as good. Cobb put on a fine show for the Texas fans, rapping two doubles and stealing two bases in Detroit's 7–1 victory. Kauff doubled once himself but dropped a fly ball and seemed generally unsure in center field.

Tastefully attired in navy-blue-trimmed uniforms, with no pinstripes running in any direction, the Giants began the season at Philadelphia by losing to Grover Cleveland Alexander, now unquestionably the National League's premier pitcher. McGraw had four former Federal Leaguers in the starting lineup: Kauff in center field, Roush in right, Rariden behind the plate, and Anderson on the mound. A few days later Bill McKechnie, still another ex-Fed, occupied third in the absence of Hans Lobert, who'd broken his leg in the annual pre-season game against Yale University.

McGraw's Giants were obviously a team in transition. Only Merkle, Doyle, Burns, Fletcher, Tesreau, and Mathewson remained from the 1913 ball club. On May 9 New York was in last place with a 2–13 record and seemed to be going nowhere. In his season's debut five days earlier, Matty had pitched courageously, yielding fourteen hits to Boston but holding on until Kauff's error lost his game in the tenth inning. However much he might think of Mathewson personally, McGraw knew that his friend's usefulness had come to an end.

Mathewson's decline was one reason for McGraw's unhappiness in the early going; bad umpiring, at least as he saw it, was another. After Bill Klem ran him out of a game on April 27 at Boston, McGraw waited under the grandstand and let go a torrent of obscenities when Klem walked by on the way to the officials' dressing room. Klem sprang at McGraw, only to be grabbed by his partner Bob Emslie and dragged away.

The 1916 Giants were a team that played strange, streaky baseball. Disgusted with their performance so far, McGraw announced that no wives, not even his own wife, would be allowed on road trips. Then the ball club left New York and won seventeen straight games, nineteen of twenty-one. Returning only a half game behind Wilbert Robinson's league-leading Brooklyns, the Giants proceeded to lose ten of fifteen at the Polo Grounds.

That would be the general pattern until September. For some mysterious reason, the Giants were a far better team on the road than at home that year. A bewildered McGraw went so far as to have a green screen hung in front of the center-field bleachers at the Polo Grounds, theorizing that the masses of white shirts in the bleachers kept his batters from seeing the ball well. The Giants still could score only twice in dropping a double-header to Philadelphia.

Drifting between fourth and fifth place, McGraw started to reconstruct his ball club in mid-season. When Garry Herrmann at Cincinnati fired Buck Herzog and sought Mathewson as his new manager, McGraw was willing to give Matty his release and throw in Edd Roush and Bill McKechnie, in exchange for getting the prickly Herzog's services for the third time.

At the time McGraw was widely praised for his generosity in clearing the way for the great pitcher to move into the managerial ranks. The two would remain good friends, but it's possible that McGraw was at least mildly irked at Mathewson for a piece published under his name in the mass-circulation magazine *Everybody's* in the fall of 1914. Mathewson had attributed the Giants' three straight losses in the World Series to their being "a team of puppets worked from the bench by a string." Unable to take the initiative, always looking to McGraw to find out what to do, the New York players had committed a succession of blunders, misjudgments, and errors that had cost them the Series. Connie Mack's players, trained to think for themselves and "stand alone no matter how big the crisis," had held together and played steady baseball, whereas the Giants had fallen apart at critical moments.[14]

Whatever McGraw may have thought about Matty's published views on his managing style, he had little reason to keep a thirty-six-year-old pitcher who'd won only four times in thirteen starts. And he wanted Herzog for his infield. Herzog probably had mixed feelings about returning to a ball club where he'd never liked the manager; at the same time, McGraw had always paid him well and now he would make $10,000 a year under a three-year contract. Mathewson's feelings were very mixed. Roush would recall that on the train to Cincinnati from Chicago (where New York had been playing when the deal was concluded), Matty kept saying that the Giants had been his home and he hated to leave,

that he thought the world of McGraw and would always be grateful to
him for making it possible for him to manage. As for Roush himself, "I
couldn't have been happier."[15]

The Giants' record was 40–41 on July 21, when Herzog's clutch single
in his first reappearance with McGraw's team beat the Cubs at Chicago.
A month later New York was two games below .500, and McGraw decided
to make more changes. Fred Merkle went to Brooklyn for catcher Lew
McCarty; Larry Doyle went to Chicago for infielder Henry "Heinie"
Zimmerman. Although he'd hated to part with Merkle and Doyle, McGraw
said, both had "slowed up badly and I had to tear the old club apart to
build up a winner."[16] His new infield consisted of Walter Holke, purchased from Rochester of the International League, at first base; Herzog
at second; Art Fletcher at shortstop; and Zimmerman at third. Burns,
Kauff, and Dave Robertson now made up the outfield; Rariden still
handled most of the catching duties; and Tesreau, Anderson, and left-
handers John "Rube" Benton, Ferdie Schupp, and Harry "Slim" Sallee
(purchased separately from Cincinnati at the time of the Mathewson deal)
did nearly all the pitching in the second half of the season.

"The Great Zim," as Zimmerman liked to refer to himself, was another
in the long succession of McGraw's bad actors—ballplayers he was
willing to take on after others had given up in exasperation. Not a hard
drinker, Zimmerman played episodically, showing bursts of brilliance
followed by periods of lassitude. In 1912 the native New Yorker had
led the National League in batting with a .372 average and belted an
extraordinary fourteen home runs. But he'd fallen off to .265 by 1915,
and this season he'd been so unreliable that he was under a ten-day
suspension for "laying down on the job" when McGraw made the deal
for him with Chicago manager Joe Tinker.[17]

McGraw's new ball club won twenty-seven of its last thirty-one games.
Twenty-six of those victories came in a row, beginning with Schupp's
win at Brooklyn on September 8. It was a dazzling run, especially for
the New York pitchers. Over one stretch of twenty-one games, they
allowed a grand total of thirty runs. Pol Perritt, never known for his
ruggedness, pitched and won both ends of a double-header with Philadelphia at the Polo Grounds, reviving memories in veteran fans of Iron
Man McGinnity's exploits. Those fans, as well as newer ones, packed
the big horseshoe day after day as the Giants, finally playing well at
home, won day after day. "The Giants," remarked the widely syndicated

political cartoonist "Tad" Dorgan, "remind me of a fighter who has been knocked out going down the aisle licking everybody in the house." McGraw called his present outfit "in many respects, the greatest baseball team I have managed in my fourteen years at the head of the organization."[18]

The record-setting streak ended on September 30, when Boston overcame Benton, who was trying to match Perritt's feat in the nightcap of a double-header after shutting out the Braves in the opener. Yet after winning twenty-six games in a row, the Giants still were only in fourth place. They might have beaten out Boston for third if they'd taken at least three of the four games they played at the end of the season with Brooklyn. Instead they dropped three of four, Wilbert Robinson's club edged Philadelphia for the pennant, and John McGraw kicked up still another big controversy that would carry over into the off-season.

After Brooklyn's Jack Coombs outdueled Schupp 2–0 at the Polo Grounds on Monday, October 2, the two teams moved to Ebbets Field for the final three games of the season. On Tuesday the Robins clinched the National League flag by beating New York 9–6 while Boston swept a double-header at Philadelphia. At the end of the fifth inning at Ebbets Field, with Brooklyn ahead 6–5, McGraw left the New York dugout and didn't return for the rest of the game. "They missed my signs, displayed miserable judgment in every department of play, and almost turned the game into a farce," he told Sid Mercer of the New York *Globe* right after the game. "I don't intend to take any of the blame. If the Giants are criticized, that is their lookout—not mine." The next day he talked with a group of reporters and accused his men of "indifferent playing" and ignoring his instructions. Especially when Perritt took a long, slow windup with Brooklyn runners on base, "I lost my patience. Such baseball disgusted me, and I left the bench. . . . I refused to be connected with it." Although McGraw had begun with the disclaimer "I do not say that my players did not try to win," it was hard to see any other meaning in his words.[19]

Every Giant queried by newsmen denied letting down against the Robins; Art Fletcher was the most vehement: "It's a damned lie!" But *Sporting Life*, among other observers, noted that what should have been easy ground balls got by the New York infielders, that the Giants ran the bases carelessly, that Perritt did in fact wind up with men on base. Grantland Rice of the New York *Tribune* thought the Giants had been "careless, listless, slipshod" throughout the game. Boston had played all out against the Phillies, whereas the New Yorkers had "failed to hustle as much as they would in an exhibition game."[20]

For public consumption, Wilbert Robinson said that "Manager McGraw's suspicions in this matter are ridiculous. His statement is very unsportsmanlike." Privately Robbie growled, "He pissed on my pennant." Ban Johnson couldn't resist the chance to slam his old enemy. "McGraw's action," pontificated Johnson, "was as cowardly as if the captain of an ocean liner were to quit in an emergency." Joe Vila agreed that while the New York manager's behavior had been "righteous," it had also been "decidedly ill-timed and entirely unnecessary."[21]

Yet like Grantland Rice and practically every other writer who witnessed the game in question, Vila thought the Giants hadn't done their best. Maybe they'd celebrated too much after their twenty-sixth victory, Vila suggested. Sam Crane of the *Evening Journal* was convinced that the Giants' "deep sentiment for their old pal" Robinson had caused them to let down. Young Jack Kofoed, in *Sporting Life*, pooh-poohed that argument, pointing out that seven of the twelve men who'd appeared in the Giants lineup on October 3 hadn't even been with the team in 1913, Robbie's last year as McGraw's coach. To Kofoed, frayed nerves and exhaustion after the twenty-six-game streak seemed a more likely explanation. Harry Dix Cole, another New York writer, claimed that going into the Brooklyn series, McGraw had received a number of telegrams warning that baseball's integrity would be in question unless New York won all four games. McGraw had held a team meeting, exhorted his men to play as hard as they could, and offered cash bonuses if they finished in third place. After Brooklyn won the first game, "the peppery leader was at white heat" during the October 3 contest. From Cincinnati, J. Ed Grillo gave still another hypothesis for McGraw's conduct: He'd lost as much as $15,000 betting on a third-place finish.[22]

Whatever was behind the Giants' shoddy play that day, McGraw would have nothing more to do with the team for what remained of the season. Leaving Herzog in charge in Brooklyn, he took in a Yankees-Washington game at the Polo Grounds, then left with Blanche by train for Baltimore, or, in McGraw's case, mostly the racetrack at Laurel, Maryland. New York won Wednesday's game at Ebbets Field, then lost the season closer on Thursday to finish with an 86–66 record, three games out of third place. With McGraw nowhere in sight, the players canceled their plans to present an expensive edition of Shakespeare's works to their manager in a ceremony at Ebbets Field, in commemoration of the twenty-six-game streak. They ended up mailing the set to his apartment.

Despite John Tener's publicly expressed preference for forgetting the whole matter, McGraw's accusations wouldn't go away. Seconded by various sportswriters, manager Pat Moran of the dethroned Phillies demanded that the National League conduct a thorough inquiry. Right after the World Series (won by the Boston Red Sox in five games from Brooklyn), Tener announced that the League's board of directors would take up McGraw's charges at the December meeting. But when that gathering took place, nothing at all happened. Having remained in New York since the end of October to testify if needed, McGraw waited all day in the hallway outside the room at the Waldorf-Astoria where the owners were meeting, but was never called in. That was the end of that. A couple of weeks later John and Blanche McGraw were off to Cuba.

When McGraw assembled his returnees and rookies at Marlin in the spring of 1917, the state of Texas was no longer in a condition of high anxiety over the prospect of war with Mexico, as had been the case a year earlier. The U.S. forces under General John J. Pershing that had plunged into northern Mexico in pursuit of the rapacious guerrilla leader Pancho Villa now were withdrawing, their expedition having failed to find Villa's army but having almost brought on full-scale conflict with the Mexican government. Now, though, the administration of President Woodow Wilson had moved the country to the verge of war with Imperial Germany. Wilson's April 2 war message to Congress was the culmination of a long series of events, of which the torpedoing of the British liner *Lusitania* two years earlier, with the loss of more than a hundred American lives, had been one of the most critical. On April 6 Congress voted overwhelmingly for war.

Meanwhile, professional baseball readied for another season, as if all that was taking place on another planet. With the Giants' spectacular late-season play in mind, the odds-makers had established them as solid favorites for the 1917 National League pennant. Apparently having forgiven his men for whatever it was they'd done in that October 3 game, McGraw was basically satisfied with his material and had left it intact over the winter. Showing his continuing happiness with McGraw's leadership, Harry Hempstead met the team at San Antonio when it played an exhibition game with the local Texas Leaguers and signed him to a new contract, even though he still had a year to go on his old one. Providing for a straight salary of $40,000 per year plus a share of the franchise's profits, the new agreement made McGraw the highest-paid person in baseball, whether manager, player, or league president.

On March 31, in Dallas, the Giants met the Detroit Tigers in the second of what was intended to be a dozen or so exhibition games the teams would play as they moved north together. In the second inning the ferocious Ty Cobb slammed into second base and knocked over Buck Herzog, ripping Herzog's pants and inflicting a minor spike wound. Cobb and Herzog and subsequently Art Fletcher as well flailed and rolled around for a bit before they were pulled apart. At McGraw's insistence, Bill Brennan, accused of favoring the Giants when he'd umpired in the National League, ordered Cobb out of the game. Despite Hughey Jennings' demands, he wouldn't also eject Herzog and Fletcher.[23] Cobb remained on the Tigers bench for the remainder of the game and periodically exhanged epithets with McGraw across the diamond.

That night, in Cobb's room at the Oriental Hotel, Herzog and Cobb staged a memorable fist fight that ended only when the Detroit trainer, acting as referee, stepped in to keep Cobb from beating his foe to death. The next morning, in the hotel lobby, McGraw cornered Cobb and cursed him roundly. Somehow keeping his rage under control, Cobb finally walked out after telling the Giants manager that he would kill him if McGraw were a younger man.

Complaining that "McGraw is a mucker and always has been and I don't intend to stand for his dirty work," Cobb refused to play in the rest of the Tigers-Giants series.[24] The teams split up anyway after snow flurries kept them from playing at Kansas City. Then the whole New York team, including McGraw, sarcastically wired Cobb, in Cincinnati waiting for the Tigers, that inasmuch as the Giants had left, it was safe for him to rejoin his teammates.

Once the season began, the Giants won six of their first seven games at Boston and Brooklyn. For six weeks they remained bunched with various teams; then on Memorial Day they swept a morning-afternoon double-header from Philadelphia before an overflow at the Polo Grounds and moved into first place. McGraw's Giants of 1917 weren't a great ball club by any means. Schupp, Sallee, Benton, Perritt, Anderson, and a fading Tesreau were a fair assortment of pitchers, but only fair. Rariden and McCarty weren't in a class with Chief Meyers or Roger Bresnahan in their primes. The infield of Holke, Herzog, Fletcher, and Zimmerman was pretty solid, and the Great Zim would drive in more runs that year (107) than anybody else in either league. But McGraw's only .300 hitters were George Burns (.302), who usually led off, and Benny Kauff, who would rebound from a poor first season in the National League to bat .308 and steal thirty bases. Dave Robertson's twelve home runs would lead the majors, but the Virginian would manage only a .259 batting average. Kauff and Robertson, moreover, were below par defensively.

In leading that basically mediocre team to a pennant, McGraw, at the age of forty-four, probably did the best managing job of his career. In the process he demonstrated that he was still the same John J. McGraw many had admired and many others had despised for a quarter-century. Early in the spring the New York *American* offered the view that in recent years McGraw had undergone "a vast change in his temperament. He is not the fire-eater of old. He has grown gray and tolerant—or at least more tolerant."[25] Events of that summer, though, would prove that rumors of McGraw's softer temperament had been greatly exaggerated.

Christy Mathewson's Cincinnati Reds, with Hal Chase on first, Edd Roush (whose .341 would lead the league that year) in center field, and Henry "Heinie" Groh, another ex-Giant, at third, had suddenly become a tough ball club. On June 6, the day designated for every male American from eighteen to forty-five to register for the recently created military draft system, the Giants lost 6–5 at Redland Field. In the course of the Registration Day game, umpire Bill Byron ejected McGraw and Hans Lobert for arguing that Roush had interfered with McCarty's throw to second on a Cincinnati steal attempt. Byron also chased four Reds for disputing ball and strike calls.

It was a fairly typical day for "Lord" Byron, as his detractors often called him. Byron was an interesting and colorful man, an umpire who liked to hum while he worked and sometimes would break into song with such lyrics as "You'll have to learn before you're older / You can't hit the ball with the bat on your shoulder."[26] But Byron wasn't a good umpire. Known for having a "quick fuse," he led the National League year after year in player ejections. He and McGraw had tangled numerous times, and neither had any use for the other.

On June 7 Slim Sallee coasted to victory behind ten New York runs in a game that was generally free of strife with the umpires. But the next day, in the sixth inning, Hal Chase veered out of the baseline to run into Fletcher and cause him to throw wildly to first, trying for a double play. McGraw charged out to claim interference; after several minutes of arguing with Ernie Quigley (working the bases) and umpire-in-chief Byron, both McGraw and Fletcher were banished. McGraw retired to a position behind an iron gate back of third base and continued to direct his team from there.

In the bottom of the ninth Jim Thorpe, whose contract McGraw had sold to the Reds some weeks earlier, singled off Fred Anderson to drive in the winning run. As the umpires came through the gate behind third on the way to their dressing quarters, McGraw confronted Byron. Pieced together from the reports of several witnesses, their colloquy went like this:

McGRAW: "Take your hands out of your pockets and I'll show you who's the better man."

BYRON: "You're a fine man to talk, when you were run out of Baltimore."

McGRAW: "Do you say that I was run out of Baltimore?"

BYRON: "That's what they say about you."

McGRAW: "Well, don't *you* say that about me."

BYRON: "Well, you *were* run out of Baltimore."[27]

At that, McGraw started swinging, landing at least one blow that cut the umpire's chin. A groundskeeper named Marty Schwab tried to separate them, only to be struck from behind by Bill Rariden and then punched and kicked as he lay on the concrete runway. Other Giants hustled McGraw and Rariden to the visitors' dressing room. In burst a policeman, sent by Reds president Garry Herrmann to arrest McGraw and Rariden. Mathewson arrived, managed to get everybody quieted, and then left to find Herrmann, whom he eventually convinced that the Giants' speedy and safe departure from town would be the best thing all around. Meanwhile, McGraw left the ballpark, found a nearby notary public, and made a sworn statement that Byron had cursed him. Rariden, Holke, and several others who'd allegedly heard everything also signed the statement.

The next morning McGraw awoke in Chicago to learn that John Tener had put him under sixteen days' suspension and fined him $500, the heaviest monetary penalty levied on any player or manager up to that time. McGraw had nothing to say for public consumption in Chicago or on a stopover at Wellsville, New York, where the local citizenry had arranged a parade and other festivities in honor of the most famous alumnus of the local minor league team. At Pittsburgh he said that he would pay the fine but that, when he returned to New York, he wanted the League to investigate what had really happened in Cincinnati. Then, in his hotel room at the Schenley, in the presence of Frank J. Finley, a local physician who'd known him in Baltimore in the nineties; Urban L. McAnerny, another Pittsburgh acquaintance; and the New York *Globe*'s Sid Mercer, one of his strongest partisans among the baseball writers, he unloaded his burden of bitter feeling.

The National League, he said, had become the "Pennsylvania league," presided over by a politican in Harrisburg who didn't attend to his job and was biased in favor of the Philadelphia Phillies. Everybody in the League was out to get the Giants; McGraw couldn't get a fair hearing anywhere. Mercer, a newsman first and last, knew a good story when he found it. He left McGraw's room, returned in a few minutes, and handed McGraw a typescript of an article built around the manager's assertions. According to what McAnerny and Finley (and in part McGraw himself) later testified, Mercer sought approval from McGraw, who held the sheets of paper in his hand for a moment without reading them and then said, "I don't give a damn what you say for me. Go as far as you like. I guess it's all right. Life isn't worth while worrying about little things like this."²⁸

Not only did Mercer's article appear in the *Globe*; he shared its essential contents beforehand with colleagues on three other New York dailies, so that within a couple of days McGraw's remarks had become a cause célèbre. On June 18, with the Giants back in town, the National League presidents met in New York to look into the whole business. After upholding Tener's action in fining and suspending McGraw, they ordered the Giants manager to appear the next morning to explain his reported slur on the League's chief executive.

It wasn't one of McGraw's bravest moments. When he came before the magnates at 10:00 A.M., he submitted a signed statement repudiating everything attributed to him in "certain scurrilous newspaper articles under the date of June 14. . . . I did not make these statements or give out by intimation any utterance that might be construed to in any way reflect upon the ability, honesty and integrity of the President of the league."²⁹ Harry Hempstead then assured the other club owners that McGraw had signed the statement under no coercion whatsoever. After that they voted to declare the affair officially closed.

By June 25 McGraw was back in uniform, at Philadelphia, in time to see Eppa Rixey throw a two-hit shutout to drop the Giants a half game behind the Phillies. Two weeks later, though, New York swept a doubleheader from defending champion Brooklyn (now floundering in sixth place) and moved out to a four-game lead over Philadelphia. On

July 4, when the Robins wistfully raised their 1916 pennant in pre-game ceremonies at Ebbets Field, McGraw and Tener shook hands and smilingly posed for cameramen.

But the string of troublesome events that had begun with McGraw's attack on Bill Byron hadn't come to an end. Outraged by McGraw's repudiation of what Sid Mercer not only had heard him say but, so Mercer contended, he'd personally okayed before Mercer published anything, the New York chapter of the Base Ball Writers' Association of America demanded that the League reopen its investigation. By that time, as Joe Vila sneeringly observed, three writers had disavowed what they themselves had written, based on Mercer's account. The *Sporting News* was unkind enough to point out that back in 1912 Horace Fogel had been banned from the National League for saying not a great deal more than McGraw had.

The BBWAA's pressure was eventually enough to bring the club owners together one more time. On July 20 McGraw, Frank Finley, Urban McAnerny, Mercer, and three other reporters testified under questioning by John Montgomery Ward, McGraw's attorney, and Martin W. Littleton, retained by the BBWAA. It came down to McGraw's word versus Mercer's, specifically McGraw's claim that he hadn't read what Mercer showed him versus Mercer's insistence that he had. Late that afternoon the club presidents adjourned, saying that they would render their ruling sometime in the next few weeks.

For those who'd followed McGraw's career and watched him in one imbroglio after another, the Byron-Tener-Mercer episode possibly had shown him at his most foolish so far. The New York fans, though, seemed totally unconcerned about the controversy in the press over who'd said or read what and when. As McGraw took his station in the coaching box at the Polo Grounds on July 7, at the start of a double-header with St. Louis, they cheered him wildly for several minutes. New York won both of those games to extend its lead over the Phillies. By the time the Giants closed their home stand on July 24, they led by eight and a half over Cincinnati, which had briefly moved into second place.

At the beginning of September the National League owners finally disposed of McGraw's case, fining him $1,000 (which superseded the earlier, still unpaid $500 fine) and officially reprimanding him. When the punishment was made public, spectators gave him sustained ovations not only at the Polo Grounds but at Ebbets Field as well. The Giants swept on to McGraw's sixth pennant, with the suspension of Buck Herzog, who'd refused to make the final road trip and gone home to Maryland complaining of a back injury, being about the only unpleasantness in the last part of the season. On September 24, Slim Sallee scattered seven hits at St. Louis in pitching the pennant clincher, and nine days later, at Philadelphia, the Giants closed the season on a high note, sweeping a double-header to finish at 98–56, eleven ahead of the Phillies.

McGraw lifted Herzog's suspension in time for the World Series. The Giants' opponents were the Chicago White Sox, managed by Clarence "Pants" Rowland. Rowland had never played major league ball and been taken as something of a joke when Charles Comiskey hired him in 1915. But with the brilliant Eddie Collins, unloaded by Connie Mack, and the great Joe Jackson, obtained from Cleveland, sparking the team and Red Faber and Eddie Cicotte emerging as top pitchers, Rowland's White Sox had finished third and then second. This year they'd won 100 games to outdistance defending champion Boston.

The White Sox were stronger in just about every way than McGraw's ball club. Maybe seeking to counter the left-handed batting prowess of Collins, Jackson, and third-baseman George "Buck" Weaver, McGraw started a left-hander in every game. Overall, Sallee, Schupp, and Benton pitched well, holding Chicago to an average of 3.5 runs per game. But Rowland's pitchers—mainly Cicotte and Faber—were even better.

The first two games, played before capacity crowds of 32,000 at Comiskey Park, went to the White Sox. A home run by Oscar "Happy" Felsch won the Series opener 2–1, Cicotte over Sallee. Jackson and Weaver led the attack the next day, as Chicago knocked around Schupp and Anderson for a 7–2 victory behind Faber. In New York on October 10, Benton pitched a five-hit shutout to best Cicotte 2–0, and Kauff's two homers behind more shutout pitching, by Schupp, evened the Series the next day. Back in Chicago the teams combined for twenty-six hits in an 8–5 White Sox victory, with Collins's single in the eighth inning scoring the go-ahead run off Sallee. Rowland and Fletcher almost came to blows when first Herzog and then Fletcher got in Weaver's way as he ran from first to third in the sixth inning.

Two days later, at the Polo Grounds, McGraw watched his Giants lose the World's Series for the fourth time in four tries since 1911. Faber held New York to six hits and two runs, while the White Sox scored four runs off Benton and Perritt, all unearned. In the top of the fourth inning occurred one of those critical mishaps that plagued McGraw throughout his years in New York. With Collins on third, Jackson on first, and nobody out, Felsch hit a high bounder right back at Benton. The pitcher whipped the ball to Zimmerman at third, catching Collins well off the bag. As Rariden moved up the line to take Zimmerman's throw and box Collins in, the lightning-quick Collins scooted past the catcher and headed for home. With the plate unattended by anybody except umpire Bill Klem, Zimmerman had no choice but to give chase. Collins scored yards ahead of the desperate Zimmerman, as, inexplicably, Benton stood near the mound and Holke remained near first base. That run put Chicago ahead to stay. Afterward, when reporters asked him why he'd pursued Collins and not thrown the ball, the Great Zim asked in return, "Who the hell was I going to throw the ball to, Klem?"[30]

It was a fair question, one nobody, least of all Benton or Holke, was prepared to answer. Again the Giants had to settle for the losers' shares out of the Series receipts. Some people questioned why McGraw started all left-handers and particularly why he'd left Sallee in while the White Sox scored five times in game five. McGraw himself was furious with Buck Herzog. Afterward he told Fred Lieb in confidence that he was convinced Herzog hadn't played the series honestly, that he'd consistently been out of position on the White Sox batters. McGraw had no proof, though, so he kept quiet. In the off-season he sent the troublesome infielder to the Boston Braves for Larry Doyle (only recently traded from Chicago) and pitcher Jess Barnes.

Baseball's first full wartime season had ended with the sport—at least at the major league level—little affected by the slow-moving mobilization of the nation's manpower and resources. A difficult season was in the offing, though. And then, having endured the ravages of war, baseball would pass through the most critical time in its history in the early post-war years. They wouldn't be easy years for John McGraw, either.

Nine

WAR, SCANDAL, AND CHARLES STONEHAM

DESPITE THE UNPRECEDENTED and unpredictable circumstances of a world war, the National Commission and the club owners in the two major leagues decided to go ahead with business as usual for 1918. They agreed to play another full 154-game schedule and keep the twenty-five-man roster limits (which had been restored after the Federal League's extinction). Fearful of declining attendances and reduced revenues, they did limit to two weeks the amount of time the teams would spend in spring-training camp, and some clubs would train closer to home. Otherwise Organized Baseball made no concessions to the war, even though several minor leagues had folded after the 1917 season and numerous ballplayers faced conscription.

John and Blanche McGraw also proceeded pretty much as usual. By late January they were again in Havana. McGraw spent most of his days at the Cuban-American Jockey Club and the Oriental Park track. At night, usually in Blanche's company, he went to such favorite spots as Dos Hermanos and a restaurant run by José Abeal, who served his *arroz con pollo* so unfastidiously that McGraw gave his place the enduring appellation "Sloppy Joe's."

Back in New York by late February, McGraw set to work getting signatures on the contracts sent to several players who wanted more money and were talking holdout. On his own he traveled to Gloversville, New York, to sign George Burns; to Higginsport, Ohio, for Slim Sallee; to Louisville for Ferdie Schupp; to Collinsville, Illinois, for Art Fletcher; to Norfolk, Virginia, for the news that Dave Robertson preferred to work for the U.S. Secret Service rather than the New York Giants. McGraw was also willing to take another chance on Jim Thorpe, recently released by Cincinnati. Although he'd become the outstanding performer and biggest gate attraction in the inchoate sport of professional football, Thorpe had managed only a .225 career average in parts of four seasons in big league baseball.

As the manager of the wealthiest club in baseball, McGraw saw no reason why the Giants ought to train any closer to New York than Marlin, Texas. On the morning of March 15, 1918, when his players, after their mile walk out from the Arlington Hotel, arrived at Marlin's little baseball park, they found McGraw already on the scene, hitting grounders and flies to a dozen or so local black kids scattered over the field.

The brightest newcomer on hand was Ross Youngs, who hadn't quite reached his twenty-first birthday. For some reason, the New York writers immediately dropped the "s" from his name, so that he would always be known to the baseball public as "Ross Young." Originally purchased by the Giants after he'd led the Western Association in batting in 1915, Youngs had been at Marlin the previous spring before McGraw assigned him to Rochester, where the switch-hitter had pounded International League pitching for a .356 average. Short, thick-legged, fast, and smart, Youngs fit what had almost become McGraw's outfielder prototype, from Mike Donlin and Josh Devore to George Burns and Benny Kauff—and later Mel Ott. Like McGraw, Youngs was combative, dedicated, and intense (and also like McGraw, he would always be a sucker for down-and-outers with hard-luck stories). "If I ever saw a coming star on the Giants," McGraw told the reporters at Marlin, "it is Young."[1]

When a team from the Air Service pilot-training center at Waco came over to play the Giants a practice game, several officers performed stunts above the Marlin ballfield in their Curtiss biplanes. Following the game McGraw wedged himself into the forward seat of an aircraft that had landed in a nearby pasture, donned helmet and goggles, and flew with the pilot back to Waco, covering the twenty-six miles in twenty minutes. When he climbed down from the Curtiss, McGraw could boast of having done what as yet only a tiny fraction of his countrymen had dared.

In the opening weeks of the 1918 season, the New York Giants appeared to be ready to fly away from the rest of the National League. McGraw's fireplug outfield of Burns, Kauff, and Youngs, along with rejuvenated Larry Doyle, led the ball club to victory in its first nine games and eighteen of its first nineteen. But after losing Doyle, who'd been hitting .426, to malaria, the Giants won only five of fourteen in the western cities and settled into a battle for the lead with the Chicago

Cubs. Bert Niehoff, obtained from St. Louis to replace Doyle, soon broke his leg, and for most of the rest of the season McGraw had to rely on a youngster named Eddie Sicking to handle second base.

That was only one of McGraw's troubles in trying to keep a major league ball club on the field. Like most other managers that season, McGraw had to watch player after player either enter military service or take jobs in shipyards, steel mills, or munitions plants. Only Burns, Youngs, Fletcher, and Zimmerman put in a full season among the regulars; Perritt was the only original starting pitcher still with McGraw at the end of the season. The Giants manager especially hated to lose Kauff, who seemed finally about to reach the stardom long predicted for him. "The most lovable chap I've ever managed," McGraw said when Kauff left for army service in June. "He is a real man, game, honest, even-tempered and kind-hearted."[2]

As if the war's toll on his players weren't bad enough, McGraw had trouble with Slim Sallee, who eventually announced that he wouldn't play for McGraw anymore and left for home, and Heinie Zimmerman, whom the manager bawled out on the field and then benched in St. Louis for not running out an infield pop-up. Late in July, McGraw got Mathewson to sell him Fred Toney, a big pitcher who was due to stand trial in Tennessee on Mann Act and draft-evasion charges.[3]

Toney was the loser in two of the four games out of five that Chicago won at the Polo Grounds early in August to take a six-and-a-half-game lead on the Giants. For all practical purposes, the pennant race ended then and there. Basically the Chicago Cubs won the pennant in 1918 because manager Fred Mitchell was able to hold on to more front-line players than the other managers in the League. In September, Mitchell's ball club was still almost intact; McGraw's was a patched-together outfit, not the same one he'd brought back from Marlin. After May 10 McGraw's continually changing assortment of ballplayers were able to win only one more than they lost.

Despite the War Department's "work or fight" order, which was supposed to bring a halt to all occupations and activities that didn't contribute directly to the war effort, the major league owners managed to keep the baseball season going until September 2, Labor Day. The season ended after that day's double-headers, with the Cubs thirteen and a half games ahead of the Giants.

At Cincinnati it had been an especially tough season for Christy Mathewson, who resigned ten games before it was over to enlist in the

Chemical Warfare Service. Fred Toney's trouble with the federal authorities was enough worry, until Mathewson sold the pitcher to McGraw. Shortly thereafter Matty found that he had two rankly dishonest ballplayers on his team. One, Lee Magee, was a journeyman infielder who'd played in both the National and American Leagues and served as player-manager for Brooklyn's Federal League entry in 1915. The other was Hal Chase, who was well traveled but hardly a journeyman ballplayer.

Chase had joined the Reds in 1916, at the age of thirty-three, after a season and a half in the Federal League at Buffalo. The native Californian had been a major-leaguer since 1905, when, with the New York Highlanders, he'd quickly made a reputation as the most skilled first-baseman in the game's history. A well-put-together six-footer and a rare left-handed thrower and right-handed batter, Chase was also a solid man at the plate, topping .300 four times and leading the National League at .339 in his first season at Cincinnati. He was a pleasant-faced, likeable, often really charming man, a popular figure among other players and fans.

But there was a twisted, malevolent side to Chase. On the New York team he'd subverted George Stallings's authority and finally convinced club president Frank Farrell to fire Stallings and give him the job. Stallings's second-place team of 1910 sank to sixth under Chase the next year. In 1913 Frank Chance, the Yankees' new manager, endured Chase as long as he could, then peddled him to the Chicago White Sox, from which he jumped to the Federals the next year.

Chase's record of disloyalty to managers was magnified by repeated doubts about his honesty on the playing field. Those suspicions followed him from team to team, league to league. Chase liked to make bets, and he knew professional gamblers all over the country. But he wasn't much for gambling. It was the sure thing he was always after. Sometimes he bet on his own ball club; often he bet on the opposition and thus left himself open to accusations that he'd deliberately let down.

Chase's unsavory reputation was well established by the time he came to the Cincinnati Reds. When Mathewson took over that ball club in mid-1916, Chase found himself playing for a man who'd been the most revered and respected player in the history of the game. It was an incongruous pairing, not likely to last.

Chase corrupted Lee Magee, as he'd no doubt corrupted other teammates on other teams. On July 25, 1918, according to what a Boston pool-room operator and gambler named James Costello would later tes-

tify, Chase and Magee each bet $500 that the Reds would lose to the
Braves that afternoon. Reds starting pitcher Pete Schneider, they said,
understood that he was supposed to lose. Before the game, though,
Schneider asked Mathewson to start somebody else. Chase wasn't in the
lineup, either, because of a cut hand, but Magee did his best to lose.
On Edd Roush's inside-the-park home run, Magee slowed down to keep
from scoring until Roush, on his heels, yelled "Run, you son of a bitch!"[4]
Both scored, Cincinnati won, and Magee stopped payment on the check
he'd given Costello. Chase let his check clear and ended up also paying
part of what Magee owed the gambler.

Mathewsón knew something was wrong in that game, in fact had
suspected Chase of playing dishonestly most of the season. Mathewson
took particular notice of how often Chase, supposedly the consummate
fielder, made poor throws to pitchers coming over to cover first on
grounders hit wide of the bag. On the Reds' eastern swing in July and
August, noted the *Sporting News* at the time, opposing players would
often yell at Chase, "Well, Hal, what are the odds today?"[5] When Chase
approached Pol Perritt with a bribe offer at the Polo Grounds on August
6, Matty finally had enough. The next day, after a bitter exchange with
Chase, the Reds manager suspended him without pay for "indifferent
playing and insubordination."[6] Chase indignantly filed suit against the
Cincinnati club for $1,650, the amount he would have drawn for the
balance of the season.

If Hal Chase's baseball future was in grave doubt that September, so
was the future of the sport as a whole. After September 11, when Carl
Mays's three-hitter clinched a poorly attended World Series for the
Boston Red Sox over the Cubs, baseball was, Joe Vila noted, "as dead
as Chelsea [Massachusetts] in all parts of the country except the ship
yards and the army camps."[7] The War Department had commandeered
the Polo Grounds as a storage site for trucks, vans, and military automobiles. The minor leagues were almost in ruins, and all the big league
teams had lost money. The Giants' season attendance for 1918 was only
about 265,000, the smallest since before McGraw came to the ball club.

American troops by the hundreds of thousands were pouring into battle
alongside the British and French, and the German forces were in stubborn retreat. It seemed, though, that many months—maybe another year
or more—would be necessary before the hated "Huns" were vanquished.
Then, much more quickly than anybody had expected, the fighting was
over. With the Kaiser having fled to Holland, the government of the new

German republic agreed to an armistice, which took effect on November 11, 1918.

It was an exceptionally significant off-season for John McGraw. For one thing, he survived an attack of influenza and thus escaped the fate of close to 700,000 Americans who succumbed in the great epidemic of that winter. Having become a member of the Lambs' Club about six years earlier (on John T. Brush's recommendation, shortly before his death), McGraw now waited on tables and otherwise helped out on those evenings when the Lambs provided dinner and variety acts to entertain maimed combat veterans brought back from France. Meanwhile, the major league owners, fearing generally uncertain post-war conditions and another poor season financially, agreed to a 140-game schedule for 1919. With the start of spring training again set back until mid-March, McGraw decided to move his training site, in the belief that the dry winds of central Texas in April hadn't been good for his players in 1918. So after eleven straight springs of hosting the New York Giants, of organizing the business and social life of the town largely around the vernal visits of McGraw and his men, Marlin, Texas, lost its connection with big-time baseball. Gainesville, Florida, would be the new training site for the Giants.

The biggest thing that happened in baseball that winter was the sale of controlling interest in the National Exhibition Company, a transaction that gave McGraw a share in the ownership of a baseball franchise for the first time since he'd left Baltimore in 1902. McGraw had long wanted to own part of the Giants; he'd been bitterly disappointed, according to Vila and others who knew him well, when Brush's will left no NEC stock to him. By mid-1918, Harry Hempstead's wife, who was Brush's daughter by his first marriage, and Else Lombard Brush, his second wife, were both ready to sell their stock in the NEC. Prospective buyers weren't scarce. The NEC's books showed that the Giants had returned an average profit of $250,000 in the period 1912–17; an annual dividend never less than 13 percent had been paid to the stockholders.

McGraw lined up two particular prospects: George W. Loft, a wealthy candy manufacturer; and a group headed by George M. Cohan, the musical comedy star, and Broadway producer Sam Harris. It was understood that McGraw would become a stockholder in whatever form the new ownership might take. For some reason the negotiations between Loft and Harry Hempstead, who was handling matters for his wife and stepmother-in-law, broke off early in 1919. By Cohan's account, he and Harris were still talking to Hempstead when they read in the newspapers that the Giants had been sold to a group in which the principal investor was Charles A. Stoneham, in partnership with Francis Xavier McQuade and John McGraw.

Impatient with the drawn-out process of getting the ball club sold, McGraw had turned to Stoneham, who was able to put together $1,030,000, by far a record price for a baseball franchise. With that, Stoneham and associates bought 58 percent of the NEC stock. A third remained in the possession of Hempstead and his business associate N. Ashley Lloyd; most of the remainder continued in the hands of the heirs of Arthur Soden, who, as owner of the Boston National League team, had helped to bail out the sinking New York franchise back in 1890.

McGraw didn't really have the funds to become part-owner of a big league team. Despite the money he'd made since coming to the Giants— at least a quarter of a million dollars from baseball alone—he had little to show for it. Partly it was a matter of gambling losses, partly it was what he gave to real or professed indigents. At the beginning of 1915 the *Sporting News* estimated that during the previous year he'd given away $2,000. He was especially generous in the spring, as the Giants traveled across the southern states. It seemed that every down-and-out old ballplayer (or his wife or offspring) came to McGraw in cities like New Orleans, Memphis, Birmingham, Louisville, Washington. Sometimes McGraw asked perfunctory questions, sometimes nothing at all, before peeling off his roll of bills.

In the fall of 1914, the city of New York had sued him for $366 in unpaid taxes for 1912 on the $20,000 assessment on the pool room he'd operated in 1908–13. McGraw swore in tax court that he'd sold his lease at a loss after paying off a $2,500 debt on the place. He owned no property, he said, besides an automobile valued at $500. In 1912 he had accumulated $8,000 in savings, but he'd also owed the Washington Heights Bank $9,500 and had since paid that off. No, he didn't have any savings at present. Asked about the value of the furniture in his apartment, he replied, "I have none. It all belongs to my wife." Blanche McGraw always had some money of her own, as a portion of the Sindall family's modest wealth. In a manner typical of the times, she left basic money management (or mismanagement) to her husband. "I never knew the exact nature of John McGraw's financial philosophy," she would say many years later, "and I never worried about it. He gave me everything I ever asked for or failed to ask for. I wanted for nothing, and so I never questioned his income or what he did with it."[7]

To afford stock in the NEC, McGraw had to go far into debt. McQuade and McGraw bought seventy shares each at $50,338 per block of shares. McGraw put up only $338.10; for the balance he gave Stoneham three promissory notes for $16,666.66 each, so that he began work under the new president of the Giants owing him $50,000.

Francis X. McQuade was a judge in magistrate's court, a prominent figure in Tammany Hall affairs, and, like many Tammanyites, a fervent New York Giants rooter. In August 1917 he'd quickly dismissed charges brought by the local Sabbath Society against McGraw and Christy Mathewson for violating the state law banning Sunday baseball when their teams played an exhibition game at the Polo Grounds, with the receipts going to dependents of the Sixty-ninth New York regiment. A longtime acquaintance of McGraw, McQuade would become treasurer of the NEC and, despite being paid a $10,000 yearly salary, insist on continuing to hold his judgeship.

Charles Stoneham was forty-two years old when he bought control of the Giants. Grossly fat and somewhat bug-eyed, he loved racehorses, gambling, and baseball, and he wasn't picky about his friends' reputations. Those traits, of course, were ones he shared with McGraw. Stoneham had made his money in a variety of ventures, some of doubtful legality. Most of all he was known for being a bucket-shop operator. Charles Stoneham and Company, with offices in the financial district on Broad Street, ostensibly dealt in the sale of stocks and bonds. What made it a bucket shop was that customers wagered on the rise and fall of securities, in the form of orders or options at current prices, without any intention of actually receiving the securities. Keeping longer hours than the stock exchanges, a bucket shop charged less commission than regular brokers, offered anybody with a few dollars the chance to "invest," and generally operated without even the loose regulations that applied to the exchanges during that period. As was typical of bucket shops, Stoneham and his associates speculated on their own with customers' funds, bet secretly against customers' guesses on securities prices, and otherwise handled other people's money without scruple or responsibility.

The way Stoneham had made his money didn't interest John McGraw, who would always be grateful to Stoneham for making it possible for him to buy into the ball club. Whatever trouble Stoneham might have later on with other NEC stockholders, McGraw, as vice-president of the NEC, would remain loyal to its president.

The second biggest news of the baseball off-season was the recruiting of Hal Chase as the new Giants' first-baseman. In mid-January, when he was still heavily involved with the final details of the ball club's sale, McGraw was also talking with Chase about why Mathewson had suspended him the previous August. McGraw had always liked the Californian, both as a ballplayer and as a man, and he was ready to be convinced when Chase assured him that Matty had had it all wrong. Some people inside baseball wouldn't have believed anything Chase said. McGraw believed him because he wanted the best first-baseman in the League on his team.

But first Chase's name had to be cleared, at least officially. Circumstances hampered the National League president's inquiry into the Mathewson-Chase affair. The League had a new president who wasn't yet sure of himself. The previous fall, in one in a series of controversies that steadily reduced the prestige and effectiveness of the National Commission, John Tener had resigned to protest the determination of Ban Johnson, supported by Garry Herrmann, to award rights to a disputed player to Connie Mack and the American League rather than the Boston Braves. In December the National League owners had chosen as their new chief executive John Heydler, who'd served faithfully for many years as League secretary. So it fell to Heydler to handle the Chase business.

On January 30, 1919, when Heydler held a hearing in his New York office, Mathewson was still in France. Heydler did have an affidavit that Matty had submitted to the League office before going overseas, but his absence obviously gave the advantage to Chase and the three lawyers who accompanied him into Heydler's office. For five hours Heydler listened to testimony from Chase; from Reds players Earle "Greasy" Neale, Jimmy Ring, and Mike Regan; and from McGraw, who admitted that the previous August, Pol Perritt had told him that he'd been propositioned by Chase. Heydler also had Perritt's deposition read into the proceedings.

On February 5 Heydler officially cleared Chase. The Cincinnati ball club had been justified in its actions, said Heydler, because Chase had "acted in a foolish and careless manner both on the field and among the players" and prompted "many rumors which arose from the loose talk of its first-baseman." But the accusations against him had all been general ones, unsubstantiated as to particulars. So Chase had to be judged innocent.[8]

As soon as Heydler gave out his ruling, McGraw was on a train for Cincinnati to make a deal for Chase with Garry Herrmann. McGraw offered Walter Holke and Bill Rariden, plus Slim Sallee if the pitcher refused to return to the Giants, but Herrmann wouldn't agree to Chase's release unless the first-baseman dropped his suit for $1,650 in back pay. After McGraw assured Herrmann that the Giants would take care of Chase's claims on the Reds, the deal was consummated.

Then came the oddest twist of all. The past fall McGraw had hired Pat Moran as his coach after he lost his job as manager of the Philadelphia Phillies, but in January Moran had signed to manage at Cincinnati. Early in March, about two weeks after he returned from Europe, Christy Mathewson signed on with McGraw to replace Moran, with the title "assistant manager."

The willingness of Mathewson, a man whose integrity had always been beyond question, to step into a situation where he'd have to be closely associated with a player whom he'd accused of crookedness and presumably despised, could be understood only in terms of his ambition eventually to manage the Giants. McGraw fed that ambition, telling the press that after a few more seasons, maybe, he wished for Matty to succeed him. For his part, Mathewson now denied that he'd ever quarreled with Chase, had ever charged him with anything but indifferent playing—of which almost every player had been guilty at some time or other. He'd only brought the matter before the League, said Mathewson, because one or two of Chase's teammates had made accusations against him.

Mathewson's extenuations sounded pretty lame. For the present, though, the New York writers, and presumably the New York fans as well, seemed satisfied. So in mid-March the unlikely trio of McGraw, Mathewson, and Chase was the prime attraction at Gainesville, Florida.

Gainesville was a strikingly different place from what it had been when McGraw had played winter ball there as a seventeen-year-old. Little more than a village then, it had grown to some 10,000 people. The University of Florida, a little backwater school in 1890–91, was now a thriving institution with decent athletic facilities. Use of the university's baseball field came free of charge for the big-leaguers.

Mathewson worked closely with the pitchers—what pitchers there were. Fred Toney would be in federal prison in Tennessee until May 1;

Sallee had obtained his release and signed with Cincinnati; and Perritt was trying to start an oil-drilling business in northern Louisiana (although he would later report and post eighteen wins). Meanwhile, McGraw worried about his elderly infield of Chase, Doyle, Fletcher, and Zimmerman, which averaged 33.5 years. The outfield of Burns, Kauff, and Youngs, on the other hand, still looked like the League's best. McGraw finally judged that he didn't need Jim Thorpe. Early in the season he would sell the famous athlete to Boston.

That spring the Giants won two games in a five-game series with the world-champion Boston Red Sox, who were based at Tampa. Babe Ruth, the top left-handed pitcher in the American League, had become such a potent force at bat that manager Ed Barrow was about ready to put him in the outfield every day. At Tampa, Ruth hit a startling home run that traveled at least five hundred feet, over the palm trees in center field. While everybody else gasped, McGraw was unimpressed. "If he plays every day," said McGraw, "the bum will hit into a hundred double plays before the season is over."[9]

McGraw's teams were known for their strong starts; the 1919 Giants were no exception, winning twenty-four of their first thirty-two games. On May 4, before a full house at the Polo Grounds, the Giants and the Phillies met in the first lawful game of Sunday baseball ever played in New York City. Legalized in that year's legislative session at Albany, mainly through the efforts of State Senator James J. Walker, a loyal son of Tammany, Sunday baseball contributed mightily to the biggest attendance surge in the history of both the Giants and the Yankees. By early June, according to Joe Vila's calculations, the Giants had already attracted some 350,000 customers, enough to cover expenses for the year and put the franchise "on velvet" the rest of the way.[10]

Record numbers of gamblers were also flocking to the Polo Grounds. Largely Jewish, these "gents from the Ghetto," as Vila termed them, attracted attention to themselves by sitting behind the visitors' dugout off third base and cheering for the opposition. In the second game of a series with St. Louis, several of them were forced to leave the ballpark. It was all right for "decent visitors" to root against the Giants, McGraw said, but if the security operatives "find persons betting and rooting against the Giants, they will drag them out of the grandstand while the game is going on."[11]

While the Giants were self-righteously expelling gambling spectators, Hal Chase continued to hold down first for them. Every time New York played in Cincinnati, the crowds were unmerciful in their verbal abuse of Chase and McGraw, as well as Fred Toney, who joined the team early in May, after leaving prison, and pitched superbly. The Cincinnati crowds also got bigger every time the Giants came into town, because on July 6 Pat Moran's Reds edged into first place, and from then on it was a two-way battle for the pennant.

It was a bitter fight, reminiscent of the Giants-Cubs struggles of the previous decade. Early in August, after his team salvaged one game in a three-game set at Redland Field, with a huge overflow, some 32,000, watching the Sunday finale, McGraw encountered a big group of hecklers as he left the park. "We beat you today and we'll be glad to get out of the home of the Huns," retorted McGraw.[12] That remark, especially inflammatory in Cincinnati, with its largely German-American population, almost provoked a riot. A park policeman took a swipe at McGraw; Chase knocked the policeman's cap off. As the angry Reds rooters moved in, the players jammed McGraw and themselves into a couple of waiting taxicabs and quickly left the scene.

In the midst of the race, McGraw made several moves to strengthen his club. A switch-hitting twenty-year-old named Frank Frisch, a native New Yorker directly out of Fordham University, appeared in his first game as a Giant on July 3. Filling in at second, short, and third, and eventually taking over for Doyle, Frisch played in fifty-four games and impressed everybody with his fielding quickness, although he batted only .226. Phil Douglas, a hulking right-hander from the Tennessee-Georgia mountains who'd been in the National League four full seasons, earning more of a reputation for drinking sprees than pitching prowess, came from Chicago in exchange for the rights to Dave Robertson, who wouldn't report to the Giants. McGraw traded sore-armed Ferdie Schupp to St. Louis for Frank "Pancho" Snyder, a dependable catcher. And to the dismay of people in Cincinnati and Giants haters everywhere, in mid-August McGraw gave the money-hungry Braves $40,000 and four little-known players for Art Nehf, a fine little left-hander.

All that, though, wasn't enough to stem the Reds' tide. By winning four games in three double-headers at the Polo Grounds, August 15–18, Cincinnati moved six and one-half games in front. Hal Chase committed four fielding errors in the August 15 twin bill, one a crucial misplay that let in three runs in the fourteenth inning and lost the opener for Nehf. In the nightcap McGraw sent up a pinch-hitter for Chase late in the game, and he played no more in the series. At the time both

Chase and McGraw said that he'd sprained his wrist reaching third base. (Chase was one of that period's few headfirst sliders.)

Chase remained with the team, coaching at first base with a bandaged wrist for a few games, returning to the lineup on August 26, and then, after supposedly reinjuring the wrist a week later, going back to the coaching lines. He was with the ball club on its last western trip, on hand to try to manipulate players and the outcome of games, despite what many baseball people had long thought and sometimes said, what even McGraw had come to believe.

The whole rotten situation revolving around Chase's presence on the New York team reached its climax during a series in Chicago. There, on September 10, Heinie Zimmerman played both games of a double-header. The next day he wasn't in the lineup. Toney pitched the first two innings on the eleventh, gave up only two hits and no runs, and left with the Giants leading. Jess Barnes came in to notch another in the twenty-five wins he would have that year. On the twelfth the Giants drove Grover Cleveland Alexander, now a Cub, from the mound and Rube Benton pitched the victory, 6–3.

Toney would later testify that Zimmerman told him at the end of the first inning of the September 11 game that it would be worth his while not to bear down on the Cubs. After another inning Toney asked McGraw to take him out so that, whatever happened, he wouldn't come under suspicion. That evening, in a northside Chicago saloon, Chase and Buck Herzog, now with the Cubs, had a few beers with Rube Benton and, Benton later related, suggested that inasmuch as Cincinnati had the pennant about wrapped up, the pitcher might as well "make some easy money" by letting Chicago win. The next night, after Benton had beaten the Cubs that afternoon, Zimmerman came up to him in the hotel lobby and said, "You poor fish, don't you know there was $400 waiting for you to lose that game today?"[13]

Unsuccessful in Chicago with Toney and Benton, in St. Louis, the next stop on the road trip, Chase and Zimmerman tried to bribe Benny Kauff with an offer of $125 per game. By that time Benton had told Art Fletcher about Zimmerman's remarks in Chicago, and Fletcher had presumably reported to McGraw. At any rate, when the Giants arrived in St. Louis, Zimmerman was under suspension, McGraw's public explanation being that Zimmerman had broken curfew. Yet while Zimmerman shortly returned to his home in the Bronx, Chase remained with the team, still in good standing. On September 15 he even pinch-hit at

Cincinnati in a 3–0 loss to Slim Sallee, who was having his best year in the majors. The next day Walter "Dutch" Ruether scattered twelve hits in a 4–3 victory that clinched Cincinnati's first championship since the old American Association.

McGraw didn't put on his uniform for the first game at Redland Field. Turning the team over to Mathewson, he left the park before Sallee finished disposing of the Giants and caught a train for New York. There, be would tell the *Sporting News* fourteen months later, he and Charles Stoneham met with Zimmerman, "called him to account" about his activities in Chicago and St. Louis, and exacted a confession.[14] Meanwhile, Chase accompanied Mathewson and the rest of the Giants to Pittsburgh and back to New York, frequently coaching at first base and, to all outward appearances, dutifully serving his ball club. He finally left the team on September 28, only one day before the Giants closed the season with a double-header win over the Phillies.

So contrary to what McGraw would subsequently claim—and what would become the accepted version of events—he didn't send Chase from the club weeks before the season ended. In fact Chase was in uniform, on the bench, and on the coaching lines up to the next-to-last game, whereas McGraw was absent after the September 15 game in Cincinnati. Presumably the Giants manager was so disgusted and dismayed by what had happened in recent weeks that he couldn't bear to be with the team. Yet while he'd suspended Zimmerman and, so he would later claim, grilled him into confessing his misdeeds, he'd never taken any formal action against Chase, never, as far as could be determined, accused him of anything untoward. McGraw's genuine fondness for a man whom he and his wife had known for thirteen years apparently kept him from acting on what, by his own account, he strongly suspected as early as that August, when Chase played so poorly at the Polo Grounds in the series against Cincinnati that really decided the pennant. "In my opinion Chase deliberately threw us down," he would say later. "I never was more deceived by a player than by Chase."[15]

Skipping the World Series, McGraw and Stoneham traveled to Texas to inspect some oil properties they'd invested in, then took a boat from Galveston to Havana. By mid-October they were the owners of the Oriental Racetrack complex, which included, besides the track, a casino, restaurant, and small hotel called the Cuban American Jockey Club. Although the price wasn't made public, it must have been a good one inasmuch as H. D. "Curley" Brown, a Texan who'd built the complex, needed to sell out before he started a prison term for shooting the son-in-law of a powerful Cuban politician.

If, financially speaking, the year 1919 had been the best of times for baseball, then because of what happened in the World Series, that year would also become, in retrospect, the worst of times for the sport that had come to mean more to more people than any other.

Almost the same exceptionally talented ball club that had beaten the Giants two years earlier, the Chicago White Sox were big favorites over Cincinnati in the first five-of-nine-game Series since 1903. It took only eight games, though, for the Reds to defeat a team that had seemed superior in nearly every way.

Within a year it would become known that of the nine White Sox who took the field at Cincinnati on October 1, five were in the employ of gamblers—two separate groups of gamblers, as it turned out. First-baseman Charles "Chick" Gandil, shortstop Charles "Swede" Risberg, left-fielder Joe Jackson, center-fielder Happy Felsch, and opening-game pitcher Eddie Cicotte had agreed to throw the Series, along with Claude "Lefty" Williams, the Sox's second-winningest pitcher, and utility in-fielder Fred McMullen. Buck Weaver, Chicago's fine third-baseman, played the games honestly but knew the fix was in and wouldn't inform on his friends.

The way the White Sox played and misplayed looked suspicious to a lot of onlookers, including Christy Mathewson. Matty shared his doubts with the Chicago sportswriter Hugh Fullerton, who in the off-season, in his columns in the Chicago *Tribune*, would help to keep those suspicions alive.

A remarkable number of people knew about the fix beforehand, including three men who'd played for McGraw that season. Hal Chase made a killing, maybe as much as $40,000, betting against Chicago. Jean Dubuc, used mainly as a mop-up pitcher by McGraw in 1919, heard about it from Bill Burns, a former teammate at Detroit and one of the gamblers involved in the plot. Rube Benton would later claim that his information came from Buck Herzog; Benton won $3,000–$4,000 betting on the Reds. Later the *Sporting News* would speculate that while McGraw himself certainly had no prior knowledge that the Series had been rigged, he probably did know within three months after it was over.

Arnold Rothstein, McGraw's onetime pool-room partner, also knew about the fix, in fact may have known more than anybody in the country. By 1919 Rothstein had become a powerful presence in the New York underworld. The bankroller of a variety of illegal and marginally legal operations, he was the biggest single figure in gambling circles. And he was the logical person for Abe Attell, former featherweight boxing champion, to come to when Attell was putting together his part of the complex World Series conspiracy. Although Rothstein evidently gave Attell only encouragement, that encouragement—and the expectation that Rothstein would put money into the venture—was probably crucial to its furtherance.

A considerable odor hung over baseball in the winter of 1919–20, but it was still basically business as usual. The owners voted to return to a 154-game schedule, amid sighs about the money they'd lost by playing fewer games in 1919. McGraw sought without success to help his team. Because Branch Rickey, the Cardinals' voluble but wily manager, insisted on Frank Frisch in addition to the $70,000 and four other players McGraw offered, the Giants didn't get infielder Rogers Hornsby, generally regarded as one of the game's rising stars. Despite his fondness for Ross Youngs, McGraw was willing to trade him to Cincinnati for outfielder Edd Roush and shortstop Larry Kopf, but Garry Herrmann and Pat Moran backed down. Nor was McGraw able to persuade Boston to let go of James "Rabbitt" Maranville, the Braves' flashy little shortstop.

McGraw had decided to switch spring training back to Texas and locate his team at San Antonio, a city that had grown to some 162,000 people. Working out at the Texas League ballpark, lodging at the well-appointed Crockett Hotel near the ruins of the historic Alamo, sampling Tex-Mex cuisine, sometimes going by streetcar south to the mineral baths at Hot Wells, McGraw's players seemed to find the new spring base quite an improvement over either Marlin or Gainesville.

As soon as he arrived from Galveston (following a second stay in Cuba), McGraw encountered queries about the status of Hal Chase and Heinie Zimmerman. "I cannot talk about the matter," he told the New York writers. "If anything is to be said, it must come from the players. As far as the Giants are concerned, Chase and Zimmerman are through."[16] Actually, according to the strategy McGraw and Stoneham had agreed to during the winter, both had received contracts for 1920, but for such little pay as to guarantee that neither would sign. Zimmerman quit baseball altogether to pursue the plumbing trade in the Bronx; Chase was playing in the strong semi-pro leagues in the San Francisco Bay area.

When they left San Antonio, the Giants hooked up for another spring tour with the Boston Red Sox, who'd trained at Hot Springs, Arkansas. Now they were the Ruthless Red Sox, because over the winter, following a season in which Babe Ruth hit twenty-nine home runs, Boston owner Harry Frazee had sold him to the New York Yankees for a quarter of a million dollars in cash and loans. Ruth was about to change the course of baseball history not only in New York but, in some sense, everywhere it was played.

Despite what one observer that spring referred to as his "aldermanic proportions," despite his almost completely white hair and a puffy face that reduced his eyes to dark beads, McGraw seemed in good health as he marked his forty-seventh birthday at a dinner given in his honor at Rocky Mount, North Carolina. And despite the undercurrent of talk about his troubles with players the previous season, his image as the little Napoleon, baseball's manager par excellence, hadn't diminished.

Again he was trying to rebuild with an unstable mix of youngsters and veterans, ready to spend money and deal anytime for anybody who might help him. Doyle and Fletcher started the season at second and shortstop, with Frisch at third and George Kelly, a tall San Franciscan brought up late the previous season after batting .356 at Rochester, given sole custody of first. Frank Snyder would divide the catching with a crusty young Arkansan named Earl Smith (called by New Yorkers, of course, "Oil" Smith). George Burns was still the left-fielder, Youngs was in right; but Kauff, badly distracted by the fact that, along with his brother, he was under indictment in New York for handling stolen automobiles, started the season in a terrible slump both at bat and afield. McGraw would try various men in center that year.

McGraw's pitching would turn out to be surprisingly strong. Still wildcatting in Louisiana, Perritt wouldn't report until the season was nearly over, but Barnes, Nehf, and Toney would all win twenty or more games, and Benton (9–16) would pitch well if often without much support. Then there was Phil Douglas, whose struggles with the bottle brought back memories of Larry McLean and Bugs Raymond. After coming to the Giants from Chicago in mid-season the previous year, Douglas had made only a couple of starts before he went on one of his periodic binges—"vacations," he called them. McGraw had suspended him for the rest of the season, the last part of which he'd spent pitching semi-pro ball in Chicago. "Shufflin' Phil," so called because of his ponderous gait, had behaved himself at San Antonio and on the trip east with the Red Sox. Decent liquor was pretty scarce that spring anyway, because the federal Volstead Act, implementing the Eighteenth Amendment to the Constitution, had taken effect on January 1, 1920. Now it was unlawful to make, distribute, or consume alcoholic beverages anywhere in the forty-eight United States. It wouldn't be long, though, before booze would be readily available through illegal suppliers in many places across the country, nowhere more so than in New York City.

Things didn't go well for the Giants over the first half of the season. Ten days into the schedule, Frisch underwent an emergency appendectomy after being stricken on the train returning from Boston. In mid-May McGraw drew a five-day suspension for haranguing Bill Klem following a game in Pittsburgh, and he sat out another three games early in June. On both occasions Mathewson handled the team, but by the end of June, Matty and his wife, Jane, were packing for a stay at the renowned tuberculosis treatment facility at Lake Saranac, upstate in the Adirondack Mountains. Matty's physicians had finally discovered that what they'd diagnosed in the spring as bronchitis was in fact the dread lung disease. Johnny Evers, the Giants' fiery nemesis when he played for the Cubs and Braves, became McGraw's new right-hand man.

On July 1 Rube Marquard, written off by McGraw five years earlier but still pitching well for Brooklyn, beat the Giants at the Polo Grounds to drop their record to 30–36. The Giants' home attendance had been respectable but only half what the Yankees were drawing in the Giants' own ballpark. Babe Ruth had become the sensation of the American sports scene and indeed a major figure in the nation's public life. Not only did Ruth obliterate his own record midway through the season and go on to amass fifty-four home runs, he batted .376, drew 148 bases on balls, scored 158 times, and batted in 137 runs. His truly awesome offensive performance kept the traditionally lackluster Yankees in the pennant race down to the last week of the season. Ruth's feats and Yankee pennant hopes brought more than a million customers into the Polo Grounds for American League games, the biggest attendance in the sport's history.

With their tenants packing in substantially more people, especially during the first half of the season, Stoneham and McGraw fumed and fussed and talked about evicting the Yankees, only to end up settling for a rent increase, from $60,000 to $100,000 a year. But the Giants president and his vice-president and manager understood fully that, for the first time, they faced powerful competition for the New York sports dollar. More than ever, the pressure was on McGraw to produce winners.

So he peddled the faltering Fletcher and a second-line pitcher to Philadelphia for Dave Bancroft, generally conceded to be the League's best shortstop. Again he sought Rogers Hornsby, this time offering $200,000 and players for the brilliant young Texan; again Branch Rickey chose to hold onto his best ballplayer.

Midway through the season Phil Douglas fell off the wagon in Chicago and again was suspended. By the time McGraw forgave him, a couple of weeks later, the Giants had become a hot ball club. With Frisch back in action and sparkling afield and at bat, Bancroft living up to expectations, Kelly driving in key runs, and Youngs spraying hits everywhere, McGraw's team won twenty of twenty-five games and climbed to third place, only three games behind front-running Brooklyn.

On Saturday, August 7, at the Polo Grounds, Chicago right-hander Claude Hendrix temporarily cooled off the Giants. That evening McGraw and his wife dined out. Afterward Blanche went back to their apartment at 109th Street and Broadway, but McGraw decided to hit a few spots where he knew there would be friends talking baseball or horses. He stayed at it all night, drinking bootleg whiskey and "home brew" beer until he was quite drunk. About daylight on Sunday, he stopped by the Lambs' Club on West Forty-fourth Street.

McGraw had no business going there, inasmuch as the club's house committee had suspended him three months earlier for fighting with a fellow Lamb, an actor named Walter Knight. He nonetheless got past the doorman and wandered into the club grill. After buying four pint bottles of whiskey, he invited the dozen or so other men in the room to join him in emptying them. As the drinking proceeded, McGraw found himself being "pestered" by a man trying to interest him in some insurance. McGraw's foul language offended William Boyd, a prominent Broadway actor, who cautioned McGraw that he shouldn't talk that way in front of the three scrubwomen who'd started to clean up. McGraw walked over to the scrubwomen, gave each of them a five-dollar bill, then turned on Boyd and, drunkenly mistaking him for Walter Knight, began to curse him. "As a man I like you, as a baseball manager I like you," Boyd replied, "but I don't like your language." The actor then hit the manager over the head with a water carafe and, by McGraw's account, kicked him in the face after he went down from the blow on the head. "It was a case of bunched hits," said McGraw later.[18]

John C. Slavin, a musical comedy performer, and Winfield Liggitt, a retired naval officer and resident Lamb, got McGraw outside and into a taxicab. They arrived at the McGraws' apartment building about 8:00 A.M. Slavin and Liggitt tried to help McGraw out, but he pushed Liggitt back into the car seat and started inside. Again his companions offered to assist, only to be told, "I don't want anyone to go in with me. I'll go by myself."[19] Liggitt started to get back into the automobile, heard a thud, and turned and saw McGraw going through the door of his building and Slavin lying face down on the sidewalk. Liggitt and the driver, William Meagan, put the unconscious Slavin into the cab and took him to St. Luke's Hospital, where he was found to have a small fracture at the base of his skull.

On Sunday police detectives quizzed McGraw, Liggitt, and Meagan. Although Liggitt insisted that neither he nor Slavin had been drinking, the police told reporters that they were convinced Slavin had just keeled over on the sidewalk. "There is nothing to indicate foul play in connection with the case," said a detective sergeant.[20] Later McGraw, wearing two black eyes, facial bruises, and cuts on his head, slipped out of the apartment long enough to go up to the Polo Grounds, meet with Johnny Evers, and put the ball club in his charge. By game time he was back home, in seclusion.

That was how he remained for the next five days, ignoring a written request from the district attorney that he come in for some questions, then refusing to admit a process server with a subpoena ordering him to come in. Meanwhile, Slavin's condition improved, enough for him to tell a visitor from the district attorney's office that he could remember nothing about how he'd been injured. Thoroughly disgusted by McGraw's antics, the Lambs' Club voted to expel him.

On August 14 McGraw finally let an assistant district attorney and a medical examiner into the apartment. Yes, he admitted from his bed, he'd bought whiskey at the Lambs' Club and consumed it "with outside help." As for the fight with Boyd, he recalled being hit over the head and kicked, nothing else until the police woke him up later that morning. He was convinced, though, that he hadn't started the fight. Slavin, he said, was "a fine fellow" who'd tried to be a peacemaker; he "would be the last person in the world I'd think of hitting." Asked whether he'd been intoxicated at the Lambs' Club, McGraw replied, "I must have been, because I never fight unless I am drunk."[21] However absurd that may have looked in print to people who'd followed McGraw's scrapes over the decades, he no doubt believed it himself at the time.

Covered in detail by the New York press, the affair was deeply humiliating to the McGraws as well as a considerable embarrassment to the New York Giants. Although the team played well under Evers and kept itself in contention, McGraw's absence during a critical stage in the race couldn't be excused. And by admitting that he'd purchased and consumed alcoholic beverages, McGraw had, in effect, confessed to a federal crime and laid himself open to prosecution.

He was still housebound five days later, when two agents from the U.S. Prohibition Enforcement Office for the city called on him. Francis X. McQuade was present, along with attorneys William Fallon and Eugene McGee, whom McGraw had retained at Stoneham's suggestion. By far the better known of the legal partners was Fallon, who was thirty-four years old, handsome, flamboyant, alcoholic, and the lover of the heiress and art patron Gertrude Vanderbilt. Already nicknamed "the Great Mouthpiece," Fallon had a clientele consisting mostly of people involved in one or another dubiously legal activity, including Arnold Rothstein and Charles Stoneham.

Fallon and McGee were on hand to see that McGraw didn't incriminate himself any more than he already had. When the prohibition agents tried to get McGraw to talk about buying whiskey, Fallon repeatedly interrupted to keep him from answering. Throughout the interview the Giants manager reclined in his Morris chair with a bandage on his head, a touch that was doubtless Fallon's idea.

That night, *sans* head bandage, McGraw took the Twentieth Century Limited to Chicago, where the next day he resumed active direction of the Giants. He saw them lose 5–1 to Alexander and drop four games behind Cincinnati, which now had possession of first. With McGraw managing from the bench in street clothes to avoid the catcalls that awaited him in the western cities, the Giants held their own on the road trip, although losing four of five at Pittsburgh hurt badly. Desperate for any kind of help, McGraw claimed Slim Sallee on waivers from Cincinnati.

McGraw's ball club had held together well despite his misadventures, but its faltering performance in the first half of the season proved too much to overcome. Wilbert Robinson's Robins, by sweeping back-to-back double-headers from St. Louis at Ebbets Field on September 10–11, while Cincinnati lost two single games at Boston, virtually killed off Pat Moran's team. By beating the Cubs, New York moved into second place, but the Brooklyns took a four-and-one-half-game lead the next day with a win over Chicago, coupled with the Giants' loss to St. Louis.

While tbe Giants continued to hold second place, Brooklyn's ten-game winning streak produced Robinson's second league championship. When Art Nehf lost to Boston 2–1 on September 29, New York fell five behind with only four to play.

In the meantime, McGraw's personal troubles took another bizarre turn. About midnight on Saturday, September 18, Wilton Lackaye, actor and Lambs' Club member, called at McGraw's apartment. Franxis X. McQuade was already there, along with a New York broker named Clarence McCormick and B. G. Pratt, a friend of McGraw's from Chicago. Lackaye later said that he'd just recently returned to New York and heard about the fight with William Boyd, and that he only wanted to ask McGraw, as an old friend, whether he intended to defame the Lambs publicly. That was none of his business, McGraw replied. Then, according to what McGraw and the others later told police, the actor became loud and abusive, so much so that Blanche McGraw came into the room and said, "I want that man out." As the others tried to escort him out the door, Lackaye kicked at Pratt and fell, injuring his left ankle. In Lackaye's version, McGraw had demanded to know who'd sent him and acted in a generally hostile manner. Taking Lackaye's right hand as if to shake it, he'd hit him with a left hook. In falling, Lackaye twisted his ankle. He got up and went home, wrapped his ankle, then saw his physician the next morning and found that he'd broken it. Interviewed at his apartment as he sat with foot on cushion, Lackaye sighed. "It looks as if I'll have at least four weeks to charge up against misguided philanthrophy," he said. [22]

Lackaye must in fact have considered himself an old friend, because he refused to press charges, even after McGraw spitefully had all passes revoked at the Polo Grounds for all Lambs. But John Slavin, finally out of the hospital, was now talking about suing McGraw, and the U.S. district attorney's office had decided to prosecute him for violating the Volstead Act. On October 28 a federal grand jury returned an indictment on the charge that McGraw had had illegal liquor in his possession at the Lambs' Club the evening of August 8. After appearing in federal district court the next day with Eugene McGee at his side, pleading not guilty, and posting $500 bond, McGraw said to newsmen, "The whole thing is a joke to me. It's not worth discussing." [23]

As if all that weren't enough, McGraw had also been called to testify before the Cook County grand jury in Chicago about gambling and baseball. After many years of hushing up, covering up, and ignoring incident after incident, the little insular society of major league baseball had finally seen the lid blow off.

It had started to blow the previous April, when Lee Magee, who'd ended the 1919 season at Chicago and then been released over the winter, brought suit against the Cubs for breach of contract, inasmuch as he'd signed to play with them through 1920. Saying he wouldn't be made a "goat," Magee threatened to "explode the biggest bomb in baseball history. . . . "[24] Although Magee didn't explode much of anything specific in court and eventually lost his suit, the commotion he made served to revive the whole gambling issue just at a time when it seemed to be fading once again.

Then on September 4 the Chicago newspapers reported a plot to fix the Cubs-Phillies game five days earlier. Having received a number of calls and wires warning of a fix, Cubs president William H. Veeck, Sr., had instructed manager Fred Mitchell to start Alexander, his ace, rather than Claude Hendrix, the scheduled pitcher. (Chicago lost anyway, 3–0.) Three days later the Cook County district attorney announced that a special grand jury would investigate not only that game but the general subject of gambling in baseball.

The hearings, which commenced on September 22, produced plenty of testimony about shady goings-on over the past two seasons. Among the luminaries called to testify were Buck Herzog, Rube Benton, John Heydler, and McGraw. The Giants manager went to Chicago at the end of the month to talk about why he'd dropped Hal Chase and Heinie Zimmerman. Yes, he'd long suspected Chase of dishonest playing, but he'd lacked any proof, so he'd kept him on his team in 1919. He'd got rid of Zimmerman when he learned about the attempt to bribe Benny Kauff. Nobody asked him, so he didn't have to try to explain why Chase hadn't been suspended, in fact hadn't left the Giants until the season was almost over. Chase himself wasn't about to travel from California to Chicago to shed light on that matter or anything else. Besides, he was busy trying to circumvent a recent Pacific Coast League directive barring him from contact with players in that circuit.

McGraw was back in Chicago on October 5, along with Stoneham, Kauff, Larry Doyle, Fred Toney, and Jean Dubuc (now managing at Toledo in the American Association). They all added to what was known about Zimmerman's and Chase's activities in 1919. By early October, though, the grand jury's focus and that of the press as well had shifted to last year's World Series.

On September 28, with much of the story already disclosed in the Philadelphia *North American*, Eddie Cicotte and Joe Jackson confessed to the district attorney that they'd thrown the Series. They implicated six others who'd been their teammates on the 1919 Chicago White Sox.[25] The biggest mess in the history of the sport could no longer be hidden.

Out of what was quickly dubbed the "Black Sox sandal" would come a radical restructuring of Organized Baseball's system of governance. Over the next several years other scandals and near-scandals would surface, and doubts would persist about the integrity of the sport. But professional baseball would survive, in fact would go on into a new era marked by record attendance and public excitement. Much of that excitement would continue to revolve around the home-run-hitting exploits of Babe Ruth, whose example would also do much to transform the game on the field.

John McGraw, too, would survive, would surmount his personal entanglements and reach new heights of professional success. Whatever doubts some people may have had about his judgment—as a man or as a manager—would soon disappear behind the unprecedented string of pennants his New York Giants were about to put together.

Ten

A TROUBLED DYNASTY

IN THE LAST MONTHS OF 1920, John Slavin made a full recovery from his skull fracture and resumed his career as a minor Broadway performer. Probably because he would have had to swear in court that he hadn't been drinking with McGraw before dawn on August 8 (and so would Winfield Liggitt), Slavin abandoned the notion of suing the Giants manager. The other complication arising from McGraw's wild night out, his prosecution under the Volstead Act, remained unresolved. In December and again in March, with McGraw in Cuba and then at spring training in San Antonio, the federal attorneys agreed to William Fallon's requests for postponements of his trial.

McGraw made two visits to the Caribbean republic that off-season. Babe Ruth was the main attraction in a group of players McGraw led to the island early in November for a series of games against the Havana and Almendares teams. Frank Frisch, Jess Barnes, George Kelly, and Fred Toney of the Giants; outfielder Emil "Irish" Meusel of the Phillies; and several lesser-known major-leaguers made up McGraw's outfit. For once McGraw didn't seem to take baseball seriously. The major-leaguers won most of the time, lost a few, and had plenty of fun at McGraw's and Stoneham's racetrack and casino. Playing before big crowds, the ballplayers did well financially, most of all Ruth. At least until the croupiers and assorted con artists got through with him, by which time he had little left of the $20,000 or so he'd gained from the trip.

In Stoneham's company, McGraw covered the 105 miles from Havana to Key West by seaplane. At the National League's annual winter meeting in New York a few days later, they made still another try for Rogers Hornsby, this time offering St. Louis $200,000 and four players for the man who'd hit .370 and won his first batting title the previous season. But because the four Giants didn't include Frisch, Branch Rickey and Cardinals president Sam Breadon still wouldn't deal.

Although Breadon and the other club owners still held virtually absolute control over their players, in important ways their power and prerogatives had diminished. That was true as well for league presidents John Heydler and Ban Johnson. Since November 15 the whole elaborate structure of Organized Baseball had been under new governance, ruled by a single commissioner to whom everybody else would be subordinate. Although discontent with the three-man National Commission had become so deep-seated that some kind of change was inevitable, the preceding September's gambling revelations had produced such fear of public repudiation among the owners that, almost in desperation, they'd quickly scrapped the old regime and made Kenesaw Mountain Landis, the fifty-four-year-old judge for the federal district of northern Illinois, virtual dictator of baseball.

White-maned, hugely egotistical, and hot-tempered, Landis had a reputation for high-handedness on the bench, for issuing sweeping decisions that won him big headlines but ended up being overturned in the higher federal courts. In other words, he hadn't been much of a judge. But he did have a passionate love for baseball, and he'd won the gratitude of the major league club owners by just sitting on a suit brought by the Federal League against Organized Baseball, until the Federals gave up and came to terms with their adversaries late in 1915.

Landis was hired (at $50,000 a year) to clean up a mess, and to a great extent he would do that. Never consistently and often on shaky evidence, he would expel more than two dozen players from Organized Baseball in the early 1920s. That included all eight Chicago White Sox implicated in the World Series scandal, even though the seven tried in Chicago in the summer of 1921 would all be acquitted. Lee Magee and Heinie Zimmerman were among the others Landis would banish, although somehow the commissioner couldn't find any reason for official action against Hal Chase. Fortunately for Landis and everybody else, Chase was too old to try a comeback in the majors.

Maybe the least deserving object of Landis's personal brand of justice was Benny Kauff. Nobody ever accused Kauff of giving anything but his best on the ballfield, but he'd been indicted in New York for being involved in his brother's auto thievery, and Landis suspended him pending the disposition of his case. At his trial in Bronx County Court in May 1921, with McGraw and John Tener, among others, serving as character witnesses, Kauff would win an acquittal. Landis would nonetheless bar him from Organized Baseball forever. Kauff's acquittal, Landis remarked to Fred Lieb, "smells to the high heaven, and was one of the worst miscarriages of justice ever to come to my attention." To Kauff he wrote, "your mere presence in the line-up would inevitably burden patrons of the game with grave apprehension as to its integrity."[1] In the fall of 1921 and again a year later, Kauff's petitions for permanent injunctions against Landis would be turned down in state supreme (district) court.

One of the earliest official actions taken by baseball's new "czar," as the sports press quickly dubbed Landis, was to put Stoneham and McGraw on notice that within six months they must dispose of their holdings in the Oriental Park track and casino. Baseball people, Landis said, had no business being involved with gamblers and gambling in any form. On July 13, 1921, Stoneham and McGraw unloaded the complex to a New Yorker named Thomas V. Monahan. Having put well over a million dollars into the venture and having yet to see any profits, Stoneham wasn't sorry to see it go. For McGraw, though, owning a piece of the Cuban enterprise, strutting around the track, and giving out twenty-five-dollar chips to guests' wives to start their evenings at the casino were important symbols of his success. He would continue to return to Cuba almost every winter, but it would never be entirely the same.

Despite Landis's apparent determination to cleanse baseball of the taint of crookedness, neither McGraw nor Stoneham was prepared to change his associates or his old habits. In October 1920 Arnold Rothstein, with William Fallon coaching his every move, had made a remarkable appearance before the Cook County grand jury. Sometimes politely, sometimes indignantly, sometimes almost casually, Rothstein turned aside any and all suggestions that he might have financed the framing of the World Series. Meanwhile, Fallon arranged to have the confessions of the Chicago players, as well as any evidence pertaining to Rothstein, disappear from the district attorney's office. Thus Rothstein would completely escape prosecution. And the following summer, with the trial of the seven White Sox under way in Chicago, Rothstein would sit as Stoneham's guest in his Polo Grounds box, the Giants president seemingly oblivious to appearances or public sentiment. Landis reprimanded Stoneham for that particular indiscretion, yet did nothing to stop Stoneham's continuing entanglement with Rothstein in a variety of enterprises.

If, with the advent of the commissioner system and the rise of Kenesaw Mountain Landis, a new era in baseball's off-the-field operations had commenced, then what was happening on the field indicated that the game itself was also undergoing fundamental changes. Before the 1920 season, both leagues had adopted a ban on the spitball and all other "trick deliveries," thereby bringing to an end a period of some sixteen or seventeen years in which ball-doctoring had been basic to the pitching craft. Seventeen spitballers, officially designated as such, would be allowed to finish out their careers throwing their favorite pitch, but nobody else anywhere in Organized Baseball could legally tamper with the ball in any way. (Until the mid-Twenties, that proscription even included applying rosin to the fingers.)

Meanwhile, most owners in both leagues, enjoying the prosperity of the post-war decade, were more willing to let spectators keep balls hit into the stands; and the umpires, presumably as instructed by league headquarters, increasingly scrutinized and discarded scuffed and stained balls. As a consequence, batters in the post–World War I decade tended to see whiter, easier-to-hit balls than in previous years.

The ball also seemed to travel faster and farther when they made contact. The Spalding company, exclusive manufacturer of baseballs for the major leagues and nearly all minor leagues, insisted that nothing had changed since 1910, when it had replaced its rubber-centered ball with one that had a cork center encased in rubber. Eventually the Spalding people did acknowledge that after 1919 they'd begun using a higher-grade woolen yarn that wound tighter around the cork-rubber core. Whatever had happened to the Spalding ball, both players and spectators were quick to see the difference. By 1920 the "dead ball" had gone the way of the legal spitter.

Babe Ruth's home runs earned him a lot of money ($41,000 for 1921, $52,000 per year in 1922–26). That elementary fact wasn't lost on the ballplayers of his generation, many of whom sought to emulate Ruth's long-distance prowess—with varying degrees of success. To aid them in driving the ball (as opposed to punching or slapping it, as had been the typical batting style), players began to use new types of bats, featuring larger knobs and thinner handles. Concentrating weight in the barrel or "fat" part, the new-style bats produced more of a whiplike effect—and more long hits. [2]

All of those factors—having to do with bats and balls, with what pitchers could and couldn't do, with what hitters were trying to do—came together to produce the biggest boost in batting statistics since 1893, when the pitching distance had been lengthened by ten feet.

In 1920 National and American League batsmen had combined for 630 home runs, against 338 in 1917 (the last previous 154-game season). By 1925 National Leaguers would clout 634 four-base hits, Americans 533—an overall increase of nearly 350 percent over 1917. Total runs scored in both leagues swelled by nearly 40 percent in 1917–25, and major league pitchers were yielding one and one-half more earned runs per nine innings in 1925 than they had eight years earlier.

Those bare statistics suggest what kind of baseball was being played in the 1920s, and what kind of adaptations John McGraw had to make in his own approach to the game. In 1911 McGraw's Giants had stolen 347 bases. In 1924 their ninety-five steals would lead the National League. The old game of base-stealing, bunting, executing the hit and run, of scratching and straining to grab a few runs and then relying on sturdy pitchers to hold a small lead, had given way to "big-inning" baseball. McGraw, who early in the century had maintained that low-scoring games bored the customers, had later exulted in "the faster, flashier" game of the pre-war years. By 1923, though, he would have to acknowledge that "with the . . . ball being hit all about the lot the necessity of taking chances on the bases has decreased. . . . A manager would look foolish not to play the game as it is, meet the new situation with new tactics. . . . there is no use in sending men down on a long chance of stealing a bag when there is a better chance of the batter hitting one for two bases, or, maybe, out of the lot." Still, he missed "the thrill . . . of seeing men shoot down the base paths, one after another, until they had stolen their way to a win. That was baseball—the kind of baseball that I learned to love when I got my first job." [3]

Under the changing potentialities and expectations of the "lively ball" era, McGraw might manage differently once the game got under way. In the more general management of his ballplayers, though, he hadn't changed much. He was still an old Oriole in the way he viewed the opposition. "I can appreciate the fine work of opposing players," he said in 1923, "but . . . I'm not much for that show of friendly feeling on the

field. . . ." He disliked fraternization between his and other teams'
players before, during, or after games. The old Orioles had shunned
enemy players; one season nobody on that team had said one word to
the hated Cleveland Spiders or Boston Beaneaters. Now, as his old Oriole
pal Hughey Jennings observed, "before a game you find the players of
the two teams in knots and groups as if they are attending a picnic."[4]

McGraw also continued to insist that if he were going to pay his men
good salaries, he had every right to expect them to remain in condition
to play at top form. And if he suspected them of drinking, wenching,
or otherwise not taking care of themselves, he felt fully justified in prying
into their lives, learning as much as he could about their conduct away
from the ballpark. He'd always been that way, but as he grew older, he
seemed to worry more than ever that his players might be doing things
off the field that he didn't know about and wouldn't approve of. Inasmuch
as he was still vain enough to believe that somehow he could reform
ne'er-do-wells on whom other managers had given up, he continued to
experience repeated frustration with men who wouldn't accept his regimen.

That regimen remained a demanding one. On road trips he required
that every player be in bed by 11:00 or 11:30 P.M., and his coaches
made room-by-room checks and dutifully reported anybody missing curfew. Those coaches also frequently served as spies, following players
around, logging their off-the-field activities, providing McGraw with
detailed rundowns. All of McGraw's players had to take their meals in
the dining room of the hotels where the team was staying, so that the
manager could keep close check on what and how much each man ate.
On home stands the Giants had to be at the Polo Grounds by nine each
morning and on the field by ten for about two hours of practice. Then
he sent them home for lunch and rest before they had to be back at the
ballpark, about two o'clock, for that afternoon's game.

"When he said something, it was McGraw," Frank Frisch recalled
about his years with the Giants. As team captain, Larry Doyle had served
as McGraw's whipping boy. "Pinhead" was one of the manager's favorite
forms of address for Doyle. A few years later, as Doyle's successor,
Frisch also had to get used to taking tongue-lashings for the whole team,
to being called "cement head" and "dumb Dutchman." Frisch learned
as well that McGraw had little patience with players' injuries. If a man
didn't get over his hurts and back in the lineup as quickly as McGraw

thought he should, McGraw would bluntly remind him that he was being paid to play baseball.[5]

So in the spring of 1921, John McGraw began his forty-ninth year on earth and his thirty-second in professional baseball as a man whose disposition, tastes, values, and general outlook were fundamentally what they'd been throughout his adult life. His twentieth season as manager of the New York Giants began on March 5, when he arrived at San Antonio with Blanche McGraw after another Cuban sojourn. He found everything going well, as indeed he'd expected to find it with Hughey Jennings in charge. Having resigned after fourteen years as manager at Detroit, Jennings had quickly found a place with McGraw as his new number-one assistant. Including Jennings, McGraw now had three coaches, the first manager to have that many.

Jennings's successor at Detroit was Ty Cobb. The bad feeling between Cobb and McGraw was still strong. Cobb also trained his Tigers at San Antonio that spring, but neither manager would hear of exhibition games between the New York and Detroit ball clubs. Nor, despite the fact that their hotels were only a block apart, was there any commingling of players—at least none that McGraw or Cobb knew about.

Larry Doyle, who, as a rookie, had gained a measure of immortality by proclaiming to the world, "It's great to be young, and a Giant," was neither by 1921. With Doyle now managing at Toronto, Dave Bancroft assumed the team captaincy—and the extra $500 that went with the job. McGraw intended to keep Frisch at second base, but the Bronx native would end up at third with Johnny Rawlings, acquired from Philadelphia during the season, playing second. "Highpockets" Kelly had possession of first, with Bancroft at shortstop. Ross Youngs had reached stardom in 1920, batting .351 with 204 base hits, second in both categories to fellow Texan Rogers Hornsby. As far as McGraw was concerned, Youngs, with "a disposition which is almost flawless," was already "a great baseball player."[6] George Burns would be McGraw's left-fielder for the ninth straight year, but with Benny Kauff in limbo, he still had a hole in his outfield. Frank Snyder and Earl Smith would divide the catching, and both would have strong batting years. Art Nehf, Jess Barnes, Fred Toney, and Phil Douglas were the mound mainstays.

In Frisch, Youngs, and Kelly, McGraw had three of the finest young players in Giants history. It wasn't an outstanding ball club otherwise, but McGraw seemed confident as he led the Giants back to New York, through a succession of exhibition-game stopovers across the upper South.

Bill Brennan again did the umpiring on the tour, under contract to the Giants, as he'd been doing for the past six springs. The fact that Brennan was still in the Giants' employ when he was about to rejoin the National League umpiring staff didn't seem to bother Landis, John Heydler, or anybody else in authority. Brennan's work on the trip, though, so bothered the Washington Senators, the Giants' opponents most of the time, that in Jackson, Tennessee, Brennan declared a forfeit to New York when manager George McBride wouldn't stop arguing in the third inning. Subsequently, under Landis's directive, Washington president Clark Griffith would have to reimburse Charles Stoneham $1,081, the amount New York had had to return to the Jackson fans as the Giants' part of the gate receipts.

Brennan was behind the plate for the Giants' first home game on April 21. Twenty-five thousand fans watched them lose to Bill Donovan's Philadelphia Phillies, 6–5. On April 30, as he was batting the ball around in infield practice, McGraw slipped in mud at home plate and badly sprained an ankle. Two days later, on crutches, with Fallon at his side, he appeared in federal district court in Manhattan to stand trial on the long-pending liquor-possession charge.

Assistant U.S. Attorney Albert B. Unger testified that when he'd questioned McGraw at his apartment on August 14, 1920, McGraw had admitted cashing a check in the Lambs' Club grill and buying several bottles of whiskey there. No, McGraw swore, he hadn't bought any liquor at the Lambs' Club, because he'd already given all the money he had with him to the scrubwomen in the room. Apparently that non sequitur didn't bother the jurors; it took them only five minutes to find McGraw not guilty. After giving them hurried thanks, the Giants manager was off to the Polo Grounds for that afternoon's game.

McGraw's exoneration may have resulted from the government's failure to present any witnesses who'd been present at the Lambs' Club, the jurors' sympathy and admiration for the famous Giants manager, or even some of Fallon's well-known skill at jury-tampering. Whatever the reason, McGraw was finally out of the clutches of the law.

But only temporarily. On the morning of July 26 an Allegheny County deputy sheriff found him at the Hotel Schenley, where the Giants always stayed when they played in Pittsburgh, and served an arrest warrant issued by a local common pleas court judge. Instead of being taken into custody, McGraw was permitted to go to the courthouse and post $3,000 bond to ensure that he would appear later in a civil suit brought against him by a Pittsburgher named George Duffy. Suing McGraw for $20,000, Duffy alleged that on the evening of June 3 (during the Giants' last stopover in Pittsburgh), Charles Stoneham had invited him to Stoneham's and McGraw's suite at the Schenley. Already drunk when they arrived, McGraw took offense at something Duffy said and proceeded to knock him unconscious. He was beaten so badly, Duffy claimed, that he had to remain in bed, under a physician's care, for several days.

On the afternoon of July 26 at Forbes Field, Bill Klem banished McGraw and Johnny Rawlings in a game the Giants eventually won in ten innings. The next morning Heydler wired that he was suspended for using profanity to an umpire. In twenty-four hours, McGraw had been arrested, ejected, and suspended.

With Jennings in charge, the Giants also won that afternoon to make it three out of four on that stay in Pittsburgh. On July 29, after a fast trip into New York to apologize to Heydler and get his suspension lifted, McGraw rejoined the team in Cincinnati, in time for a double-header sweep of the Reds that gave the Giants the League lead for the first time over Pittsburgh.

McGraw's outfield, unsettled since 1919, now seemed set with Youngs in right, Burns shifted to center, and "Irish" Meusel in left. Suspended at Philadelphia for lackadaisical play, Meusel had just come to the Giants in exchange for three benchwarmers and $30,000. Earlier in the season, also from Philadelphia, McGraw had obtained not only Rawlings but Charles Dillon "Casey" Stengel, a ten-year-veteran outfielder. The irrepressible Stengel was so happy to be traded to McGraw's team that, when told of the deal after that day's game in Philadelphia, he left for New York right then. "I wasn't taking no chances," he would later explain. "I didn't want anybody to change their mind."[7]

Another of McGraw's deals didn't go through because Judge Landis wouldn't permit it. Heinie Groh, Cincinnati's fine little third-baseman, was a holdout. He would sign with the Reds, Groh announced, only on condition that he be traded. McGraw reached an agreement with Garry Herrmann whereby Groh would sign, then go over to the Giants in exchange for $100,000 and three players. Landis ordered Groh to stay in Cincinnati, contending that it was "an unhealthy situation if a dissatisfied player could dictate his transfer to a strong contender before he agreed to sign a contract."[8] If Groh was frustrated and Herrmann, who could have used the money, was disappointed, McGraw was furious with Landis. For the second time in the six months since he'd become commissioner, Landis had told him what he could and couldn't do, first with his own money, then with the ball club's. Things hadn't been done that way under the old regime.

In the first three weeks of August, George Gibson's roistering, high-living Pittsburgh Pirates not only regained first place but pulled away from the Giants. By the evening of August 23, when they came into New York, they'd built a comfortable seven-and-a-half-game lead. Barney Dreyfuss, the Pirates' owner, had approved plans for adding more seats at Forbes Field, in anticipation of a World Series. Charley Grimm, strumming his left-handed banjo in the dugout; Rabbit Maranville, as fun-loving off the field as he was volatile on it; Dave Robertson, who'd never liked playing for McGraw; and various other Pirates did little to conceal their contempt for McGraw and his ball club.

What followed over the next five days was one of those bursts of energy and excitement that determine the course of a long and often plodding baseball season. With McGraw haranguing them daily, the Giants won all five games. On Wednesday the twenty-fourth, George Kelly homered behind Art Nehf in the Giants' 10–2 victory in the first game of a doubleheader. In the nightcap Phil Douglas, only recently reinstated after another of his "vacations," pitched splendidly, gaining a 7–0 shutout. On Thursday, Fred Toney pitched and batted New York to a 5–2 win, and the next day Douglas, with only a day's rest, outdueled Earl Hamilton 2–1, Frisch and Youngs driving in the Giants' runs. On Saturday 35,000 people watched Nehf throw a four-hitter and Meusel drive home the go-ahead runs in a 3–1 triumph, Nehf's sixth of the season over the Pirates.

Although they left town still ahead by two and a half, the Pirates were badly shaken. By mid-September, when the Giants arrived for three games, Pittsburgh had fallen back by a game and a half. Knowing that the series would probably decide the pennant race, McGraw took no chances. He had Jennings; Alvin "Cozy" Dolan and Jesse Burkett, his other two regular coaches; and even Hans Lobert, hired for late-season duty, keep his players secluded at the Schenley. The Giants weren't allowed to leave the hotel for any reason except to go—as a group—to nearby Forbes Field. McGraw even ordered sealed bottles of water from a local malt company (formerly a brewery, like many such places in the Twenties) for use in the visitors' locker room and dugout.

Those stringent precautions may have been more McGravian theater than anything else. In any case, the Giants won two of three, despite periodic barrages of pop bottles and threats of even greater mayhem from the Smoke City faithful. That gave New York sixteen wins in the season's twenty-two games against the Pirates. Ten days afterward the idle Giants learned that in St. Louis, the Pittsburgh team had just dropped a double-header to the Cardinals, clinching New York's seventh National League pennant under McGraw.

The 1921 World Series, opening on October 5, was the third straight under a five-of-nine format and the first to take place entirely in one ballpark. Miller Huggins's Yankees, with Babe Ruth slamming fifty-nine homers, driving in 171 runs, and scoring 177, had won their first American League pennant—and again drawn substantially more people into the Polo Grounds than the Giants. McGraw didn't like that, didn't like Ruth's influence on the game, in fact didn't like anything about the New York Yankees. With McGraw determined to reestablish the Giants' supremacy on the New York baseball scene, the first all–New York World Series would be a bitterly fought one.

It didn't get off well for the Giants. "Shufflin' Phil" Douglas, a fifteen-game winner despite his mid-summer absence, pitched well enough to win the opener, but the Yankees' Carl Mays shut out the Giants. In game two, despite furious harassment from the Giants' bench, Waite Hoyt also threw a shutout, a three-hitter, to best Art Nehf. After he'd retired the Giants midway through the game, Hoyt was on his way back to the Yankees' dugout when he was almost hit by a bar of soap, a token of his recent commercial endorsements. The young pitcher fired the soap bar at the Giants' bench (whence he assumed it had come), barely missing McGraw himself.

"I am anything but discouraged," said McGraw after a second straight blanking.[9] He knew his team, which had averaged nearly .300 for the season, would start hitting. As they did the next day, hammering Bob Shawkey and three other Yankees pitchers for twenty hits and thirteen runs, including an eight-run barrage in the seventh inning. Ruth, more-over, ripped his elbow so badly sliding into a base that the next day, with his arm infected, he swung the bat with difficulty. He was still able to put one into the bleachers in the ninth inning off Douglas, but it wasn't enough, Shufflin' Phil outpitching Mays 4–2.

Ruth was in even worse shape by game five, yet he managed to beat out a bunt to trigger a late-inning rally, as Hoyt pitched another gem, again at Nehf's expense. On October 11 Jess Barnes came on in relief of Toney and struck out ten Yankees in an 8–5 Giants victory that tied the Series.

With Ruth unable to play anymore except to pinch-hit one time, the Yankees could score only a single run in the next two games. Douglas, in his third distinguished outing of the Series, gained his second win, a taut 2–1 duel with Mays. The Giants closed it out on Thursday, October 13. Again both Nehf and Hoyt pitched superbly, but in their third meeting Nehf had the better luck, the Giants scoring the game's only run on a first-inning error by shortstop Roger Peckinpaugh. It ended on a brilliant double play. Rawlings dived to knock down Frank Baker's hot smash in short right field, then scrambled up and threw to Kelly to nip Baker. Aaron Ward, who'd been on first and apparently thought the ball had gone through, headed for third, where Kelly's peg to Frisch cut him down for the Series' last out.

"I have the greatest baseball club in the world," proclaimed McGraw in the clubhouse. "And unquestionably the gamest."[10] Although only 25,410 came out for the eighth and final game (convincing Landis that the five-of-nine format tired the fans), the full houses for the first four games made it the richest Series yet for the players. And despite being outdrawn by their tenants, it had still been the most profitable year in the history of the Giants franchise. Joe Vila's cautious estimate was that the National Exhibition Company had cleared $400,000 in 1921, including receipts from the World Series and the Army-Navy game played that autumn at the Polo Grounds.

McGraw also should have been financially better off than ever. Besides his Series share and a nice little dividend on his NEC stock, he'd just finished the last year of a five-year contract at $40,000 a year, and in January 1922 Stoneham would sign him for another five years—at $50,000. For 1922 the only people in baseball making a bigger annual salary than McGraw would be Babe Ruth and Kenesaw Mountain Landis.

Yet he still couldn't show much in the way of a bank account. Besides the thousands of dollars he gave away to charity-seekers and lost at racetracks and casinos, that fall he had to settle out of court with George Duffy in the Pittsburgh lawsuit. The amount of the settlement was never disclosed, but it must have been at least $5,000, a quarter of the figure specified in Duffy's suit. Presumably McGraw also had to pay back at least part of the $50,000 Stoneham had loaned him three years earlier so he could buy into the NEC, although it's possible that Stoneham may eventually have written off most of the loan.

Late in 1920 the McGraws had acquired one major tangible asset— a ten-room brick house on Edgewood Avenue in Pelham, a newly developed residential area in Westchester County. It was the first residence McGraw had owned since he and his first wife lived in adjoining row houses with the Wilbert Robinsons in Baltimore more than twenty years earlier. Never having learned to operate an automobile, McGraw depended on Edward James, a young black man whom he'd befriended and brought from San Antonio, to chauffeur him the nine or ten miles from Pelham to the Polo Grounds. Also living at the house in Pelham was Mildred Jefferson, a hefty black woman who became the McGraws' cook and maid shortly after they moved in.

Despite his differences with commissioner Landis, McGraw had him out to Pelham for dinner in 1921. Dave and Edna Bancroft were also frequent guests, and during his two and one-half years with the Giants, Casey Stengel, still a bachelor, spent much of his time at the McGraw house. Often in the early morning hours, Blanche McGraw would awaken to the sounds and smells of Stengel and her husband in the kitchen, frying bacon and eggs and still talking baseball. Those long nighttime sessions were part of the education under McGraw that Stengel would cite when, many years later, people asked how he'd become one of the winningest managers in the game's history.

Before he left for Cuba, McGraw finally landed Heinie Groh, paying the Reds at least $50,000 and also giving up Miguel Gonzalez, the Cuban catcher, and George Burns, the last man left from the 1911–13 champions. Groh, McGraw announced, would be his third-baseman; Frisch would take over at second. The Giants also paid San Francisco of the Pacific Coast League $75,000 for outfielder Jimmy O'Connell, a Santa Clara College product (like Hal Chase), who'd performed brilliantly in his first season of professional ball. McGraw decided to leave O'Connell at San Francisco for 1922.

When the manager arrived at San Antonio at the end of February, Phil Douglas wasn't yet on hand. Despite his three fine appearances in the World Series, Douglas had been the subject of trade talk all winter; club secretary James J. Tierney had openly referred to him as "a bad actor." At San Antonio, McGraw said that he'd doubled Douglas's salary, but whether he drew the extra money depended "on his behaving and

keeping in condition. . . . If he won't behave I don't want him around.
I won't put up with behavior like last year's." Douglas's fifteen wins in
1921, he added, were "no record at all. Why, I can take any one of the
young pitchers on the staff last year and make them win that many."
When Douglas finally arrived a month later, he acknowledged that he
hadn't liked the conditions written into his contract, but "that's all past
and buried now."[11]

Except for Frank Frisch, who missed the first month of the season
with a badly infected foot, the result of a spring-training spiking, the
Giants got off to a flying start, winning sixteen of their first twenty. In
the season's second game, Douglas, McGraw's only designated spitballer, outpitched Brooklyn's Arthur "Dazzy" Vance, and in succeeding
weeks the big Southerner continued to look better than he ever had. The
main disciplinary problem McGraw had wasn't Douglas but Earl Smith,
who liked to frequent speakeasies, miss curfew, and talk back when the
manager chided him. Finally he fined the catcher and sent him home
to Arkansas to meditate on his misdeeds. Smith was back within ten
days, although with Frank Snyder outhitting every other catcher in the
majors, he'd definitely become number-two man.

McGraw was so bothered by sinusitis that spring that he stayed in the
dugout in street clothes well into June. Losing Ralph Shinners, his
promising new center-fielder, did nothing for his physical or mental well-
being. At the end of May, Shinners, playing well in his rookie season
after being purchased from Indianapolis, was almost fatally beaned by
George Smith of the Phillies. Hospitalized for two weeks, Shinners was
back in uniform by late June. By then, though, McGraw had solved his
center-field problem by platooning the left-handed Stengel and the right-
hand-hitting Bill Cunningham.

On June 29 Shinners and McGraw were both watching a game against
the Phillies from the bench in the Giants' bullpen in right center field.
George Smith, just lifted for a pinch-hitter, walked past on his way to
the visitors' dressing room and met a shower of McGraw's choicest
obscenities. Smith swung at McGraw and missed, whereupon Shinners
rushed between them and took a right to the jaw for his troubles. As
Smith and Shinners rolled on the ground, McGraw tried to land a blow
on the Phillies pitcher, only to miss and cut Shinners's cheek. By then,
players from both bullpens had arrived to break it up. Commissioner
Landis was present, but from his box behind first, he complained, he
hadn't been able to see much of the fracas. If he'd known there was

going to be a fight, "I would have been on hand [out there] for the excitement."[12] No, he didn't think any disciplinary action was in order.

By winning that day, the Giants improved their record to 42–24 and enjoyed a lead of five and one-half games over St. Louis. In July, though, things took a bad turn. Groh reinjured a long-troublesome knee and was disabled for six weeks. After a poor road trip that included dropping three of four before record National League crowds in St. Louis, the Giants came home leading Branch Rickey's club by only half a game.[13] McGraw's nagging upper-respiratory complaint had developed into bronchitis and lung congestion, and he'd been hospitalized for two days in Cincinnati. Despite his physicians' insistence that he remain at home, he watched from the exit gate in right center at the Polo Grounds as his team defeated the Cardinals four times in five games to gain some breathing room.

For pennant insurance, McGraw gave Fred Toney, two rookies, and $100,000 to Boston for Hugh "Red" McQuillan, a right-hander who'd had a totally undistinguished career with the Braves but had the makings of a first-rate pitcher—or so McGraw believed. And he took on Jack Scott, another veteran right-hander, who'd developed a sore arm and been released by Cincinnati. Scott showed up at the Polo Grounds at the end of July and convinced McGraw to give him a trial. McGraw staked him to fifty dollars, watched him throw, liked what he saw, and gave him a contract. After pitching a couple of relief innings, Scott got his first start on August 4, when he outdueled the great Alexander of Chicago 2–1 at the Polo Grounds.

Meanwhile, Phil Douglas was headed toward disaster. Over the first half of the season he'd been McGraw's most reliable pitcher, posting eleven wins and the staff's lowest earned-run average. It seemed that at age thirty-two the big spitballer might have finally found himself. Then, after losing to Pittsburgh at the Polo Grounds on July 31, Douglas eluded Jesse Burkett, who'd been one of the National League's great hitters in the Nineties but now was paid mainly to serve as Douglas's off-the-field "keeper." Early the next morning, a Tuesday, police found the pitcher, dead drunk, at a place on the Upper West Side, not far from where Douglas lived with his wife and two children. At the 135th Street station, Burkett took him in tow, then called Francis X. McQuade. They admitted him to a private sanitarium on Central Park West, where he was put under heavy sedation. McGraw visited him there a couple of days later.

Released on Saturday the fifth, a dried-out and depressed Douglas found that he had to pay the $225 bill for his sanitarium stay. McGraw summoned him to the Polo Grounds, cursed him at length, and fined him $100 plus five days' pay. The next day, as the Giants fell 7–3 to Cincinnati, Douglas lumbered into the press box section behind home plate and threatened a local sportswriter who'd reported that he'd been fined. After other writers gathered around the pitcher and pressured him into admitting that the report was correct, he left quietly and disconsolately.

Two days later, sitting in the Giants' clubhouse and using club stationery, Douglas penned a letter to Leslie Mann, St. Louis outfielder and Douglas's former teammate at Chicago. "I want to leave here," he wrote, "but I want some inducement. I don't want this guy [McGraw] to win the pennant and I feel if I stay here I will win it for him." If "the fellows" (Mann and other Cardinals) would "send a man over . . . with the goods," then he would go home "to fishing camp and stay there."[14]

On Monday, August 14, Douglas and Burkett were to follow the Giants to Pittsburgh, where McGraw reportedly intended to lift the pitcher's suspension and start him on the sixteenth. On the Saturday before they left, William Bender, M.D., the Giants' team physician, called at Douglas's home and gave him another injection of a sedative, presumably to make him sleep, possibly to counteract his alcoholic withdrawal. At Penn Station on Monday evening, Douglas looked well and seemed quite upbeat, flashing a new diamond ring to Frank Graham of the *Evening Sun* and bragging that he wasn't going to end up broke like a lot of ballplayers.

Les Mann, a graduate of Springfield College, a well-known figure in national Y.M.C.A. affairs, and a ballplayer whose honesty had always been above suspicion, did what everybody, with the possible exception of Phil Douglas, would have expected him to do. He went directly to Branch Rickey with Douglas's letter. Rickey contacted Landis in Chicago, and by Wednesday morning, August 16, the commissioner was in Pittsburgh, in McGraw's room at the Schenley, telling the Giants manager that Douglas had to go. Landis and McGraw called in Douglas, who admitted writing the letter to Mann. At that, Landis told him that it was all over, that he was out of baseball for good.

In announcing Douglas's expulsion to the press later that morning, Landis described the whole business as "tragic and deplorable," then sat with a pained expression on his face as McGraw waxed righteously indignant. "He will never play another game in Organized Baseball," declared McGraw, "and not a league will knowingly admit him to its parks. Winning games is not everything. . . . it will be a fine thing for the sport—this exposure of another 'shady' player. Personally I am heartily glad to be rid of him." When McGraw added that "Without exception, he is the dirtiest ballplayer I have ever seen," the scribes in the room must have wondered whether he could possibly have forgotten the shenanigans of Hal Chase and Heinie Zimmerman.[15]

With $100 in his pocket, given him by club secretary Tierney on McGraw's order, Douglas left for New York that evening in the silent company of Jesse Burkett. At his apartment, for the newspaper people, he dolefully went over the whole train of events, acknowledging that he'd written to Mann, adding that when he'd realized how dumb that had been, he'd tried to get in touch with Mann and have him destroy the letter. Douglas also hired a lawyer named Edward Lauterbach, who petitioned Landis for a hearing, only to be told that Lauterbach had to come up with new evidence. After a protracted period of bedridden depression, Shufflin' Phil took his family home to Cowan, Tennessee. More than a decade later, he would still be pitching semi-pro ball in towns across the Appalachian South.

If Douglas's fall wasn't "tragic," as Landis described it, then it was still deeply pathetic. Douglas loved three things: whiskey, his family, and baseball—probably in that order. And he'd come to despise John McGraw, a man who'd reviled and humiliated him for three years. Although a certain number of imponderables would always cloud the affair, Shufflin' Phil's motives were fairly simple, as well as simpleminded. The *Sporting News* was cruel but nonetheless basically accurate when it described Douglas as being "sub-normal, at his best, from which you may guess his mentality after a two-weeks' debauch. . . ."[16]

Although most of the Giants had liked Douglas and hated to see him go, his passing and the accompanying publicity seemed to have no effect at all on their performance on the field—except maybe to improve it. After winning the last two games in the Pittsburgh series, they went on to take nine of eleven on the road trip. When they returned to New York at the end of August, St. Louis, Chicago, and Pittsburgh were bunched six or seven games back of them. After losing five of seven to Brooklyn at Ebbets Field and the Polo Grounds, the Giants' lead was still intact—

as it remained until September 25. A 5–4, ten-inning victory over St.
Louis that day clinched another League title, McGraw's eighth with the
Giants.

McGraw's pitching staff, shaky much of the season, still showed the
lowest earned-run average (3.45) in the League. Nehf led the staff with
nineteen wins; rookie Bill "Rosy" Ryan hung up seventeen victories.
As a team the Giants batted .305 (second in the league to St. Louis).
Every regular except Heinie Groh hit at least .321, and Stengel and
Cunningham, dividing the time in center field, batted .368 and .328,
respectively. With 132 runs batted in, Irish Meusel, brother of the
Yankees' equally heavy-hitting Bob, had only four less than Rogers
Hornsby, who also led the League in batting average (.401) and home
runs (forty-two). If it wasn't a great team, it was a very good one, a
talented, experienced, smart bunch of ballplayers, virtually all of whom
readily accepted the common estimate that, whatever his faults as a
man, John McGraw was the greatest manager who'd ever lived.

The upcoming World Series would be the first to be broadcast over
the new communications marvel, the radio. Stations WJZ in Newark and
WYG in Schenectady would transmit the progress of each game from
the Polo Grounds, with Grantland Rice, who'd become one of the country's best-known sportswriters, on hand to provide a play-by-play narrative that would be broadcast "live" out of Newark and as it was telegraphed
to Schenectady. Although Rice's accounts would reach into only a few
thousand homes and other places with radio "receiving sets," they marked
the beginning of baseball's electronic age, a period in which people
would rely increasingly on electronic rather than print media for their
day-to-day coverage of the sport.

The 1922 Series offered another all-Manhattan matchup. With Ruth
out of the lineup much of the time for one reason or another, the Yankees
had just squeezed past the St. Louis Browns, who that year fielded the
strongest team in their fifty-two-year history in the American League.
But the Babe was in fine fettle for the Series opener on October 5, joking
and posing before the game with McGraw, who wore street clothes (as
he had during the last part of the season), including a topcoat against
the damp and chill. For the first time McGraw's players sported the
white stockings with red-and-blue stripes that would be the Giants'
trademark through the mid-1920s.

Among the 37,000 at the Polo Grounds were Christy Mathewson, his
tuberculosis in remission; General John J. Pershing, the nation's foremost

military figure; and Tammany's own Alfred E. Smith, former governor and budding presidential aspirant. They saw Irish Meusel single home two runs and then drive in the game-winner with a sacrifice fly off Joe Bush as Nehf and Ryan combined to hold the Yankees to two tallies.

Game two ended in confusion and controversy when plate umpire Ernie Hildebrand and Bill Klem, senior official on the field, agreed at the end of ten innings, with the score 3–3, that it might become too dark to complete another inning. With the game called and the sun still high, angry fans jostled Landis and his wife and pelted them with wadded paper as they made their way out of the ballpark. Furious with the umpires and with suggestions that the game had been called to give the owners an extra day of big profits, Landis announced that night that the entire second-game receipts, some $120,500, would be turned over to New York area charities.

That ten-inning tie was as close as the American Leaguers came to victory in the Series. Jack Scott, who'd won eight and lost two in the pennant stretch drive, threw a four-hit shutout to beat Waite Hoyt in game three. The next day Red McQuillan, unimpressive since coming to the Giants, was good enough to best Carl Mays, 4–3; and on October 8, 38,551, the biggest crowd in New York history, were on hand to see the Giants end it. Kelly's single in the eighth inning sent home the winning runs; Bush lost again and Nehf won again, 5–3.

It was probably McGraw's supreme moment in baseball. "We yield to none in acknowledging the Napoleonic qualities of McGraw," proclaimed the *Sporting News* in the aftermath of the Giants' victory. The secret of the outcome was that Giants pitching neutralized Ruth, who went hitless in the last three games and managed only a .118 average for the Series as a whole. Afterward the legend would grow that McGraw called every pitch his moundsmen threw, and that a steady diet of slow curve balls steadily foiled the Babe. McGraw may indeed have called every pitch, standing on the step of the Giants' dugout, holding a bat in both hands. As McQuillan would relate in later years, "If the right hand was on top, a fast ball; the left hand, a curve ball; both hands down the bat, a changeup; bat across hands, a slow curve." And it was slow curves, "curve balls into the dirt, at Ruth's feet," as McQuillan put it, that got the greatest slugger in the game's history out. Yet as McGraw himself later admitted, "we caught Ruth in one of his slumps. . . ."[17] If in fact McGraw's slow curves had proved to be Ruth's permanent weakness, then American League pitchers would have got the word, and Ruth wouldn't have battered them as he did in subsequent years—a .393 average, forty-one homers, 131 runs batted in in 1923, for example.

At the time, though, McGraw reigned as the unquestioned master of the game. "McGraw came as near to perfection in his strategy as man probably ever will come in baseball," vapored H. G. Salsinger, the respected Detroit sportswriter. After Ross Youngs caught Aaron Ward's fly ball for the final out of the Series, McGraw emerged from the dugout to have his hat knocked off, his back pounded, and his cheek kissed by adoring fans. A big number of them waited until he emerged from the clubhouse on the Eighth Avenue side of the bleachers. He said a few words of thanks and shook the hand of an elderly woman who'd pushed through the crowd. "I can go home now," she announced. "I've seen the greatest manager in baseball."[18]

As indeed he seemed to just about everybody that winter. And not only had McGraw and his Giants utterly vanquished the Yankees, the American League upstarts were now banished as well. The previous spring, after being told that 1922 would be the last year they could lease the Polo Grounds, Yankees owners Ruppert and Huston had announced plans for a great new sports facility to be built in the extreme south Bronx, in fact almost directly across from the Polo Grounds, on the other side of the Harlem River bridge. Ruppert (who bought out Huston right after the World Series) would push construction through the off-season to have what people were already calling "the Yankee Stadium" ready by April 1923.

Despite undergoing surgery for the removal of cartilage blocking his nasal passages (a condition dating back to 1903, when Dummy Taylor's errant throw had smashed his nose), McGraw passed a generally pleasant off-season. Late in October he returned to Baltimore for another reunion of the old Orioles, arranged as part of the annual civic festival. Although McGraw's relations remained distant with Wilbert Robinson (at whose house on Charles Street the onetime heroes gathered first), he delighted in seeing Ned Hanlon, Dirty Jack Doyle, Steve Brodie, and Sadie McMahon, and in riding through the streets with them (and Hugh Jennings) in a tally-ho driven by Bernard Gough, who'd been their batboy. Dan Brouthers, employed as a gatekeeper for several years at the Polo Grounds, was too ill to attend, and Wee Willie Keeler, confined to his home in Brooklyn, would soon die of heart disease.

Rarely one to stand pat, even with a world's champion, McGraw first fired Jesse Burkett, who'd failed to keep Phil Douglas out of trouble, then put aside his lingering resentment toward Baltimore owner-manager Jack Dunn for not giving him first choice on Babe Ruth, at least long enough to pay Dunn $65,000 and three players for Jack Bentley. Bentley's performance in three years in the International League had convinced many people that he was the next Ruth. Besides batting .349 as a first-baseman–outfielder the past season, Bentley had won thirteen times in fourteen decisions as a pitcher. His pitching record since 1920 had been an amazing 41–5.

With McGraw's enthusiastic approval, Christy Mathewson returned to baseball that winter. Along with Emil Fuchs, a New York attorney who'd often represented the Giants (and more recently Benny Kauff), and Bostonian James McDonough, Mathewson bought the Boston Braves for $300,000 and became the club's new president.

McGraw also gave his blessing to Rube Benton's return to the National League. The past season Benton had won twenty-two games in pitching St. Paul to an American Association pennant, and Cincinnati had purchased his contract. Despite the well-publicized fact that Benton had known beforehand about the 1919 World Series fix, Landis had let him stay in Organized Baseball and hadn't objected to his moving back up with the Reds. McGraw praised Benton's conduct back in August 1919 in reporting to Art Fletcher that Heinie Zimmerman had tried to bribe him. The Giants leader also acknowledged that he'd contacted St. Paul owner Pat Kelly the past August about buying Benton when Douglas was banned, but Kelly had refused to name a price. Various commentators disputed the decision to let Benton pitch in the majors again when Buck Weaver and others who'd shared his "guilty knowledge" remained barred. Landis apparently saw no inconsistency in his actions.

The McGraws were in Cuba with Hugh Jennings and his second wife, Ada, when McGraw's reminiscences, first syndicated in various major newspapers, were published in book form by the adventuresome house of Boni and Liveright. Entitled *My Thirty Years in Baseball*, McGraw's book was informative on some aspects of his life, disingenuous on others, and simply mistaken on still others. In other words, it was a fairly typical book of its kind.

The McGraws and Jenningses were among about one hundred Giants-connected people—ballplayers, club officials, writers, and wives—who descended on San Antonio in early March 1923. McGraw had close to forty players on hand; thirty years earlier he'd been one of only fourteen

Orioles with Ned Hanlon at Charleston, South Carolina. Miffed over the reluctance of several men to sign their contracts, McGraw declared that except for Rogers Hornsby and Edd Roush, he had the twelve highest paid performers in the National League. All of the reluctant signees shortly came around, but then McGraw learned that some of his players had been enjoying the city's largely illegal attractions to such an extent that they'd missed curfew. After interrogating his suspects, he fined Jack Scott one hundred dollars and "Oil" Smith twenty-five dollars, assigning Smith to the rookie squad as an added indignity. Scott was an ingrate in McGraw's estimation, while Smith had been "an anarchist with no respect for law and order." McGraw would trade the catcher if anybody cared to have him. "I don't want a fellow like that around me," he said disgustedly.[19]

Besides his players' nighttime habits, McGraw fretted over Jack Bentley's waistline, Heinie Groh's knee, and Jack Bancroft's slow recovery from a bout with pneumonia. Yet he was out in uniform every day, slapping grounders to the infielders, keeping close watch on Jimmy O'Connell and Travis Jackson, his other prize rookies, and looking generally chipper despite his advancing years and own advancing girth. At Memphis, on the way east with the Chicago White Sox, he gave a party for himself on his fiftieth birthday.

When the Giants played their home opener on April 26, the Polo Grounds was still undergoing renovation and enlargement. At a cost of $400,000, Stoneham had decided to increase its seating capacity to some 52,000, mainly by tearing down the old wooden bleachers and extending the double-decked grandstand around into center field from both sides. New narrow bleachers, wedged in at the ends of the grandstand, would flank a new four-story structure housing dressing facilities and club offices. Already eccentric, the Polo Grounds' outfield distances would become even more so. Down the right-field line, it would be only 256 feet to the twelve-foot wall; down the line in left, 279 feet. Yet because of the park's horseshoe configuration, a ball would have to carry more than 400 feet to reach the stands in left and right center, and approximately 500 feet to the steps of the new clubhouse in dead center. In the era of the lively ball, the Polo Grounds would obviously become a haven for extreme pull hitters, especially left-hand-batting ones.

About 41,000 seats were available for the home opener, of which no more than 25,000 were filled. (Eight days earlier, some 60,000 had seen Babe Ruth christen Yankee Stadium with a game-winning home run.)

The Giants-Braves game offered plenty of nostalgia, with McGraw and Mathewson embracing during the pre-game ceremonies and Rube Marquard, 198 major league wins behind him but only three ahead, starting for Boston. Marquard lasted until the seventh inning in what ended up as a 7–3 Giants victory.

The 1923 season brought a third straight pennant, and a relatively easy one. The Giants didn't pull away from the rest of the League as they had in other years, but they were never out of first place and never seriously threatened. At the end of May, with the Giants having run up a 26–9 mark and built a comfortable lead over Pittsburgh, Joe Vila was ready to proclaim them "the most powerful ball team ever put together. . . ."[20] If they weren't that, they were decidedly a powerhouse. Frisch batted .348, Youngs 336; Kelly and Bancroft were the other regulars above .300, while Stengel, who started platooning with Cunningham midway through the season after the disappointing O'Connell was benched, hit .339. Kelly, Frisch, and Meusel all drove in more than a hundred runs, with Meusel's 125 leading the League. McQuillan, Scott, Nehf, and Ryan each posted 13–16 wins; Jack Bentley, besides winning thirteen games, batted .427 in eighty-nine times at bat and seemed well on his way to confirming predictions that he would be the most talented all-around ballplayer since Ruth.

After appearing before the biggest crowd in National League history— some 41,000 for the afternoon half of the Memorial Day double-header versus Brooklyn—the Giants embarked on their first western swing playing .750 baseball. By then Groh's chronic knee problem had forced him to give way to nineteen-year-old Travis Jackson. Recommended to McGraw by Kid Elberfeld, who'd managed him at Little Rock in the Southern League, the Waldo, Arkansas, native was a natural shortstop with a rifle arm, speed afoot, and a sharp batting eye.

By then McGraw had found a way to get rid of Earl Smith, trading him along with Jess Barnes, his frequent co-carouser, to Boston for catcher Hank Gowdy and pitcher John "Mule" Watson. If George Washington Grant (whose indebtedness to Stoneham for the capital to buy the Braves in 1919 had been an open secret) was no longer on hand to deal players to the Giants, Matty and associates seemed prepared to be equally accommodating. As the *Sporting News* wryly noted, "the Giants and Braves are still 'related.' . . ."[21] At least now, under Landis's new ruling, such deals had to take place before June 15, no longer in the decisive period of a pennant race.

Overcoming injuries to various key men, the Giants held a lead of eight and a half games over Pittsburgh in mid-August. Yet despite their sparkling performance thus far, attendance at the Polo Grounds had fallen off considerably. In the opinion of Joe Vila and quite a few other observers, that had much to do with the sleazy and shady image of the Giants' ownership.

A couple of years earlier, having accumulated a fortune of perhaps ten million dollars, Charles Stoneham had supposedly divested himself of his bucket-shop operations. Two of the firms to which he'd supposedly sold out failed in 1922 and 1923. In E. D. Dier and Company, lawyers for its creditors claimed, Stoneham had continued to hold stock; the other, Fuller and Company, had received his loan of $172,500, secured with stock from the National Exhibition Company. In August 1923, after pleading guilty in federal district court to stock fraud and receiving two-year prison sentences, the two partners in Fuller and Company were jailed indefinitely for contempt of court because they'd destroyed the firm's records. Anxious to begin their regular sentences and get that over, they decided to disclose for U.S. attorneys the contents of the incinerated records. What they told served as the basis for an indictment of Stoneham on August 31 for perjury, in that he'd denied putting NEC funds into Fuller and Company; by that transaction he'd become a quarter-interest partner and thus both criminally and civilly liable for its misdeeds. Subsequently William J. Fallon, lawyer for Stoneham as well as for Fuller and Company, was indicted for trying to bribe a federal juror and taking part in the destruction of company records. Fallon went into hiding to avoid trial.

Commissioner Landis refused to discuss the case publicly when, on September 8, he came to New York to confer with Stoneham and John Heydler. Amid rumors that the other National League owners might form a pool to buy the Giants, Stoneham had reportedly put a price tag of three million dollars on the franchise. He certainly ought to go, said the *Sporting News*, but getting rid of him wouldn't be easy.

Branded a liar and a crook by a federal grand jury, Stoneham had no intention of giving up the Giants. In fact, the rotund wheeler-dealer loved owning the ball club, loved the glamor and excitement of seeing them power their way into still another World Series. That they did, clinching at the Polo Grounds on September 28 when Nehf shut out Brooklyn. It was one of the relatively few complete games McGraw had gotten out of his pitchers all year. By the end of the season, of the 153

games the Giants had played, his starters had finished only sixty-two—
further indication of how much of their pre–1920 advantage the moundsmen had lost.

It would be another all–New York World Series. The Yankees had
easily outdistanced Ty Cobb's Detroit Tigers and Tris Speaker's Cleveland Indians. The Series would no longer be all-Manhattan, though. In
their huge new ballpark in the Bronx, the Yankees had again drawn
more customers than their National League rivals, even though the enlarged Polo Grounds now loomed almost as impressively on the south
side of the Harlem River as Yankee Stadium on the north.

McGraw's animosity toward the Yankees had grown even stronger.
He turned thumbs down on Jacob Ruppert's and Miller Huggins's request
to substitute young Lou Gehrig, up from the Eastern League, for Wally
Pipp, the Yankees' ailing first-baseman. Even though Gehrig had joined
the Yankees too late in the season for regular Series eligibility, Landis
thought it would be all right; such substitutions for injured players had
been made in the past. But McGraw wouldn't hear of it, thereby prompt-
ing charges of poor sportsmanship and intensifying bad feelings between
the Yankees and Giants and especially between Gehrig and McGraw.[22]

A throng of 55,307 saw the opening game on October 10. Before that
and succeeding games scheduled at Yankee Stadium, McGraw disdained
the Yankees' dressing facilities and had his players don their uniforms
at the Polo Grounds, then go by taxis over to what sportswriters had
already dubbed "the house that Ruth built." The opener was a thriller,
won on Stengel's two-out, inside-the-park homer in the ninth inning into
deep left center field, over Bob Meusel's head. Rosy Ryan, in relief of
Watson, sat down the Yankees in the bottom of the ninth to save the
Giants' 5–4 victory.

Managing again from the bench in street clothes, McGraw then had
to endure four losses in the next five games. This year Ruth wasn't to
be stymied by slow curves or much of anything else. His two homers
off McQuillan were the difference in game two, which the Yankees won
4–2. The third game, before 62,430 at the Stadium, provided more
heroics by Stengel. His homer into the right-field bleachers off Sam
Jones was the game's only run; Nehf yielded six hits but wouldn't let
the Yankees score.

Then came three straight Yankees victories and the American Leaguers' first world championship. A record crowd at the Polo Grounds,
46,802, saw what McGraw later termed "a rotten ballgame. . . ."[23] The

Yankees bombarded Scott and Ryan for six runs in the second inning.
It ended 8–4, McGraw using three more pitchers and four pinch-hitters
in an effort to get back into the game. The next day it was even worse.
Third-baseman Joe Dugan led a fourteen-hit attack on Jack Bentley and
three others that produced eight runs for Joe Bush, off whom the Giants
could manage but three hits and a run.

Before game six McGraw delivered one of his legendary locker-room
tirades. In a misty rain that held the Polo Grounds turnout to 34,172,
Ruth became the first man to homer three times in a World Series, lifting
one of Art Nehf's curve balls into the right-field stands in his first at
bat. Going into the eighth inning, though, the Giants led 4–1. Then
Nehf uncharacteristically lost his control, walking in two runs before
McGraw waved in Ryan. Ruth hit into a force-out at home, but Bob
Meusel followed with a single over second base. Three runs scored, the
last on Cunningham's wild throw past third. Sam Jones came on to
preserve the victory for Herb Pennock.

"You fellows beat us fairly," McGraw told Miller Huggins and his
players afterward in the visitors' dressing room.[24] And roundly, he might
have added. The Yankees batted .293 as a team, the Giants only .233.
Ruth's .368 average and three homers were a vindication of sorts for his
ineptness at the plate in the previous year's Series. Wally Pipp, both
legs taped hip to ankle, played every game, handled first errorlessly,
and chipped in with five singles. As the victors, the Yankees took home
the biggest players' shares up to then—$6,161 per man. The Giants'
shares—$4,113 apiece—were also the biggest the losers had ever re-
ceived.

The Series defeat convinced McGraw that his team would only get
older, not any better. Jack Dunn at Baltimore wouldn't take the $75,000
that McGraw offered for another of his prodigies, a fireballing left-hander
named Robert Moses "Lefty" Grove. (A year later Dunn would take
$100,000 for Grove, but from Connie Mack and the Philadelphia Ath-
letics.) When Mathewson and his associates in Boston sought Dave
Bancroft to manage the lowly Braves, McGraw, sold on Travis Jackson's
potential, put together a trade package. As his reward for starring in
the Series, Stengel went to Boston, along with Bancroft and Bill Cunningham, for outfielder Billy Southworth and Joe Oeschger, a journeyman
pitcher. But still another try for Rogers Hornsby (again the League's
batting champ at .384) got nowhere because Branch Rickey and Sam
Breadon still insisted on the inclusion of Frank Frisch in any deal for

Hornsby. "So far as I am concerned," snapped McGraw to reporters, "the proposed deal for Hornsby is off for all time. . . . I wouldn't trade Frisch for Hornsby or any other player in baseball."[25]

In mid-November, John and Blanche McGraw and Hugh and Ada Jennings sailed for Europe. Ill with influenza going over and then for a few days in Paris, McGraw had to pass up Berlin and a tour of the Belgian-French battlefields of the recent war. While the Jenningses traveled to Rome for an audience with Pope Pius XI, the McGraws remained in Paris. Recovering sufficiently to take in the horse races at Auteuil, McGraw bet a thousand francs (about $50) on each of six events and picked five winners. "There are too many ciphers on these bills," he complained of the French currency. "I always feel I'm betting beyond my means."[26]

After two weeks in London, the two couples returned on the *Leviathan* too late for the winter baseball meetings. Wearing recently acquired horn-rimmed reading glasses, McGraw talked enthusiastically about organizing an expedition after the 1924 season to spread the gospel of baseball to the Europeans. Whether or not the Europeans wanted the gospel to be spread apparently didn't much concern McGraw.

In January, Charles Stoneham's legal troubles deepened. A federal grand jury returned a second indictment against him, this time for mail fraud in connection with the operations of the defunct E. D. Dier and Company. Stoneham's position in baseball nonetheless remained secure. In November the stockholders in the National Exhibition Company, in their annual meeting in Jersey City, had reelected him president by acclamation, as they had vice-president McGraw, treasurer McQuade, and secretary James Tierney. "I am in baseball to stay permanently," said Stoneham, "and that's all there is to it."[27]

Stoneham was frequently and cheerfully in evidence that winter at the NEC's new headquarters on West Forty-fourth Street, as was McGraw after he got back from Europe and until he and Blanche left in mid-February for a couple of weeks of relaxation in Cuba. McGraw was so anxious to get out of New York that he was uncharacteristically inattentive to the arrangements for spring training. For 1924 the Giants had shifted to Sarasota, Florida, joining eight other big league teams training in that state.

Persuaded to move his team to the little Gulf Coast town by his friend John Ringling, whose famous circus troupe wintered there, McGraw himself had never been to the place. Nor did he send anybody ahead to check out the accommodations. As a result, the first group of about twenty players and ten New York writers found the hotel where the Giants party was booked to be generally rundown and far too small. Francis McQuade scurried around town and finally located space for most of the baseball people at the Hotel Miramar, overlooking Sarasota Bay, although several rookies had to stay elsewhere. On short notice, Giants groundskeeper Henry Fabian could do little about the ballfield, which consisted mostly of deep sand. So everybody started out disgruntled—ballplayers, writers, and also quite a few Sarasotans, whose civic pride was wounded by complaints about the town's cuisine and hostelries in the New York newspapers.

Weighing 220 pounds, more than he ever had, and accepting at least part of the responsibility for the confusion over accommodations, McGraw arrived at Sarasota on March 2 on Ringling's yacht. Frank Frisch had succeeded Bancroft as team captain and now was being paid $17,500 a year, which put him among the top two or three highest-salaried players in the League. Ross Youngs signed a two-year contract at $16,000 per year. An avid and proficient golfer, Youngs brought along his clubs and looked forward to breaking in the recently finished local course, as did Frisch and other golfing Giants. But like Ty Cobb, whose team was training at Augusta, Georgia, McGraw decreed a season-long ban on golf. "The first-class baseball player," he contended, "must think, talk and eat baseball in addition to playing it, and I don't want any of my players sitting around and talking nothing but golf in the heat of the pennant race."[28]

Three particularly impressive rookies were on hand that spring. Twenty-five-year-old Bill Terry had pitched in the Texas League, then stayed out of Organized Baseball three full years before, in 1922, McGraw gave him $5,000 to play at Toledo in the American Association—as a first-baseman. The previous year Terry had batted .377 at Toledo. Lewis Wilson, not quite twenty-four, was only 5′ 6″ tall and had tiny feet, but was massively muscled from the waist up—so much so that the others quickly nicknamed him "Hack," after a well-known professional wrestler named Hackenschmidt. In 1923 Wilson had led the Virginia League in hitting. The third notable newcomer was Chicagoan Fred Lindstrom. Only eighteen years old but already starting his third season in professional ball, Lindstrom had been with Terry at Toledo, where he batted only .270 and led American Association third-basemen in errors. But McGraw liked the kid's agility around third, strong throwing arm, speed on the bases, and facility for hitting to all fields—with surprising power.

After a great deal of arduous exhibition-game travel back and forth across Florida—by rail, by steamboat, sometimes by automobile over dirt roads through tropical forests—the Giants came home to lose the season opener to Brooklyn before some 45,000, the biggest opening-day crowd the League had seen. For the first time, McGraw began a season out of uniform, which meant that Jennings and Frisch would have to convey his protests to the umpires once the game started.

As had happened several times in the past, McGraw had a mishap early on that put him out of action. Five weeks into the season, he stepped off a high curb outside the ballpark in Chicago, fell in the street, and badly injured the same scarred right knee that Dick Harley had slashed in Baltimore in 1902. He made it to Pittsburgh on crutches, only to be ordered home by physicians who examined him there. Laid up at his house in Pelham with the knee in a cast, McGraw acknowledged that he was overweight and that, in his physicians' judgment, he probably wouldn't have hurt himself otherwise. But neither then nor in years to come would he be prepared to go on a diet.

By early June, still on crutches, McGraw could watch the games from his office window in the center-field clubhouse and order pitching changes and pinch-hitters over a telephone line into the home dugout. Jennings handled the team on the field. In McGraw's absence the Giants put together a ten-game winning streak and moved into a lead of four and one-half games over Chicago, seven over Brooklyn. When Billy Southworth went out with a broken hand, Hack Wilson became the regular center-fielder. Batting and fielding beyond McGraw's expectations, Wilson became a favorite of the Polo Grounds crowds.

Noticeably limping, McGraw returned to the bench on July 8, in St. Louis, at the start of a road trip on which the Giants built their lead to nine to twelve games over Pittsburgh, Chicago, and Brooklyn. But Ross Youngs, the team's leading hitter, had to be hospitalized when the team returned to New York. Delicately described as "intestinal trouble," Youngs's ailment was actually a severe urinary tract infection, the consequence of the migration of an earlier streptococcal throat condition into his kidneys.[29] Accompanied by a specialist, Youngs felt well enough to travel west with the team in mid-August, and he was back in the lineup in Pittsburgh. But he would never again be wholly sound.

On that stay in Smoke City, the Giants lost four straight; from then on they had to battle desperately to hold off the persistent Pirates and resurgent Robins. Again New York's pitching was lackluster. Bentley and rookie Virgil Barnes, younger brother of the departed Jess, won sixteen games apiece but often needed bullpen help, as did Nehf and McQuillan, each a fourteen-game winner. Brooklyn, by contrast, had a powerful combination in Dazzy Vance, who ran up twenty-eight victories and, in that period of heavy hitting, held opponents to 2.16 runs per nine innings, and spitballer Burleigh Grimes, who won twenty-two. Bill McKechnie's staff at Pittsburgh was also stronger overall than McGraw's.

At nightfall on September 20, after the Pirates had pushed over a run in the eleventh inning to beat Vance at Ebbets Field and the Giants had lost in twelve to Chicago and Alexander, New York led both Pittsburgh and Brooklyn by only a game and a half. Then three straight losses at the Polo Grounds, at the hands of McQuillan, Virgil Barnes, and Nehf, blasted the Pirates' pennant chances. On September 27 Boston, winning for only the fifty-third time all year, knocked Brooklyn out of the race, while over at the Polo Grounds, Jack Bentley easily handled the seventh-place Phillies, 5–1. That put New York two up with a single game left. After losing to Philadelphia in the season's finale, the Giants finished at 93–60 to Brooklyn's 92–62 and Pittsburgh's 90–63.

McGraw had achieved something that neither Connie Mack, Ned Hanlon, Frank Selee, Frank Chance, nor anybody else had been able to do: lead a ball club to four consecutive league championships. Yet that triumph, like others he'd gained in past years, was marred by elements of suspicion and scandal. The specter of corruption that had hung over the Giants much of the time during McGraw's regime still troubled the New York team and baseball as a whole.

On Tuesday morning, September 30, Art Fletcher, now managing Philadelphia, and John "Heinie" Sand, the Phillies' shortstop, met with League president John Heydler in his Manhattan office. By noon Landis had the information they'd given Heydler, and that evening the commissioner began questioning a number of people at the Waldorf-Astoria, where he'd established headquarters in preparation for the World Series. The next afternoon Landis announced that Giants outfielder Jimmy O'Connell and coach Cozy Dolan were both ineligible to participate in the upcoming Series against the Washington Senators. Landis's explanation was that O'Connell and Dolan had tried to bribe Heinie Sand into throwing the previous Saturday's game at the Polo Grounds.

As Sand had reported to Fletcher, and as they'd then related to Heydler, during pre-game practice on September 27, O'Connell had approached Sand near the third-base line. They'd known each other personally since 1922, when O'Connell had played at San Francisco and Sand at Salt Lake City in the Pacific Coast League. The situation in the pennant race at that moment was that either the Giants had to win two out of three games in the season-ending series with the Phillies, or Brooklyn had to lose a game to Boston.[30] "How do you feel about the game?" asked O'Connell. "We don't feel. We're going to beat you" was Sand's reply. O'Connell then said, "I'll give you $500 if you don't bear down too hard." "Nothing doing," said the Phillies shortstop. At that O'Connell returned to the Giants' dugout across the infield and reported to Dolan that Sand had turned him down. Dolan said, "Well, Jimmy, forget it."[31] The Giants won the game anyway, with O'Connell, playing for only the fifty-first time that season, hitting a double in four times at bat. Sand was hitless and handled three chances errorlessly.

O'Connell not only didn't deny Sand's account; he readily, almost eagerly, confirmed it to both Landis and the press. Dolan, he said, had put him up to the bribe attempt at morning practice on the twenty-seventh, assuring him that the whole team would pitch in to make up the $500 pot, and that Frank Frisch, Ross Youngs, and George Kelly, the three most respected men on the ball club, knew all about it. When, as O'Connell told the story, he'd asked Youngs what he thought, Youngs had said, "Go to it." Frisch had told him to give Sand whatever he wanted. Kelly hadn't replied directly when O'Connell sought his advice, but "I could tell he had been let in on it by Dolan the way he talked."[32]

At the same time that he suspended O'Connell and Dolan, Landis cleared Frisch, Youngs, and Kelly. All three had vigorously denied knowing anything about a bribe attempt until Landis called them in on the evening of September 30. Said Landis, "Their testimony, in the Commissioner's opinion, was a clear refutation of [O'Connell's] charge, which, standing alone, was exceedingly unreasonable." As for Dolan, all he could say in reply to Landis's questions was "I don't remember." That didn't satisfy Landis, even though, so Dolan would later maintain, what he'd been trying to say was that he didn't know anything.[33]

O'Connell was bereft when he showed up at the Giants' clubhouse late in the afternoon on October 1, shortly after Landis's announcement. A $75,000 letdown in his two seasons with the Giants, he realized that his career in Organized Baseball was probably finished. "They're making a goat out of me," he protested. "I've been a damned fool. They were all in on it and they deserted me when they found I was caught."[34]

O'Connell sat on a rubbing table as the players trooped in from practice. Except for Irish Meusel, who patted him on the back and muttered a few sympathetic words, his teammates ignored him.

McGraw told reporters that early Tuesday evening he and Stoneham had been summoned by Landis to his suite at the Waldorf. After being told that O'Connell had confessed to trying to bribe Sand the previous Saturday, McGraw had advised Dolan and the other players to come clean. No, McGraw said, he didn't think O'Connell and Dolan were part of a gambling ring. "The only explanation I can give is that they are a couple of saps. If you search the country over, you probably couldn't find two bigger ones."[35]

On October 7, after meeting again first with O'Connell and then with Dolan, Landis announced that as far as he was concerned nothing had changed. He'd keep an open mind, though, and remain "ready to go to the bottom of any new developments."[36]

By then the "O'Connell-Dolan affair," as the press called it, had been crowded off the front pages of the newspapers by the World Series. Like the 1920 Brooklyn-Cleveland Series, which came on the heels of the Black Sox revelations, the 1924 meeting between the Giants and Washington took place amid doubts about the integrity of the nation's favorite athletic pastime and plenty of unanswered questions about the behavior of the people in it. Yet also like that of 1920, this year's Series would feature such exciting, suspenseful baseball that by the time it was over, millions of fans had once again put aside whatever misgivings they may have entertained about the sport's fundamental soundness.

In Washington, where it started on October 4, much of the population had gone frantic over the team that had given the nation's capital its first baseball championship in any league. Managed by twenty-eight-year-old Stanley "Bucky" Harris, who was also their regular second-baseman, the Senators had finished torridly to outdistance the Yankees by three games. Now, to the delight of fans everywhere, Walter Johnson, one of the best-liked men in baseball history, would finally get his chance in a World Series after eighteen years of toil with mostly losing teams.

In vested suit, watch chain stretched across his rotundity, McGraw posed before the game with the youthful, black-haired Harris. Some 36,000 people, by far the biggest turnout Washington had ever seen, packed the regular stands and the temporary bleachers erected around the outfield. Johnson, his fabled sidearm fastball no longer overpowering, nonetheless gave them twelve brave, stubborn innings—but then so did Art Nehf. Youngs's two-run single finally beat Johnson.

The Senators won the next day on Roger Peckinpaugh's double off Jack Bentley, which sent home the winning score in the bottom of the ninth. With shouts of "Where's Jimmy O'Connell?" and "Put Cozy Dolan on the coaching line" occasionally rising from the record crowd of 47,608 in the Polo Grounds, the Giants won game three 6–4. Mule Watson came in to get the final two outs and save the game for Rosy Ryan, who in turn had relieved McQuillan in the fourth.

McGraw used four pitchers in that game, and throughout the Series he would not only use everybody on the staff but juggle his other players more than he ever had. Against Johnson and Washington's other right-handers, he put Terry on first, sent Kelly to center field, and moved Wilson over to left. Against lefties, he kept Kelly at first and played Southworth in center and Meusel in left. Moreover, with Groh barely able to walk because of his bad knee, McGraw had no choice but to rely on young Lindstrom to cover third.

The right-hand-oriented lineup produced four runs off southpaw George Mogridge in game four, but Leon "Goose" Goslin, Washington's star outfielder, hit Virgil Barnes's high fastball into the right-field seats with two on base for the difference, 7–4. The Polo Grounds' first standing-room-only turnout, maybe 50,000, included a large number of once loyal fans who now spent the afternoon hooting the Giants and their manager. "The enemy was a New York team playing on the home field before New York fans," reported one observer.[37] Afterward McGraw didn't win any new friends when he publicly criticized the popular Jennings for sending home Meusel on Wilson's hit in the eighth inning. Meusel was tagged out to stifle a Giants rally.

The next day many Polo Grounders pulled unabashedly for Johnson, but the "Big Train," as sportswriters had long ago nicknamed him, gave up thirteen hits and six runs. Bentley, who pitched seven innings and got the win, helped himself with a two-run homer. Back home on October 9, though, the Senators evened the Series when Tom Zachary outdueled Nehf 2–1.

That set up what would prove to be one of the most thrilling World Series games ever—and one of the strangest. Harris used a novel strat-agem, starting right-hander Warren "Curly" Ogden but having him pitch to only one batter before bringing in lefty Mogridge. Thereby Harris induced McGraw to remove Terry, who'd batted .429 for the Series. Mogridge and then Fred Marberry yielded three runs, but at the end of eight, aided by Harris's homer off Barnes, Washington had tied it.

Then the young manager called in Johnson. Amid shouts of "Walter! Walter!" the great hurler held the Giants scoreless over the next four innings. In the bottom of the twelfth, with Bentley now on the mound for New York, Frisch threw out the Senators' first batter. Herold "Muddy" Ruel, their catcher, lifted a foul to the left of home plate. Hank Gowdy tossed away his catcher's mask, then managed to step in the mask, stumble, and miss the ball. Ruel followed that gaffe with a line-drive double to left center. Always capable with the bat, Johnson hit for himself and grounded to shortstop Travis Jackson, who couldn't come up with the ball. Outfielder Earl McNeely then slapped a double-play grounder to Lindstrom at third, but the ball hit a pebble and bounded high over his head. Ruel dashed home with the winning run. As jubilant Washingtonians spilled onto the field from all directions, Calvin Coolidge, the country's taciturn president, stood in his first-base box, waved his scorecard, and managed a thin smile. "A close observer," wrote Grantland Rice, "reports that the vocal cords of Mr. Coolidge twitched."[38]

Again, freakish happenings—in the tradition of Merkle's failure to touch second, Snodgrass's muff, Zimmerman's futile pursuit of Eddie Collins across home plate—had deprived McGraw of a championship. That evening, soft-spoken and downcast, the Giants boarded their train for the 250-mile ride back to New York. McGraw himself, though, seemed almost light-hearted. "As the train was nearing New York," Rosy Ryan would remember, "McGraw told us to call our wives—there would be a party that night at the Hotel Biltmore. It was gala and John McGraw led the singing with stars of Broadway shows. . . . George M. Cohan was there and other celebrities."[39]

That would be the Giants' last post-Series party, whether in victory or defeat, under John McGraw. The little Napoleon (as some of the older sportswriters still called him) had built a true dynasty in 1921–24. Yet it had been a repeatedly troubled dynasty both on and off the baseball field. The ball club's troubles would make plenty of news in the off-season of 1924–25 and continue to do so in subsequent off-seasons. Questions would persist in the O'Connell-Dolan case—and never really be answered. Charles Stoneham, still facing prosecution under two federal perjury indictments in the fall of 1924, would take on more legal woes when, a few years later, the Giants' top officials began to fight among themselves. Carrying on as Giants manager, McGraw would narrowly miss a couple more pennants and continue to enjoy renown and high regard within and without baseball. Much of what he would experience, though, would also involve frustration and disappointment.

Eleven

SEASONS OF FRUSTRATION

AMERICAN LEAGUE PRESIDENT Ban Johnson, still unreconciled to the superimposition of the commissioner's authority, had his personal reasons for wanting to embarrass Kenesaw Mountain Landis. In light of the O'Connell revelations, Johnson had declared, Landis ought to call off the 1924 World Series and invite a federal investigation of gambling in baseball. Ignored by Landis, Johnson boycotted the October spectacle. Barney Dreyfuss, who'd feuded with John McGraw for more than twenty years, agreed that the Series should be canceled and termed the notion that O'Connell and Cozy Dolan would have tried to bribe somebody on their own, out of their own pockets, "an insult to the intelligence of the public. . . ." Convinced that the whole Giants operation was thoroughly unscrupulous, Dreyfuss added that in the fall of 1923 McGraw had "tampered" with Harold "Pie" Traynor, Pittsburgh's star third-baseman, by having Dolan urge Traynor to hold out for at least $15,000—in the hope that Dreyfuss would then seek to trade him.[1]

Given Johnson's and Dreyfuss's personal antagonisms, one might at least partly discount what they had to say. But the venerable baseball scribe John B. Sheridan held no grudges against Landis, McGraw, or anybody else involved in the controversy. Sheridan expressed what great numbers of baseball followers were thinking when he contended that there was no excuse for any manager—whether McGraw now or Kid Gleason with the 1919 Chicago White Sox—not to know what was going on among his players. "It is almost incredible to me," said Sheridan, "that [a] man could manage a baseball club, be about his players when crooked dealing was in the air and not 'feel' it, not know it."[2] Yet by their own accounts, neither McGraw nor Ross Youngs, Frank Frisch, or George Kelly, not even Cozy Dolan, had any inkling what O'Connell was about to do when he walked over to Heinie Sand before the September 27 game.

Late in October, Dolan held a press conference in William J. Fallon's office to make public that Fallon was now representing him. Only a few weeks earlier, Fallon had given himself up to federal authorities and declared that he was prepared to stand trial on the indictments for jury-tampering and destroying material evidence arising out of the Fuller and Company prosecution in 1923. With even more than his customary wit, eloquence, and genius for dissemblance, the Great Mouthpiece had convinced the federal jury of his innocence. Officially cleared and back in business, Fallon said that as a friend and baseball fan, he'd wanted to help Dolan, who'd gotten "badly rattled" when questioned by Landis. In answering that he didn't remember, said Fallon, Dolan had really meant, "I don't remember any such incident." "I always use that expression," added Dolan.[3]

Dolan, a mediocre infielder in 1911–15 with four major league clubs, had been McGraw's chief spy since coming to the Giants in 1921. The players sneeringly referred to him as "the night watchman" and "McGraw's man Friday." Semiliterate at most and always modestly salaried, Dolan, as everybody who knew him was aware, had little money. Neither Fallon nor Dolan would say who was paying the famous attorney's fees; everybody assumed that it must be John McGraw or maybe Charles Stoneham.

Meanwhile, out in San Francisco, Jimmy O'Connell had retained his own lawyer. "I was working for the Giants and I thought the management wanted me to do it," he continued to insist.[4] But he wasn't about to return to New York to take part in any criminal investigation without being granted immunity from prosecution beforehand.

The statutory authority for such an investigation existed, inasmuch as in 1921 the New York legislature had outlawed bribery to affect the outcome of sporting events. In January 1925, at the request of state district attorney Joab H. Banton, Landis turned over the evidence he'd gathered. That consisted almost entirely of the 15,000-word transcript of the testimony Landis had taken from O'Connell, Dolan, Frisch, Kelly, and Youngs—and had already released to the press the previous November. Nothing in the transcript indicated that Landis had questioned Stoneham or McGraw for the record. The commissioner then left for a vacation in the Canal Zone.

Assistant District Attorney George Brothers, put in charge of the investigation, questioned Sand, Art Fletcher, Youngs, Kelly, Frisch, Dolan, and Horace "Hod" Ford, the Phillies' second-baseman, who'd been standing close enough on September 27 to hear what had passed between O'Connell and Sand. O'Connell's attorney wired from San Francisco, "No immunity, no testimony." No effort was made to query either McGraw, Stoneham, or John Heydler. Landis, of course, had blithely skipped town. On February 4, Brothers delivered to Bantom a report exonerating everybody but O'Connell, who might be indictable, and Dolan, who'd "brought suspicion upon himself" by the way he'd answered questions.[5] After conferring with Landis, who returned on February 16, the district attorney said that he hadn't made up his mind whether to go to the grand jury.

He never did go. In fact, he didn't have anything beyond what Landis had been able to gather hurriedly five months earlier. Nor did Dolan ever sue Organized Baseball, as from time to time over the winter months he hinted he might. In the spring of 1925, O'Connell and his lawyer threatened to sue for O'Connell's lost 1924 World Series share, but nothing ever came of that, either. O'Connell and Dolan were never officially banished from baseball, only kept in the ineligible category— forever. Once the new season got into full swing, the celebrated O'Connell-Dolan affair, like other shadowy, ultimately unresolved episodes in baseball's history, ceased to be newsworthy.

Might it all have been a practical joke that got out of hand? Pat Ragan, a coach with the Phillies, thought so. According to Ragan, both Sand and O'Connell had repeatedly been the target of teammates' pranks. "Why not buy Sand?" somebody had jokingly said in the Giants clubhouse, and Dolan had suggested O'Connell as the unwitting collaborator in the mischief.[6]

Maybe. Certainly O'Connell, a young player struggling to make it with the Giants, would have been anxious to ingratiate himself with captain Frisch and the club's other two acknowledged leaders, Kelly and Youngs. Many years later Travis Jackson would comment, "I was a young player on the team, and if Frisch or Kelly or Youngs had asked me to contribute to some kind of pot or even do what O'Connell did, why, I probably would have."[7] Yet if it was a joke, then Frisch and the others could have told Landis as much, at a cost that undoubtedly would have been nothing worse than a private chastisement from the commissioner.

Was it somehow a plot to get Cozy Dolan? If so, then it was fully successful, inasmuch as Dolan was driven from baseball. But surely whoever might have wanted to ambush Dolan wouldn't have also been willing to sacrifice the innocent O'Connell. And if Dolan was blameless, then why didn't he go public with everything he knew or suspected? If he was paid for his silence, then of course the whole business takes on a sinister cast. It becomes a question of whether and to what extent the three Giants stars—on their own or maybe under their manager's instigation or at least encouragement—sought to make what looked like a sure fourth-straight pennant an even surer thing.[8]

Less than twenty-four hours after Earl McNeely's pebble-deflected single ended the World Series, McGraw, red-eyed from sleeplessness and booze, left on a trip that would put three thousand miles between himself and the O'Connell-Dolan controversy. With cooperation from the aging Charles Comiskey, he led a baseball expedition to Europe. Eleven Giants plus Boston's Casey Stengel (whom McGraw especially wanted along for his company) and two Philadelphia Phillies made up McGraw's team; Comiskey led a group consisting of the same numbers of Chicago White Sox and other American Leaguers. A dozen or so wives were in the party, including Blanche McGraw and Stengel's and Ross Youngs's new spouses. Fifteen-year-old Sindall Schryver, son of Blanche's widowed and remarried younger sister Jeannette Van Lill, was the wide-eyed guest of his aunt and famous uncle.

Poorly planned and hurriedly organized, the tour was a bust financially and promotionally. In Liverpool, Dublin, Paris, and practically everywhere else, the Americans were received with "cold indifference." On only two occasions did decent crowds show up for "Giants" and "White Sox" exhibitions—both times in England and, as in 1914, both times drawn by the presence of royalty. The Duke of York (the future George VI) greeted the lined-up players at the Stamford Bridge soccer stadium on October 24; two weeks later King George V, Queen Mary, and the Prince of Wales were there, sharing the royal box with U.S. Ambassador Frank B. Kellogg. George Bernard Shaw, the renowned playwright, was also on hand to record his impressions for the London *Evening Standard*. Although Shaw found baseball quite boring, in John McGraw he had "at last discovered the real and authentic Most Remarkable Man in America. . . ."[10]

In Paris the McGraws and a few others put up at the Grand Hotel while the rest scattered to various places in western Europe. A New York friend who'd come along for the fun would later recall that one night McGraw picked up the checks for everybody in a Paris restaurant, and that he also paid for the transportation home of a group of "stranded actors" (no doubt some of the numerous young Americans flocking to Paris in the Twenties in search of a freer artistic and social environment).[11]

The would-be baseball evangelists were back in New York harbor by December 2. Although he'd lost $20,000 on the trip and convinced himself that "It is out of the question to make ballplayers out of adult Europeans," McGraw was undaunted. His main object had been to "give the boys a good time." Maybe next year he would go back to Europe, maybe even take a couple of teams to the continent of South America.[12]

As far as the New York ball club was concerned, said McGraw, the O'Connell-Dolan matter was closed. Looking forward to the coming season, he declared himself quite satisfied with his present personnel and especially Jackson, Terry, Lindstrom, and Wilson, all outstanding young players with great potential.

Things were generally better at Sarasota that spring. The palm trees still lined the outfield, but Henry Fabian had had time to sod and otherwise improve the playing surface. Everybody, even the New York writers, could be accommodated in the Hotel Sarasota, one of the new landmarks in a mushrooming town that now claimed a population of 10,000. Early in the stay at Sarasota, the news arrived that, following a seven-week trial in federal district court in Manhattan, Charles Stoneham had been acquitted of the mail-fraud charge involving the transfer of customers' accounts from his former company to E. D. Dier and Company. Having lost that case, the federal prosecutors would subsequently also drop their perjury charges against Stoneham, so that by mid-1925, for the first time in nearly five years, neither the Giants president nor the team's vice-president—manager was in any kind of legal jeopardy.

After cruising for a few days off Florida's Gulf Coast aboard John Ringling's yacht, the McGraws got into Sarasota late on February 25. The next morning McGraw was at the ballpark looking over the pitchers, catchers, and rookies, but he passed up the afternoon practice to look at real estate—an interest that would take up many of his afternoons that spring. Like a lot of other Americans in the mid-1920s, he'd fallen victim to the lure of the great Florida land boom.

Through a prominent local resident named Phocion Howard, McGraw had become acquainted with Louis M. Polakov and Israel B. Perlman, two hustlers from Chicago who convinced him that with his famous name and their business savvy they could all get rich. It seemed a credible prospect in view of what had already happened at other places in Florida. Land values in Palm Beach, Coral Gables, and Miami had skyrocketed, inflating in some instances from $800 to $150,000 per acre. By 1925 an estimated one-third of the 75,000 people residing in Miami were dealing in real estate. At Sarasota, John Ringling had his own huge development under way on Long Key, on the southwest side of Sarasota Bay.

Of course, McGraw knew little if anything about developing property—about clearing complicated land titles, draining swampland (which was the condition of much of the property in the Sarasota vicinity), or dealing with sharp building and paving contractors and public officials. Polakov, Perlman, and a Sarasota developer named A. S. Skinner, a subsequent partner, were supposed to handle all that. McGraw was to be the front man for what, at his wish, would be called Pennant Park— a development on the north side of the bay near Bradenton. But as the president of the McGraw–Pennant Park Corporation, he would be liable for any and all claims against the enterprise.

Ebullient that he'd finally gotten in on something that would set him up for life, McGraw put in fourteen-to-sixteen-hour days at Sarasota, cajoling Bill Terry and others dissatisfied with their contracts, working out in uniform with his players, finding a little time for Christy Mathewson when he showed up looking frail and walking with a cane, poring over blueprints for Pennant Park. With streets named after his best-known early Giants—Mathewson Park and Bresnahan Boulevard, for example—the development would offer lots at prices ranging from $2,500 to $5,000. Many of the lots fronted the bay; all buyers were assured that they would have use of an opulent yacht club.

Having retained a flock of fast-talking salesmen, McGraw took the Giants north on a highly profitable exhibition tour with the Washington Senators. Back in New York, with the Giants having taken five of six games from the world champions, McGraw pronounced his team stronger than last year's. Indeed it was a ball club rich in talent. Seven 1925 Giants—Frisch, Terry, Youngs, Kelly, Lindstrom, Wilson, and Jackson—would eventually be voted into baseball's Hall of Fame.

Yet McGraw's pitching staff was unreliable, like most others in the mid-1920s. Besides that, Frank Snyder was well past his prime, and Ross Youngs, now chronically afflicted by malfunctioning kidneys, would slump to .264, ninety-two points below his 1924 average. Travis Jackson would be disabled for much of the season with torn knee cartilage, and Hack Wilson would play so poorly that he would end up at Toledo in the American Association.

The Pittsburgh Pirates, a tough ball club the previous year, were still tougher in 1925. With an array of slashing hitters and fast base runners such as Pie Traynor, Glenn Wright, Max Carey, and Hazen "Kiki" Cuyler, and with spacious Forbes Field as their home ballpark, the Pirates specialized in triples (an average of 107 a year, 1921–30, about twenty or thirty a year more than anybody else). As a team the 1925 Pirates would bat .307 and score 912 runs, tops in the majors.

Sinusitis again put McGraw out of commission in the first part of the season. The surgery he'd undergone late in 1923 to clear his nasal passages hadn't really done much good. Evidently allergic to pollen and varieties of vegetational growth and decay, he suffered every spring and late summer from what was at best irritating upper-respiratory congestion and discharge, at worst infected sinuses, bronchitis, low-grade fever, and general misery. As with Youngs's increasingly frequent struggles with infected kidneys, little could be done for McGraw's ailments in a period before the development of antibiotics and (in McGraw's case) antihistamines. His players got used to the sight of the gray, fat little man, his feet not quite touching the dugout floor, sitting uncomfortably at the end of the bench, coatless, his silk Cuban-made shirt sweat-soaked, fanning himself with his straw hat and sneezing and coughing into his handkerchief. Travis Jackson would never forget seeing McGraw in June 1925 in his hotel-room bed in Cincinnati, with his face all puffy, his eyes swollen nearly shut, and his nose running blood, as he went over how to pitch to the Reds' batting order.

McGraw had been too sick to start that road trip in St. Louis; when he did join the team in Chicago, watching from the visitors' field box, it was in a slump that ran to six games in Pittsburgh. In Smoke City he had to suspend Virgil Barnes, who'd proved to be about as much of a night owl as his older brother Jess. Barnes had sprained his ankle on some kind of nocturnal misadventure, although he insisted that he'd slipped in his bathtub—at least until McGraw pointed out to him that his room didn't have a bath.

Finally back on the bench on June 23, for a double-header split with Brooklyn that began a homestand, McGraw still had his team in first by a game and a half over Pittsburgh. Irked by persistent rumors that poor health would force him to resign in favor of Hugh Jennings, he told reporters he intended to manage the Giants "as long as I live. Why should I retire? Baseball has been my profession for more than thirty years and it has given me a good living. I wouldn't know what to do with myself if I quit the game now or any other time. The game is my life. That's all there is to it!"[13]

For six weeks New York and Pittsburgh remained no more than a couple of games apart. But early in August the Giants lost six times in eight tries in St. Louis and Cincinnati, and found themselves five back. The Pirates' visit to the Polo Grounds later that month offered no replay of their disastrous stay almost exactly five years earlier. In Saturday-Sunday double-headers before crowds in excess of 50,000, Pittsburgh won three times, then finished the series on Monday by hammering Wayland Dean, a much-touted but disappointing rookie, 9–2. When they moved on, manager Bill McKechnie's charges enjoyed a six-game advantage.

Enraged at their play in the Pittsburgh series, McGraw, so Joe Vila reported sometime later, had vowed to his players in the clubhouse, "I won't manage this team next year."[14] Still in a foul mood and bothered by renewed sinus trouble, he didn't accompany the club when it went west for the last time on September 14. Nine days later, when the Giants dropped the opener of a double-header at St. Louis while Pittsburgh won for the ninth straight time, beating Philadelphia, the pennant race was over. McGraw showed up when they returned to close out the season with two games in Brooklyn. At the end Pittsburgh's margin was eight and one-half games.

In Pittsburgh, before the opening game of the World Series between the Pirates and repeat-winner Washington, McGraw smilingly shook hands with Ty Cobb, and the two patched up the feud that had originated in Dallas more than eight years earlier. The next day, October 8, the wire services carried the news that at the age of forty-five, at Lake Saranac, Christy Mathewson had finally succumbed to tuberculosis. After that day's game McGraw left for Lewisburg, Pennsylvania, the home of Bucknell College, Matty's alma mater. There, on October 10, Matty was buried in the college cemetery. McGraw served as a pallbearer.

McGraw had no intention of living up to what he'd said in a moment of anger and disgust after the fatal Pittsburgh series in August. Following the Pirates' triumph over Washington (won in seven games, the valiant Johnson failing in a rain-soaked finale), McGraw sought to make trades with various clubs but was able to conclude only one. Jack Bentley, who

no longer reminded anybody of Babe Ruth either on the mound or at
bat, went to Philadelphia along with Wayland Dean; the Giants got Jimmy
Ring, a right-hander with a losing record in ten years but, according to
McGraw, "one of the best pitchers in the League and a glutton for work."[15]

For the second winter in a row, the McGraws didn't make it to Cuba.
The Pennant Park scheme kept McGraw traveling back and forth between
New York and Sarasota. It was still no more than a scheme; its tangible
existence consisted of sign posts, a few sidewalks, and an office in
Sarasota and another in New York in the Hart Building at 104 West
Forty-second Street, the same building in which the National Exhibition
Company had recently reestablished itself. Jack Bentley worked for
McGraw over the winter in New York, processing orders for Pennant
Park lots. Unwilling to go to the trouble and expense of title searches,
McGraw and associates provided no deeds, only certificates of "own-
ership." And none of the money flowing in went to pay off the $307,431
mortgage they'd taken out in buying the property.

In January 1926 newspapers in New York and in various other cities,
including the *Sporting News*, carried a full-page advertisement for Pennant Park. Underneath a picture of himself in uniform, McGraw touted
"the greatest winning combination I have ever managed." While he
couldn't promise investors "enormous profits," he could promise "a good
honest run for your money."[16] By that time McGraw had even had a new
home built for Blanche and himself on the northern edge of Sarasota,
at a cost of $35,000. He'd also persuaded a number of his racing-set
friends to put money into Pennant Park, as well as Jack Bentley, Irish
Meusel, nineteen-year-old Fred Lindstrom, and Hugh Jennings, who
invested more than he could afford to lose—at the worst possible time.

During the past season, in which Jennings had been in charge of the
Giants on the field close to half the time, he'd often seemed moody,
distracted, and easily upset. In the late fall, at his home in Scranton,
Pennsylvania, he suffered a nervous breakdown. His physicians sent
him to Winyah Sanitarium at Asheville, North Carolina. There he would
remain for the next year. While he responded well to his psychological
treatment, a physical checkup revealed that he had tuberculosis. Although he signed and sent in his contract, he had to let McGraw know
that he couldn't possibly be with the team in 1926. In February, Roger
Bresnahan was hired to assume Jennings's duties as coach and assistant
manager.

Pennant Park still made heavy demands on McGraw's time, but at the beginning of March, wearing khakis, windbreaker, and straw hat, he threw himself into the twice-a-day workouts. To the *New York Times*'s Harry Cross, he appeared to be in "splendid health," and "His stentorian voice rang across the ball diamond as it has not been heard . . . in many years."[17] McGraw still liked to take a few swings at the start of morning practice, demonstrating for newcomers that he could still foul off pitch after pitch, just as he had in the old days with the Orioles.

McGraw expected much from outfielder Al Tyson, purchased from Louisville, and a rookie right-hander from Kansas named Fay Thomas. Thomas must have been a wonder in practice, because McGraw thought he had "more stuff than [any] young pitcher I have seen since Mathewson."[18] He had even more reason to be excited about Melvin Ott, a left-hand-hitting catcher from Gretna, Louisiana, who turned seventeen during spring training. Sent to New York at the end of the previous season by Mississippian Harry Williams, an acquaintance of McGraw who'd had Ott on his lumber company team, the youngster stood 5″ 9′, weighed about 160 pounds, and, with good shoulders and thick legs, reminded McGraw of Ross Youngs, Benny Kauff, and Mike Donlin. When he saw the kid hit, cocking his right leg at least six inches off the ground, dropping his hands, and then snapping his whole body into a beautifully fluid swing, McGraw knew that he had a prize. "Ott is the best looking young player at bat in my time with the club," he reported enthusiastically to Stoneham. "I am going to make an outfielder of him."[19]

As the Giants again played their way north with the Washington Senators, McGraw detoured to Asheville to see Jennings. As they'd often done over the past thirty-five years, they celebrated their birthdays together. On April 2, 1926, Jennings turned fifty-six; five days later McGraw was fifty-three. When McGraw arrived Jennings was resting in bed, but he jumped up and greeted his old comrade joyously. Afterward McGraw remarked to reporters that Jennings looked heavier and generally fitter than when he'd last seen him back in October.

Bill Terry, having batted .319 and made first base his own the previous year, thought he was worth a two-year contract at a thousand dollars more per year. Unsigned, he remained at his home in Memphis when James J. Walker, New York's natty new mayor, threw out the first ball of the season on April 12. Brooklyn's Jess Pelty blanked the Giants and Virgil Barnes 3–0 before some 45,000 in a game that was heard by many thousands more, as described by Graham McNamee and broadcast over three different radio hookups. After that, though, the Giants were off to one of McGraw's patented fast starts, winning seven straight before the bothersome Pelty stopped them at Ebbets Field.

Despite that auspicious beginning, the season quickly turned sour. Events both on and off the field would make it one of McGraw's toughest. Again plagued by springtime sinusitis, he stayed home when the team went to Philadelphia. Bill Terry met the Giants there and signed a one-year contract (for about $6,500), but because of assorted injuries he would appear in only ninety-eight games. Travis Jackson hurt his knee again and missed a fourth of the season, and Pancho Snyder, seemingly bent on the destruction of himself or somebody, first fought Burleigh Grimes under the Ebbets Field stands; then, two days later, threatened to brain Robins catcher Mickey O'Neill with a bat, and in mid-summer broke both hands in a fight with Pittsburgh coach Jack Onslow. Art Nehf couldn't get anybody out and was sold to Cincinnati; Heinie Groh was released in May; Al Tyson, playing solid baseball, went out with a broken arm; and McGraw dealt Billy Southworth to St. Louis for another out-fielder, Clarence "Heinie" Mueller.

McGraw was so angry at club secretary Jim Tierney that he wouldn't let him accompany the team on its first western swing. The previous fall Tierney had neglected to do the routine paperwork in placing Hack Wilson on the Giants' spring roster for 1926, so that the Chicago Cubs, finding Wilson still at Toledo, simply drafted him. In his first season with the Cubs, Wilson would bat .321, with twenty-one homers and 109 runs batted in. To soothe his manager's feelings, Stoneham met McGraw in Chicago on May 7 and signed him to a new three-year contract to supersede his present one, which was due to expire at the end of the season.

McGraw was going to need every penny of his continuing $50,000 salary and more, too, because by late summer the Pennant Park pipe dream was no longer even that. Orders had fallen off badly and values had started to sink several months before two hurricanes—one that devastated Palm Beach, another that first hit Miami and then raked the state's west coast—provided the coup de grace to the great Florida boom. The holders of the mortgage on the Pennant Park property foreclosed. McGraw found himself besieged by creditors and buyers demanding at least something on the dollar, and he discovered that because his name had been used in promotions and sales done through the U.S. mails, he might even be liable to federal prosecution for fraud. The McGraws' fine new home at Sarasota, not yet completed and never occupied, had to be sold. Throughout August and September and far into the off-season, McGraw had to deal embarrassedly, painfully, sometimes acrimoniously with people who, in many cases, had invested in what he'd promised solely because of their personal fondness for him.

With his players able to win barely half their games, McGraw, harassed and foul-tempered, publicly criticized several of his veterans. Ross Youngs was above reproach; sometimes barely able to make it to the ballpark, he nonetheless played in ninety-five games and batted a remarkable .306. But Irish Meusel, complained McGraw, had "value only as a hitter" and wasn't hitting; George Kelly wasn't either hitting or hustling; Frank Frisch wasn't providing any leadership as captain. "The trouble with the team," he said, "is due to the indifference of certain players and the downright insubordination of others." What bothered him most was "lack of appreciation from some of the successful players on my team. . . . At first they are meek enough, glad to get a trial, proud to play on the Giants. Then success goes to their heads." Some of them thought they were bigger than the team; if told to hustle, "they don't take it the way younger players do." And when players who'd been with him for years acted like that, "it hurts you."[20]

Without Youngs, who'd finally had to put himself into a hospital in New York, the Giants went west on August 10 with a record of 56–51, in fourth place but trailing League-leader Pittsburgh by only five and one-half games. In Chicago, though, they dropped two out of three, then moved to St. Louis and dropped three in a row. The third defeat in St. Louis, on Friday, August 20, marked the downfall of Frank Frisch as a New York Giant.

Errors by Mueller and Kelly were major elements in the Cardinals' 6–2 win that day. Frisch, playing second base with sore legs, made two hits, played errorlessly, and also made a nice over-the-head catch in short right center. But in the bottom of the seventh inning, with Cardinals on first and third, McGraw signaled for the pitcher to intercept the catcher's peg if the runner on first tried to steal, so as to prevent a double-steal attempt. Missing the sign, Frisch broke for the bag when Bob O'Farrell started for second, and thus was out of position when Tommy Thenenow slapped a grounder between first and second, driving home the run. "Every man on the team caught the signal except the captain," fumed McGraw later on.[21] After the game he berated Frisch unmercifully in front of his teammates.

That evening at the Hotel Chase, after dinner, Frisch reached a decision: "I made up my mind I was finished with the Giants. I wouldn't take it anymore."[22] Frisch had a bellhop buy a ticket to New York and told him to have his bags in the lobby by ten-thirty. The next morning he paid his own bill at the hotel and boarded the train.

While Frisch, sore-legged, fighting a cold, and generally run down, went to bed at his home in the Bronx, McGraw fined him $500 for leaving the team and complained to reporters that he'd missed signs "many times" and "never satisfied me" as team captain.[23] It was a bitter experience for Frisch, a New York boy who'd grown up idolizing McGraw and been one of McGraw's favorites almost from the time he joined the Giants out of Fordham back in 1919.

When the Giants lost a three-game set at Pittsburgh, they fell into fifth place, thirteen and one-half games off the pace. The Pirates were having their own internal troubles. Max Carey led a faction of malcontents who were determined to get both manager Bill McKechnie and coach Fred Clarke fired (as indeed they would succeed in doing in the off-season). The St. Louis Cardinals, now managed by Rogers Hornsby, shot past the Pirates and everybody else in the last month of the season. Beating out Jack Hendricks's almost equally hot Cincinnati Reds by two games, they brought St. Louis its first pennant in the National League. The Cardinals clinched it at the Polo Grounds on September 24 on Billy Southworth's homer. Frisch played at second, having rejoined the team more than two weeks earlier. Watching from the stands were an ailing Ross Youngs and a resentful Irish Meusel, recently given his outright release.

A 74–77 record and a fifth-place finish amounted to the worst showing for a McGraw-led team since the debacle of 1915. Nearly every Giant fell off from his previous year's performance. Youngs and Jackson were exceptions, but then they both missed much of the season. Fred Fitzsimmons, a hefty right-hander who'd come up from Indianapolis in time to post a half-dozen victories in the previous year, led the staff with only fourteen in 1926. One bright spot was Melvin Ott. Used occasionally as a pinch-hitter and with games either safely won or lost, the teenager made twenty-three hits in sixty at-bats, a .383 average.

On December 20 McGraw finally got the player he'd been seeking for seven years. Rogers Hornsby came to the Giants in exchange for Frank Frisch and Jimmy Ring. It was probably the most sensational trade in baseball history up to then. Many had expected Frisch's departure after his late-season troubles with McGraw. Ring, a throw-in in the trade, had pitched no better with the Giants than he had at Philadelphia. But Hornsby was coming off not only a pennant in his first full season as a manager but also a brilliant seven-game triumph over the Yankees in the World Series. Although his managerial cares had evidently hampered his hitting in 1926, Hornsby was still the National League's reigning star, its biggest since Honus Wagner.

Hornsby, though, needed lots of money, more than tight-fisted Sam Breadon and Branch Rickey were willing to pay. They offered him $50,000 to continue as player-manager for 1927; Hornsby demanded that amount for each of the next three years. The sometimes brutally blunt-spoken Texan had developed an antagonistic relationship with both men. Despite having turned the Cardinals over to him in May 1925, Rickey had continued to meddle in on-the-field matters—or so Hornsby claimed. Breadon had bestowed a $25,000 bonus on Rickey for putting together a pennant winner, yet wouldn't give Hornsby a multi-year contract.

"The Rajah," as the St. Louis writers had crowned him, was thirty years old, a veteran of eleven full seasons. A shortstop in the early years, Hornsby possessed no more than a mediocre arm and had eventually settled at second base. Though a generally capable man at that position, he would never overcome a weakness on pop flies hit behind him. Hornsby's greatness was in his bat. A two-hundred-pounder, slightly under six feet tall, he positioned himself in the back corner of the right-hand batter's box and, from a closed stance, stepped into the pitch and drove the ball to all fields—with plenty of power. He'd already topped .400 three times; his .424 average in 1924 was a twentieth-century high. The forty-two homers he'd hit in 1922 were more than anybody besides Babe Ruth had totaled so far.

Dedicated to his profession, Hornsby shunned alcohol and tobacco and, to safeguard his eyesight, stayed away from motion pictures and refused to read anything, even the sports pages, during the baseball season. He did love ice cream, a minor vice, and he was perhaps the most inveterate horse player in baseball. If McGraw bet habitually and moderately, Hornsby bet obsessively and immoderately. His losses were so big that, despite making salaries exceeded only by Ruth's, he nearly always owed money. At the time he was traded, he was about to be sued for $70,075 by Frank L. Moore of Newport, Kentucky, who said that the past winter he'd put down that amount for Hornsby at the local track, out of his own pocket. Hornsby had picked a string of losers and never compensated Moore.

Saying "I'm mighty glad to be with John McGraw," Hornsby signed a two-year contract with the Giants at nearly $40,000 a year. McGraw also made him team captain. "Frisch," said McGraw, unable to resist a dig at his former favorite, "used to think his day's work was over when he handed the umpire the batting order. If I wanted to call his attention to something during the game, he generally was looking for his cap or a bird flying around or anything except the field."[24]

McGraw made two other major deals. Burleigh Grimes, one of the last of the legal spitballers, came over from Brooklyn in a complicated three-way arrangement that also brought outfielder George Harper from Philadelphia. At odds with George Kelly since mid-summer, McGraw traded the tall San Franciscan to Cincinnati for Edd Roush, who, unlike Hornsby, was anything but glad to be with McGraw—in Roush's case, back with McGraw. A two-time batting titlist, Roush owned a career .335 average in the National League and was also the circuit's finest center-fielder. But he'd always been a tough man at contract time, as well as a superbly conditioned athlete who kept himself that way year-round. Roush still didn't like McGraw, didn't look forward to being railed at when in uniform and spied upon when not. As soon as he heard about his trade, he wrote McGraw, "I'm not sure you and I would ever get along. . . . I don't want to be awakened by some trainer or housedick knocking on my door at midnight to find out if I'm in. By that time I'm asleep."[25] When Roush received his Giants contract, for $19,000, he sent it back unsigned.

That winter McGraw continued to work to placate unhappy Pennant Park investors. Although the federal authorities left him alone, he had plenty of trouble talking the losers out of bringing civil actions. A few filed suit anyway, but McGraw was able in each instance to arrange some kind of out-of-court settlement. It was a wearing, sometimes degrading, always costly process that would stretch over the next several years. At the end, when he would finally be able to tell his wife, "Well, the last one is paid," he would have lost close to $100,000 on the ill-conceived Florida venture.[26]

At the end of January 1927, though, the McGraws temporarily put all that aside and returned to Cuba, where they spent three enjoyable weeks. Still another tropical storm delayed their departure for Sarasota.

Roger Bresnahan was already on duty, having again signed on as McGraw's senior coach. Meanwhile, Hugh Jennings, at his home in Scranton, Pennsylvania, was losing his fight against tuberculosis.

Jennings had also lost heavily in the collapse of Pennant Park, although McGraw had promised to repay him. McGraw, Jennings said, had been "my real friend" who'd "stuck with me all the way." Toward the rest of the Giants organization, though, Jennings was bitter. After he'd worn himself out for the club in 1924–25, Charles Stoneham, Francis X. McQuade, and Jim Tierney had "deserted me," "shunned me in every way," not paid him a penny in 1926 even though he'd been under contract. "They cast me aside as one who would be of no further use to them," complained Jennings.[27] McQuade and Stoneham both pointed out that Jennings hadn't been able to fulfill his contract, and they both protested that they would have helped him if they'd known he needed help. Jennings remained unreconciled; the whole thing amounted to bad public relations for the prosperous New York Giants.

Jennings was struggling to stay alive at Scranton and now, in a San Antonio hospital, so was Ross Youngs. Over the winter the little outfielder's condition had deteriorated rapidly. That April, severe alcoholism and attendant malnutrition killed William J. Fallon at age forty-one. Penniless by the time he died, Fallon was buried in a casket that, according to a widely believed rumor, John McGraw paid for.

But if dying friends reminded McGraw of his own mortality, it was still a baseball springime, a period of renewed hope—and he had Rogers Hornsby. The Texan's presence dominated the weeks at Sarasota. McGraw was delighted that Hornsby had immediately assumed the full responsibilities of his captaincy, organizing and directing the practice sessions and otherwise lightening McGraw's workload. Yet Hornsby presumed too much as far as some of his new teammates were concerned. "He had a good way of making everybody irritated," Travis Jackson would remember. When Hornsby called down Fred Lindstrom for throwing too hard on the first day out, Lindstrom shot back: "Who do you think you are? You're no more than a rookie on this ball club as far as we're concerned. We're playing for McGraw, and he's sittin' over there on the bench. And what's more, how the hell can you tell anybody about fielding? Listen, if you lost that bat tonight you'd be in the bushes tomorrow."[28]

For a time it looked as if Hornsby might not be eligible to start the season for the Giants. He still owned 1,167 shares in the St. Louis

Cardinals, and he was holding out for $105 a share. League president Heydler ruled that Hornsby couldn't play for one team while continuing to own stock in another. No such restriction existed in writing, argued McGraw, and Heydler was making up rules to suit himself. In a special meeting of the League's club owners in Pittsburgh on April 8, only four days before the Giants were to open in Philadelphia, Hornsby rejected Breadon's offer of $100,000. With Stoneham dissenting, the owners then voted 7–1 to uphold Heydler. When he got back to New York, though, Hornsby went into conference with McGraw, Stoneham, and Heydler, and emerged to announce that he'd take Breadon's offer. It turned out that Hornsby would actually receive $112,000 for his Cardinals stock.[29]

So on April 12 Hornsby was at second base in Philadelphia, homering along with Terry and George Harper in a 15–7 rout of the "futile Phillies." Edd Roush, having met with McGraw at Chattanooga when the Giants moved north and accepted $70,000 for three years, started the season in center field. But Jackson, hospitalized in Memphis for an emergency appendectomy, was lost for six weeks. Little Eddie Farrell, a graduate of the University of Pennsylvania dental school, filled in ably for a while. Early in June, though, McGraw continued his quest for reliable pitching by trading Farrell and pitchers Red McQuillan and Kent Greenfield to the obliging Boston Braves for right-hander Larry Benton, who'd been the ace of a dreadful staff.

Cheered lustily at the Polo Grounds, Hornsby responded with lusty hitting. He led a potent attack that kept the Giants bunched with St. Louis, Pittsburgh, and Chicago, despite a pitching staff that yielded more runs than any in the League besides Boston's and Philadelphia's. In mid-June, though, McGraw's team fell into a slump that dropped them seven and one-half games behind pace-setting Pittsburgh. Despite Stoneham's emphatic assurance that "John McGraw can manage the Giants as long as he likes!" rumors persisted that he would step down in favor of Hornsby. "The Giants are through," thought Richards Vidmer of the *New York Times*. "They're not going any place, unless it's down to the . . . second division." Vidmer attributed the Giants' problems largely to "a fear of censure," the kind of devastating criticism with which McGraw had broken young Kent Greenfield's self-confidence before he traded him. For all their talent, the Giants no longer believed in themselves as a team.[30]

Two proud and pleasant occasions lightened what had become another tough season for McGraw. On June 1 he brought the Giants to Olean,

New York, for a game with the St. Bonaventure College nine that would be the climactic event in dedication ceremonies for his alma mater's new athletic field. Upon learning that the site would be named after him, he insisted that it be called "McGraw-Jennings Field," to give equal honor to the man who'd once roomed, coached, and studied with him at St. Bonaventure. The Reverend Thomas Plassmann, president of the college, readily agreed, and made an announcement to that effect at the luncheon for students, faculty, and Giants in the college dining hall.

The other occasion was the Silver Jubilee for McGraw at the Polo Grounds on July 19, 1927, commemorating his quarter-century as Giants manager. Although too many activities were planned and it started to rain, McGraw appeared to enjoy himself. It was good to see some of his early Giants players again as well as Hugh Jennings, who'd wanted to remain in the stands but, at the behest of the crowd, come down to stand with McGraw at home plate. Not the least of the day's satisfactions was being publicly honored by the Lambs' Club, which had kicked him out back in 1920 after his fracas with William Boyd. Although the Lambs had quietly restored his membership in 1924, now everybody would know about it.

Two days after his Silver Jubilee, McGraw demonstrated that, whatever people might say about his gray hair, his waistline, or the state of his health, some of the old fire still burned. In a game against St. Louis, he blistered umpire Frank Wilson from the dugout until Wilson ordered him out of sight. It was the first time he'd been ejected since he stopped managing in uniform three years earlier.

A week later, though, his sinuses were bothering him so much that he sent the team to Chicago with Hornsby in charge. Enforcing a strict curfew and forbidding beer drinking, smoking, or even reading in the clubhouse, Hornsby led his teammates to seven victories in nine games in Chicago and St. Louis. With McGraw back for the series in Cincinnati and Pittsburgh, the Giants lost only four games out of nineteen in the West and came home trailing the Pirates by a game and a half.

From then on it was a three-way struggle. With his sinusitis having developed into an infection of an eye and the side of his face, McGraw stayed home in Pelham for most of the homestand, on which his team won seventeen out of twenty. After a Labor Day split with Boston in front of a capacity-plus crowd at the Polo Grounds, the Giants left for the West with McGraw still disabled and Hornsby in command.

It was on that trip that Hornsby blew whatever future he may have had with the New York Giants. In Pittsburgh, on September 22, the Giants and Pirates split a double-header. Though remaining three and a half behind the Pirates, New York yielded second to St. Louis. That evening club secretary Jim Tierney came to Hornsby's room at the Schenley and launched into a denunciation of Travis Jackson for being out of position on a particular play. Hornsby cursed Tierney, told him he didn't know what he was talking about, and ordered him out. Later that night Stoneham arrived with McGraw, who was ready to resume direction from the dugout. Stoneham was livid when he learned that the club secretary, who was also his close friend, had been bawled out by a ballplayer, even if that ballplayer was Rogers Hornsby. From that moment Stoneham was Hornsby's enemy.

The Giants won the remaining two games at Forbes Field and left again only a game and a half out of first. But McGraw's pitching staff was in tatters. On September 25 Frank "Dutch" Henry, a retread left-hander in his first year with the Giants, battled Brooklyn's Jess Pelty to a scoreless tie that, combined with Pittsburgh's double-header sweep at Chicago, shoved New York two and a half down. Two days later Jim Faulkner, just up from the minors, and then Burleigh Grimes couldn't stop the Phillies' onslaught. Philadelphia's fiftieth victory that season and another Pirates win at Chicago made the margin three and a half with only four to play.

On September 30 McGraw watched from his office window in the Polo Grounds clubhouse, more than five hundred feet from home plate, as Brooklyn battered Henry, Barnes, and Fitzsimmons, while Dazzy Vance held on to eliminate the Giants. By being rained out two days later, even though the Giants won from Philadelphia, St. Louis ended up in second place by half a game. New York, with a 92–62 record, finished two behind Pittsburgh.

Still running a fever at season's end, McGraw passed up the Yankees' four-game sweep of the Pirates. Within a couple of weeks, though, he felt well enough to start going to the racetracks in the area. The Giants had won forty-five of their last fifty-seven games, under Hornsby's field management most of the time. Given McGraw's persistent health difficulties and his heavy reliance on Hornsby this past season, it seemed a real possibility that he might yield the job to the Texan. But before that could happen, said Hornsby with customary tactlessness when he returned to St. Louis, some changes in the Giants' ownership would have to take place.

Nothing much that was newsworthy emanated from the Giants' front office for the rest of 1927. In St. Louis, Hornsby's attorneys defended him successfully in the civil suit brought by Frank L. Moore, basing their defense on the ethically dubious grounds that inasmuch as Hornsby's bets had originated in Missouri, where gambling was illegal, Moore couldn't recover losses from an illegal transaction.

Then, about 10:00 P.M on January 10, 1928, Jim Tierney called reporters for the New York papers to the National Exhibition Company offices and handed them copies of a typewritten statement signed by Charles Stoneham alone. Rogers Hornsby had been traded to the Boston Braves "for the best interest of the New York Giants. . . ." New York would receive Jimmy Welsh, an outfielder, and Francis "Shanty" Hogan, a young catcher. Neither Stoneham nor McGraw was present for the announcement. The McGraws had left that afternoon for Miami and then Havana. Queried the next day in New York, Stoneham said, "It dawned on me that . . . to prevent any possible conflict in authority, it would be best to send Hornsby elsewhere." Caught by reporters in Miami, McGraw's only comment was "The trade has been made and that's all there is to it."[31]

If Giants fans and baseball followers everywhere were bewildered, Hornsby seemed equally so. Except for maybe keeping his mouth shut more of the time, he must have wondered what he had to do to stay with a ball club. In 1926 he'd managed the Cardinals to a pennant and World Series victory—and been traded. The past season he'd carried the managerial burden for McGraw much of the time and still batted .361 (runner-up to Pittsburgh's Paul Waner), clouted twenty-six home runs, driven in 125 runs, and scored 133 times. If he and Stoneham hadn't gotten along, the Polo Grounds fans had loved him and his relations with McGraw had been the best. "I still can't understand that deal," Hornsby said a month after the trade, "but I know it wasn't McGraw's doing, and I still consider Mac the greatest manager in baseball."[32]

Trading Hornsby wasn't McGraw's doing, but it was done with his acquiescence. As various observers suspected at the time, the decisive power within the Giants organization had passed from McGraw to Stoneham. McGraw would continue to have Stoneham's confidence and admiration, but the Hornsby deal should have left no doubt that when the

Giants president wanted something done, McGraw wouldn't or couldn't stand in his way.

Like Hornsby, Burleigh Grimes must have asked himself what he had to do to satisfy his employers. After a poor start, Grimes had won thirteen straight games during the second half of the season, nineteen in all, tops on the Giants staff. In February, though, McGraw, from Havana, gave his approval by telephone to a trade with Pittsburgh: Grimes for fifteen-game-winner Vic Aldridge. It was another mysterious deal, one that prompted the New York *Tribune*'s Heywood Broun to compare the Giants' present close-mouthed operations with the way things used to be. Back in 1915 at Marlin, as Broun remembered it, "any Giant would tell you anything you wanted. It didn't even matter whether you did want; he would tell you anyhow."[33]

Tired of Sarasota and its reminders of real estate promotions that had washed out (both literally and figuratively), McGraw based his 1928 spring practice at Augusta, Georgia, Ty Cobb's residence. Readying for what would be his twenty-fourth and last year as a player, Cobb worked out a few late afternoons with some of the Giants rookies before leaving to join Connie Mack's Philadelphia Athletics at Fort Myers, Florida. Cobb and McGraw, on good terms for the past couple of years, could exchange regrets over the passing of Hugh Jennings, who'd died at his home on February 1. Cobb had played for Jennings at Detroit for fourteen years and had about as much feeling for him as he ever did for anybody in baseball.

McGraw's sadness over Ross Youngs's death, at the age of thirty, in San Antonio the previous October, was different. Besides Christy Mathewson, Youngs had been McGraw's favorite Giant, in many ways his ideal of what a ballplayer ought to be. In his nine full seasons with the Giants (1918–26), Youngs had averaged .322 at bat and been the best-liked player on the team. A notoriously easy mark for alms seekers, he'd died with his many debtors owing him around $16,000.

Saddened by the deaths of Jennings and Youngs, resigned to doing without Hornsby, McGraw nonetheless began spring practice enthusiastically and expectantly, as he always did. Russell "Red" Reeder, a catcher reporting to Augusta fresh from the U.S. Military Academy at West Point, would later describe McGraw's appearance: ". . . the famous New York Giant peppermint candy stockings covering his powerful calves, an old, gray cardigan buttoned over that paunch. He looked his part: an old ball player." Lectured McGraw to the rookies (as quoted by Reeder): "You will hit only balls in the strike zone. I had such a sharp eye that I never struck at a bad ball." Then: "Now, while I have you here—there's too much running 'round in the dark. I want your minds on the game. On the old Baltimore Orioles, Hughie Jennings, Willie Keeler and I sat up nights figuring out new plays so we could win. On the Orioles, I realized that a ball player's career hinges on one thing— is he a winner?"[34]

After running up an exhibition-game record of 22–5 and keeping everybody healthy, the Giants met Hornsby and the Boston Braves on a cold, overcast opening day in front of some 30,000 Polo Grounders. Before the game Hornsby posed with little Andy Cohen, the young man who'd replaced him. A Baltimore native who'd grown up in Laredo, Texas, and attended the University of Alabama, Cohen had played at Waco in the Texas League, spent part of 1926 with the Giants, and starred in the International League the previous year at Buffalo. Cohen, McGraw fervently hoped, would become the outstanding Jewish player he'd sought for a long time as an attraction for the huge numbers of actual and potential Jewish baseball fans in the New York area.[35]

The rest of the Giants infield still consisted of Terry, Lindstrom, and Jackson, McGraw's new captain. Roush was again in center field, flanked by George Harper and thirty-one-year-old Frank "Lefty" O'Doul, who'd failed as a pitcher in the American League, converted to the outfield, and battered Pacific Coast League pitching the past two years. Catcher Shanty Hogan, only twenty-one, hit the ball with power and showed reasonable agility and a strong arm, but he already weighed around 220 pounds and would never be able to keep his appetite or weight under control. McGraw would exhort and berate him and go over his restaurant tabs meal by meal, all to no avail.

McGraw, looking a bit trimmer himself, was in uniform for a regular-season game for the first time in nearly five years. The Giants won the game 5–2, with Cohen making two hits, scoring twice, and fielding flawlessly. At the end of the game his new admirers carried him from the field to the clubhouse.

Cohen's play sparkled over the first month of the season. He might even be better than Hornsby, some wildly suggested. "It ain't fair to the kid," commented Hornsby. "As soon as I get going, I'll lose him."[36] As indeed the Rajah did. Cohen would tail off to .274; Hornsby would hit

.387 and capture his seventh batting title while managing the Braves for the last two-thirds of the season. (They would still win only fifty games and finish next to last.)

The Giants played little better than .500 baseball into late July, a fact that mystified many observers. Practically everybody hit well. Lindstrom's and Terry's bats were especially potent; and once McGraw traded George Harper to St. Louis for catcher Bob O'Farrell and installed Mel Ott in right field, the nineteen-year-old quickly established himself as a major-leaguer, batting .322 with eighteen home runs. Bolstered by Larry Benton, on his way to twenty-six wins, and Fred Fitzsimmons, who would win twenty, McGraw's pitching was substantially improved— even though Vic Aldridge, a holdout until May, proved a complete bust.

Meanwhile, trouble surfaced in the upper reaches of the Giants' hierarchy—a bitter quarrel between Charles Stoneham and Francis X. McQuade that led to McQuade's dismissal as club treasurer. Although McGraw loyally sided with Stoneham, many people wondered whether he might not be the next to go. To squelch such speculations, Stoneham summoned reporters to his hotel room in Cincinnati on May 2 and announced that he'd again torn up McGraw's existing contract and given him a new one, this time, at McGraw's request, for only two years (1929– 30). He'd turned down another five-year contract, said McGraw, because "I'm fifty-five years old now and I don't know how I'll feel when I'm sixty." But he wanted everybody to know that "I am getting the complete support of Mr. Stoneham. . . . there have been stories around, most of them propaganda, that he and I didn't agree and were having trouble. They said McGraw was slipping. Well, you can say for me that is absolutely untrue."[37]

Two weeks later McGraw's remarkable accident-proneness again manifested itself. On the same street outside the ballpark in Chicago where he'd injured his knee in 1924 stepping off a curb, McGraw was struck and knocked down by a roadster as he, Bresnahan, and Hans Lobert tried to thread their way to a waiting taxi. Mad only at himself, McGraw told everybody it hadn't been the driver's fault and hobbled on to the taxi.

From Chicago, where an estimated 96,000 people saw the Cubs sweep four games, McGraw proceeded with his team to St. Louis. When his leg began to swell and the pain worsened, he left for New York. X-rays there showed that the leg was broken. On crutches, he met the Giants when they stopped off in Brooklyn before returning to the Polo Grounds. Bresnahan handled the team while he sat in the visitors' field box.

McGraw was out of commission for six weeks, during which the Giants performed indifferently. Bresnahan and Edd Roush quarreled when Roush refused to play in Philadelphia. A subsequent medical examination showed that he had good cause—a hernia in the groin region. That finished him for the season; Jimmy Welsh took over center field full time.

In July the Giants could manage no better than a 6–10 record in the western cities. McGraw was back on the bench in street clothes. Much of the time on that trip, Vincent DeAngelis, just graduated from Erasmus Hall High School in Brooklyn and named "Most Valuable Schoolboy Baseball Player" by the New York *Telegram,* was by his side. At the expense of the newspaper, and of course with McGraw's consent, young DeAngelis took part in pre-game workouts; mixed with the players; sometimes ordered double desserts on his own meal tab for Shanty Hogan; and listened raptly as, during the course of a game, McGraw patiently explained the various moves he was makng.

One of the high points of Vincent DeAngelis's life, that trip marked the low point of the 1928 season for the New York ball club. The Giants returned in fourth place, nine off the pace being set by St. Louis. But then it turned around. By winning fifteen of nineteen at home and then taking three straight at St. Louis, the Giants climbed all the way to the top. Jimmy Welsh's fine all-around play, Shanty Hogan's robust hitting, and Mel Ott's emergence were key factors. Another was the arrival in mid-June of Carl Hubbell, a twenty-five-year-old left-handed pitcher from Missouri who'd knocked around the minor leagues for nine years.

Hubbell had been found earlier in the month by Dick Kinsella, who happened to be an Illinois delegate to the Democratic Party's national convention in Houston. Taking a break from the convention tedium one afternoon, Kinsella saw a Texas League game in which Hubbell, pitching for Beaumont, throttled the locals. He quickly telephoned McGraw, who took Kinsella at his word—as he always had—and arranged Hubbell's purchase from Beaumont. Throwing his reverse-breaking "screwball," which was simply a left-handed version of Mathewson's fabled fadeaway, Hubbell won his first major league game on August 11 when he shut out Philadelphia. He would win nine more before the season was over.

Week after week through August and September, New York, St. Louis, and Chicago fought for the lead. Suffering less than usual from his annual upper-respiratory torments, but still ailing, McGraw drove his men toward just one more pennant. On September 20, having won eleven of their last twelve games but still trailing St. Louis by two, the Giants hosted the Cardinals in a double-header. A record Polo Grounds weekday crowd watched George Harper hit three home runs in the Cardinals' victory in the opener. Harper, who'd overheard McGraw refer to him as "a dumb bastard" back in May, just before the Giants traded him, thumbed his nose at McGraw on his first trot around the bases, did the same and jumped on home plate the second time around, and, after the third homer, did a double nose-thumb and bounced his bottom off the plate.[38] Polo Grounders who'd been hooting McGraw and the slumping Andy Cohen over the Hornsby trade loved Harper's antics. But Shanty Hogan pleased even more people by hitting one into the left-field seats with two aboard to win the nightcap for Hubbell.

The Giants won again the next day to close to one game, then beat Cincinnati twice. They trailed the Cardinals by half a game when Joe McCarthy's Chicago Cubs, still within reach of the pennant themselves, came in for a double-header. In the opener, before 40,000 on a Thursday afternoon, the venerable Art Nehf outpitched Hubbell. The game's crucial moment—maybe the season's as well—came in the bottom of the sixth inning. With runners on second and third, one out, and the Giants behind 3–2, Hogan hit back to Nehf, who threw to third-baseman Clyde Beck to trap Andy Reese (Cohen's replacement) off the base. Reese started homeward, only to find big Gabby Hartnett, the Cubs' catcher, astride the baseline. The two collided, Hartnett grabbing Reese as he fell. Beck ran down and tagged Reese, who was still struggling to free himself from Hartnett's grasp. Plate umpire Bill Klem called Reese out.

McGraw, who couldn't advance beyond the dugout steps in his street clothes, jumped up and down and screamed interference while Bresnahan, Lobert, captain Jackson, and other Giants swarmed around Klem. League president John Heydler, on hand to unveil memorial tablets to Christy Mathewson and Ross Youngs, saw it all. When Nehf retired the next batter and held the Giants scoreless the rest of the way, McGraw filed an official protest with Heydler. The fact that Joe Genewich, a right-hander obtained from Boston in June for Virgil Barnes, shut out the Cubs in the nightcap did nothing to console McGraw.

The next day Heydler denied the Giants' protest, citing base umpires Barry McCormick and Charley Moran, who supported Klem's contention that Hartnett had been as much entitled to the baseline as Reese. While McGraw choked on that ruling, the Giants lost to Chicago and the Cardinals beat Boston to extend their lead to two games. When St. Louis won again at Braves Field on September 29 and Fitzsimmons couldn't stop the Cubs at the Polo Grounds, it was all over. A season-closing victory over St. Louis the next day made the final margin two games. The Cardinals thereby earned the chance to suffer the same fate as Pittsburgh in 1927: a four-game sweep at the hands of the murderous Yankees of Ruth, Gehrig, and company.

Meanwhile, by Bill Klem's account, McGraw "encouraged a campaign of abuse in the newspapers" against him. Despite their many rows on the diamond, Klem and McGraw had often drunk together, spent time at the racetracks together, and otherwise remained on friendly terms. But when Klem encountered McGraw at one of the tracks that fall, the umpire warned, "We're through this time, for all time." Klem left New York after putting Heydler on notice that he wouldn't be back next year, but over the winter, after Heydler raised his salary, baseball's senior umpire changed his mind. He would never change his mind about McGraw, though.[39]

As for John McGraw and the New York Giants, again they'd fallen a couple of games short of McGraw's eleventh National League championship. As with Fred Merkle's failure to touch second twenty years earlier (also in a critical meeting with the Cubs), a single controversial play had made the difference in a whole season—so McGraw would always believe. Again he'd been victimized by shoddy umpiring.

Despite his age and frequent infirmity, McGraw would keep trying. He had, though, already come closer to that elusive eleventh pennant than he ever would again. His best times were behind him, more and more the "old times" that fewer and fewer people could remember. But as he'd acknowledged a few years earlier, baseball had been his life, and he wouldn't know what to do with himself without it. So he would stay on—for a while longer, anyway.

Twelve

GIVING IT UP

HE WOULD NEVER FORGIVE Bill Klem for what many agreed was a lousy call on the Reese-Hartnett collision. McGraw would keep a photograph of the play on the wall in his Polo Grounds office, alongside pictures of Mathewson and Youngs. That call had kept his Giants out of the 1928 World Series, he would always believe, just as he was convinced that they would have made a much better showing against the Yankees than had Bill McKechnie's St. Louis Cardinals.

Still, that was last season, and as always, McGraw studied what moves he might make to strengthen his chances for next year. Lefty O'Doul had batted .319 in 1928, but McGraw judged him too old and slow and not serious enough about his work. So off went the colorful San Franciscan, along with a check, to the indigent Phillies for the stolid Fred Leach, who was almost the same age but a better outfielder. Roger Bresnahan, tired of the stresses of being the Giants' part-time manager, decided to remain in his native Toledo, where he was a major stockholder in the local American Association franchise. McGraw's new first lieutenant would be Ray Schalk, the American League's premier catcher for many years, recently fired after two seasons managing the Chicago White Sox.

In the off-season the McGraws remained prominent personages in New York's night life. Occasionally McGraw accompanied Blanche to a Broadway play, although his tastes continued to run to musical reviews and vaudeville. Many of the city's vaudeville houses, though, had already closed, unable to compete with the motion pictures, the new mass-entertainment medium that in the Twenties became a bigger factor in Americans' leisure-time existence than baseball had ever been.

The McGraws never cared much for the movies, nor were they caught up in the Twenties vogue of slumming at Harlem cabarets like Small's World and the Cotton Club, with their all-black performers and all-white clientele. Sharing a fondness for fine food, they liked to frequent Mama Leone's, then at Thirty-eighth Street and Seventh Avenue, or any of a number of other notable Italian restaurants. Billy LaHiff's tavern on West Forty-eighth was another haunt. There they might encounter "Hizzoner" Jimmy Walker, fight promoter Tex Rickard, heavyweight boxing champ Jack Dempsey, or such journalistic lions as the *Daily Graphic*'s Ed Sullivan, the *American*'s Damon Runyon, or the *Tribune*'s Heywood Broun and Grantland Rice. Wherever McGraw was, with whatever group of friends, and despite his well-known Florida financial woes, he continued to be an inveterate "check-grabber." New acquaintances quickly learned to defer to that aggressive and sometimes disagreeable trait.

On November 6, 1928, Arnold Rothstein, the man with the big bankroll, died of a gunshot wound inflicted two nights earlier by a hoodlum named McNamara who owed him a big gambling debt. At the time of his death Rothstein, arguably the most powerful underworld figure in American history up to then, was only forty-six years old.

Meanwhile Charles Stoneham, one of many fast operators who'd benefited at various times and in various ways from Rothstein's bankroll, was doing better than ever. Although he would never talk numbers, Stoneham acknowledged to the *Sporting News* that the 1928 Giants, despite having the biggest payroll in the club's history, had made more money than in any year since he'd been its president except 1919, his first.

In fact, the Giants had become such a lucrative enterprise that William F. Kenney, a New York building contractor and close friend of Francis X. McQuade, deposed club treasurer, paid a half million dollars for 20 percent of the National Exhibition Company's stock. What Kenney bought consisted mainly of the shares held by the heirs of Arthur Soden, who'd owned the Boston Beaneaters and, along with Cincinnati's John T. Brush, Chicago's A. G. Spalding, and other National League magnates, had bailed out the sinking Giants franchise in 1890. Although Kenney's buy-in was seen in some quarters as a move by McQuade ultimately to gain control of the NEC, Kenney denied that he wanted "to meddle with the affairs of the Giants. . . ." As for Stoneham, no, he wouldn't consider selling out. "Baseball had come to be my pet hobby," said the jowly Giants president, "and I have no intention of giving it up." Of some incidental interest was the fact that with Kenney's purchase of the Soden heirs' stock, the NEC was owned wholly by New Yorkers for the first time. Its value, estimated the *Sporting News,* was now $3,750,000.[1]

Right after New Year's the McGraws, accompanied by nephew Stephen Van Lill, left New York harbor on the S.S. *President Roosevelt,* bound directly for Havana. It would be one of their lengthiest stays, lasting until mid-February. After playing a lot of golf (and of course a lot of horses and a few roulette wheels), McGraw returned to his office in the Hart Building feeling, he said, "better than I have in years."[2]

It was back to San Antonio for spring training in 1929. On the morning of February 27, McGraw, in uniform, jogged out at the head of his players to start another baseball season. Good weather, no holdouts, no major illnesses or injuries, and no serious disciplinary problems made the weeks at San Antonio one of the smoothest spring-training periods in his career. Returning to New York at the end of an exhibition series with Washington, he pronounced his team stronger than last year's.

The Giants started the season in the cold and damp of the increasingly run-down Philadelphia Phillies ballpark by rallying for six runs in the ninth inning to give Carl Hubbell an inelegant 11–9 victory. In dark topcoat and snap-brim hat, McGraw watched Lefty O'Doul hit two homers over the short, high right-field fence. From then on O'Doul's prowess at the plate would make the Leach deal look worse and worse. Setting a new National League record for base hits in a season, O'Doul would lead the majors with a .398 average, belt thirty-two homers, and drive in 132 and score 152 runs. Mainly because of his presence and that of a young slugger playing his first full year in the majors named Chuck Klein, the Phillies would have their best record (71–82) since 1917 and finish in fifth place. Leach began the season on the bench, and wouldn't play much until June, when McGraw swapped Jimmy Welsh back to Boston for Eddie Farrell. In 113 games Leach would end up batting .290, a lackluster mark in a year in which the average for the League as a whole was nearly .300.

O'Doul was only the latest ex-Giant to disprove McGraw's judgment. Hack Wilson, George Harper, Art Nehf, and Burleigh Grimes (a twenty-five-game winner at Pittsburgh in 1928) all had made Giants fans wonder why McGraw had let them go. Of course, the most inexplicable departure had been Rogers Hornsby's. By contrast, Hornsby's recent off-season move from the Boston Braves to the Chicago Cubs—for $200,000 in cash and five nondescript players—was simply a matter of the Braves' inability to draw enough fans to pay their bills.

The addition of Hornsby made the Cubs, a good team for the past few years, into the most powerful in the League. Scoring nearly a thousand runs, the Cubs would bat .303 as a team and hit 140 home runs, forty of them by Hornsby and thirty-nine by Hack Wilson. Besides Hornsby (.380) and Wilson (.345), Chicago's heavy hitters included Riggs Stephenson (.362) and Kiki Cuyler (.360). It would have been an even more potent lineup if Gabby Hartnett hadn't been disabled early in the season. In Pat Malone, Charley Root, and Guy Bush, manager Joe McCarthy also had the League's three best pitchers that year.

Drawing 1,485,000 fans at home, the Cubs set a National League attendance record that would stand for seventeen years. The crowds at what was now officially Wrigley Field (after William K. Wrigley, the Cubs' principal owner) saw their favorites pull away from the Cardinals, Giants, and Pirates in the last part of July. At the end Chicago would be ten and one-half games ahead of Pittsburgh, thirteen and one-half and twenty better than New York and St. Louis, respectively.

With his ball club's pennant chances dimming early, McGraw spent a particularly unhappy season. Again sinusitis and upper-respiratory infections kept him at home or confined to his clubhouse office much of the time. At the end of May he missed a return visit to St. Bonaventure with his team. Late in July, with the Giants already nine games behind Chicago, McGraw left Schalk in charge while he did some personal scouting for ballplayers through Tennessee and the Carolinas. When the Giants went west for the last time in mid-September, McGraw didn't go with them, nor was he on the bench at the Polo Grounds for the last few games of the year.

As a team the 1929 Giants, finishing with an 84–67 record, had been a thorough disappointment. Individually, though, they hung up some impressive numbers. Terry batted .372 and drove in 117 runs; Edd Roush batted .324; and Travis Jackson's twenty-one homers were more than any shortstop had ever hit. At the age of twenty, Mel Ott arrived as a full-fledged star. Having made himself a master at pulling pitches into the short right-field corner at the Polo Grounds, Ott tied Hornsby's League home-run mark with forty-two, driving home 151 runs and batting .328. In his first full major league season, Hubbell notched eighteen wins. Left-hander Bill Walker, used sparingly in 1928, became a de-

pendable starter, winning fourteen games and leading the League with
a highly creditable 3.09 earned-run average.

McGraw covered the World Series for John Wheeler's North American
Newspaper Alliance, traveling to Chicago for the first two contests, then
back to Philadelphia to see Connie Mack's Athletics wrap it up in five
games. Mack's splendid ball club, built patiently over the past five years
until it was finally strong enough to dethrone the Yankees, probably
wasn't that much better than the Cubs. What really decided the Series
was the Athletics' ten-run explosion in the eighth inning of game five
after Chicago had built an 8–0 lead. That so demoralized the National
Leaguers that the 3–2 clincher two days later (after the obligatory Sunday
off in Philadelphia) was almost anticlimactic.

McGraw was back in New York, selling Andy Cohen, the would-be
Jewish phenomenon, to Newark; firing Ray Schalk, whose handling of
the team during his various absences hadn't pleased him; and hiring
Dave Bancroft as his new chief coach, when the stock market collapse
of late October 1929 occurred. The McGraws didn't own any stock apart
from his seventy shares and her five in the NEC (which of course wasn't
listed on the exchange), so that the Great Crash didn't affect their
personal financial situation. By the coming spring, though, it would be
increasingly apparent that what President Hoover and many others had
been prepared to dismiss as mostly a liquidation of speculators and a
"readjustment" in stock values had become a severe and generalized
economic downturn. As banks failed, factories and mills closed, and
agricultural prices plummeted, the nation would sink rapidly into the
worst depression in its history.

None of that was at all clear in the baseball off-season of 1929–30.
That winter, at the Travers Island restaurant and sports facility owned
by the New York Athletic Club, McGraw was reconciled with Frank
Frisch, who'd overcome the initial hostility he'd met in St. Louis to
become the Cardinals' sparkplug and displace Rogers Hornsby in the
affections of their fans. The McGraws were entertaining friends at dinner
when Blanche McGraw spied Frisch several tables away and went over
to invite him to come by their house in Pelham later that evening. Frisch
hesitantly agreed. When he rang the doorbell, McGraw, to his surprise,
met him with a big smile and grabbed his hand. The next two hours,
spent sipping chilled wine and talking about nearly everything but baseball, "were the most enjoyable I ever spent in my life," Frisch would
say long afterward.[3]

After the usual Cuban sojourn, the McGraws left Havana by steamer for Galveston and then San Antonio. Besides Dave Bancroft, McGraw had taken on as a coach Irish Meusel, who'd played the past couple of years in the Pacific Coast League. Edd Roush, his three-year contract expired, wouldn't accept a pay cut for 1930. He and McGraw would never come to terms that spring, and Roush would sit out the whole season.

Roush's recalcitrance was one reason why the stay at San Antonio wasn't nearly as pleasant as the previous year's. The weather, which was wet much of the time, was another. McGraw fretted and fumed over Roush, the soggy ballfield, and many other matters. Grantland Rice described him as having become "gray, portly, [and] quieter" in recent years. Yet he was "still quick of tongue and keen of brain," still outspoken, still great copy for the baseball journalists. And his knowledge of the talent available in the minor leagues, Rice said, remained unmatched. "I'm sort of a permanent fixture, like home plate and the flag pole," was the way McGraw would characterize himself later that year.[4]

With rookie Eddie Marshall, up from Bridgeport of the Eastern League, at second base and Wally Roettger, hurriedly obtained from St. Louis for Eddie Farrell, taking Roush's place in center field, the Giants started off with a 3–2 win over Boston at the Polo Grounds. Bill Walker went the distance for New York. The 50,000 or so paying customers came away satisfied with the outcome and also talking about the Polo Grounds' new electrically amplified loudspeaker system, which had informed them not only about the starting batteries but the entire starting lineups, each batter's name as he came to the plate, and any lineup changes in the course of the game. A similar hookup had been installed at Shibe Park in Philadelphia.

Such information was particularly helpful to new fans, inasmuch as putting numbers on the backs of the players' uniforms wasn't yet the usual practice in the major leagues. Just that year, in fact, three American League teams—New York, Washington, and Cleveland—had started wearing numbers. Some of the National League teams would adopt numbers in 1931, but McGraw, believing that real baseball fans got to know the players well enough by sight, had no use for that innovation.

The Giants won their first seven games of the season, then settled into a pace that by mid-June had them in third place, six games behind Wilbert Robinson's surprising Brooklyn team and nearly even with Chicago. Feeling that he needed more experience at second, McGraw persuaded Garry Herrmann at Cincinnati to take the fading Larry Benton in an even swap for Hughey Critz, one of the League's best infielders. Critz wasn't much at bat, but with the kind of attack he'd put together that year, McGraw thought he could afford to have a man in the lineup mainly for his glove.

That attack was a potent one, the most potent since the old Orioles of 1897 in terms of team batting average. But the Giants' .319 team mark was only one indication of the kind of hitting that went on in 1931. The whole National League averaged .303, fifty-four points higher than in 1917. The Phillies, with a .315 team average, scored 944 runs but could win only fifty-two times with a pitching staff that permitted the opposition an average of nearly seven earned runs per game. St. Louis topped a thousand runs scored and averaged .314; Chicago set a new major league record with 171 home runs, even though Rogers Hornsby missed most of the season with an injured foot. Hack Wilson set a League home-run record with fifty-six and a majors runs-batted-in record with 190, both of which would still stand more than half a century later. The overall American League average wasn't as high, at .288, but three teams hit better than .300. The Yankees piled up 1,062 runs while finishing only third.

At .401, Bill Terry led the National League, followed by Floyd "Babe" Herman of Brooklyn at .393, Philadelphia's Klein and O'Doul at .386 and .383, respectively, and New York's Lindstrom at .379. On the Giants, Ott, Jackson, Hogan, and Leach each batted at least .327. In Carl Hubbell, Bill Walker, and Fred Fitzsimmons, McGraw had three first-rate pitchers, but like all the other moundsmen that year, they had to try to get people out with a ball that everybody agreed was livelier than ever.

McGraw was dismayed by it all. In May, after watching nine homers fly out of Wrigley Field in one Giants-Cubs game, he complained that "nowadays, the game has become a case of burlesque slugging, with most of the players trying to knock home runs and many of the pitchers becoming discouraged. Numerous games have been played this year that should not be seen in the big leagues." A few weeks later he came out in favor of shortening the pitching distance to fifty-eight feet, presumably unmindful of the even greater peril from wicked line drives such a change would hold for pitchers. One day he showed Joe Vila a ball that had higher stitching and a little looser cover than the 1930 ball. Scuffed and stained, the ball McGraw held in his hand, he said, had been one of only three used in a Giants game back in 1916.[5]

Yet if McGraw yearned for the old-style baseball—in his words, "tight pitching, sensational fielding, team play at the bat, base stealing and scientific methods"—the present hit-happy game was drawing record crowds.[6] In spite of the rippling economic slowdown, more people spent their money on baseball tickets in 1930 than ever before in the sport's history. Another easy Athletics pennant and a distant third-place finish didn't keep the Yankees from drawing 1,600,000 customers. In the National League a good race for most of the season distributed the prosperity more evenly.

Throughout July and August the Giants stayed within reach of first place, occupied by Brooklyn in the first part of the season, then taken over by Chicago, with the Robins a close second. McGraw's health had held up pretty well, although when the Giants left on a western swing in mid-August, Bancroft was in charge. Suffering once again from infected sinuses, McGraw also stayed behind to straighten out the business affairs of his brother James, who'd died in the spring. The last surviving male in McGraw's immediate family besides himself, James McGraw had also been the one sibling with whom John McGraw had stayed in fairly close contact over the years. At the time of his death James McGraw was secretary of the Toledo American Association ball club, a job secured through his famous brother's influence with Roger Bresnahan.

The Giants moved past Brooklyn into second place on that trip, although they dropped three of four in Chicago before big crowds. McGraw looked on and telephoned directions from his office window in the Polo Grounds when the team split four games with Brooklyn to start a homestand. On September 4 he was in New York, signing a new five-year contract, while the Giants divided a double-header at Boston. The new contract, remarked Charles Stoneham, was intended "to dispel all the foolish rumors of Mr. McGraw ever leaving the National League."[7] As always, Stoneham wouldn't discuss specific figures. Some of the writers closest to the organization put the total amount at $70,000 a year—$50,000 for managing, the rest for serving as NEC vice-president.

In the last month of the season the St. Louis Cardinals, now managed by Charles "Gabby" Street, came on with the same kind of rush that had carried them to their first pennant four years earlier, under Hornsby. Boasting a starting lineup made up entirely of .300-plus hitters (with captain Frank Frisch having one of his best years), the Cardinals took the lead in mid-September after sweeping a three-game series at Ebbets Field. Meanwhile, Pittsburgh virtually put the Giants out of the running, winning both ends of a double-header before 45,000 at the Polo Grounds. That left New York five and one-half games down, in fourth place, with only twelve left. In what remained of the season, McGraw, still managing from his office in the faraway clubhouse, saw the Giants kill the Cubs' chances, then slip past Brooklyn and occupy third place. There they finished: eighty-seven wins, sixty-seven losses, a game ahead of Brooklyn, three behind Chicago, five away from the champion Cardinals.

"I don't care a rap about winning pennants," Stoneham told reporters near season's end. "It's McGraw's health that concerns me." He'd urged McGraw to leave the team altogether, just take a vacation and forget baseball. But McGraw had insisted on sticking it out, "even though it's been impossible for him to sit on the bench."[8]

As had usually been the case in past years, once the stresses of the pennant struggle were over, McGraw's health improved quickly. He looked quite fit in Philadelphia, where he attended the sixth and final game of the World Series. For the fourth straight year, the American League representative was the winner. Of the nineteen World Series games played since 1927, the National Leaguers had managed to win three.

In the fall of 1930 John McGraw showed no inclination to give up his managing chores. Although he had a new five-year contract and would be making upwards of $70,000 a year, he and Blanche had decided to move to smaller quarters. A smaller house, Blanche McGraw hoped, would discourage her husband from bringing home so many overnight guests. In October they sold the place in Pelham and moved into "a Colonial-type brick dwelling" at 620 Ely Avenue in nearby Pelham Manor.[9] Formerly occupied by an investment trust executive and his family, the house had nine rooms and three baths and sold for $65,000. Although McGraw gasped at the size of the mortgage, the sale of the bigger house in Pelham, according to Blanche McGraw, covered most of it.

It was in the process of clearing out the old place that she first became fully aware of the magnitude of her husband's generosity to those who'd sought his help over the decades. She found him before the fireplace, burning "a fantastic collection of checks and notes and apologies." When she asked how much debt was represented in all that paper, he answered, "I don't know . . . ten or fifteen thousand, I guess. . . ."[10]

The McGraws' move in 1920 from their apartment in upper Harlem to a new residential development beyond the New York City limits, then to a still newer area ten years later, typified what hundreds of thousands of New Yorkers did in the 1920s. By the beginning of that decade central Harlem was already predominantly black, most of its Jewish, Italian, and German residents having moved into the Bronx, Queens, or Brooklyn. A decade later "black Harlem" extended as far north as 110th Street, the northern boundary of Central Park. While the total population of the borough of Manhattan declined in the Twenties, its black residents increased by 115 percent, to some 328,000.

As black Harlem advanced steadily north, the area around the Polo Grounds would become increasingly undesirable to most white New Yorkers. Another obstacle the Giants francise would face in the decades to come was the absence of parking space for the growing number of people who reached the Polo Grounds not by subway or elevated railway but by private automobile. The piece of land known as Manhattan Field, adjacent to the ballpark, already had proved insufficient to accommodate auto-borne customers.

For all of that, the New York Giants remained a highly attractive property in 1930. If in fact William F. Kenney's purchase of a one-fifth interest in 1928 had been some kind of power move on Francis X. McQuade's part, nothing came of it. Kenney had subsequently sold his stock in the National Exhibition Company to Harry McNally, another wealthy contractor. In June 1930 Stoneham purchased half of McNally's holdings, 230 shares in all, thereby increasing his ownership to 69 percent of the NEC.

In the meantime, McQuade had initiated what would become a protracted court fight to win back his lost position as NEC treasurer and the $10,000 annual salary that went with it. Late in 1929 McQuade and twenty other stockholders had filed suit in state supreme (district) court in Manhattan, asking for an accounting of NEC funds. The plaintiffs charged that in the period 1919–25, Stoneham had made loans—in the form of checks drawn against the company's treasury—to the Cuban-American Jockey Club, an oil-lease company in which he and McGraw had been involved, and various other parties, including a $3,500 personal loan to the Giants manager. The total amount loaned was $410,000, on which no interest was ever paid. Leo G. Bondy, one of Stoneham's attorneys and McQuade's successor as NEC treasurer, acknowledged that Stoneham had made loans with the company's money, but he maintained that all of it had been repaid at interest. Besides, added Bondy, sometimes Stoneham had also loaned money to the NEC, interest-free.

Charging that McQuade had "willfully and maliciously" tried to "wreck and destroy" the NEC, Stoneham, McGraw, and the other directors countersued McQuade for $250,000.[11] McQuade formally sued for reinstatement as NEC treasurer on January 7, 1930, basing his claim on a document that he, Stoneham, and McGraw had signed at the time they bought the Giants, by which each pledged to strive to protect the official positions of the other two. Supreme Court Justice Schmuck threw out McQuade's action because the NEC, as a New Jersey–chartered corporation, couldn't be sued in the New York state courts. When he carried his case to the appellate division, though, McQuade won a ruling that the three-way agreement among himself, Stoneham, and McGraw was valid, and that inasmuch as the NEC did business exclusively in New York State, its New Jersey incorporation was immaterial. McQuade was entitled to reinstatement as NEC treasurer.

Reinstatement, though, wasn't McQuade's main concern, and he was content to let Leo Bondy keep the treasurer's job. His goal was to regain the salary he'd lost when he was ousted. So the battle among the former friends and allies, once the big three of the Giants operation, would continue in court and in the press. It was an embarrassing business all around, detrimental to the morale of the team and to John McGraw's ability to keep his mind on winning ballgames.

At the National League's annual winter meeting at the Waldorf-Astoria, McGraw finally shook hands and made up with the first real friend he'd had in the major leagues, Wilbert Robinson. The two old Orioles finally were able to forget the bitter words they'd exchanged in the aftermath of the Giants' 1913 World Series defeat. Now sixty-six, bespectacled, even more rotund than McGraw, Robinson had won two pennants at Brooklyn and finished a strong fourth this past season. Yet his employers and some of his players were convinced he'd become too old and slow. Another fourth-place showing in 1931 would cost him his job.

McGraw didn't rehire Irish Meusel for 1931. George Burns and Chief Bender joined Dave Bancroft at San Antonio as McGraw's coaches. When Edd Roush still wouldn't report to the Giants, McGraw sold him to Cincinnati. Bill Terry wasn't at San Antonio; unhappy with his contract, as usual, he remained at his Memphis home until the Giants came through on the way to New York, when he signed for about $22,500. Terry's was the highest salary on a ball club whose total payroll, by Joe Vila's reckoning, was about $300,000. Like most sportswriters in that period, Vila tended to side with management in contract disputes, pointing out "the tremendous expenses entailed in running the Giants," including the $200,000 annual rent on the Polo Grounds property and adjacent Manhattan Field.[12]

Excited over his plan to make Lindstrom into a full-time outfielder and Johnny Vergez, purchased from Oakland of the Pacific Coast League for $60,000, into his regular third-baseman, McGraw predicted that "the Giants will be decidedly stronger this year than they have been in the past few seasons."[13] He hoped that Harry Rosenberg, an outfielder bought last year from San Francisco, just might become the Jewish star he was still seeking. By the time the Giants got back to New York, though, Rosenberg would be at Newark, starting the season in the International League.

Ban Johnson died that March in St. Louis at the age of sixty-seven. Forced out by the American League owners after the 1927 season, he'd spent a quiet retirement since then. Asked to comment on Johnson's passing, McGraw was more gracious than people old enough to remember their combat thirty years earlier might have expected. "Johnson was a great fighter and organizer," said McGraw, and the American League was "a monument to his genius."[14]

Each passing year reduced McGraw's links to his past. In the fall of 1929 Joe McGinnity had died at fifty-eight, only three years after he pitched eighty-five innings in the Mississippi Valley League (where he'd been manager and part-owner at Dubuque). Garry Herrmann, Ban Johnson's reliable ally on the old National Commission, died in April 1931. McGraw's longtime American League friend Charles Comiskey would follow in the fall and Barney Dreyfuss, his longtime National League enemy, the next year.

The baseball played in 1931 would look a little more like the kind of game whose passing McGraw had often lamented in recent years. Two changes produced substantial drops in overall major league batting statistics. The horsehide covering on the Spalding-made baseball was slightly thicker than in 1930, and the stitching was higher. As a consequence the ball was both a little deader and easier to grip, especially for curveball pitchers. The second change was in scoring rules: elimination of the sacrifice fly, so that henceforth a run-scoring fly ball would be recorded as a regular time at bat and count against a hitter's average.

For 1931 the National League's aggregate batting average would be twenty-six points lower than for the previous year. Home runs would decline 44 percent. With 20 percent fewer runs being scored, the League earned-run average would shrink by more than a run. Lesser but significant changes would also show up in the American League's statistics. By mid-summer 1931 baseball's officialdom was expressing satisfaction that the delicate balance between pitcher and batter had been pretty much restored.

Yet talent was still talent, regardless of changes in the baseball or the scoring rules. Defending champion St. Louis, the Giants, and Chicago (with Rogers Hornsby having displaced Joe McCarthy) still had the National League's most talented teams. All three started well, with the Giants winning fourteen of their first twenty games. The three clubs jockeyed for the lead until early June, when the Giants dropped three of four at Sportsman's Park and two of three at Chicago. After that New York was never in first place again. In July, Lindstrom, who'd ended up in right field with Ott shifted to center, broke his ankle in Philadelphia. Critz missed most of the season with a shoulder injury.

By mid-July the Giants were eight and one-half games out of first place, occupied by St. Louis, and McGraw was thoroughly down on his team. He often began his interviews with the complaint that "the men don't get out and fight for the games like they used to—that's what is wrong with baseball." One sports columnist recalled how, in the old days, "everybody knew there'd be plenty of excitement to stir the blood" when the Giants came into town. Now, though, McGraw's men were "just another ball club."[15]

Maybe McGraw's players had lost the combative spirit, but not McGraw himself. He could still flare with the old-time fury, as he demonstrated in St. Louis in July. On a Saturday, Bill Walker threw a shutout. By the time he retired the last Cardinal, though, McGraw was no longer in the dugout. In the top of the eighth inning, when umpire Bob Clarke called out a Giants runner trying to score, McGraw was beside himself. Clarke ran him out of sight, along with coach George Burns. McGraw's language had been sufficiently abusive that, when he received Clarke's report, John Heydler hit the Giants manager with a three-day suspension—the first time that had happened since McGraw stopped wearing a uniform.

On Sunday, McGraw paced back and forth outside the Sportsman's Park press gate, snarling and snorting and waving Heydler's telegram, which the League president had sent from St. Louis, after his arrival the previous night. By the time Heydler started through the press gate, a crowd of reporters and fans had gathered around McGraw. Heydler stuck out his hand, only to be met by a staggering verbal barrage. Why hadn't Heydler called him last night to get his side of the run-in with Clarke? Why did Heydler persist in protecting incompetent umpires, like Klem back in 1928? McGraw then stormed off, on his way back to the Hotel Chase to sit in his suite and await Dave Bancroft's report on that day's double-header.

It was a double defeat for the Giants. Their 7–10 record on that western trip put them so far behind that only a total Cardinals' collapse would have made much difference from then on. During most of the August home stand, McGraw remained at his new home in Pelham Manor, again bedeviled by inflamed and infected sinuses, and he was too sick to accompany the team when it left for Pittsburgh.

That September the Giants played two games with the Yankees—first at Yankee Stadium, then at the Polo Grounds—that signified what had happened in the New York area and across the country. What people would soon start calling the Great Depression had already caused massive layoffs of workers in the cities and industrial towns. In the immediate pre–New Deal years, voluntarism and localism remained the guiding principles in public assistance, as evidenced in the mayor's unemployment fund in New York. Part of the struggle to help the growing number of the city's needy was the staging of the September 9 and 24 Yankees-Giants exhibitions. The games drew a total of 84,000 paid admissions for the local jobless fund.

On September 16 the Giants, now firmly in possession of second place but still way behind St. Louis, lost a double-header at Cincinnati, despite the presence of a suffering McGraw. The Cardinals won at Philadelphia to give Gabby Street's outfit its second pennant in a row. The season mercifully ended with St. Louis thirteen games in front of New York, seventeen ahead of Hornsby's Cubs. By that time Ott was back home in Louisiana, recovering from a beaning by Burleigh Grimes (now one of the stalwarts of Street's staff); Lindstrom, having finally convinced

McGraw that his broken ankle hadn't healed, had returned to New York; and Shanty Hogan was home in Somerville, Massachusetts, sulking over a protracted suspension McGraw had laid on him for being drunk on the final road trip.

Was the once-vaunted little Napoleon losing his grip? Some of his players and some of the writers may have thought and even said as much—in private conversation. McGraw himself was again planning for next year, looking to better times. Jim Mooney, a rookie who'd posted a 7–1 record in the last part of the season for the Giants, would become "one of the greatest southpaws ever seen in the majors," declared McGraw.[16] And Charles Stoneham was still committed to McGraw as his manager. It was an odd friendship and professional association: one man who'd made a fortune taking advantage of people, another who'd made being taken advantage of a basic part of his life.

It wasn't a happy off-season for McGraw *or* Stoneham. Despite several big crowds, attendance at the Polo Grounds had fallen off. Except for the truncated 1918 season, it was the first time since the stormy years of Andrew Freedman that the Giants had lost money. Moreover, the dispiriting litigiousness that had started two years earlier continued that winter.

In December the trial on Francis X. McQuade's suit against Stoneham and McGraw for retroactive payment of his NEC treasurer's salary began before Justice Philip McCook in supreme court. By then they'd dropped their damage suit against McQuade, but Stoneham remained determined to thwart their onetime crony and had hired the renowned trial attorney Arthur Garfield Hays. McQuade was represented by Isaac N. Jacobson. McQuade repeated his charges that Stoneham had made interest-free loans from NEC funds—the figure now specified was $155,000—to various other businesses he was interested in. He'd insisted that Stoneham either repay the money at interest or put up security for the loans; that had been the origin of Stoneham's vendetta against him. McGraw had once told him, said McQuade, that if he would just "lay off Stoneham," he wouldn't have to worry about keeping his treasurer's job.[17] Hays got McQuade to admit that he'd also profited from some of Stoneham's nonbaseball investments.

When the defendants' turn came, Leo G. Bondy testified that the source of the Stoneham-McQuade feud was McQuade's resentment at having to pay interest on IOUs he'd given Stoneham for NEC stock, whereas Stoneham didn't charge McGraw interest on his notes. Bondy also talked about McQuade's efforts to transfer the Polo Grounds concessions contract to a friend of his, his profligate distribution of passes, and his insistence on being paid a 10 percent commission simply for collecting the $81,500 that promoter Tex Rickard had paid to rent the Polo Grounds for the 1923 Dempsey-Firpo prizefight. McQuade had assaulted him, added Bondy, when he stepped between McQuade and Stoneham to keep them from fighting in the Giants clubhouse in 1926.

McGraw took the stand to recount that at the time of Stoneham's trial on federal mail-fraud charges, McQuade had said, "If that guy goes to Atlanta [to the federal penitentiary], we will get the ball club." "Stoneham," McGraw quoted McQuade as saying, "is worth more to us dead than alive. I'll put a pill in his soup." McGraw also testified that in the spring of 1920 in New Orleans, where the Giants were playing an exhibition date, McQuade had drunkenly insulted Blanche McGraw and struck his own wife. Finally, McGraw revealed that it was he himself who, at the NEC directors' meeting in December 1927, had first raised the question of McQuade's behavior. "I'm sick and tired of McQuade's abuse and something must be done about it," McGraw remembered saying to his associates.[18] The next spring McQuade had been voted out.

Jacobson called McQuade's estranged wife to rebut McGraw's testimony about what McQuade had done in 1920 in New Orleans. No, McQuade hadn't punched her in the face, said Lucille McQuade, and besides, "McGraw would not have known anyway, because he was so intoxicated that evening that he had to be carried to his room by players." Asked whether McGraw was conscious or unconscious, she reflected a moment, then replied, "Semi."[19]

In his summing up, Hays accused McQuade of disloyalty and perjury. Jacobson characterized Stoneham, McGraw, and McQuade as being "of the same ilk and none was an angel. They were all drinking men, all cursing men, all fighting men." It had been "common knowledge that the management of the Giants was in the hands of a rough element." Still, that didn't justify the way McQuade had been mistreated.[20]

Justice McCook agreed. He decided in favor of McQuade, ruling that Stoneham and McGraw had broken a valid contract to keep their associate in the treasurer's office; they owed him $10,000 per year going back to May 1928, with interest. Hays filed notice of appeal in behalf of Stoneham and McGraw with the state appellate division, so that McQuade still couldn't get his money. He needed it, too, inasmuch as the Seabury Committee, originally set up under the appellate division to investigate corruption in the magistrates' courts in Manhattan and the Bronx, had uncovered enough to force the resignations of McQuade and a number of other magistrates. By late 1931 the Seabury Committee, now working under the authority of the state legislature and reporting to Governor Franklin D. Roosevelt, was also making matters most uncomfortable for Mayor Jimmy Walker.

On the baseball front, McGraw abandoned another hope for a Jewish gate attraction when he gave Harry Rosenberg, three other players, and $75,000 to Indianapolis for outfielder Len Koenecke, who'd feasted on American Association pitching in 1931. Koenecke, prophesied McGraw, "will be a bright star in the National League. . . ." With the McQuade trial over, McGraw and Blanche left for Miami and Havana. At the train station, McGraw told reporters, "I can't recall a winter when I have looked forward more hopefully to a successful season. . . . I feel confident we will be in the thick of the fight from start to finish." His only problem, he said, was to "make Hogan behave himself."[21]

As he'd been able to do with John T. Brush in the off-season of 1906–1907, McGraw convinced Charles Stoneham that the Giants could make a lot of money from exhibition games if they did their spring training at Los Angeles and played up and down the Pacific Coast. The McGraws traveled directly from Havana to Los Angeles—by ship to New Orleans, then via the Southern Pacific across the deserts to the Coast.

In New Orleans, McGraw met with Bill Terry, who'd come down from Memphis solely for that purpose. Last year Terry's batting average had fallen to .349 (from .401 in 1930), but then nearly everybody else had batted less, and Terry had still missed the hitting title by only a fraction of a percentage point. But retrenchment was the watchword on all the ball clubs. Terry's new contract provided a salary cut of 20 percent, nearly $5,000. Fred Lindstrom, Mel Ott, and various other Giants took their cuts, but Terry sent his contract back unsigned, along with the word that he was "thoroughly disgusted." But McGraw locked himself and Terry in his suite at the St. Charles Hotel and somehow convinced his first-baseman to take what the club had offered. When Terry came down to the lobby, where Ott was chatting with Blanche McGraw, he had only a curt "Well, I guess so" to a reporter's query as to whether he was satisfied.[22] In fact, Memphis Bill was anything but satisfied. He didn't make it to spring training for another two weeks, and when he did he refused to speak to McGraw.

Described as "ruddy of complexion and exuding good cheer," McGraw arrived in Los Angeles on February 23.[23] Wearing a Giants cap and windbreaker and street slacks, he hit to the infielders; visited with Mike Donlin, who for a number of years had made a living off bit roles in the movies; and talked optimistically about the new season. Except for being way overweight, he did look good. In fact, though, he was under his physicians' stern admonitions to watch his diet and liquor intake and get sufficient rest. Partly that medical counsel pertained to his excess poundage and marginally high blood pressure; mainly it had to do with the prostatitis that had been diagnosed a year or so earlier.

His close newspaper friend Bozeman Bulger used the time spent with McGraw in Los Angeles as the basis for a three-part *Saturday Evening Post* piece. Bulger described McGraw as "a well-educated man" who "enters his sixtieth year in a thoughtful mellowness," although he could be short and impatient with uninformed admirers. He was also generous with time and information for young sportswriters, yet downright rude to those who didn't exhibit a proper deference. McGraw, wrote another journalist who interviewed him that spring, "seldom uses the first personal pronoun: it is usually 'McGraw.' " Despite his age and health difficulties, he still "gives the impression of pride, confidence, something of disdain and something of arrogance. It may not be Napoleonic, but it is certainly . . . the conqueror."[24]

"Maybe I don't move around as fast as I once did," said McGraw in Los Angeles, "but I'm just as active mentally. I don't know whether I can think any more rapidly than I could a few years ago, but I know I don't think any more slowly." Yet Travis Jackson would remember that McGraw no longer handled his pitchers effectively, that he often stayed with a starting pitcher too long, that he took too much time to make up his mind, that "his stubbornness cost us games." And reserve catcher Bob O'Farrell, who'd succeeded Hornsby at St. Louis, then given way to Bill McKechnie and come over to the Giants for George Harper in 1928, would recall playing for McGraw as a generally unpleasant experience: "You couldn't seem to do anything right for him, ever. If something went wrong, it was always your fault, not his. Maybe it was because he was getting old and was a sick man, but he was never any fun to play for. He was always so grouchy. . . ."[25]

One reason for McGraw's grouchiness in the spring of 1932 was the disappointing turnouts at Wrigley Field in Los Angeles, on Santa Catalina Island twenty-one miles offshore (where the Chicago Cubs were based), and at San Diego and San Francisco. The players didn't like Los Angeles,

either. The sprawling metropolis made for expensive cab fares from the
Hotel Biltmore to the ballpark, to Aguas Calientes racetrack, or almost
anywhere else they wanted to go. Everybody was unhappy with the trip
eastward, which consumed three nights and two days through the Sierras
and Rockies before the Giants arrived at Kansas City for a game with
the Detroit Tigers. By that time Fred Leach was in Florida, sold to the
Boston Braves, and Shanty Hogan was under orders from McGraw to
trim down to 228 pounds or ride the bench indefinitely.

After playing thirty-two exhibition games (winning twenty-three), the
Giants returned to New York for the start of McGraw's thirtieth season
as their manager, his forty-third in professional baseball. It was a sorry
beginning. A congratulatory telegram from President Hoover, whose
administration seemed helpless to do anything about the ever-worsening
hard times, might have been an ill omen. McGraw himself, bundled
against the chill in topcoat and high-crowned fedora, was helpless to do
anything about the Giants' inept performance. The Philadelphia Phillies
knocked out Bill Walker and went on to pile up thirteen runs on seventeen
hits. The Giants helped out with five errors, which matched the runs
they could muster off "Fidgety Phil" Collins. A crowd of somewhat more
than 20,000 at the Polo Grounds was about average for the opening-day
games in both leagues, but that average was 11,000 below the inaugural
turnouts a year earlier. Baseball attendance would continue to sag
throughout the year.

The Giants lost five of their first six games, ten of their first fifteen.
Over those fifteen games they committed fifty-eight errors, including
eight in one particularly horrendous outing against Boston. Only Hubbell
among the regular moundsmen pitched with any effectiveness, although
a young right-hander named Hal Schumacher, a recent graduate of St.
Lawrence University, soon worked his way into the starting rotation.
Nobody was hitting much, either, except for Bill Terry. In a four-game
stretch against Boston and Philadelphia, Terry crashed six home runs.

The New York team looked good in winning three of four from the
world-champion Cardinals to start their first western swing. McGraw had
made the trip to St. Louis, but sinusitis put him to bed in Cincinnati.
He showed up before the third game of the Cincinnati series just long
enough to bawl out Bill Klem for not calling off the previous day's water-
logged Reds victory, then returned to the hotel. Adding to his woes was
an attack of ptomaine poisoning, the result of eating some bad fish in
Pittsburgh. He finally gave up and went back to New York.

While he stayed home in Pelham Manor, the Giants continued to struggle at the Polo Grounds, under Bancroft's direction. On June 1, before they met Philadelphia, he visited the players in the center-field clubhouse and tried one of his old-fashioned pep talks on them. It didn't do much good. McGraw looked on from his office window until the third inning, when Terry lifted his eleventh homer into the seats. After he went home, Bill Walker yielded two late-inning runs and the Giants lost another one.

That left their record at 17–23. In last place, they were still only eight games behind the League-leading Cubs, but it didn't seem likely that things would get much better. McGraw was discouraged, at a loss to explain his team's poor play. For two weeks he'd mulled over his situation. His sinuses were giving him a lot of trouble, as they almost always did starting about May. His prostate was bothering him, too, causing him discomfort and difficulty in urinating. Soon the Giants would leave on another road trip; he would either have to send them off in Bancroft's care or endure another two weeks of train rides, hotel stays, watching what his players ate and what they did at night, concentrating as much energy as he could, for two hours plus in the afternoons, on winning another ballgame. No, he'd finally had enough—enough self-doubt, enough of being a part-time manager, enough of a life that was designed for healthy young athletes, not a fat and sickly man nearing sixty.

But who would take over? Bancroft had worked devotedly and probably thought he deserved the job full-time, but Banny had failed as a manager at Boston and Stoneham lacked confidence in him. Frank Frisch was McGraw's first choice, or so he would tell Joe Vila later on. But when McGraw felt out Branch Rickey about a deal for Frisch, the Cardinals' general manager turned thumbs down. So it came down to Bill Terry.

On Thursday, June 2, it rained so much in the early afternoon that the Giants' game at the Polo Grounds with the Phillies had to be called off. Terry was in the clubhouse when McGraw called him into the manager's office. It was the first time they'd spoken since February. Closing the door behind Terry, McGraw put the question to him directly: Did he want to manage the Giants? Momentarily stunned, Terry recovered to say yes, he wanted the job, but he also wanted McGraw's assurance that he would be the boss, not a front man for McGraw. He would be the boss, replied McGraw.

The next day, after another rainout, McGraw was at home when Jim

Tierney called reporters into Stoneham's office and, with Terry, Stoneham, and Leo Bondy present, handed out copies of a typewritten statement signed by McGraw. The statement explained that McGraw's physicians had advised against any more road trips. It was impossible for him to manage under those circumstances, he and Stoneham had agreed. He'd wanted a successor "who was thoroughly familiar with my methods and who had learned his baseball under me." Bill Terry was such a man. Terry would have "full and complete charge and control of the team and will have to assume entire responsibility therefor. . . . I am turning over a good team to Terry, who I believe will capably handle it." His health permitting, he would help Terry as much as requested. He would also continue as club vice-president and stockholder, and as a "general advisor and counsellor in business as well as baseball matters."[26]

Running his hand through his thick black hair, the thirty-three-year-old Terry wondered aloud whether he would turn gray as he'd seen other managers do. When he'd agreed to take over the team, said Terry, McGraw had "looked like a man who had a forty-pound weight lifted from his head." He intended to let the players "relax a bit. . . . They won't have to report to the park at ten o'clock in the morning or go to bed at any certain hour."[27] Bancroft was already gone, having resigned within hours after McGraw's resignation was announced. Terry also quickly got rid of Leonard "Doc" Knowles, the Giants' trainer and McGraw's faithful spy for the past two years.

On Saturday, June 4, the Giants debuted under Terry by sweeping a double-header from Philadelphia. They won four more games in a row to climb out of the cellar for good. That streak, though, didn't presage any kind of spectacular shift in their fortunes. Terry's Giants would play only 55–59 baseball the rest of the way and finish in sixth place, eighteen games behind the pennant-winning Cubs. Hughey Critz was healthy for the whole season, but Travis Jackson missed most of it with a broken leg. In July, Terry optioned Len Koenecke to Jersey City, bringing up skinny Joe Moore to begin a solid ten years in the New York outfield. Lindstrom, claiming that McGraw had promised the manager's job to him (despite his being still only twenty-six), quarreled with Terry and went into a batting slump—and would find himself with Pittsburgh the following spring. Hubbell was Terry's only reliable pitcher, winning eighteen games with a 2.50 earned-run average. Some thought he might win even more with a more mobile catcher than the beefy Hogan. Re-

stored to good graces under Terry, Hogan had another productive year
at the plate.

McGraw stayed out of the way, watching games from his five-hundred-
foot-distant perch, sometimes puttering around his house, spending most
of August with Blanche at Saratoga Springs, where he was a daily wagerer
at the local track. Relieved of his managerial responsibilities, he found
that his sinuses had pretty well cleared up, so that he felt better in late
summer than he had in many, many years. Visiting George M. Cohan,
who was hospitalized for a while in nearby New Rochelle, he remarked
that it had been a long time since he'd felt so relaxed.

At season's end, McGraw persuaded Stoneham to give Terry a two-
year contract, despite the team's lackluster showing under his leadership
and a total attendance of only about 400,000, the second smallest at
the Polo Grounds since the early years of the century. Passing up both
the Yankees-Cubs World Series and the National League's December
meeting, McGraw left for Cuba with Blanche. Back at the beginning of
February to be the guest of honor at the annual dinner of the New York
chapter of the Baseball Writers Association of America, he then spent
another month in Cuba before returning for the resumption of the legal
wars with Francis X. McQuade.

On March 17, 1933, the court for the New York appellate division,
first department, upheld Justice McCook's ruling fourteen months earlier:
McQuade was entitled to $42,827 in back pay and interest, because
he'd been illegally deprived of his position as National Exhibition Company treasurer in 1928. Again Stoneham and McGraw appealed, this
time to the state court of appeals in Albany.

A month later, for the first time since 1902, the New York Giants
began a baseball season without John McGraw as their manager. Another
smallish Polo Grounds opening-day crowd nonetheless cheered heartily
as McGraw joined the traditional procession of players and managers to
the flag pole in center field. Jimmy Walker was no longer part of the
scene. In 1932 he'd resigned in the midst of the Seabury Committee's
disclosure of widespread and multifarious corruption within the city's
government. The man who, maybe more than anybody else, had sym-
bolized the gaudiness and glitter of New York in the high-riding Twenties
was finished politically, and in 1933 the Tammany Hall organization
itself would fall from power (temporarily) with the election of a reform
ticket headed by Fiorello La Guardia.

Other voices from McGraw's glory years had faded as well. Bozeman Bulger, who'd probably done more than any sportswriter to promote the McGraw mystique, had died in the spring of 1932, just as the *Saturday Evening Post* published his last paean to the "genius of the game." Dan Brouthers died the following August; Kid Gleason succumbed in January 1933; Mike Donlin, out in Hollywood, had only about six months to live.

Much had already changed on the Giants. When they returned from another spring training in Los Angeles, Terry continued to disdain morning practices, follow a liberal curfew policy, and name his starting pitchers a day or more ahead of time (something McGraw had usually refused to do). Terry had even abandoned the busy McGraw-designed uniforms, with their white caps, pinstripes, and striped stockings, in favor of a more subdued motif: all-blue caps and stockings, no pinstripes. Not only Lindstrom but Hogan, Walker, Mooney, and various others were gone from the previous year's team. Knee surgery would keep Jackson out the whole year, but John "Blondy" Ryan would fill in adequately at shortstop. Gus Mancuso, a cat-like catcher obtained from the Cardinals, would be one of the big reasons why Carl Hubbell would win twenty-three games, with a remarkable 1.66 earned-run average.

Terry had that team in close contention with Pittsburgh, Chicago, and St. Louis early in June, when Arch Ward, sports editor of the Chicago *Tribune*, announced that his newspaper would sponsor a game between selected stars of the two major leagues, to be played at Chicago's Comiskey Park in July. The contest would be staged as a feature of the city's Century of Progress exposition, with proceeds going to a fund for indigent old baseball players. The *Tribune* named McGraw to manage the National League All-Stars, Connie Mack to handle the Americans.

It would be McGraw's last time in the spotlight. Broadcast by both the Columbia and NBC radio networks, the game took place on July 6. Forty-nine thousand people nearly filled Comiskey Park, producing net receipts for the players' charity of $51,000. Chosen in balloting held at newpapers across the country, the two squads of twenty players each offered the greatest concentration of baseball talent (at least white talent) ever assembled in one place up to then.

Before the game seventy-year-old Mack towered over sixty-year-old McGraw as they posed doing the old hands-over-hands routine on a bat. McGraw was sharply turned out in brown linen suit and straw boater; Mack was his usual dignified self in vest and high collar, seemingly oblivious to the ninety-degree temperature. McGraw named the starting National League lineup, but once the game began, he sat quietly in the third-base visitors' dugout and left the decisions up to Bill Terry and Frank Frisch (who would soon succeed Gabby Street as Cardinals manager).

It was a good ballgame. The American Leaguers scored once in the bottom of the second inning when "Wild Bill" Hallahan of St. Louis, starter for the Nationals, walked two men and the Yankees' Vernon "Lefty" Gomez, Hallahan's counterpart, hit a single. In the third Babe Ruth, in one of his last moments of glory, homered into the right-field upper deck following another walk by Hallahan. In the top of the sixth, pitcher Lon Warneke (Cubs) scored on an infield out, and Frisch followed with a home run off Washington's Alvin Crowder to make it 3–2. Warneke yielded a run in the bottom of that inning, Cleveland's Earl Averill singling in Washington player-manager Joe Cronin. Hubbell and Lefty Grove of the Athletics pitched shutout ball the rest of the way, although Ruth had to make a fine catch against the right-field wall to kill a Nationals rally in the eighth. The first in what would become an annual mid-summer baseball extravaganza had gone to the American Leaguers, 4–2.

When Grove struck out Brooklyn's Tony Cuccinello to end the game, McGraw bounded out of the dugout and headed for the American League dressing room to congratulate everybody. "It was a splendid game, wasn't it?" he bubbled. "Ruth? He was marvelous. That old boy certainly came through when they needed him." Then players from both leagues crowded around McGraw and Mack with baseballs for the two elder statesmen to autograph. When somebody mentioned the possibility of McGraw's managing again, he replied quickly, "I'm through with it. I have quit."[28]

At the time of the All-Star game, the Giants had moved out to a six-game lead over Pittsburgh. McGraw talked excitedly about Terry's rebuilt pitching staff, whose sturdy foursome of Hubbell, Fitzsimmons, Schumacher, and rookie Roy Parmalee reminded him of his 1905 stalwarts: Mathewson, McGinnity, Wiltse, Ames, and Taylor. He was at the Polo Grounds frequently during the last half of the season, watching now from Stoneham's office on the top level of the clubhouse building and appearing to be genuinely delighted with the team's turnaround under his young successor. When the Giants clinched the pennant, McGraw was on hand for the celebration at City Hall and spoke a few words into the radio microphones.

He saw the first two games of the World Series, played at the Polo Grounds. The Giants won both games from the Washington Senators. Despite being tired and having difficulty sitting for long periods, he traveled to Washington for the next three games, which were all the Giants needed. Mel Ott's home run in the tenth inning of game five made the Giants world champions for the first time in eleven years.

That winter John and Blanche McGraw didn't pack their trunks and embark on their usual journey to the warm sunshine and relaxed atmosphere of Havana. By the fall of 1933 McGraw was dying. He may have realized it, although in line with the medical conventions of the time, he hadn't been told. Blanche, and a few very intimate friends with whom she shared her distress, had known since the previous spring.

After their return from Cuba, McGraw had gone in for a checkup. A routine rectal examination of his prostate revealed that it was now considerably enlarged. A biopsy showed the presence of cancerous cells; X-rays indicated that the malignancy had already spread beyond the prostate to the kidneys and stomach. Dr. Louis B. Chapman, McGraw's personal physician, had to inform Blanche that nothing could be done; her husband probably wouldn't last more than another year.

The McGraws spent Christmas 1933 and New Year's 1934 in Pelham Manor. Sometimes chauffeur Edward James drove him all the way into midtown Manhattan to the National Exhibition Company offices in the Hart Building, but he was suffering more and more now and unable to spend much time away from the comfort and privacy of 620 Ely Avenue. Early in February he started to get into his tuxedo for the Baseball Writers Association dinner but became exhausted and had to go to bed. Two days later, though, he felt strong enough to be driven to the Waldorf for the National League winter meeting. That evening, per tradition, Charles Stoneham, as the pennant-winning club owner, gave a banquet for the other teams. McGraw could stay only about an hour before pain and fatigue forced him to leave. The next week he made a brief appearance at the Hart Building to sign a few papers, but was soon in such agony that he told Edward James to get him home as quickly as possible.

Dr. Chapman had him admitted to New Rochelle Hospital, only a couple of miles from his house, on Friday, February 16. His immediate difficulty, said Chapman, was uremia. That meant (although Chapman didn't say as much publicly) that the cancer had so damaged McGraw's kidneys that he was no longer getting rid of toxicants normally passed through the system. In other words, McGraw was steadily poisoning himself. By the twentieth he seemed improved, still running a temperature of 103 but "less stuperous"—improved enough for his wife to go home for a good sleep.

McGraw was comfortable and alert the next day, when, of all people, Francis X. McQuade paid him a visit. Just a month earlier the New York State Court of Appeals had overturned the decisions in the two lower courts on McQuade's suit for the NEC treasurer's salary he'd lost. Chief Justice Cuthbert W. Pound, in a unanimous opinion, wrote that under the laws of the state, prohibiting a city magistrate from engaging in outside business affairs, McQuade had illegally held the NEC treasurer's job in 1919–28. His agreement with Stoneham and McGraw, whereby they'd pledged to keep each other in office, had no legal force. While Pound acknowledged that McQuade had been "shabbily treated as a purchaser of stock from Stoneham," he was entitled to no recompense of any kind.[29]

Yet McQuade held no hard feelings toward McGraw, he said. He wasn't in such bad shape. Last fall Tammany had arranged his appointment as assistant corporation counsel for the city, so that he could qualify for his pension. He shook McGraw's hand and parted as his friend.

On February 22, a Thursday, McGraw felt well enough to have a shave. Stoneham visited him for the second time and was encouraged by his appearance and spirits. Within forty-eight hours, though, McGraw had begun to hemorrhage from his intestines and fallen into a coma. Two specialists called in from Manhattan advised that he was too weak to take blood transfusions, but he was put under oxygen to facilitate his breathing. That evening, at Blanche's request, a local priest administered the Roman Catholic sacrament of extreme unction.

Overnight it began to snow heavily. Blanche's younger sister Jeannette Van Lill, Christy Mathewson's sister Bess Cregar, and Frank Belcher, an actor and very old friend, kept the vigil with her. Stoneham arrived early in the morning. Father Vincent de Paul Mulry, pastor at St. Catherine's Church in Pelham, the McGraws' parish, led the group in prayer in the corridor outside the dying man's room. Then they, together with the three attending physicians, waited by his bedside until 11:50 A.M., when Chapman shook his head and told the others that it was all over. McGraw had died on Sunday, February 25, 1934, forty-one days short of his sixty-first birthday.

The body was taken to a New Rochelle mortuary for embalming, then to the red-brick house in Pelham Manor. Vehicles could barely navigate streets clogged with snow that by late afternoon measured nine inches. Nonetheless, people began coming as soon as they heard, as many as could make it, given the weather. On Ely Avenue workmen with shovels and cinders, dispatched by the town authorities, tried to keep the street passable. Many more people came on Monday and Tuesday to view McGraw's remains, which lay in a plain mahogany casket, his hands holding a crucifix. Frank Frisch and Bill Terry (who'd left the Giants in spring training at Miami Beach as soon as he got the news) stood together for a long time beside the casket.

Tributes came in from around the country. Terry hailed McGraw as "far and away the greatest baseball manager of all time" and attributed his own success to "the solid groundwork of baseball which I learned under him." Frank Snyder, now a coach for Terry, said that "He had a baseball mind that was in a class by itself." For Kenesaw Mountain Landis, McGraw typified "the virile competitive spirit of baseball"; out in Atherton, California, Ty Cobb characterized him as a man who "put everything he had into baseball, both as a player and manager. . . . The game needs more like him." Said Mel Ott at Miami Beach, "He treated me as though I were his son and I have also looked on him as a second father. . . . I have lost the best friend I ever had."[30]

At 8:30 A.M. on February 28, in biting cold, the funeral cortege started into midtown Manhattan for services at St. Patrick's Cathedral. The McGraws had never been truly pious Catholics, but they had sometimes attended Mass at St. Catherine's in Pelham, and John McGraw had considered himself a faithful son of the Church. So he would be memorialized in the Church's best-known edifice in North America. A police motorcycle escort led the cortege through the Bronx and across the river to Fifth Avenue, then down the spine of Manhattan Island, past Central Park and the new Rockefeller Center, finally to St. Patrick's. The mourners, estimated at 3,500 and overwhelmingly male, filled the cathedral and spilled out onto Fifth Avenue. As they stood in the cold, some of them swapped stories about McGraw's many beneficences.

Her brother Frank Sindall escorted Blanche McGraw to her place near the flower-free catafalque. Two of McGraw's sisters, Nelly Donnelly of Camillus, New York, and Anna Gray of New Canann, Connecticut, were also on hand. The last survivors in McGraw's immediate family, they'd rarely had any contact with their brother in the past thirty years.

The Reverend Mulry celebrated a High Requiem Mass, with the

Reverend Henry Hammer, assistant rector at St. Patrick's, giving the eulogy. "In life," said Hammer, "our comrade had some faults, like all of us. But remember that charity covers a multitude of sins." McGraw, he went on, "lives gloriously at this moment" as "baseball's highest inspiration."[31]

Following the services, a party of about thirty people, including Stoneham, Terry, Leo Bondy, and Christy Mathewson, Jr., accompanied Blanche by train to Baltimore, where the body was to be entombed. At the Pennsylvania Station in Baltimore they were met by a delegation of Elks, the lodge that had made McGraw an honorary member when he was a player in the city. Police motorcycles then led the line of automobiles out Edmonson Avenue to the New Cathedral Cemetery on the west side. At the cemetery the Reverend Timothy B. Kenney, who as a young priest had assisted at the McGraws' marriage, read the ritual of interment, and the body was placed in a vault to await burial in the spring. At six that evening the funeral party returned to New York, where, at the age of fifty-three, Blanche McGraw, always happy to be known simply as John McGraw's wife, settled into her new role as his widow.

Postlude

— · —

NAMES WITH NO NUMBERS
IN A FARAWAY PLACE

NEVER REMARRYING, she would live the role of John McGraw's widow for the next twenty-eight years. Sometimes called "the first lady of baseball," she would be satisfied to serve as the principal living connection between the present and the ever-receding golden age of the New York Giants. John McGraw's will—drawn up only three days before his death, written on a piece of New Rochelle Hospital stationery, and signed with a barely legible scrawl—left all of his property to his wife. That consisted almost wholly of his seventy shares in the National Exhibition Company and the house in Pelham Manor. After a couple of years, Blanche McGraw sold the house and moved back into Manhattan, into an apartment at 30 Fifth Avenue in Greenwich Village. With interest from her savings, NEC stock, and income from family sources, she lived not lavishly but comfortably. The year after McGraw's death, she had the family tomb in New Cathedral Cemetery in Baltimore rebuilt in marble and granite, then had McGraw's remains placed near those of her father and mother.

Blanche McGraw was present at the Polo Grounds on April 17, 1934, for the season's first game, when a bugler played taps in John McGraw's memory during pre-game ceremonies. Three months later she was part of the near-capacity crowd at the Giants ballpark for the second All-Star game. Forever remembered for Carl Hubbell's feat of consecutively striking out Babe Ruth, Lou Gehrig, Jimmy Foxx, Al Simmons, and Joe Cronin, the game was also the occasion for the unveiling of a memorial tablet to McGraw in front of the clubhouse in center field.

Other tributes to McGraw's memory came along as the years passed. In August 1938 the Giants ball club took a train to Cortland, New York,

316

then rode a school bus up to Truxton for a game with the semi-pro Truxton Giants. All proceeds from the game went to pay for the erection of a monument in the village to the "son of these hills" who'd been "spawned for Destiny and Fame."[1] The game took place at John J. McGraw Field, on property purchased with money McGraw had given the village. A reported 7,650 people were there, drawn from many miles around and sitting in bleachers trucked in from Cornell and Syracuse universities. The monument itself, a relief bust carved in a granite shaft and topped by a granite baseball, was set in place in October 1942. It stood in the center of the village, exactly where, on that rain-drenched night long ago, little Johnny McGraw had fled across the road to escape his father's rage and seek refuge at Mary Goddard's hotel.

In June 1939 the National Baseball Hall of Fame and Museum was dedicated in all-day ceremonies and festivities at Cooperstown, New York, some fifty miles east of Truxton. Situated where, according to the sport's official mythology, young Abner Doubleday had invented baseball a hundred years earlier, the Hall of Fame would "enshrine" its "immortals" and serve as a central repository for its records and artifacts. McGraw had been chosen in 1937 in the second round of balloting by members of the Baseball Writers Association of America. All told, the BBWAA picked fourteen men, all still living except for McGraw, Christy Mathewson, and Willie Keeler.[2] Blanche McGraw was there to receive the honors for her husband and congratulate Ty Cobb, Babe Ruth, Connie Mack, and the other admittees. Going to Cooperstown for subsequent induction ceremonies would become almost an annual event for her.

In 1944 she went to the Bethlehem Steel Corporation's shipyard at Baltimore to break a champagne bottle across the prow of a newly finished military transport ship christened the *John J. McGraw*. And two years later she and millions of other Americans heard the *Cavalcade of America*, a popular network radio series sponsored by the Du Pont Corporation, carry a half-hour dramatization entitled "The Great McGraw." Starring the well-known actor Pat O'Brien and derived from Frank Graham's biography, published in 1944, the program presented a succession of scenes from McGraw's career, such as Fred Merkle's blunder, Mathewson's death, and a wholly fictional episode in which the manager fines a player named "Larry" for hitting a home run after missing a bunt sign.[3]

Blanche McGraw provided her own memorial to her husband in 1953, when her reminiscences of their years together were published as *The Real McGraw*. Unstintingly adoring, her account nonetheless provided a full narrative and would prove indispensable for anybody seriously interested in his life.[4]

Holding a lifetime pass to a box at the Polo Grounds, Blanche McGraw often saw the Giants in action. Sometimes older fans would come over and visit during a game. She received several letters a week asking for McGraw's autograph, most of which she satisfied by cutting off the bottoms of canceled checks he'd signed. As long as the Giants trained in Florida, she frequently went down for a week or so; when, in the early 1950s, they shifted to the Phoenix area, she still sometimes made the long trip to sit in the sun and hear the *thwack!* of bat on ball once again. In the off-seasons she liked to visit the Mel Otts in New Orleans, and she remained close to Frank and Ada Frisch and some of the other ex-Giants couples, as well as Jane Mathewson and her sister-in-law Bess Cregar. "She was the nicest, sweetest person you'd ever want to meet," was the way Mary Jackson would remember her.[5]

As long as they were still the New York Giants, the memory of McGraw lived in the recollections of fans and what they passed along to their progeny, in the traditions of the team, in the Polo Grounds itself, indeed in the entire ambience of New York City baseball. But within twenty-three years following his death, they were no longer the New York Giants.

Over those twenty-three years, the Giants had plenty of great moments. Bill Terry led them to back-to-back pennants in 1936–37, although they managed only three wins in two World Series against Joe McCarthy's Yankees juggernaut. Terry stopped playing after 1936, but Mel Ott remained the club's main offensive threat and Carl Hubbell was still its ace. Ott succeeded Terry after the 1941 season. For four wartime seasons Ott struggled to keep a respectable team on the field, but in 1943 the Giants finished last for the second time since 1902. Mild-mannered and well-liked by his players, Ott lacked the driving temperament that McGraw and to some extent Terry as well had brought to their jobs. After another cellar finish in the first peacetime season, Ott's 1947 Giants set a new major league home-run record but still could make it no higher than fourth place.

Leo Durocher, who came over from the hated Brooklyn Dodgers in the middle of the 1948 season, reminded people a lot of John McGraw. Outspoken, scrappy, a gambler and night-lifer, controversial both on and off the field, and bringing a reputation for getting the most out of his material, Durocher revived the Giants' dreary fortunes and made them a contender. With baseball's color line finally broken, Durocher could do what McGraw had often wanted to but hadn't been willing to try (not after the Charley Grant episode): sign outstanding players from the black professional teams. In 1951 Negro-league veteran Monte Irvin and twenty-year-old Willie Mays were vital to the Giants' pennant drive, which culminated in a historic victory in the rubber game of a three-game playoff with Brooklyn (necessitated when the teams tied at season's end). Three years later Mays's magnificent all-around play lifted New York to another pennant, with Ruben Gomez, a racially mixed Puerto Rican, pitching seventeen victories. A stunning World Series sweep of the Cleveland Indians, winners of a record 111 games in the American League, was undoubtedly the pinnacle in the Giants' post-McGraw history.

Yet they weren't long for New York. The area around the Polo Grounds was increasingly rundown and crime-infested; parking was always a massive problem; and the ballpark needed a major fixing-up. Durocher was fired after a poor third-place finish in 1955. The next year the Giants fell to sixth and remained there for still another season. Attendance sagged to Depression-era levels. Horace Stoneham, president of the club since his father's death in 1936, followed the lead of Walter O'Malley, Brooklyn owner, who'd decided to abandon New York for the riches supposedly awaiting major league baseball on the rapidly populating Pacific Coast.

The New York Giants played the last game in their history on September 29, 1957. A crowd of 11,606 watched with morbid curiosity as the Pittsburgh Pirates won 9–1; then many of them swarmed onto the field to rip up bits of turf and whatever other souvenirs they could collect from the old ballpark. Blanche McGraw was there to receive a dozen long-stemmed roses in pre-game ceremonies. "New York can never be the same for me," she said.[6]

The next April she was the honored guest of Horace Stoneham and the new San Francisco Giants when they opened their first major league season in Seals Stadium, formerly occupied by the city's Pacific Coast League team. Apparently braced by the cool Pacific air, they climbed to third place in 1958. Although they drew well for a decade and more after they moved to the Coast, the Giants never found the pot of gold in the Bay area that O'Malley immediately discovered with his Los Angeles Dodgers.

By 1961 the Giants were playing in a new stadium on cold and windswept Candlestick point, south of the city. Being regularly chilled,

especially during night games, didn't seem to bother their fans at all in
1962, when the Giants, powered by the great Mays and newer black
and Hispanic stars such as Willie McCovey, Orlando Cepeda, and Juan
Marichal, overcame their Los Angeles rivals in a grueling struggle that
resulted in another tie over the regular season and another Giants victory
in a three-game playoff. After that came a tough seventh-game loss to
the Yankees in the World Series. Two and one-half weeks later, in New
York, Blanche Sindall McGraw died at the age of eighty-one.

As for the Polo Grounds, the historic horseshoe proved serviceable
for a few more years, first for the grimly inept New York Titans of the
new American Football League, then for the laughably inept New York
Metropolitans, one of two franchises added to the National League for
1962. The Polo Grounds had seen some strange baseball over the decades, but nothing as persistently awful as Casey Stengel's "Mets," whose
40–120 record in their first season gave them the worst winning percentage in the twentieth century. With the departure of the Mets to their
new stadium in Flushing for 1964, big league baseball again vanished
from Manhattan Island. Demolition crews arrived at the Polo Grounds
on April 10, 1964. Thanks to somebody's perverse sentimentalism, the
wrecking ball was the same one used to knock down Ebbets Field four
years earlier.

As the San Francisco Giants grew older, their connections with their
earlier New York incarnation became ever more tenuous. Ironically, it
was in the early 1980s, at a time when sparse attendance at Candlestick
Park had stirred much talk about their leaving the Bay area, that the
Giants organization began to exhibit greater concern with the team's lofty
ancestors. Not only were the uniform numbers for Mays, Marichal, and
McCovey retired and plaques bearing their names and numbers affixed
to the outfield fence, but the same was done for Bill Terry (3), Mel Ott
(4), and Carl Hubbell (11). Christy Mathewson's name was also displayed
on a plaque, although Matty had never worn a number to go with the
name. Finally, the Giants (apparently settled at San Francisco for the
time being) proclaimed August 9, 1987, "John McGraw Day." Besides
giving out posters of McGraw to the first several thousand people entering
the ballpark, the Giants staged ceremonies to retire his uniform shirt,
which of course had never borne a number. A plaque with his name
would now hang alongside those of Mathewson, Terry, Ott, Mays, Marichal, and McCovey.

So in that faraway place, three thousand miles from where the Giants had originated, two names with no numbers would be on display for Bay area fans, few of whom had even been born at the time of McGraw's death. Some of them, having bothered to learn something about the long history of the sport they watched, might be able to enlighten others who asked about those names on the outfield fence. For most, though, the distant past was the time of Mays, muscling home runs into the stiff wind from left field at Candlestick; of Marichal, kicking his left leg above his head and snapping off his sweeping overhand curve; of McCovey, lifting towering drives beyond the right-field fence. They probably wouldn't know or care much about stubby Ott's 511 career homers, Terry's .341 career batting average, Hubbell's 256 victories (twenty-four straight in 1936–37), Mathewson's 373 wins and eighty-three shutouts. Nor about McGraw, once the little Napoleon of baseball.

No, McGraw would have to belong to history—and to those who cared about it. He would always be considered among the handful of truly great managers, along with Connie Mack, Ned Hanlon, Joe McCarthy, Miller Huggins, maybe Frank Chance, Fred Clarke, and Frank Selee, certainly McGraw's pupil Casey Stengel, who surmounted unhappy stints at Brooklyn and the Boston Braves to direct the Yankees to ten pennants and seven world championships in twelve seasons (1949–60).

How good was McGraw? With Baltimore and St. Louis in the National League and Baltimore in the new American League, he was a very good player, never a great one. Only a fair third-baseman, he excelled at getting on base and scoring runs—more than a thousand in a career that included no more than five fully played seasons. Although he compiled his lifetime .334 batting average mostly in an era when foul balls didn't count as strikes, home plate was only a foot wide, and the pitchers were adjusting to throwing from 60' 6", McGraw's batting statistics are still impressive.

As early as 1911–13, when his Giants brought him his third, fourth, and fifth pennants since he'd come to New York, McGraw was being widely acclaimed as the greatest manager in baseball history. Outside of Mathewson, Joe McGinnity, Mike Donlin, and Roger Bresnahan, his early winners weren't notably talented. But McGraw seemed to exact more productivity from players with limited abilities than other managers. That, his admirers explained, was a consequence of his success in staying on top of every aspect of the game, drilling his men to execute his wishes without regard for personal glory, and infusing in them a passion for winning.

Probably the chief reason for McGraw's reputation as a baseball genius was that he was the first manager who insisted on trying to control everything that happened on the field. Often he went so far as to call every pitch (something others were willing to leave to their catchers). By the time of his death, the wire-pulling aspect of McGraw's managerial style was well on the way to becoming the norm in the major leagues. Managers would not only signal for nearly everything their players did; most would be wedded to "platooning" (left-handed batters against right-handed pitchers and vice versa, defensive specialists in late innings). Casey Stengel's success in making maximum use of his abundant Yankees talent did much to establish incessant player manipulation (push-button managing and overmanaging, critics said) as the essential baseball of the late twentieth century.

McGraw also went further than his predecessors in trying to control what his ballplayers did off the field. Managing in a period when, under the reserve clause, players were little more than chattels, McGraw had a free hand to enforce his dictates on personal behavior. He had mixed success, experiencing frustration with a succession of incorrigibles—from Mike Donlin to Shanty Hogan. If Hack Wilson had remained Giants property, he might have hit even more prodigiously than he did with the Chicago Cubs. But no doubt he would have boozed prodigiously as well, and McGraw would have failed to reform Wilson, just as he'd failed with such assiduous topers as Bugs Raymond, Larry McLean, and Phil Douglas.

In general, though, McGraw's players accepted his discipline in and out of uniform, and they won and won—at least in the National League. In the World Series the Giants were successful only three times in nine tries. Partly, as everybody acknowledged, that was a matter of plain bad luck and quirky plays. But it was also, critics said, because he disdained bunting to move runners into scoring position and because, in Mathewson's view, his players weren't trained to take the initiative and improvise, as it was often necessary to do, especially in a short series.

In the 1920s McGraw managed differently, no longer relying on basestealing and the hit-and-run play, accommodating his strategy to the new era of heavy hitting and high scoring. He won an unprecedented four straight pennants, but in 1923 the Giants lost the battle of New York to the Yankees in the World Series, just as they'd already lost the battle of the turnstiles to Babe Ruth's outfit.

McGraw's 1921–24 pennant winners had less talent than his teams of the late Twenties—at least as measured by subsequent Hall of Fame admissions. Yet the Giants came close to a pennant only twice more, in 1927–28. Part of what happened was that McGraw's judgment in players, supposedly unmatched, repeatedly failed him in the Twenties. It had happened occasionally in earlier years, of course. He'd given up too soon on Al Demaree and Rube Marquard, who were instrumental in winning Philadelphia's and Brooklyn's pennants in 1915 and 1916, respectively. McGraw could hardly be blamed for losing Hack Wilson in 1925, unless one assumes that he should have been looking over the club secretary's shoulder to make sure he did his paperwork. Losing Rogers Hornsby after the 1927 season wasn't something over which McGraw had any control. Charles Stoneham decreed Hornsby's banishment; McGraw, heavily in debt to the Giants president, struggling to pay off the Pennant Park investors, and needing the big salary he was getting, had to go along. But getting rid of Art Nehf, George Harper, Burleigh Grimes, and Lefty O'Doul amounted to a mistake in each instance. Sooner in some cases, later in others, they all came back to haunt him.

McGraw also never really grasped the significance of what Branch Rickey was doing at St. Louis. Knowing that the Cardinals would never be wealthy enough to buy a lot of well-developed talent, as the Giants did, Rickey began to build a farflung "farm system" of minor league teams, sometimes controlled by the Cardinals, sometimes linked to St. Louis by working agreements. Signing huge numbers of raw youngsters and paying them a pittance to start out in the lowest minors, the Cardinals then carefully scouted, graded, and advanced their best prospects, until they were finally ready for major league competition. Starting in 1926, Rickey's grand design produced nine National League pennants and six world championships over the next twenty-one seasons. Meanwhile the Giants, despite acquiring the Bridgeport Eastern League franchise in the late Twenties, lagged far behind not only the Cardinals but a number of other major league organizations in building a farm system. To the end McGraw saw putting together a winning team as mainly a matter of spotting and buying the best talent in the higher minors and buying and trading for what was available in the majors.

McGraw should have quit managing at least five years before he did. Illness and infirmity kept him away from his team at least a third of the time, beginning about 1924. Hugh Jennings, Roger Bresnahan, Rogers Hornsby, Ray Schalk, and finally Dave Bancroft handled the job in his numerous absences, generally without either appreciation or additional recompense. Long before he finally resigned, McGraw had ceased to be able to carry his managerial burdens effectively.

Vanity, a life in baseball and an inability to imagine life outside it, big money and the need for even more, maybe most of all, an obsession with winning just one more time—that's what kept him at it year after year, through a great deal of physical discomfort and more than a little emotional distress. McGraw simply couldn't bear being a loser. When at last he had to admit to himself that that was what he'd become, he gave it all up, quietly and with dignity.

McGraw retired with an overall managerial record of 2,840 victories, 1,984 defeats, a .589 winning percentage. When Connie Mack finally quit in 1950, after fifty-three years of managing, his teams had won more games (3,776), but because only one of his last sixteen clubs finished as high as fourth place, Mack's won-lost percentage had dropped to .484. Joe McCarthy, in twenty-four major league seasons, finished with a .614 percentage, while Frank Selee, in his sixteen years with Boston and Chicago in the National League, saw his teams win .598 percent of the time.

So whatever else might be said about him, McGraw was one of the great winners in American sports history. Throughout his career, whether as player or manager, he remained willing to do anything—or almost anything—to win a ballgame. That ethic made him a relentless, ruthless, sometimes less-than-honest man, sometimes also a very stupid one. Demanding and dictatorial with his players, he could also be cruel and unjust. Off the field he often exhibited those same traits, at the same time that he could show abiding kindness and outrageous generosity. A bon vivant and a genuine international celebrity, he took little care of his health, lived his life generally as he pleased, and probably enjoyed himself most of it. He wasn't of our time—he probably wouldn't have wanted to be. But he's worth remembering.

NOTES

PRELUDE: A SOGGY JUBILEE

1. For accounts of the McGraw Silver Jubilee, see *New York Times*, July 20, 1927, pp. 4, 20; *Sporting News*, July 21, 1927, p. 2.

2. McGraw managed the Giants for the second half of the 1902 season and resigned about a third of the way through the season in 1932. He had been player-manager at Baltimore in the National League in 1899 and in the American League in 1901–1902. Mack managed Pittsburgh in the National League, 1894–96.

3. Quoted in Mrs. John J. [Blanche] McGraw, *The Real McGraw*, ed. Arthur Mann (New York: David McKay Co., 1952), p. 310.

4. *New York Times*, March 18, 1931, p. 31; Frank Frisch tape-recorded interviews with J. Roy Stockton, reel 7, National Baseball Library, Cooperstown, N.Y.; Edward Lyell Fox, "What Is Inside Baseball?" *Outing*, LVIII (July 1911), p. 497.

5. John J. McGraw, *My Thirty Years in Baseball* (New York: Boni and Liveright, 1923), p. 175; Hugh Bradley, "McGraw," *American Mercury*, XXVI (August 1932), pp. 461–62.

6. Latham quoted in McGraw, *My Thirty Years in Baseball*, p. 114; Sheridan in *Sporting News*, April 6, 1926, p. 7; April 13, 1926, p. 4.

7. *Sporting News*, November 2, 1916, p. 8; New York *World-Telegram*, February 28, 1934, clipping in John J. McGraw Collection, National Baseball Library.

8. *Sporting News*, April 14, 1926, p. 4.

9. *Sporting News*, August 15, 1896, p. 4.

10. *Sporting News*, October 13, 1900, p. 4.

11. Frisch tapes, reel 1A; Arthur Mann, *Branch Rickey: American in Action* (Boston: Houghton Mifflin Co., 1957), p. 102; Chicago *Journal*, September 1, 1908, quoted in G. H. Fleming, ed., *The Unforgettable Season* (New York: Penguin Books, 1982), p. 200.

12. New York *World-Telegram*, June 4, 1932, clipping in McGraw Collection.

13. Christy Mathewson, "Why We Lost Three World's Championships," *Everybody's*, XXXI (October 1914), p. 544; *Sporting News*, December 31, 1926, p. 3.

CHAPTER 1: "AS GOOD AS THEY COME"

1. New York *Evening Telegram*, April [?], 1913, clipping in John McGraw Collection, National Baseball Library, Cooperstown, N.Y.
2. *Sporting News*, March 8, 1934, p. 6.
3. *Sporting News*, April 4, 1891, p. 1; May 9, 1891, p. 4.
4. *Sporting News*, April 25, 1891, p. 2.
5. Mrs. John J. [Blanche] McGraw, *The Real McGraw*, ed. Arthur Mann (New York: David McKay Company, 1952), p. 55.
6. *Sporting News*, September 1, 1900, p. 6.
7. *Sporting News*, August 29, 1891, p. 5.
8. Quoted in Sherry H. Olson, *Baltimore: The Building of an American City* (Baltimore: Johns Hopkins University Press, 1980), p. 148.
9. John J. McGraw, *My Thirty Years in Baseball* (New York: Boni and Liveright, 1923), pp. 47–48.
10. Baltimore *Sun*, August 27, 1891, p. 6; *Sporting News*, September 1, 1900, p. 6.
11. The 1891 Association season was a nominal 140 games long. Because of rainouts and occasional difficulties with railroad travel, teams in the Nineties rarely played all of their scheduled games.
12. *Sporting News*, September 24, 1892, p. 5.
13. The 1892 season was scheduled for 154 games.
14. In 1892 Boston, first half winner, defeated Cleveland, leader over the second half, in post-season play.
15. Given the geography of the National League in the Nineties, divisional alignment should have worked out almost perfectly: Boston, New York, Brooklyn, Washington, Baltimore, and Philadelphia in the east; Pittsburgh, Cleveland, Cincinnati, Louisville, St. Louis, and Chicago in the west. Besides encouraging regional rivalries, such an arrangement would have greatly reduced travel costs.
16. Cincinnati led in attendance with a little less than 200,000.

CHAPTER 2: THE OLD ORIOLES

1. Joe A. Broderick to Father Thomas [Plassman], January 14, 1944, McGraw-Jennings items, John J. McGraw Collection, St. Bonaventure University, St. Bonaventure, N.Y.
2. Quoted in Fred Lieb, *The Baseball Story* (New York: G. P. Putnam's Sons, 1950), p. 113
3. Broderick to Plassman.
4. Various explanations have been given over the years for why 60' 6" (rather than sixty feet or sixty-one feet) became the new pitching distance, but nobody really knows for sure—and nobody ever will.
5. Although technically the "pitcher's box" was done away with under the 1893 rules changes, the term remained in use for many years as a synonym for either slab or mound. The 1893 changes also provided that a batter wouldn't be charged a time at bat on a sacrifice bunt or fly, and that foul *bunts* would be counted as strikes.
6. New York *Clipper*, May 20, 1893, p. 4.
7. Lieb, *Baseball Story*, pp. 139–40.
8. *Sporting News*, November 4, 1893, p. 2.

9. Baltimore *Sun*, August 26, 1901, p. 6; John J. McGraw, *My Thirty Years in Baseball* (New York: Boni and Liveright, 1923), p. 56.

10. *Sporting News*, April 14, 1894, pp. 2–3; April 21, 1894, p. 1.

11. As late as 1915, the average size of major league players was 5′ 9½″ and 174 pounds. See Arthur Macdonald, "Statistics of Baseball," *Scientific American*, CXII (May 1, 1915), p. 418.

12. *Sporting News*, February 17, 1921, p. 8.

13. McGraw, *My Thirty Years in Baseball*, pp. 68, 71.

14. *Sporting News*, June 30, 1894, p. 2.

15. *Sporting News*, October 6, 1894, p. 1.

16. *New York Times*, October 9, 1894, p. 8; Baltimore *Sun*, August 20, 1895, p. 6.

17. Baltimore *Sun*, January 26, 1895, p. 7; February 2, 1895, p. 6; *Sporting News*, November 10, 1894, p. 5; March 2, 1895, p. 5.

18. Apparently until Hanlon came along, it had never occurred to anybody connected with the club that the appropriate colors for a team named the Baltimore Orioles should be those of a Baltimore oriole.

19. *Sporting News*, September 21, 1895, p. 1; July 27, 1895, p. 1.

20. Baltimore *Sun*, July 10, 1895, p. 6; July 19, 1895, p. 6; *Sporting News*, August 3, 1895, p. 1.

21. Cleveland *Plain Dealer*, October 9, 1895, p. 1.

22. *Catalogue of St. Bonaventure's College, 1895–1896*, p. 27, in McGraw Collection, St. Bonaventure University.

23. Baltimore *Sun*, January 4, 1896, p. 6.

24. New York *Clipper*, February 15, 1896, p. 795.

25. Baltimore *Sun*, May 12, 1896, p. 6.

26. Baltimore *Sun*, June 28, 1896, p. 6.

27. In the 1890s, to make up for an earlier missed playing date, teams sometimes played an additional game on top of a regularly scheduled double-header.

28. *Sporting News*, September 26, 1896, p. 6.

29. Baltimore *Sun*, November 19, 1896, p. 6; *Sporting News*, November 21, 1896, p. 3.

30. Baltimore *Sun*, February 4, 1897, p. 2.

31. New York *Clipper*, January 9, 1897, p. 719; January 30, 1897, p. 767.

32. *Sporting News*, July 3, 1897, p. 4.

33. Baltimore *Sun*, July 8, 1897, p. 6; *Sporting News*, August 20, 1898, p. 5.

34. *Sporting News*, February 3, 1899, p. 4.

35. Ibid.

36. *Sporting News*, September 4, 1897, p. 5.

37. Quoted in Fred Lieb, *The Baltimore Orioles* (New York: G. P. Putnam's Sons, 1955), p. 68.

38. *Sporting News*, October 9, 1897, p. 3.

CHAPTER 3: TWO CITIES, TWO LEAGUES, AND THREE JOBS

1. Quoted in Robert Kelly, *The Shaping of the American Past* (2nd ed., Englewood Cliffs, N.J.: Prentice-Hall, Inc., 1978), p. 469.

2. David Quentin Voight, *American Baseball: From Gentleman's Sport to the Commissioner System* (Norman: University of Oklahoma Press, 1966), p. 230.
3. New York *Clipper*, March 5, 1898, p. 9; *Sporting News*, March 12, 1898, p. 2.
4. New York *Clipper*, April 9, 1898, p. 97; April 2, 1898, p. 79.
5. *Sporting News*, July 30, 1898, p. 1; Baltimore *Sun*, July 26, 1898, p. 8.
6. *Sporting News*, July 30, 1898, p. 1.
7. Baltimore *Sun*, September 30, 1898, p. 6; *Sporting News*, August 28, 1898, p. 4.
8. Baltimore *Sun*, October 17, 1898, p. 8; *Sporting News*, October 22, 1898, p. 4.
9. Baltimore *Sun*, October 24, 1898, p. 8.
10. The nickname came from the frequency with which, in past years, Brooklyn pedestrians had been struck by horse-drawn trolleys.
11. Quoted in *Sporting News*, October 29, 1898, p. 5.
12. New York *Clipper*, March 25, 1899, p. 71; Yager quoted in *Sporting News*, May 6, 1899, p. 5.
13. *Sporting News*, October 14, 1899, p. 6; June 2, 1900, pp. 4, 5.
14. *Sporting News*, September 2, 1899, p. 1.
15. Baltimore *Sun*, September 5, 1899, p. 6; *Sporting News*, September 9, 1899, p. 1.
16. *Sporting News*, February 24, 1900, p. 2.
17. *Sporting News*, March 24, 1900, p. 1.
18. *Sporting News*, April 14, 1900, p. 1.
19. St. Louis *Post-Dispatch*, April 13, 1900, p. 7.
20. *Sporting News*, June 2, 1900, p. 3.
21. St. Louis *Post-Dispatch*, August 20, 1900, p. 5.
22. Quoted in Eugene C. Murdock, *Ban Johnson: Czar of Baseball* (Westport: Greenwood Press, 1982), p. 39.
23. Of course, with the competition for playing talent from the new league, nearly all of those who'd played as National Leaguers in 1900 delayed signing contracts for the coming year.
24. Baltimore *Sun*, January 2, 1901, p. 6.
25. Quoted in Fred Lieb, *The Baseball Story* (New York: G. P. Putnam's Sons, 1950), p. 153.
26. Quoted in Lee Allen, *The American League Story* (New York: Hill and Wang, 1962), pp. 21–22.
27. Quoted in Mrs. John J. [Blanche] McGraw, *The Real McGraw*, ed. Arthur Mann (New York: David McKay, 1953), p. 145.
28. McGraw, Comiskey, and Mack did go along with the wider, five-sided home plate adopted in the National League for 1901, as well as the older league's new rule requiring the catcher to play closely behind the bat at all times. The American League added the foul-strike rule in 1903.
29. Seymour hadn't come directly from the National League but by way of the Chicago Americans, to which he'd jumped near the end of the past season. Steve Brodie, who'd played at Chicago in the American League in 1900, signed as a free agent with McGraw.
30. *Sporting Life*, May 18, 1901, p. 7.
31. Baltimore *Sun*, June 4, 1901, p. 6.

32. *Sporting Life,* June 22, 1901, p. 5.
33. *Sporting Life,* June 29, 1901, p. 5; *Sporting News,* June 29, 1901, p. 7.
34. Baltimore *Sun,* July 27, 1901, p. 6; July 31, 1901, p. 6; August 3, 1901, p. 7; August 10, 1901, p. 7.
35. Baltimore *Sun,* August 31, 1901, p. 6; *Sporting Life,* September 14, 1901, p. 7.
36. Baltimore *Sun,* September 30, 1901, p. 6.

CHAPTER 4: THE MAIN CHANCE

1. Mrs. John J. [Blanche] McGraw, *The Real McGraw,* ed. Arthur Mann (New York: David McKay Co., 1953), pp. 1–2.
2. Ibid., p. 11.
3. Ibid., p. 10.
4. *Sporting Life,* January 18, 1902, p. 11; *Sporting News,* November 11, 1962, p. 6.
5. *Sporting News,* December 7, 1901, p. 4; Baltimore *Sun,* March 7, 1902, p. 6.
6. Fraser handled things his own way, simply jumping back to his old club, the Phillies.
7. *Sporting News,* May 24, 1902, p. 7; Pittsburgh *Press,* quoted in *Sporting News,* May 3, 1902, p. 5.
8. McGraw, *Real McGraw,* p. 20.
9. Baltimore *Sun,* June 23, 1902, p. 6.
10. Fred Lieb, *The Baltimore Orioles* (New York: G. P. Putnam's Sons, 1955), p. 114; Bozeman Bulger, "Genius of the Game: III," *Saturday Evening Post,* CCV (July 9, 1932), p. 26.
11. Baltimore *Sun,* July 1, 1902, p. 6; *Sporting Life,* July 5, 1902, p. 5. Johnson lifted Kelley's suspension after four days; he was back in the lineup for a July 4 double-header at Boston.
12. *Sporting Life,* July 12, 1905, p. 4.
13. Baltimore *Sun,* July 8, 1902, p. 6.
14. *Sporting News,* July 12, 1902, p. 1; *Sporting Life,* July 19, 1902, p. 5.
15. *Sporting News,* July 12, 1902, pp. 4, 5; July 19, 1902, p. 1; *Sporting Life,* July 19, 1902, p. 4.
16. *Sporting News,* July 19, 1902, p. 4; Lieb, *Baltimore Orioles,* p. 114; Lieb, *Baseball Story,* p. 158.

CHAPTER 5: THE TOAST OF NEW YORK

1. Mrs. John J. [Blanche] McGraw, *The Real McGraw,* ed. Arthur Mann (New York: David McKay Co., 1953), p. 182.
2. *New York Times,* July 18, 1902, p. 6.
3. Baltimore *Sun,* July 21, 1902, p. 6.
4. Taylor was the second deaf-mute to play in the major leagues. In 1902 William "Dummy" Hoy finished a fifteen-year career as an outfielder in the American Association and the National, Players, and American leagues.
5. *Sporting Life,* October 4, 1902, p. 7.
6. *Sporting News,* October 29, 1904, p. 2.
7. *Sporting News,* April 4, 1903, p. 7.
8. *Sporting Life,* September 27, 1902, p. 5.
9. What's been forgotten is that in McGinnity's two wins over Brooklyn on August 8,

by scores of 6–1 and 4–3, Oscar Jones, Brooklyn's little rookie right-hander, went all the way in the first game and relieved after three innings of the nightcap, for a total of fifteen innings pitched on the same day.

10. *Sporting Life*, October 31, 1903, p. 4.

11. *Sporting Life*, April 16, 1904, p. 2.

12. Donlin came to the Giants in a three-way trade, outfielder Harry McCormick going to Pittsburgh while the Pirates sent outfielder Harry Sebring to Cincinnati.

13. Chicago *News*, August 31, 1908, quoted in G. H. Fleming, *The Unforgettable Season* (New York: Penguin Books, 1982), p. 199.

14. " 'Czar' McGraw," *Literary Digest*, XLVIII (January 20, 1914), pp. 1501–1502.

15. *Sporting News*, October 15, 1904, p. 6.

16. *Sporting Life*, October 1, 1904, p. 6.

17. *Sporting Life*, October 15, 1904, p. 6.

18. John J. McGraw, *My Thirty Years in Baseball* (New York: Boni and Liveright, 1923), p. 157; *Sporting Life*, November 5, 1904, p. 4; November 26, 1904, p. 4.

19. *Sporting Life*, December 24, 1904, p. 5.

20. Bozeman Bulger, "Genius of the Game: III," *Saturday Evening Post*, CCIV (July 9, 1932), p. 60.

21. McGraw, *My Thirty Years in Baseball*, p. 159.

22. *Sporting News*, April 29, 1905, p. 1.

23. William J. Klem and William J. Slocum, "Umpire Bill Klem's Own Story," *Collier's*, CXXVII (April 7, 1951), p. 50.

24. *Sporting News*, May 6, 1905, p. 1.

25. *Sporting Life*, June 3, 1905, p. 1.

26. Fred Lieb, *The Baseball Story* (New York: G.P. Putnam's Sons, 1950), p. 171.

27. Lieb, *The Baseball Story*, p. 172; *Sporting Life*, June 10, 1905, p. 1; Harold Seymour, *Baseball: The Golden Age* (New York: Oxford University Press, 1971), p. 26.

28. "Table of Baseball Cases: John J. McGraw and National Exhibition Co. v. Harry H. Pulliam, individually and as president of the National League, and Umpires Henry O'Day, Robert Emslie, George Bausewine, William Klem, James Johnstone, Superior Court, Boston, Mass.," typescript in John J. McGraw Collection, National Baseball Library, Cooperstown, N.Y.

29. *New York Times*, September 23, 1905, p. 6.

30. *Sporting Life*, November 11, 1905, p. 4.

CHAPTER 6: REBUILDING AND BARELY MISSING

1. *Sporting Life*, January 13, 1906, p. 3.

2. *Sporting Life*, May 19, 1906, p. 3; *Sporting News*, February 14, 1918, p. 4.

3. *New York Times*, August 8, 1906, p. 4; August 9, 1906, p. 4; August 22, 1906, p. 8.

4. *Sporting Life*, August 18, 1906, p. 4; August 25, 1906, pp. 1, 8.

5. *Sporting News*, October 24, 1906, p. 4.

6. *Sporting News*, December 8, 1906, p. 3.

7. *Sporting Life*, June 8, 1907, p. 1.

8. Mrs. John J. [Blanche] McGraw, *The Real McGraw*, ed. Arthur Mann (New York:

David McKay Co., 1953), p. 18; Lieb, in *Sporting News,* November 17, 1962, p. 6.
9. *Sporting News,* March 8, 1934, p. 2.
10. Branch Rickey, *The American Diamond: A Documentary of the Game of Baseball* (New York: Simon and Schuster, 1965), p. 25.
11. *Sporting News,* January 2, 1908, p. 2; G. H. Fleming, *The Unforgettable Season* (New York: Penguin Books, 1982), p. 20.
12. Fleming, *The Unforgettable Season,* p. 19.
13. *Sporting Life,* May 9, 1908, p. 6; Fleming, *The Unforgettable Season,* p. 37.
14. After hitting only .240 that year, McGann was released by Boston. Two years later, at the age of thirty-eight, he took his own life in his native Louisville.
15. *Sporting News,* October 3, 1908, p. 3.
16. William J. Klem and William J. Slocum, "Umpire Bill Klem's Own Story," *Collier's,* CXXVII (April 14, 1951), p. 51.
17. *New York Times,* September 30, 1908, p. 8.
18. *New York Times,* October 4, 1924, p. 8.
19. Fleming, *The Unforgettable Season,* p. 297.
20. Christy Mathewson, *Pitching in a Pinch* (reprint ed., New York: Stein and Day, 1977), p. 195.
21. John Carmichael, ed., *My Greatest Day in Baseball* (New York: A. S. Barnes, 1946), p. 175.
22. Lee Allen, *The National League Story* (New York: Hill and Wang, 1961), p. 119; Klem and Slocum, "Umpire Bill Klem's Own Story," *Collier's,* CXXVII (April 7, 1951), p. 30.
23. Carmichael, ed., *My Greatest Day in Baseball,* p. 176; *New York Times,* October 9, 1908, p. 1.
24. Mathewson, *Pitching in a Pinch,* pp. 185–86.
25. Carmichael, ed., *My Greatest Day in Baseball,* p. 178; New York *American,* October 9, 1908, in Fleming, *The Unforgettable Season,* p. 315.
26. Fleming, *The Unforgettable Season,* p. 319.
27. *Sporting Life,* October 21, 1908, p. 8; Mathewson, *Pitching in a Pinch,* p. 205.
28. *Sporting News,* April 22, 1909, p. 1.
29. *Sporting Life,* May 13, 1909, p. 1.

CHAPTER 7: THE LITTLE NAPOLEON
1. *Sporting Life,* June 12, 1909, p. 9.
2. " 'Czar' McGraw," *Literary Digest,* XLVIII (June 20, 1914), p. 1502.
3. Lawrence Ritter, *The Glory of Their Times* (rev. ed., New York: William Morrow and Co., 1984), p. 94.
4. Until 1912 National League statistics didn't include earned-run averages.
5. *Sporting Life,* July 3, 1909, p. 3; John Lardner, "That Was Baseball: The Crime of Shufflin' Phil Douglas," *The New Yorker,* XXXII (May 12, 1956), p. 141.
6. *Sporting Life,* July 3, 1909, p. 3.
7. J. J. McGraw to Otis Crandall, August 23, 1909, copy in John J. McGraw Collection, National Baseball Library, Cooperstown, N.Y.
8. *Sporting News,* November 15, 1909, p. 4.
9. *Sporting News,* February 24, 1910, p. 4.

10. James Hopper, "Training with the Giants," *Everybody's*, XX (June 1909), p. 741.
11. "Big Leaguers in Training," *Literary Digest*, XLIV (March 30, 1912), p. 657.
12. *Sporting News*, April 7, 1910, p. 1.
13. *Sporting News*, February 2, 1911, p. 4.
14. Ritter, *The Glory of Their Times*, pp. 15, 91, 131, 174.
15. Ibid., p. 91.
16. *New York Times*, April 4, 1911, p. 8.
17. *Sporting Life*, August 5, 1911, p. 6.
18. *Sporting Life*, September 2, 1911, p. 15.
19. *Sporting Life*, September 30, 1911, p. 6.
20. *Sporting News*, September 21, 1911, p. 1.
21. Mrs. John J. [Blanche] McGraw, *The Real McGraw*, ed. Arthur Mann (New York: David McKay, 1953), p. 235.
22. Fred Lieb, *The Story of the World Series* (New York: G.P. Putnam's Sons, 1965), p. 79.
23. *Sporting Life*, October 28, 1911, p. 2.
24. Quoted in Christy Mathewson, *Pitching in a Pinch* (reprint ed., New York: Stein and Day, 1977), p. 115.
25. *Sporting News*, November 30, 1911, p. 5.
26. John B. Holway, "Cuba's Black Diamond," *Baseball Research Journal* (1981), p. 144; *Sporting Life*, December 16, 1911, p. 6; *Sporting News*, January 25, 1912, p. 4.
27. McGraw, *The Real McGraw*, p. 247.
28. *Sporting Life*, July 27, 1912, p. 3.
29. *New York Times*, August 13, 1912, p. 10; September 29, 1912, p. 1; Harold Seymour, *Baseball: The Golden Age* (New York: Oxford University Press, 1971), p. 31.
30. C. H. Claudy, "Managers and Their Work," *St. Nicholas*, XL (July 1913), p. 803.
31. Fred Lieb, *The Baseball Story* (New York: G.P. Putnam's Sons, 1950), p. 193.
32. *Sporting Life*, December 7, 1912, p. 8.
33. *Sporting Life*, November 2, 1912, p. 4.
34. Bozeman Bulger, "Genius of the Game: III," *Saturday Evening Post*, CCIV (July 9, 1932), p. 62; *Sporting Life*, December 21, 1912, p. 14.
35. *Sporting News*, July 3, 1913, p. 4.
36. William J. Klem and William J. Slocum, "Umpire Bill Klem's Own Story," *Collier's*, CXXVII (April 14, 1951), p. 51.
37. "Baseball's Generals," *Literary Digest*, XLIV (March 2, 1912), p. 446; Claudy, "Managers and Their Work," p. 802.

CHAPTER 8: AROUND THE WORLD, INTO THE CELLAR, BACK ON TOP

1. Mrs. John J. [Blanche] McGraw, *The Real McGraw*, ed. Arthur Mann (New York: David McKay Co., 1953), p. 250.
2. *Sporting Life*, January 31, 1914, p. 12.
3. Strang's true name was Samuel Strang Nicklin. Because his father (co-owner of the Nashville Southern League club, strangely enough) sternly disapproved of his becoming a baseball player, he played under the name Sammy Strang.

4. *Sporting Life,* February 28, 1914, p. 6.

5. *New York Times,* August 29, 1914, p. 7. McGraw's reference was to Kaiser Wilhelm II of Germany, who found himself facing French and British forces to the west, Russian to the east.

6. *Sporting News,* November 26, 1914, p. 1.

7. *Sporting Life,* June 5, 1915, p. 4.

8. *Sporting Life,* October 25, 1913, p. 6.

9. *Sporting Life,* June 19, 1915, p. 4.

10. *Sporting News,* June 17, 1915, p. 4; *Sporting Life,* August 14, 1915, p. 2.

11. Lawrence Ritter, *The Glory of Their Times* (rev. ed., New York: William Morrow and Co., 1984), p. 16.

12. *New York Times,* September 10, 1915, p. 12.

13. *Sporting Life,* March 25, 1916, p. 13.

14. Christy Mathewson, "Why We Lost Three World's Championships," *Everybody's,* XXXI (October 1914), p. 544.

15. Ritter, *The Glory of Their Times,* p. 224.

16. *Sporting News,* September 7, 1916, p. 5.

17. *New York Times,* August 31, 1916, p. 12.

18. Dorgan quoted in Frank Graham, "The New York Giants," in Ed Fitzgerald, ed., *The Book of Major League Baseball Clubs: The National League* (New York: A.S. Barnes, 1952), p. 229; McGraw in *Sporting News,* October 5, 1916, p. 4.

19. *Sporting News,* October 5, 1916, p. 4.

20. *Sporting Life,* October 28, 1916, p. 8; *Sporting News,* October 5, 1916, p. 4.

21. *New York Times,* October 5, 1916, p. 12; Harold Seymour, *Baseball: The Golden Age* (New York: Oxford University Press, 1971), p. 287; *Sporting Life,* November 4, 1916, p. 7; *Sporting News,* October 5, 1916, p. 1.

22. *Sporting News,* October 5, 1916, p. 4.

23. Brennan had jumped from the National League to the Federal League in 1914. In 1916 he'd caught on in the American Association, and within a few years he would be back in the National League.

24. Charles C. Alexander, *Ty Cobb* (New York: Oxford University Press, 1984), p. 132.

25. Quoted in "McGraw Collects," *Literary Digest,* LIV (May 5, 1917), p. 1358.

26. John Durant, *The Story of Baseball* (New York: Hastings House, 1947), p. 142.

27. Cincinnati *Enquirer,* June 9, 1917, p. 6; *New York Times,* June 9, 1917, p. 12; *Sporting News,* June 14, 1917, p. 2.

28. *New York Times,* July 21, 1917, p. 12; *Sporting News,* July 12, 1917, p. 1; July 19, 1917, p. 1.

29. Cincinnati *Enquirer,* June 20, 1917, p. 6; *New York Times,* June 20, 1917, p. 12.

30. Frank Graham, *The New York Giants* (New York: G.P. Putnam's Sons, 1952), p. 102.

CHAPTER 9: WAR, SCANDAL, AND CHARLES STONEHAM

1. *New York Times,* March 18, 1918, p. 10.

2. *Sporting News,* June 13, 1918, p. 1.

3. The federal Mann Act, passed by Congress in 1910, forbade the transportation of persons across state lines for immoral purposes.

4. Lee Allen, *The Cincinnati Reds* (New York: G. P. Putnam's Sons, 1948), p. 127.
5. *Sporting News*, August 22, 1918, p. 2.
6. *Sporting News*, September 26, 1918, p. 1.
7. *Sporting Life*, October 24, 1914, p. 18; Mrs. John J. [Blanche] McGraw, *The Real McGraw*, ed. Arthur Mann (New York: David McKay Company, 1953), pp. 251–52.
8. *Sporting News*, February 13, 1919, p. 5; *New York Times*, February 6, 1919, p. 12.
9. Robert Creamer, *Babe: The Legend Comes to Life* (New York: Simon and Schuster, Inc., 1974), p. 190.
10. *Sporting News*, June 12, 1919, p. 1.
11. *Sporting News*, July 17, 1919, p. 1.
12. Cincinnati *Enquirer*, August 4, 1919, p. 11.
13. *New York Times*, September 24, 1920, p. 2.
14. *Sporting News*, November 11, 1920, p. 1.
15. *Sporting News*, November 4, 1920, p. 8; November 11, 1920, p. 1.
16. *Sporting News*, March 11, 1920, p. 1.
17. *Sporting News*, April 1, 1920, p. 3.
18. *New York Times*, August 17, 1920, p. 6. The William Boyd involved in the Lambs' Club fracas shouldn't be confused with the Hollywood film actor William "Bill" Boyd. William Boyd the Broadway figure died in 1936; "Bill" Boyd enjoyed a long and lucrative movie career first as a romantic lead, then as the star of numerous "Hopalong Cassidy" Westerns.
19. *New York Times*, August 12, 1920, p. 10.
20. *New York Times*, August 9, 1920, p. 1.
21. *New York Times*, August 17, 1920, pp. 1, 6.
22. *New York Times*, September 25, 1920, p. 1; September 26, 1920, p. 15.
23. *New York Times*, October 30, 1920, p. 6.
24. *Sporting News*, April 1, 1920, p. 1.
25. Chick Gandil and Fred McMullen were no longer in Organized Baseball in 1920.

CHAPTER 10: A TROUBLED DYNASTY
1. Quoted in Fred Lieb, *The Baseball Story* (New York: G. P. Putnam's Sons, 1950), p. 229; J. G. Taylor Spink, *Judge Landis and 25 Years of Baseball* (New York: Thomas Y. Crowell Co., 1947), p. 91.
2. John B. Sheridan, who'd covered baseball for forty years and wrote a regular column for the *Sporting News* in the 1920s (until his death in 1926), was one of the few contemporary observers who called attention to the significance of changes in bat configuration.
3. "Baseball Has Changed Some in Thirty Years, Says John McGraw," *Literary Digest*, LXI (May 10, 1919), p. 96; John McGraw, *My Thirty Years in Baseball* (New York: Boni and Liveright, 1923), pp. 207, 210.
4. McGraw, *My Thirty Years in Baseball*, p. 175; *Sporting News*, March 31, 1921, p. 2.
5. Frank Frisch tape-recorded interviews with J. Roy Stockton, Reel 1A, National Baseball Library, Cooperstown, N.Y.
6. *New York Times*, March 19, 1921, p. 12.

7. Quoted in Robert Creamer, *Stengel: His Life and Times* (New York: Simon and Schuster, 1984), p. 143.

8. Quoted in Spink, *Judge Landis and 25 Years of Baseball*, p. 93.

9. *New York Times*, October 7, 1921, p. 12.

10. *Sporting News*, October 20, 1921, p. 6.

11. *New York Times*, January 21, 1922, p. 12; March 2, 1922, p. 18; March 24, 1922, p. 10; *Sporting News*, March 9, 1922, p. 1.

12. *New York Times*, June 30, 1922, p. 12.

13. In 1922 the Cardinals had finally abandoned their little wooden ballpark on Natural Bridge Road and become the tenants of the Browns in Sportsman's Park.

14. Quoted in Tom Clark, *One Last Round for the Shuffler* (New York: Truck Press, 1979), p. 84.

15. *New York Times*, August 17, 1922, pp. 1, 10; John Lardner, "That Was Baseball: The Crime of Shufflin' Phil Douglas," *The New Yorker*, XXXII (June 12, 1956), pp. 136, 150.

16. *Sporting News*, August 24, 1922, p. 3.

17. *Sporting News*, October 12, 1922, p. 5; Cy Kritzer typescript, John J. McGraw Collection, St. Bonaventure University, St. Bonaventure, N.Y.; McGraw, *My Thirty Years in Baseball*, p. 4.

18. "When 'Babe' Ruth Was Beaten by John J. McGraw," *Literary Digest*, LXXV (December 2, 1922), p. 61; *New York Times*, October 9, 1922, p. 12.

19. Frank Graham, *McGraw of the Giants* (New York: G.P. Putnam's Sons, 1944), p. 162; *New York Times*, March 23, 1923, p. 22.

20. *Sporting News*, May 31, 1923, p. 1.

21. *Sporting News*, June 21, 1923, p. 8.

22. That bad feeling went back to 1921, when Gehrig, having just graduated from high school in New York City and received a football scholarship from Columbia University, signed a contract with the Giants and was assigned to Hartford under the name "Henry Lewis," in a futile effort to conceal his professionalism from collegiate authorities. Gehrig left Hartford after only twelve games. He lost his scholarship benefits for 1921–22; then, with scholarship restored, starred at Columbia in football and baseball the next year. Signed by the Yankees in the spring of 1923, Gehrig again went to Hartford, then came up to the Yankees near the end of the season. Gehrig would always believe that in refusing to approve his eligibility for the 1923 World Series, McGraw was spiting him for leaving Hartford two years earlier.

23. *New York Times*, October 14, 1923, sec. I, pt. 2, p. 2.

24. *Sporting News*, October 25, 1923, p. 1.

25. *New York Times*, November 11, 1923, sec. I, pt. 2, p. 1.

26. *New York Times*, November 26, 1923, p. 21.

27. *Sporting News*, November 22, 1923, p. 1. The NEC's annual corporate meeting had to take place in New Jersey because it was chartered in that state, not New York.

28. *New York Times*, March 4, 1924, p. 14.

29. For this information, I am indebted to Jesse H. DeLee, M.D., of San Antonio, who has thoroughly investigated Youngs's medical history.

30. Of course, Brooklyn lost that day at Ebbets Field to the Braves to give the pennant to the Giants. The Giants' last scheduled game of the year, on Monday, September

29, was rained out, so that only two games in the Phillies series actually took place.

31. *Sporting News*, October 9, 1924, p. 2; *New York Times*, October 2, 1924, p. 8.

32. *Sporting News*, October 9, 1924, p. 2.

33. *New York Times*, October 2, 1924, p. 8.

34. Ibid.; *Sporting News*, October 9, 1924, p. 2.

35. *Sporting News*, October 9, 1924, p. 2.

36. *New York Times*, October 7, 1924, p. 13.

37. *New York Times*, October 8, 1924, p. 1.

38. "Washington's Big Day in Baseball," *Literary Digest*, LXXXIII (October 25, 1924), p. 58.

39. Kritzer typescript.

CHAPTER 11: SEASONS OF FRUSTRATION

1. *New York Times*, October 10, 1924, p. 8.

2. *Sporting News*, October 9, 1924, p. 4.

3. *New York Times*, October 22, 1924, p. 24; Gene Fowler, *The Great Mouthpiece* (New York: Blue Ribbon Books, 1931), p. 127; *Sporting News*, October 30, 1924, p. 1.

4. *Sporting News*, October 30, 1924, p. 6.

5. *New York Times*, February 5, 1925, p. 16.

6. Washington *Post*, October 9, 1924, p. 8.

7. C.C.A. interview with Travis Jackson, Waldo, Arkansas, December 3, 1985.

8. The closest student of the O'Connell-Dolan affair has concluded that gamblers had nothing to do with it. Rather, it was "an ill-considered, near spur-of-the-moment player-instigated bribe scheme." Frisch, Youngs, and Kelly were "supporting players," while "it is not improbable that McGraw was behind the 1924 incident." Lowell Blaisdell, "Mystery and Tragedy: The O'Connell-Dolan Scandal," *Baseball Research Journal* (1982), pp. 44–48.

9. *Sporting News*, October 3, 1924, p. 5.

10. Mrs. John J. [Blanche] McGraw, *The Real McGraw*, ed. Arthur Mann (New York: David McKay Company), p. 293.

11. John J. Loftus to Rev. Thomas Plassmann, January 19, 1944, McGraw-Jennings misc. items, John J. McGraw Collection, St. Bonaventure University, St. Bonaventure, N.Y.

12. *New York Times*, November 30, 1924, sec. X, p. 1; December 3, 1924, p. 17.

13. *Sporting News*, July 9, 1925, p. 1.

14. *Sporting News*, November 26, 1925, p. 1.

15. *New York Times*, January 9, 1926, p. 20.

16. See *Sporting News*, January 21, 1926, p. 6.

17. *New York Times*, March 9, 1926, p. 19; March 14, 1926, sec. X, p. 1.

18. Sent down after appearing in nine games with no record for the Giants in 1926, Thomas made it back to the majors in 1931. Pitching in three seasons for three different teams, he showed a 9–20 record.

19. J. J. McGraw to Charles Stoneham, March 11, 1926, John McGraw Collection, National Baseball Library, Cooperstown, N.Y.

20. Quoted in *Sporting News*, July 29, 1926, p. 3; Cullen Cain, "The Manager,"

Saturday Evening Post, CXCVIII (June 19, 1926), pp. 177–78; *New York Times,* July 22, 1926, p. 18.

21. *New York Times,* August 22, 1926, sec. IX, p. 1.
22. Frank Frisch tape-recorded interviews with J. Roy Stockton, Reel 1A, National Baseball Library.
23. *New York Times,* August 22, 1926, sec. X, p. 1.
24. *New York Times,* January 8, 1927, p. 18; March 7, 1927, p. 24.
25. Quoted in Lee Allen, *The Hot Stove League* (New York: A. S. Barnes Co., 1955), p. 135.
26. McGraw, *The Real McGraw,* p. 298.
27. *Sporting News,* December 16, 1926, p. 4; *New York Times,* December 2, 1926, sec. X, p. 1.
28. Jackson interview; *Sporting News,* April 11, 1929, p. 4.
29. Made up of $86,000 from Breadon, $2,000 from each of the other seven National League clubs, and an extra $12,000 contributed by the Giants. But Hornsby had to use most of his profit paying off the $50,000 he'd borrowed to buy the stock a couple of years earlier.
30. *Sporting News,* June 23, 1927, p. 1; *New York Times,* July 3, 1927, sec. IX, p. 3.
31. *New York Times,* January 11, 1928, p. 1; January 13, 1928, p. 31; *Sporting News,* January 21, 1928, p. 1.
32. *New York Times,* February 15, 1928, p. 17.
33. Quoted in "The Great Hornsby Mystery," *Literary Digest,* XCVI (February 25, 1928), p. 58.
34. Russell P. Reeder, Jr., "The McGraw I Knew," *NRTA Journal* (July–August 1974), p. 65, in McGraw Collection, NBL.
35. Later that spring the Giants would lose the chance to acquire the greatest Jewish ballplayer who'd ever come along, when Henry "Hank" Greenberg, fresh from James Monroe High School in Manhattan, couldn't secure a tryout at the Polo Grounds, supposedly because he couldn't get past club secretary Tierney. Whether or not McGraw knew anything about Greenberg is uncertain. Greenberg would go on to achieve stardom with the Detroit Tigers in the American League and membership in baseball's Hall of Fame.
36. Quoted in Daniel Okrent and Harris Lewine, ed., *The Ultimate Baseball Book* (Boston: Houghton Mifflin Company, 1984), p. 151.
37. *Sporting News,* May 10, 1928, p. 1; *New York Times,* May 4, 1928, p. 19.
38. Roscoe McGowen, "Here's the McGraw That I Knew," *Sporting News,* July 12, 1961, clipping in McGraw Collection, NBL.
39. William J. Klem and William J. Slocum, "Umpire Bill Klem's Own Story," *Collier's,* CXXXII (April 14, 1951), p. 69.

CHAPTER 12: GIVING IT UP

1. *Sporting News,* November 29, 1928, p. 2; January 10, 1929, p. 1; *New York Times,* December 30, 1928, p. 5.
2. *New York Times,* February 17, 1929, p. 18.

3. Quoted in Mrs. John J. [Blanche] McGraw, *The Real McGraw*, ed. Arthur Mann (New York: David McKay Company, 1953), p. 320.

4. Grantland Rice, "The Firebrand," *Collier's*, LXXXV (April 5, 1930), p. 13; *Sporting News*, November 20, 1930, p. 2.

5. *Sporting News*, May 22, 1930, p. 3; July 17, 1930, p. 2.

6. *Sporting News*, May 22, 1930, p. 3.

7. *New York Times*, September 4, 1930, p. 19.

8. *Sporting News*, September 27, 1930, p. 1.

9. *New York Times*, September 6, 1930, p. 20.

10. McGraw, *The Real McGraw*, p. 325.

11. *New York Times*, December 25, 1929, p. 1.

12. *Sporting News*, February 20, 1931, p. 2; March 5, 1931, p. 2.

13. *New York Times*, February 28, 1931, p. 25.

14. *Sporting News*, April 2, 1931, p. 4.

15. *Sporting News*, December 17, 1931, p. 4; February 2, 1933, p. 2.

16. *Sporting News*, October 8, 1931, p. 1. Mooney's record in four major league seasons, two each with the Giants and Cardinals, would be 17–20.

17. *New York Times*, December 15, 1931, p. 21.

18. *New York Times*, December 19, 1931, p. 17; *Sporting News*, December 24, 1931, p. 2.

19. *New York Times*, December 8, 1931, p. 2.

20. *New York Times*, December 23, 1931, p. 18.

21. *Sporting News*, November 12, 1931, p. 1; December 17, 1931, p. 2; *New York Times*, January 1, 1932, p. 57.

22. *New York Times*, January 12, 1932, p. 29; February 20, 1932, p. 20.

23. *New York Times*, February 24, 1932, p. 21.

24. Bozeman Bulger, "Genius of the Game," *Saturday Evening Post*, CCIV (May 28, 1932), p. 11; Hugh Bradley, "McGraw," *American Mercury*, XXVI (August 1932), pp. 464–65.

25. Bradley, "McGraw," p. 467; C.C.A. interview with Travis Jackson, Waldo, Ark., December 5, 1985; Lawrence Ritter, *The Glory of Their Times* (rev. ed., New York: William Morrow and Co., 1984), pp. 255–57.

26. *New York Times*, June 4, 1932, p. 10; *Sporting News*, June 9, 1932, p. 1.

27. *New York Times*, June 4, 1932, p. 10.

28. *New York Times*, July 7, 1933, p. 12; *Sporting News*, July 13, 1933, p. 3.

29. *New York Times*, January 19, 1934, p. 6.

30. *New York Times*, February 26, 1934, p. 23; March 1, 1934, p. 27; *Sporting News*, March 1, 1934, p. 7.

31. *New York Times*, March 1, 1934, p. 19; *Sporting News*, March 8, 1934, p. 2.

POSTLUDE: NAMES WITH NO NUMBERS IN A FARAWAY PLACE

1. Joseph H. Adams, "John McGraw Goes Home," in *Memorial Baseball Game: New York Giants vs. Truxton Giants* . . . (n.d.), in possession of C.C.A.

2. The other original BBWAA choices were Ty Cobb, Babe Ruth, Walter Johnson, Honus Wagner, Tris Speaker, Grover Cleveland Alexander, Cy Young, George Sisler,

Napoleon Lajoie, Eddie Collins, and Connie Mack. Several other figures from baseball's early history were named by a Special or "Veterans' " Committee.

3. The script was prepared for Du Pont by the advertising firm of Batten, Barton, Durstine, and Osborn, Inc., and produced on April 15, 1946. Mimeographed copies are in the McGraw collections at the National Baseball Library, Cooperstown, N.Y., and St. Bonaventure Library, St. Bonaventure, N.Y.

4. Mrs. John J. [Blanche] McGraw, *The Real McGraw*, ed. Arthur Mann (New York: David McKay Co., 1953).

5. C.C.A. interview with Mary [Mrs. Travis] Jackson, Waldo, Ark., December 5, 1985.

6. Quoted in Joseph Durso, *The Times of Mr. McGraw* (Englewood Cliffs, N.J.: Prentice-Hall, Inc., 1969), p. 218.

BIBLIOGRAPHY

Archival Resources:
Frank Frisch tape-recorded interviews with J. Roy Stockton, National Baseball Library, Cooperstown, New York.
Garry Herrmann Papers, National Baseball Library, Cooperstown, New York.
Hugh Jennings Collection, National Baseball Library, Cooperstown, New York.
Willie Keeler Collection, National Baseball Library, Cooperstown, New York.
John McGraw Collection, National Baseball Library, Cooperstown, New York.
John J. McGraw Collection, St. Bonaventure University Archives, St. Bonaventure, New York.
McGraw-Jennings Collection, St. Bonaventure University Archives, St. Bonaventure, New York.
Christy Mathewson Collection, National Baseball Library, Cooperstown, New York.

Government Documents:
U.S. Congress, House of Representatives, *Organized Baseball: Report of the Subcommittee on the Study of Monopoly Power of the Committee of the Judiciary Pursuant to H. Res. 95*. 82nd Cong., 2nd sess. (1952).

Newspapers:
Baltimore *Sun*, 1891–1902.
Cincinnati *Enquirer*, 1917–19.
Cleveland *Plain Dealer*, 1895–1900.
Independent Villager (Marathon, New York), 1986.
New York *Clipper*, 1890–1900.
New York Times, 1894–1962.
St. Louis *Post-Dispatch*, 1899–1900.
San Francisco *Chronicle*, 1986.
Sporting Life, 1901–17.
Sporting News, 1890–1962.
Washington *Post*, 1924.

Personal Communications:

Interview, Jesse C. DeLee, M.D., San Antonio, Texas, March 25, 1987.

Interview, Mary Jackson, Waldo, Arkansas, December 5, 1985.

Interview, Travis Jackson, Waldo, Arkansas, December 5, 1985.

Interview, James W. Sindall, Severna Park, Maryland, August 5, 1985.

Interview, Frank Steele, Fort Washington, Pennsylvania, September 22, 1985.

Interview, Andrew H. Tei, Truxton, New York, March 27, 1986.

Interview, Stephen J. Van Lill III, M.D., Severna Park, Maryland, August 5, 1985, and telephone conversations, August 12, 1985, and July 8, 1987.

Interview, Ross Youngs II, Canyon Lake, Texas, December 4, 1984.

Books:

Allen, Lee. *The American League Story* (New York: Hill and Wang, Inc., 1962).

———. *The Cincinnati Reds* (New York: G. P. Putnam's Sons, 1948).

———. *The Hot Stove League* (New York: A. S. Barnes Company, 1955).

———. *The National League Story* (New York: Hill and Wang, Inc., 1961).

Asinof, Elliott. *Eight Men Out: The Black Sox and the 1919 World Series* (New York: Holt, Rinehart, and Winston, 1963).

Axelson, Gustav. *"COMMY": The Life Story of Charles A. Comiskey* (Chicago: Reilly and Lee, 1919).

Beirne, Francis E. *The Amiable Baltimoreans* (New York: E. P. Dutton and Company, 1951).

Brown, Warren. *The Chicago Cubs* (New York: G. P. Putnam's Sons, 1946).

———. *The Chicago White Sox* (New York: G. P. Putnam's Sons, 1952).

Carmichael, John P., ed. *My Greatest Day in Baseball* (New York: A. S. Barnes Company, 1946).

Clark, Tom. *One Last Round for the Shuffler* (New York: Truck Books, 1979).

Corn, Joseph J. *The Winged Gospel: America's Romance with Aviation, 1900–1950* (New York: Oxford University Press, 1983).

Creamer, Robert. *Babe: The Legend Comes to Life* (New York: Simon and Schuster, Inc., 1974).

———. *Stengel: His Life and Times* (New York: Simon and Schuster, Inc., 1984).

Dickey, Glenn. *The History of American League Baseball Since 1901* (New York: Stein and Day, 1980).

———. *The History of National League Baseball since 1876* (New York: Stein and Day, 1982).

Durant, John. *The Story of Baseball* (New York: Hastings House, 1947).

Durso, Joseph. *The Times of Mr. McGraw* (Englewood Cliffs, N.J.: Prentice-Hall, Inc., 1969).

Ehrenberg, Lewis. *Steppin' Out: New York Nightlife and the Transformation of American Culture, 1890–1930* (Chicago: University of Chicago Press, 1981).

Ellis, John Tracey. *Francis Cardinal Gibbons: Archbishop of Baltimore* (2 vols., Milwaukee: Bruce Publishing Company, 1952).

Evers, John J., and Hugh S. Fullerton. *Touching Second: The Science of Baseball* (Chicago: Reilly and Britton, 1910).

Farrell, James T. *My Baseball Diary* (New York: Vanguard Press, 1959).

Fitzgerald, Ed., ed. *The Book of Major League Baseball Clubs: The National League* (New York: A. S. Barnes Company, 1952).

Fleming, G. H., ed. *The Unforgettable Season* (New York: Penguin Books, 1982).

Foster, John B. *Spalding's Official Base Ball Record [Guide]* (New York: American Sports Publishing Company, 1907–32).

Fowler, Gene. *Beau James: The Life and Times of Jimmy Walker* (New York: Viking Press, 1949).

————. *The Great Mouthpiece: A Life Story of William J. Fallon* (New York: Blue Ribbon Books, 1931).

Graham, Frank. *The Brooklyn Dodgers* (New York: G. P. Putnam's Sons, 1945).

————. *McGraw of the Giants* (New York: G. P. Putnam's Sons, 1944).

————. *The New York Giants* (New York: G. P. Putnam's Sons, 1952).

————. *The New York Yankees* (New York: G. P. Putnam's Sons, 1943).

Hirschfeld, Charles. "Baltimore, 1870–1900: Studies in Social History," *Johns Hopkins University Studies in Historical and Political Science,* LIX, series 59 (Baltimore: Johns Hopkins University Press, 1941), pp. 9–176.

Honig, Donald. *Baseball's Ten Greatest Teams* (New York: Macmillan Company, 1982).

————, and Lawrence Ritter. *Baseball: When the Grass Was Real* (New York: Coward, McCann, and Geoghegan, Inc., 1975).

Kahn, James M. *The Umpire Story* (New York: G. P. Putnam's Sons, 1953).

Katcher, Leo. *The Big Bankroll: The Life and Times of Arnold Rothstein* (New York: Harper and Row, 1959).

Leitner, Irving. *Baseball: Diamond in the Rough* (New York: Abelard-Schuman, 1972).

Lieb, Fred. *The Baltimore Orioles* (New York: G. P. Putnam's Sons, 1955).

————. *Baseball as I Have Known It* (New York: Tempo/Grosset and Dunlap, 1977).

————. *The Baseball Story* (New York: G. P. Putnam's Sons, 1950).

————. *The Boston Red Sox* (New York: G. P. Putnam's Sons, 1947).

————. *The Story of the World Series* (New York: G. P. Putnam's Sons, 1965).

Lowry, Philip J. *Green Cathedrals* (Cooperstown: Society for American Baseball Research, 1986).

McFarlane, Paul, ed. *Daguerreotypes of Great Baseball Stars* (St. Louis: Sporting News Publishing Company, 1981).

McGraw, John J. *How to Play Baseball* (New York: Harper and Brothers, 1914).

————. *My Thirty Years in Baseball* (New York: Boni and Liveright, 1923).

McGraw, Mrs. John J. *The Real McGraw,* edited by Arthur Mann (New York: David McKay Company, 1953).

Mack, Connie. *My 66 Years in the Big Leagues* (New York: John C. Winston Company, 1950).

Mann, Arthur. *Branch Rickey: American in Action* (Boston: Houghton Mifflin Company, 1957).

Mathewson, Christy. *Pitching in a Pinch* (reprint ed., New York: Stein and Day, 1977).

Mead, William B., and Harold Rosenthal. *The 10 Worst Years of Baseball* (New York: Van Nostrand Reinhold, 1982).

Meany, Tom. *Baseball's Greatest Pitchers* (New York: A. S. Barnes Company, 1952).

————. *Baseball's Greatest Teams* (New York: A. S. Barnes Company, 1949).

Memorial Baseball Game: New York Giants vs. Truxton Giants . . . (n.d.).

Moreland, George C. *Balldom: "The Britannica of Baseball"* (New York: Balldom Publishing Company, 1914).

Morris, Lloyd. *Incredible New York* (New York: Random House, Inc., 1951).

Murdock, Eugene C. *Ban Johnson: Czar of Baseball* (Westport, Conn.: Greenwood Press, 1982).

Obojski, Robert. *Bush League: A History of Minor League Baseball* (New York: Macmillan Company, 1975).

Okrent, Daniel, and Harris Lewine, eds. *The Ultimate Baseball Book* (Boston: Houghton Mifflin Company, 1984).

Olson, Sherry H. *Baltimore: The Building of an American City* (Baltimore: Johns Hopkins University Press, 1980).

Osofsky, Gilbert. *Harlem—The Making of a Ghetto: Negro New York, 1890–1930* (New York: Harper and Row, 1966).

Peterson, Robert. *Only the Ball Was White: A History of Legendary Black Players and All-Black Professional Teams* (rev. ed., New York: McGraw-Hill Book Company, 1984).

Polner, Murray. *Branch Rickey* (New York: Atheneum Publishers, 1982).

Povich, Shirley. *The Washington Senators* (New York: G. P. Putnam's Sons, 1954).

Reichler, Joseph L., ed. *The Baseball Encyclopedia* (5th ed., New York: Macmillan Company, 1982).

Reichler, Joseph, and Ben Olan. *Baseball's Unforgettable Games* (New York: Ronald Press, 1961).

Rice, Grantland. *The Tumult and the Shouting: My Life in Sport* (New York: Dell Publishing Company, 1954).

Rickey, Branch. *The American Diamond: A Documentary of the Game of Baseball* (New York: Simon and Schuster, 1965).

Riess, Steven. *Touching Base: Professional Baseball and American Culture in the Progressive Era* (Westport: Greenwood Press, 1980).

Ritter, Lawrence. *The Glory of Their Times* (rev. ed., New York: William Morrow and Company, 1984).

———, and Donald Honig. *The Image of Their Greatness* (New York: Crown Publishers, 1979).

Rogosin, Donn. *Invisible Men: Life in Baseball's Negro Leagues* (New York: Atheneum Publishers, 1983).

Ruth, Claire Hodgson, and Bill Slocum. *The Babe and I* (Englewood Cliffs, N.J.: Prentice-Hall, Inc., 1959).

Ruth, George Herman (Babe), and Bob Considine. *The Babe Ruth Story* (New York: E. P. Dutton and Company, 1948).

Seymour, Harold. *Baseball* (2 vols. to date, New York: Oxford University Press, 1960—).

Shannon, Bill, and George Kaminsky. *The Ballparks* (New York: Hawthorne Books, 1975).

Smelser, Marshall. *The Life That Ruth Built: A Biography* (New York: Quadrangle/New York Times Book Company, 1975).

Smith, Myron J. *Baseball: A Comprehensive Bibliography* (Jefferson, N.C.: McFarland and Company, 1986).

Spalding, Albert G. *America's National Game* (New York: American Sports Publishing Company, 1911).

Spink, J. G. Taylor. *Judge Landis and Twenty-five Years of Baseball* (reprint ed., St. Louis: Sporting News Publishing Company, 1974).

Sullivan, Ted. *History of the World's Tour, Chicago White Sox and New York Giants* (Chicago: M. A. Donahue and Company, 1914).

Thorn, John. *Baseball's Ten Greatest Games* (New York: Four Winds Press, 1982).

Veeck, William, Jr., and Ed Linn. *Veeck as in Wreck* (New York: Bantam Books, 1963).

Voight, David Quentin. *American Baseball* (3 vols., Norman: University of Oklahoma Press; State College: Penn State University Press, 1966–84).

————. *America Through Baseball* (Chicago: Nelson-Hall, Inc., 1976).

Works Progress Administration, Federal Writers' Project. *New York City Guide* (New York: Random House, Inc., 1939).

————. *New York Panorama* (New York: Random House, Inc., 1938).

World Tour, National and American League Base Ball Teams, October 1913–March 1914: The Triumph of Organized Base Ball (Chicago: S. Blake Willsden and Company, 1914).

Zucker, Harvey M., and Lawrence J. Babich. *Sports Films: A Complete Reference* (Jefferson, N.C.: McFarland and Company, 1987).

Articles:

Axelson, Gustav W. "Enlightening the World with Baseball," *Harper's Weekly*, LVIII (April 4, 1914), pp. 24–26.

Barber, Frederick Courtenay. "The Star Ball-Players and Their Earnings," *Munsey's*, XLIX (May 1913), pp. 213–21.

"Baseball and the Crooks," *Outlook*, CXXXVIII (October 15, 1924), pp. 235–36.

"Baseball Has Changed Some in Thirty Years, Says John J. McGraw," *Literary Digest*, LXI (May 10, 1919), pp. 96–101.

"Baseball's Generals," *Literary Digest*, XLIV (March 2, 1912), pp. 445–47.

"Base-Stealing's Sensational Decline," *Literary Digest*, LXXIII (April 29, 1922), pp. 41–42.

"Big League Superstitions," *Literary Digest*, XLVIII (May 9, 1914), pp. 1151–54.

"Big Leaguers in Training," *Literary Digest*, XLIV (March 30, 1912), pp. 654–57.

Blaisdell, Lowell. "Mystery and Tragedy: The O'Connell-Dolan Scandal," *Baseball Research Journal* (1982), pp. 44–48.

Bluthardt, Robert F. "Fenway Park and the Golden Age of the Baseball Park, 1909–15," *Journal of Popular Culture*, XXI (Summer 1987), pp. 43–52.

Boren, Steve. "The Bizarre Career of Rube Benton," *Baseball Research Journal* (1983), pp. 180–83.

Bradley, Hugh. "McGraw," *American Mercury*, XXVI (August 1932), pp. 461–69.

Bulger, Bozeman. "Genius of the Game," *Saturday Evening Post*, CCIV (May 28, 1932), pp. 10–11; (June 25, 1932), p. 26f.; CCV (July 9, 1932), p. 24f.

Burkholder, Edwin V. "How Charley Faust Won a Pennant for the Giants," *Reader's Digest*, LVII (October 1950), pp. 79–82.

Busch, Thomas S. "Searching for Victory: The Story of Charles Victor(y) Faust," *Baseball Research Journal* (1983), pp. 82–85.

Cain, Cullen. "The Manager," *Saturday Evening Post*, XCCVIII (June 19, 1926), pp. 20–21.

"Changes in Baseball Rules for This Season," *Literary Digest*, LXV (May 29, 1920), pp. 98–99.

Claudy, C. H. "The Battle of Baseball," *St. Nicholas*, XXXVIII (April 1911), pp. 531–37; (May 1911), pp. 611–18; (June 1911), pp. 707–13; (July 1911), pp. 803–809; (August 1911), pp. 881–89; (September 1911), pp. 997–1003; (October 1911), pp. 1092–98.

———. "Managers and Their Work," *St. Nicholas*, XL (July 1913), pp. 799–804.

———. "The World Series," *St. Nicholas*, XL (August 1913), pp. 884–90; (September 1913), pp. 1006–12; (October 1913), pp. 1109–15.

"Crack of the Baseball Bats Goes Echoing around the World," *Current Opinion*, LV (November 1913), pp. 308–10.

Creamer, Robert. "John McGraw, Manager," *Sports Illustrated*, LIV (April 13, 1981), p. 61.

" 'Czar' McGraw," *Literary Digest*, XLVIII (June 20, 1914), pp. 1499–1502f.

"Dr. Arlington Pond, Public Health Official," *Baseball Research Journal* (1980), pp. 12–13.

Dubbs, Gregg. "Jim Sheckard: A Live Wire in the Dead-Ball Era," *Baseball Research Journal* (1980), pp. 134–39.

———. "The 1892 Split Season," *Baseball Research Journal* (1981), pp. 179–81.

Erb, Hugh. "Forty Years of Bona's Baseball," *The Laurel*, XLVII (Spring–Summer 1950), pp. 12–15.

Evans, Billy. "Why the Giants Win," *Harper's Weekly*, LIX (July 25, 1914), p. 82.

"The Exciting Close of the Baseball Season," *Current Literature*, LI (November 1911), pp. 468–70.

"Explaining the Athletics' Victory," *Literary Digest*, XLVII (October 25, 1913), pp. 780–82.

Fay, Bill. "Muggsy's Legacy," *Collier's*, CXXIV (October 15, 1949), pp. 46f.

"Finis to Story of Giants' McGraw," *News Week*, III (March 3, 1934), p. 21.

"Fortunes Made in Baseball," *Literary Digest*, XLV (July 20, 1912), pp. 119–25.

Foster, John B. "John T. Brush: A Power in Baseball," *Baseball Magazine*, III (May 1909), pp. 17–20.

———. "The Magnificent New Polo Grounds," *Baseball Magazine*, VII (October 1911), no pagination.

Foster, Mark. "Foul Ball: The Cleveland Spiders' Farcical Final Season of 1899," *Baseball History*, I (Summer 1986), pp. 4–14.

Fox, Edward Lyell. "South with the Ball Teams," *Outing*, LX (April 1912), pp. 24–34.

———. "What Is Inside Baseball?" *Outing*, LVIII (July 1911), pp. 488–97.

"A Frenzied Baseball Year," *Current Literature*, XLV (November 1908), pp. 487–91.

Fullerton, Hugh S. "Baseball: The Business and the Sport," *American Review of Reviews*, LXIII (April 1921), pp. 417–20.

————. "Deciding Moments of Great Games," *American Magazine*, LXVIII (June 1909), pp. 106–16.

————. "Earnings in Baseball," *North American Review*, CCIX (June 1930), pp. 743–48.

————. "Freak Plays That Decide Baseball Championships," *American Magazine*, LXXIV (May 1912), pp. 114–21.

————. "On the Bench," *American Magazine*, LXVIII (August 1909), pp. 401–405.

————. "Winning Baseball Pennants," *Collier's*, XLIII (September 11, 1909), pp. 13–14f.

Gershman, Michael. "Wooden Weapons," *Sports Heritage*, I (July–August 1987), pp. 25–32.

"Giants and Sox in Japan," *Literary Digest*, XLVIII (February 14, 1914), pp. 331–33.

Graber, Ralph S. "Jack Bentley's Sad Tale: Victim of Circumstances," *Baseball Research Journal* (1986), pp. 23–25.

"The Great Hornsby Mystery: Was the Rajah Too Ambitious?" *Literary Digest*, XCVI (February 25, 1928), pp. 57–60.

Greenwell, Paul. "John McGraw and Pennant Park," *Baseball Research Journal* (1980), pp. 128–30.

Hanna, William B. "Baseball's Eventful Week," *Harper's Weekly*, LII (October 10, 1908), pp. 12–13.

Harlow, Alvin F. "McGraw, John Joseph," in Harris E. Starr, ed., *Dictionary of American Biography: Supplement One* (New York: Charles Scribner's Sons, 1944), pp. 529–30.

Henry, Lyell D., Jr. "Alfred W. Lawson, Aviation Pioneer," *Baseball Research Journal* (1980), pp. 9–12.

Hoie, Robert C. "The Hal Chase Case," *Baseball Research Journal* (1981), pp. 34–41.

Holway, John B. "Cuba's Black Diamond," *Baseball Research Journal* (1981), pp. 139–45.

Hopper, James. "Training with the 'Giants,' " *Everybody's*, XX (June 1909), pp. 739–49.

"How the Two Big Leagues Compared in 1924," *Literary Digest*, LXXXIV (March 28, 1925), pp. 58–64.

"Humors and Tragedies of Baseball Training-Time in Dixie," *Literary Digest*, LIX (April 9, 1921), pp. 63–68.

Hurlburt, Gordon. "The Worst Season Ever," *Baseball Research Journal* (1979), pp. 129–34.

"Is New York Getting Too Many Pennants?" *Literary Digest*, LXXIX (October 13, 1923), pp. 72–76.

Jennings, Hugh A. "Reminiscences," *The Laurel*, XVII (1925–1926), pp. 326–27.

"John McGraw Will Bawl Out No More Umpires," *Literary Digest*, CXIII (June 18, 1932), pp. 32–33.

Kennedy, John B. "Pillars of Sport," *Collier's*, XC (September 3, 1932), pp. 28–29f.

Klem, William J., and William J. Slocum. "Umpire Bill Klem's Own Story," *Collier's*, CXXVII (March 31, 1951), pp. 30–31f; (April 7, 1951), pp. 30–31f.; (April 14, 1951), pp. 30–31f.; (April 21, 1951), pp. 30–31f.

Kofoed, Jack. "A Dirge for Baseball," *North American Review*, CCVIII (July 1929), pp. 106–10.

———. "The Secret of the Giants' Twenty-six Straight Wins," *Baseball Magazine*, XVIII (January 1917), pp. 45–48.

Krueckeberg, Dan. "Take-Charge Cy," *National Pastime*, IV (Spring 1985), pp. 7–11.

Lancaster, Donald G. "Forbes Field Praised as a Gem When It Opened," *Baseball Research Journal* (1986), pp. 26–29.

Lane, F. C. "John McGraw, Manager," *Baseball Magazine*, VIII (April 1912), pp. 21–24.

Lardner, John. "That Was Baseball: The Crime of Shufflin' Phil Douglas," *The New Yorker*, XXXII (May 12, 1956), pp. 136f.

"Lively Controversy over the Lively Ball," *Literary Digest*, CIII (October 5, 1929), pp. 78–81.

Macdonald, Arthur. "The Psychology of Baseball," *Scientific American*, CXIII (August 28, 1915), pp. 188–89.

———. "Statistics of Baseball," *Scientific American*, CXII (May 1, 1915), p. 418.

McGeehan, W. O. "Baseball: 'Business as Usual,' " *North American Review*, CCIV (March 1927), pp. 119–24.

McGraw, John. "Baseball Changes of Thirty Years," *Baseball Magazine*, XXII (May 1919), pp. 11–14f.

———. "Rooting to Victory," *Collier's*, XLVII (July 15, 1911), pp. 18f.

"McGraw Collects," *Literary Digest*, LIV (May 5, 1917), p. 1358.

McNeill, Don. "That Man McGraw," *Coronet*, XXXVI (June 1954), p. 77.

"The Manager's Part in Making a Ball Team," *Literary Digest*, XLVI (March 29, 1913), pp. 731–34.

"Marquard and His Predecessors," *Literary Digest*, XLV (July 6, 1912), pp. 36–38.

Mathewson, Christy. "How I Became a Big League Pitcher," *St. Nicholas*, XXXIX (May 1912), pp. 605–15.

———. "Why We Lost Three World's Championships," *Everybody's*, XXXI (October 1914), pp. 537–47.

"Matty," *Literary Digest*, XLV (November 16, 1912), pp. 932–33.

Moss, Edward Bayard. "The Greatest Baseball Series Ever Played," *Harper's Weekly*, LVI (November 2, 1912), p. 10.

———. "Rulers of the Game: Some Famous Baseball Umpires and Their Ways," *Harper's Weekly*, LIII (August 21, 1909), pp. 13–14.

"The National League Pennant Race," *Literary Digest*, XLVI (June 7, 1913), pp. 1291–93.

"The Passing of the Super-Pitcher," *Literary Digest*, LXXX (February 16, 1924), pp. 72–77.

Price, Bill. "Braves Field," *Baseball Research Journal* (1978), pp. 1–6.

Puff, Richard A. "George Burns: A Star in the Sunfield," *Baseball Research Journal* (1983), pp. 119–25.

Rice, Grantland. "The Firebrand," *Collier's*, LXXXV (April 5, 1930), p. 13.

Rothe, Emil H. "Was the Federal League a Major League?" *Baseball Research Journal* (1981), pp. 1–10.

"Sad Decline of Base-Thievery in Baseball," *Literary Digest,* LXXXII (August 2, 1924), pp. 52–53.

Sangree, Allen. "Fans and Their Frenzies: The Wholesome Madness of Baseball," *Everybody's,* XVII (September 1907), pp. 378–87.

————. "The Strategy of the Ball Field," *Everybody's,* XV (October 1906), pp. 509–16.

"Sentiment and Matty," *Literary Digest,* LIII (August 12, 1916), p. 363.

Shutt, Timothy Baker. "Year of the Booming Bat," *Sports History,* I (September 1987), pp. 26–33.

"Some Prize Moments in the National Game," *Literary Digest,* LXXIV (September 9, 1922), pp. 50–53.

Stewart, Charles D. "The United States of Baseball," *Century,* LXXIV (June 1907), pp. 307–19.

"Tesreau, Giant of the Giants," *Literary Digest,* XLV (October 5, 1912), pp. 596–97.

"Thorpe in Baseball," *Literary Digest,* XLVI (February 15, 1913), p. 363.

Vance, Dazzy, with Furman Bisher. "I'd Hate to Pitch Nowadays," *Saturday Evening Post,* CCVIII (August 20, 1955), pp. 27f.

"Washington's Big Day in Baseball," *Literary Digest,* LXXXIII (October 25, 1924), pp. 50–58.

Weir, Hugh C. "Baseball: The Men and the Dollars Behind It," *World To-day,* XVII (July 1909), pp. 752–61.

"When Babe Ruth Was Beaten by John J. McGraw," *Literary Digest,* LXXV (December 2, 1922), pp. 57–61.

"Why Matty Lasts," *Literary Digest,* XLVII (August 1913), pp. 299–300.

Yaff, Lawrence. "Reminiscences of an Era Most Have Forgotten," *Baseball Research Journal* (1986), pp. 60–61.

INDEX

John Joseph McGraw

major league playing career, 1891–1906

year	team	games	AB	R	H	RBI	2b	3b	HR	B.Ave.	SB	BB	SO	Position
1891	Balt	115	17	31	14	12	3	5	0	.270	4	12	17	ss-21, Of-9, 2b-3
1892	Balt	79	286	41	77	26	13	2	1	.269	15	32	21	of-34, 2b-34, ss-8, 3b-3
1893	Balt	127	480	123	154	64	9	10	5	.321	38	101	11	ss-117, of-11
1894	Balt	124	512	156	174	92	18	14	1	.340	78	91	12	3b-118, 2b-6
1895	Balt	96	388	110	143	48	13	6	2	.369	61	60	9	3b-95, 2b-1
1896	Balt	23	77	20	25	14	2	2	0	.325	13	11	4	3b-18, 1b-1
1897	Balt	106	391	90	127	48	15	3	0	.325	44	99	—	3b-105
1898	Balt	143	515	143*	176	53	8	10	0	.342	43	112*	—	3b-137, of-3
1899	Balt	117	399	140*	156	33	13	3	1	.391	73	124*	—	3b-117
1900	StL	99	334	84	115	33	10	4	2	.344	29	85	—	3b-99
1901	Balt	73	232	71	81	28	14	9	0	.349	24	61	—	3b-69
1902	Balt	20	63	14	18	3	3	2	1	.286	5	17	—	}ss-34, 3b-19
	NY	35	107	13	25	5	0	0	0	.234	7	26	—	
1903	NY	12	11	2	3	1	0	0	0	.273	1	1	—	of-2, 2b-2, ss-1, 3b-1
1904	NY	5	12	0	4	0	0	0	0	.333	0	3	—	ss-2, 2b-2
1905	NY	3	0	0	0	0	0	0	0	—	1	0	—	of-1
1906	NY	4	2	0	0	0	0	0	0	.000	0	1	—	3b-1
Career		**1,099**	**3,924**	**1,024**	**1,309**	**462**	**121**	**70**	**13**	**.334**	**436**	**836**	**74**	**3b-782, ss-183, of-60, 2b-48, 1b-1**

*—led league

John Joseph McGraw

major league managing career, 1899, 1901–1932

year	team/league	Wins	Losses	Position	Pct.
1899	Balt/N	86	62	4	.581
1901	Balt/A	68	65	5	.511
1902	Balt/A	26	31	7(8)*	.456
	NY/N	25	38	(8)8**	.397
1903	NY/N	84	55	2	.604
1904	NY/N	106	47	1	.693
1905	NY/N	105	48	1	.686
1906	NY/N	96	56	2	.632
1907	NY/N	82	71	4	.536
1908	NY/N	98	56	2 (tied)	.636
1909	NY/N	92	61	3	.601
1910	NY/N	91	63	2	.591
1911	NY/N	99	54	1	.647
1912	NY/N	103	48	1	.682
1913	NY/N	101	51	1	.664
1914	NY/N	84	70	2	.545
1915	NY/N	68	83	8	.454
1916	NY/N	86	66	4	.566
1917	NY/N	98	56	1	.636

year	team/league	Wins	Losses	Position	Pct.
1918	NY/N	71	53	2	.573
1919	NY/N	87	53	2	.621
1920	NY/N	86	68	2	.588
1921	NY/N	94	59	**1**	.614
1922	NY/N	93	61	**1**	.604
1923	NY/N	95	58	1	.621
1924	NY/N	61	48	1	.560
1925	NY/N	86	66	2	.566
1926	NY/N	74	77	5	.490
1927	NY/N	70	52	3	.574
1928	NY/N	93	61	2	.604
1929	NY/N	84	67	3	.556
1930	NY/N	87	67	3	.565
1931	NY/N	87	65	2	.572
1932	NY/N	17	23	8(6)*	.425
Career; 33 yrs.		**2,784**	**1,959**		**.587**

Notes:
Won-loss records are for the games McGraw officially managed; when as in 1924, he managed only part of the season, totals are for McGraw's games only.
If the digit for final standing is in **bold type,** team went on to win the World Series.
*—First digit is team standing when McGraw left; second digit is final standing.
**—First digit is team standing then McGraw joined the club; second digit is final standing.